INDONESIA

INDONESIA

*Selected Documents on Colonialism
and Nationalism, 1830-1942*

Edited and translated by
Chr. L. M. Penders

UNIVERSITY OF QUEENSLAND PRESS

Published by University of Queensland Press,
St. Lucia, Queensland, 1977

© Christiaan Lambert Maria Penders, 1977

This book is copyright. Apart from any fair dealing
for the purposes of private study, research, criticism,
or review, as permitted under the Copyright Act, no
part may be reproduced by any process without
written permission. Enquiries should be made to
the publishers.

Typeset, printed and bound by Academy Press Pty. Ltd.,
Brisbane

Distributed in the United Kingdom, Europe, the
Middle East, Africa, and the Caribbean by
Prentice-Hall International, International Book
Distributors Ltd., 66 Wood Lane End, Hemel
Hempstead, Herts., England

National Library of Australia
Cataloguing-in-publication data

Indonesia: selected documents on colonialism and
   nationalism 1830—1942.

   ISBN 0 7022 1324 1.
   ISBN 0 7022 1029 3 Paperback.

   1. Dutch in Indonesia — History — Sources.
   2. Netherlands — Colonies — Administration —
   Sources. 3. Indonesia — Politics and government —
   Sources. 4. Nationalism — Indonesia — History —
   Sources. I. Penders, Christiaan Lambert Maria,
   1928—, ed.

325.349209598

Acknowledgment is made to W. W. Norton & Company, Inc., and
William Heinemann Ltd. for permission to use extracts from
Letters of a Javanese Princess by Raden Adjeng Kartini, translated
from the Dutch by Agnes Louise Symmers. Edited by Hildred
Geertz. Copyright 1920 by Agnes Louise Symmers.
Copyright renewed 1948 by Agnes Louise Symmers.
Copyright © 1964 by W. W. Norton & Company, Inc.

To my daughter Monica

Contents

PREFACE ... xiii

PART I COLONIALISM ... 1

INTRODUCTION ... 3

THE CULTURE SYSTEM, 1830–70 ... 5

1. **J. van den Bosch**: Report on his activities in the Indies, 1830–33 ... 8
2. **J. C. Baud**: Criticisms of van den Bosch and the Culture System in the Netherlands and the Indies, 1832 ... 15
3. **J. van den Bosch**: Despatch to de Eerens, 30 April 1836 ... 19
4. **L. Vitalis**: The system of forced cultivation in Java, 1851 ... 22

THE IMPACT OF LIBERALISM ON DUTCH COLONIAL POLICY, 1848–1900 ... 31

5. **W. R. van Hoevell**: Parliamentary speech, 8 December 1851 ... 34
6. **Multatuli**: Max Havelaar, 1860 ... 39
7. Deliberations by the learned society Indisch Genootschap about the Culture System, 1866 ... 43
8. **J. H. Boeke**: Budget studies in Koetoardjo, 1886 and 1888 ... 50
9. **J. Homan van der Heide**: Economic studies and criticisms, 1901 ... 56

THE ETHICAL POLICY, 1901–42 ... 61

Economic policy ... 61

10. **P. Brooshooft**: The Ethical direction in colonial policy, 1901 ... 65
11. **C. J. Hasselman**: General survey of the results of the investigation into economic prosperity in Java and Madura, held in 1904–5 ... 78
12. **W. Huender**: Survey of the economic conditions of the indigenous people of Java and Madura, 1921 ... 91

13	**J. H. Boeke**: Budget studies in various parts of Java, 1924–25	97
14	**L. H. Huizenga**: Some results of the Coolie Budget Investigations, 1939–40	113

Political and administrative decentralization   121

15	Promises of political reforms in the Indies, 1918	126
	1. Idenburg to van Limburg Stirum, 15 November 1918	126
	2. Van Limburg Stirum to Idenburg, 19 November 1918	126
	3. Van Limburg Stirum to Idenburg, 1 December 1918	126
16	Conservative reaction in the Netherlands	128
	1. Idenburg to van Limburg Stirum, 11 December 1918	128
	2. De Graeff to van Limburg Stirum, 17 February 1919	130
	3. Creutzberg to van Limburg Stirum, January 1924	132
17	Conservative reaction in Indonesia	133
	De Graeff to van Limburg Stirum, 26 October 1927	133
18	**H. Colijn**: On political reforms, 1918	135
19	Commentaries on the views of Colijn	139
	1. De Graeff to van Limburg Stirum, 15 April 1918	139
	2. Van Limburg Stirum to Pleyte, 14 July 1918	139
	3. Idenburg to van Limburg Stirum, 8 October 1918	140
	4. Van Limburg Stirum to Idenburg, 14 October 1918	141
	5. Idenburg to van Limburg Stirum, 16 October 1918	141
20	The Petition Sutardjo	141
	Van Helsdingen to First and Second Chambers of the States-General, 1 October 1936	141
21	Reply to Sutardjo	142
	Stachouwer to Welter, 14 September 1938	142
22	Rejection of an Indonesian parliament	147
	Welter to the Queen, 13 February 1941	147
23	Declaration of the Netherlands Government in exile in London, 27 January 1942	149

Education policy   149

24	**J. Habbema**: The political and economic importance of education for the native people, 1904	155
25	**C. Snouck Hurgronje**: The ideal of association, 1911	157
26	**J. W. T. Cohen-Stuart**: The Indonesiasation of the colonial service, 1907	165
27	Controvery on mass education	166
	1. **D. Fock**: On mass technical education, 1905	166

	2. **C. Snouck Hurgronje**: On the fallacy of mass education, 1905	166
	3. **J. B. van Heutz**: On Fock's plans, 1907	166
28	Obstacles to vernacular education	167
	1. **J. H. Gunning**: On the progress of village schools, 1919	167
	2. **C. O. van der Plas**: On forceful methods in education, 1919	167
29	**P. Post**: The need to adapt village schools to local demands and culture, 1927	168
30	The indigenous literacy rate — from the 1930 Census	169
31	**The Resident of Besuki**: Education and radical nationalism, 1924	170
32	**J. Meyer Ranneft**: Speech on education and radical nationalism, 1927	170
33	**Suroso**: Speech on the right of Indonesians to receive Dutch-language education, 1927	174
34	The Depression and education	175
	1. Minister of Colonies to the Governor-General, 10 October 1930	176
	2. Governor-General to the Minister of Colonies, September 1932	176
35	**J. F. H. A. de la Court**: A postscript on the principle of *concordantie*, 1945	176

PART II NATIONALISM 177

ANTI-COLONIAL MOVEMENTS IN THE NINETEENTH CENTURY 179

36	**J. A. B. Wiselius**: The prophecies of Jojobojo, 1872	183
37	**T. Roorda**: The beginning of the Rebellion of Diponegoro, according to a Javanese manuscript, 1860	188
38	**H. J. J. L. de Stuers**: Memoirs of Tuanku Imam Bondjol, 1850	202
39	**H. T. Damste**: *Hikajat Prang Sabi*, 1928	207

THE GENESIS OF THE MODERN INDONESIAN NATIONALIST MOVEMENT 215

40	The social origin of S.T.O.V.I.A. students and graduates, 1875–1904	218
41	**R. A. Kartini**: Letters of a Javanese Princess	219
42	**Ahmad Djajadiningrat**: Memoirs, 1936	223
43	**Soewarno**: Letter of Secretary of Founding Committee of *Budi: Utomo* to the press, 23 July 1908	225

| 44 | **E. F. E. Douwes Dekker**: The Indies Party, its nature and objectives, 1913 | 228 |

The Indische Partij in action

| 45 | 1. **R. M. Soewardi Soerjaningrat**: If only I were a Netherlander, 1913 | 232 |
| | 2. **Tjipto Mangoenkoesoemo**: Power or fear, 1913 | 234 |

THE ISLAMIC MOVEMENT 236

46	**C. Poensen**: Letters about Islam from the country areas of Java, 1886	241
47	**J. A. van der Chijs**: Report of 1831 on indigenous education	248
48	**Ahmad Djajadiningrat**: Reminiscences about life in a *pesantren*, 1936	252
49	**Tjokroaminoto**: Speech at the *Sarekat Islam* Congress, 1916	255
50	Report of the meeting of the *Partij Sarikat Islam* held on 26 January 1928, to commemorate its fifteen years of existence.	257
51	*P.S.I.I. Congress* held at Palembang, January 1940	261
52	Report of the 23rd Congress of *Muhammadyah* held at Jogjakarta, July 1934	264
53	Proceedings of the 3rd Congress of the *Jong Islamieten Bond* (Young Muslims League), held 23–27 December 1927	267
54	Government report on *Nahadatul Ulama*, 1928	270

COMMUNISM 273

55	**Tan Malaka**: Letters to D. J. L. van Wijngaarden, 1920–21	275
56	**H. J. Benda and R. T. McVey**: Communist uprisings, 1926–27	284
57	**The Resident of Kediri**: Communist disturbances in Blitar, 1927	288
58	**The Assistant Director of Education and Religion**: The educational background of arrested Communist leaders, 1927	291

THE INDONESIA-CENTRIC NATIONALIST MOVEMENT, 1922–42 301

59	Report of a meeting of the *Partij Nasional Indonesia*, held 27 October 1929	305
60	**Sukarno**: The quest for national unity, 1926	308
61	**Sukarno**: Towards the Brown Front, 1927	311
62	Report of the 2nd *P.P.P.K.I.* Congress held at Solo on 25 December 1929	314

63	Report of the first public meeting of Partindo in Batavia, 12 July 1931	317
64	Open letter from the *Perhimpunan Indonesia*, 3 November 1931	320
65	**Mohammad Hatta**: The crisis of the *P.P.P.K.I.*, 1930	326
66	**Sutan Sjahrir**; *Out of Exile*, 1949	327
67	Report of the 2nd Congress of *Parindra*, December 1938	329
68	Report of the *Perhimpunan Indonesia* closed meeting held at Leiden on 12 June 1936	332
69	Manifesto of the *Gaboengan Politiek Indonesia*, 20 20 September 1939	334
70	Indonesian People's Congress, 23–25 December 1939	335
71	Petition of G.A.P.I. to the Governor-General, 9 August 1940	338
72	Views of an indigenous lawyer on the Indonesian political situation in 1940	340

GLOSSARY 349

INDEX 355

Preface

As basic source materials on modern Indonesian history are almost entirely in Dutch and Bahasa Indonesia, the vast majority of English-speaking students taking courses in this field are severely handicapped. This is particularly true of the Dutch colonial era and the genesis and evolution of the Indonesian nationalist movement, periods in which students are almost totally dependent on a few often-outdated textbooks in English, usually based on secondary sources, and on an even smaller range of more specialized works.

The aim of this book is to reduce the deficiency somewhat by providing tertiary and upper-grade high school students with a representative selection of mainly primary sources. A single volume of this kind, which tries to cover more than a century of rather eventful history, has to be highly selective and, of course, can hardly do more than present a glimpse of the immense wealth of primary material, as yet largely untapped, that is stored in the various archives and libraries of the Netherlands and Indonesia. Yet it is hoped that the authenticity of this material will enable students to gain a more vivid picture and a deeper understanding of some of the more important events, movements, and personalities.

With the exception of documents 41, 56, and 66, all extracts were translated by myself. I should like to thank Dr. Subardi of the Australian National University for his help with some of the translations from Javanese and Indonesian. Indonesian words in the documents have kept their original spelling.

Chr. L.M. Penders
Brisbane
November 1975

Part I
Colonialism

Introduction

The Portuguese were the first Europeans to gain a foothold in the Indonesian Archipelago. Fired by a mixture of religious zeal, hatred of Islam, zest for adventure, and strong desire for wealth, they succeeded at the beginning of the sixteenth century in establishing a number of fortified trading posts, the most important of which were at Malacca and in the Moluccas (the Spice Islands). Although causing some important chain reactions in the commercial and political life of the Archipelago, the Portuguese impact was decidedly less significant than some of the earlier colonial historians have tried to convey.

The Dutch East India Company, which ousted the Portuguese during the early decades of the seventeenth century, was solely concerned with making the largest possible profits, and showed very little interest in either missionary activity or territorial aggrandizement. On the Portuguese model, the Dutch established a chain of fortified trading posts in strategically important areas, from which they tried to impose a monopoly on the Archipelago's trade and commerce. Usually contracts were signed with local princes or chiefs, who were forced to accept the Dutch as overlord and to deliver certain categories and quantities of produce to the exclusion of all other competitors. The control of internal affairs was left as much as possible in the hands of the traditional indigenous authorities. Exceptions were the Moluccas and later parts of Java, where the Company established its own rule, although it still made use of traditional leaders such as the *bupati* or regents (the former viceroys of the Javanese kings) for the execution of its policies. In the Moluccas closer supervision was needed to safeguard the all-important spice monopoly, while in Java the Dutch gradually brought the island under their control in order to stop the chronic internecine warfare that affected Dutch profits. In their own territories the Dutch also interfered in production: in the Moluccas growers were forced to burn down trees whenever the price of spices was falling on the world market, while for similar reasons in the Priangan regencies (West Java), where the Company had introduced a system of forced cultivation of coffee, growers were compelled to regulate their crops.

The Dutch East India Company showed little interest in converting the native population to Christianity. Fearing socio-political disturbances, it actively discouraged missionary activity in predominantly Muslim areas such as Java and Sumatra. Only in some parts of Eastern Indonesia, where Islam had not yet fully penetrated or where the Portuguese had made converts to the Catholic faith, were Dutch Reformed Ministers given a freer hand. The Company provided elementary education with a strong Dutch Reformed bias to the children of its own officials and of Indonesian Christians only. In 1795 about five thousand Indonesian children were attending Company schools, mainly in the Moluccas.

For about a century and a half the Dutch East India Company proved to be a highly successful venture. But from the middle of the eighteenth century onwards, suffering from old age and increasing internal corruption, it started to decline. The Company finally expired in 1799 when its vast debts were taken over by the Netherlands Government.

The Culture System, 1830-70

During the first three decades of the nineteenth century successive colonial governments, influenced by the ideas of the French Revolution and free-trade theories, attempted to break with the policies of the Dutch East India Company and introduce a more liberal system of colonial administration. Free trade, free labour, and free production, together with a more enlightened governmental system, were considered to be the most effective means of restoring the finances of the Indies and of making the colony profitable again to the mother country.

Governor-General Daendels, a Dutch army general in the pay of Napoleon, was the first to try to implement some of these principles. As a first step he reduced the feudal power of the indigenous nobility and chiefs and tried to transform them into a salaried corps of civil servants. Daendels, however, was mainly concerned with bringing Java into a state of defence against an expected British attack. Holland at the time was being forced more and more into the orbit of France and finally lost the last vestige of its independent status in 1808 when it became an inseparable part of France.

In 1811 the British occupied Java and the Moluccas and Sir Stamford Raffles was appointed lieutenant-governor of Java. Raffles was extremely critical of previous Dutch colonial rule, which he described as harsh and unfeeling, and introduced a more liberal and what he termed a more humane system of colonial administration. One of his best-known measures was the land-rent system of taxation under which indigenous farmers were left free to decide how to use their labour and what crops they wanted to plant. However, they were to hand over to the government, preferably in cash, from one-half to two-fifths of their crops, depending on the fertility of the land.

Raffles's policies turned out to be financially disastrous, and his plans for the establishment of a British East Indies empire were ruined by the decision of the British Government, in 1814, to return to Holland some of its former colonial empire, including the East Indies.

The Commissioners-General appointed by the Dutch King to take over the Indies from the British arrived in Java in 1816. Together with Governor-General van der Capellen (1818-24), they continued the policies started by Daendels and Raffles. But the financial results were again disastrous. Free trade had to be abandoned because Dutch shipping and commerce were in no position to compete successfully with the British. Export production lagged behind because most Javanese farmers were not interested in producing for export. Moreover the Dutch were plagued by low prices for tropical produce on the world market and they had to cope with many costly rebellions and wars in various parts of the Archipelago.

By 1824 the colony was on the verge of bankruptcy and Governor-General van der Capellen in desperation offered the Indies as collateral to the British firm of Palmer and Co. of Calcutta for a substantial loan. When news of this reached the Netherlands it stung the Dutch Government into action, and large loans were advanced to the Indies in 1826 and again in 1828. At the same time a controversy raged in The Hague about what system would be most efficient in bringing the colonies back to a durable prosperity. The strongly liberal-minded entourage around the King advocated the granting of large parcels of land to Europeans and the establishment of a European-owned and European-run plantation economy in which Indonesians could find employment on a voluntary basis. A more conservative and pragmatic party advocated a return to the Company system of forced cultivation and labour.

Gradually coming to the fore in this dispute was General J. van den Bosch, whose ideas about colonial administration had been shaped during a sojourn in the Indies (1798-1810) as a young officer in the Engineers Corps. He had become impressed by the policies of the Company, which he felt should be continued after the checking of abuses that had crept in. He was on bad terms with Daendels, who in 1808 granted him an honourable discharge from the army with the rank of colonel and in 1810 ordered him to leave the colony. In 1813 van den Bosch was back in the Netherlands, where he took an active part in the liberation of the country from the French. In 1815 he was promoted to major-general and put in charge of the logistics of the colonial army. He had retained his strong interest in colonial affairs and in 1815 published a pamphlet criticizing Daendels's policies; in 1818 he put out a two-volume work on the Dutch colonies, in which he took Raffles and his system severely to task.

Van den Bosch was a hard-headed businessman, a patriot, and an excellent organizer, but he was also a humanitarian of note. With characteristic singlemindedness and enthusiasm he had thrown himself heart and soul into the business of the *Maatschappij of Weldadigheid* (the Society for Charitable Works) and with some considerable success conducted the vast experiment of resettling on reclaimed lands in the eastern provinces thousands of paupers who were cluttering up the Dutch city slums.

His obvious organizing talents as well as his writings on colonial policy attracted the attention of the King, who in 1827 appointed van den Bosch Commissary-General for the West Indies, with the task of putting the sagging financial affairs of these colonies into order again. In the West Indies van den Bosch dismissed liberal ideas of free labour and free cultivation as chimerical and instead introduced a system of government-controlled negro labour on the plantations.

On his return from the West Indies van den Bosch was able gradually to wean the King away from the liberal colonial faction, and finally convinced him that his system of forced cultivation and consignment would produce immediate results, while the measures suggested by the liberals would at best only produce a very slow economic recovery. In October 1828 van den Bosch was promoted to lieutenant-general and appointed governor-general of the Netherlands Indies, with the task of making the colony profitable again to the mother country as quickly as possible. Van den Bosch departed for the Indies in July 1829 with two million guilders in cash and another two million in credit.

Immediately on his arrival in Batavia, van den Bosch set out with his usual energy and singlemindedness to introduce his so-called Culture System, which in many ways signalled a return to the policies and practices of the Dutch East India Company. In the more fertile areas of Java and later also in parts of West Sumatra and North Sulawesi (Minahasa), farmers were forced to set aside one-fifth of their land for the production of export crops such as sugar, coffee, indigo, and spices, which were to be delivered to the Netherlands Trading Company for low prices. This company, in which the King invested heavily, had been set up in 1824 in order to further Dutch commerce and trade. It was now given the monopoly of the buying, transporting, and selling of government produce on the European market and also acted as a banker to the Dutch Government, granting loans on the security of future crops in Java.

Van den Bosch ran Java as a business venture (*see* documents 1 and 3) and accordingly kept overheads as low as possible, only allowing government expenditure on projects that would increase profitability, such as improvements in communications. Soon the chronic budget deficits of the previous half-century were turned into *batige sloten* (surpluses). And between 1831 and 1877, 832.4 million guilders in budget surpluses were remitted from the Indies to the Home Treasury, greatly to the benefit of the Netherlands economy as a whole.

Document 1 contains a justification by van den Bosch of his

system. It should be noted that some of the points he stresses, such as the paternalistic concern with indigenous civilization and the need for indirect rule, remained important features of Dutch colonial rule until the end. Document 2 is taken from a despatch by J.C. Baud, Secretary-General of Colonial Affairs in The Hague and a strong supporter of the Culture System; it shows the widespread opposition to van den Bosch and his policies by liberal-minded politicians and colonial officials. The fear, however, that the Culture System would turn the indigenous population into a mass of paupers and drive them into rebellion appears to have been unfounded, at least during the early years of the system. And in spite of the considerable sabotaging efforts in some areas by both European and native officials (*see* first part of document 4), the claim of van den Bosch that his system would also benefit the Javanese people appears to have some foundation. Judging from a marked rise in the consumption of imported goods, particularly textiles, there was a rise in native prosperity until the mid-1830s. However, as is shown in document 4, which is taken from a pamphlet by Vitalis, Inspector of Forced Cultivation from 1833 to 1838 in Cheribon, it was after 1836 that a number of excesses crept into the system. And the instructions of van den Bosch designed to safeguard the basic interests of the Javanese, such as leaving the peasants sufficient time to grow rice and for other means of livelihood, were often ignored by European as well as native officials. The excessive drive by these officials to increase production for export resulted in some areas in serious famines and large-scale emigration of peasants to areas where the Culture System was not in force.

1 J. van den Bosch: Report on his activities in the Indies, 1830-33

It was in particular the political situation in Java that influenced my actions and achievements. The term "political situation" in this context means first of all the relationship between the native population and the European government, and secondly the ways and means used to make this relationship beneficial to us.

The Netherlands holds these regions as tribute. And whatever the size of the territory ceded contractually [by the native people] to [the Dutch], the people remain separate from us and they are subjected to European rule. Thus the relationship between the government and the people is determined by the power the former exercises and the physical and intellectual means it has at its disposal to assert and reinforce this authority. The princes are no different in this respect, because they are mere vassals of the government. In the year 1825 began the Java War, which has only recently ended. [The Java War, 1825-30, was a fierce and bloody struggle led by the Javanese prince Dipanegara. *See* document 37.]

This war has clearly shown that the people in these former principalities were strongly opposed to the rule of our government. This is obvious from the great following the rebellious prince Dipanegara was able to gain so quickly. It also explains the fact that the people continued to give their support in spite of the many disasters they had to suffer and the many sacrifices they had to make ...

This ill-feeling could not have resulted from maltreatment by us because, in the regions where the rebellion broke out and where it spread most widely and was continued most stubbornly, there had hardly been any contact with the European administration.

So there must be other reasons for this hate. It probably resulted partly from the aversion which normally every people holds for foreign rule and partly from the religious hate fostered by the Muslim sect against all people who are considered to be unbelievers. This feeling of hate was incited particularly by fanatical priests [van den Bosch uses this word although Islam does not have priests]. And in the Jogjakarta area it became much greater than anywhere else in Java because the old sultan, Sepoe, who has ruled this principality for so long, has always treated Europeans with the greatest disdain ...

Our policies have done nothing to overcome this popular hate towards us. On the contrary it has increased whenever we have come into closer contact with the people. Further proof of this is to be found in the peaceful conditions reigning in Java between 1755 and 1806, when the native chiefs were left in control of internal affairs. During that fifty-year period not a trace of rebellion or riot could be found in the areas under government control, because at that time the principle of non-interference in the internal affairs of the people was consistently adhered to. Since this principle has been abandoned we have had to fight and suppress nine rebellions in Java over the last twenty-five years ...

During the regime of the Company the native chiefs retained all the privileges they enjoyed earlier under their own kings. We treated them honourably and the position of regent was made hereditary in their families. This situation is preferred by them in every way to the time when they were under their own kings. As a result these chiefs remained faithful to the government even under the most difficult circumstances.

Later, after the introduction of a more European type of government ... the privileges of the native chiefs were gradually curtailed, and often they were treated with far less reverence than of old. This went even further, and in the belief that it was in the best interest of the people, the native chiefs were made government officials who could be ordered around indiscriminately—they were even transferred from one regency to another.

Surely it should be easy to prove that we can govern the Javanese only through the medium of their own chiefs ... It is dangerous to weaken their power and authority, even if this were done with the loftiest ideals in mind.

Looking at it superficially, it would appear that the government could obtain the support of the people by protecting them against the suppression and arbitrariness of the native chiefs. In fact this idea is entirely unrealistic, as experience has shown. The weakening of this prestige and authority, which is supposed to be in the government's interests, must be condemned as politically insane, because it cannot be done without offending the feelings of the Javanese and without deeply insulting something that they revere highly ... [Van den Bosch then attempts to show the policies and achievements of the Dutch East India Company in a much more favourable light than liberal opponents would have cared to. He condemns the policies of Daendels and makes a vicious attack on Raffles, whom he considers a hypocritical upstart.]

I feel confident that I have shown the real facts about the so highly praised reforms of Raffles and also to have clearly shown that there is no justification in maintaining that his system was better than the one followed by the Company ... Finally his [Raffles's] three years of administration resulted in a deficit of ten million guilders. In the light of this it should be easy to judge the usefulness of his activities, which seem to have been considered more satisfactory by the credulous general public than by his own government. This is evident from his dismissal before the colony was surrendered to the Netherlands Government and his appointment as Resident of Bencoolen, a very small and unimportant post on the west coast of Sumatra, which is now part of this colony ...

The Commissioners-General desired to maintain the system of land rent and internal administration that they found on their arrival. They were motivated in this by something they felt to be of great importance, i.e. the attractive, though false, prospect raised by Daendels and Raffles. Other reasons were the unfavourable regard in which the old colonial system was held, although only the financial side of the matter seems to have been considered, and the spirit of the times that demanded the introduction of so-called liberal institutions (it had not yet been determined what was liberal and what was not in the Javanese context). [The Commissioners] further argued that even if they had wanted to it would have been impossible to turn the clock back. The earlier ties between the native chiefs and the people had been broken, a new set of interests had developed, and to change the system of native administration would probably cause a dangerous situation. In any case it was considered very uncertain whether another system would be more profitable financially ...

The Commissioners-General were clearly working towards achieving the following objectives: the Javanese were to be ensured the freedom of their person and freedom to dispose of their land and labour; industry was to be encouraged; and trade was to be liberalized as much as possible, allowing even foreigners a chance to compete fairly.

In all fairness it must be admitted that the Commissioners-General have shown great diligence, perseverance, and unselfish consideration, in trying to realize the objectives outlined above for the benefit of the Javanese.

However, it does not matter how much everyone wants to agree in the abstract with these principles; the fact remains that such principles cannot be unconditionally applied in all societies ...

Only after a sound knowledge of the economic system of a country has been gained is it possible to apply a certain principle, while at the same time allowing exceptions necessary to safeguard the particular interests of that country.

The situation is different when dealing with a people whose social institutions and language are not understood, and where no two districts can be found with the same socio-economic system. In such cases it is obvious that even with the best intentions mistakes can be made when applying general principles, and that often things are damaged or sacrificed which in the public interest should not have been touched.

Another difficulty that will be encountered is the creation of a sound legal system. How is it possible to devise a just legal code for such a nation? Mutual rights in a society are usually based mainly on convention and it would be completely impracticable to subject the Javanese to and familiarize them with laws and regulations which, while acceptable to us, are squarely opposed to their sense of law and justice. The law in this country must whenever possible be administered in line with local and age-old customs. These laws differ widely from area to area and Europeans who are called upon to dispense justice are usually not very familiar with them. So it often happens that matters are decided in an arbitrary manner ... In many ways it is the more hateful to the Javanese because for centuries they have been accustomed to subject themselves in such cases to the decisions of their chiefs. They therefore object to foreigners taking it upon themselves to obstruct and sell them short of what they consider is justice.

Theoretically, of course, it is possible to introduce a legal system that ostensibly fulfils all requirements. In its practical application, however, many clashes would occur owing to the peculiar and often different values held by the Javanese. Sensitivities and other special interests would often be hurt. Surely one cannot demand that a whole nation abandon its ancestral legal concepts and values and be forced by foreigners to accept a new social system that is not understood and cannot even be disseminated among the masses. Is it not natural for people to feel injured when they see that what they consider to be justice is no longer recognized as such? Furthermore it should be realized that the difference in religion, and the hate of the priests, whose privileged interests in this matter would be curtailed, would result in an even more unfavourable reception. And it should not be too difficult to see how dangerous would be the position of a handful of Europeans wanting to superimpose their wisdom and concepts on a people who cannot even understand them ...

A system of free trade, while most suitable in European societies for effective industrial development, does not have the same application in societies that are structured on differend principles. For example, Java under the strict monopoly system of the Company developed industrially much more than the surrounding countries where the people were not subject to these restrictions ...

In establishing a system of free trade in this country, considerations other than the traffic in goods must be kept in mind. These have been overlooked. One should have taken account of the fact that the mother country sacrificed considerable sums of money in order to reoccupy and maintain control of these lands. Therefore free trade, which tended to cut off trade with the mother country or caused it to be unprofitable, negated the reasons for having possessions and turned this colony into a useless financial burden. In these circumstances it would have been better to abandon the colony ...

Soon after taking office, the Commissioners-General realized that the free disposal of land and labour did not lead by any means to an increase in production, particularly of coffee. It was therefore decided to use gentle persuasion to turn the Javanese in the desired direction. This is certainly a rather euphemistic way of describing a breach of an accepted principle ... In fact this gentle persuasion ... meant in practice nothing less than a definite command to the Javanese to plant coffee ...

The intellectual development of the average Javanese does not reach beyond that of our children of twelve to fourteen years, while in general knowledge he is left far behind by them. His chiefs are a little more advanced, but in comparison with the European middle classes they have as yet not progressed very far intellectually.

To give to such people institutions suitable for a fully grown society is just as absurd as to give children the rights of adults and to expect that they will put them to good use. It was mainly mistakes of this kind that were responsible for the many calamities suffered by the Javanese during the last twenty-five years.

One desired to be liberal and one wanted the impossible ... Only a patriarchal government suits the Javanese. The government must take care of them and must not allow them to do things for themselves, because of their limited capabilities. This, of course, must be done with fatherly consideration. In so far as this is possible, the function of the government is to bring [the Javanese] to the kind of happiness they are striving for within their own restricted view of the world.

The interests of the government should always be made identical with those of the Javanese. The restricted ideas of the Javanese should always be respected and, as far as possible, measures intended for the benefit of the government should be taken only when the people are agreeable.

The application of this rule is not difficult. The Javanese are attached to their ancestral customs, feeling duty-bound to whatever is prescribed by them. And whatever burdens are attached, they will bear them willingly. One should make careful use of this cooperative spirit, for their own good and to improve their conditions ...

In particular one should not try to speed up by artificial means the intellectual development of the Javanese. The germ of civilization that is inherent in every society often develops through circumstances independent of human control. In the same way as we cannot accelerate the process of germination in plants, we cannot within a short period of time cause whole societies to make spectacular progress in civilization.

One should not attempt to subject the happiness and contentment of a people to schemes that too often have proved to be chimerical and therefore can be considered only with mistrust. I myself therefore have not indulged in experimental measures of this kind and have left the intellectual development of the Javanese to the course of time and the natural evolution of things ...

The only successful productive system in Java is the one that does not interfere with the people's existing mode of economic life ...

In addition to the attachment to their own institutions, there is nothing more pleasing to the Javanese than to be in a position where they will have to work less. This is the result of climatic conditions. Moreover, in common with most other human beings, they want to gain as much profit as possible from the labour they are compelled to perform. These two attitudes had to be taken account of in introducing the new system. In addition to basing it on age-old custom, it was necessary to provide landholders in particular with the opportunity either to work less or to obtain a greater return with the same labour input.

Accordingly, the following principles have been adopted. A *desa* [village] is to be exempted from paying land rent if it sets aside one-fifth of its rice fields for the production of crops suitable for the European market, the cultivation of which may not require more work than the cultivation of rice. Furthermore, where the price obtained for the product is higher than the amount of land rent to be paid, the difference is to be paid to the *desa*. Crop failures, providing they are not caused by laziness or a lack of diligence on the part of the Javanese, are to be borne financially by the government. Clearly this policy was instituted solely for the benefit of the Javanese so that they could gain more profit from their land ...

In order to obtain products that were marketable in Europe, crops first had to be prepared in factories. This required considerable capital, knowledge, and other things that could not be expected from the Javanese. In order to ensure that the crops were properly treated, European and Chinese capital had to be brought into the business.

In some cases, such as sugar cultivation, it was found necessary to introduce division of labour in order not to overburden the people. Some were required to grow the crop, others to harvest it, and others again to transport it to the factories in case no day labour was available.

The Javanese do not like to work under the supervision of Europeans and prefer to be directed by their own chiefs. This was taken into consideration and supervision by European officials was restricted as much as possible to such matters as ensuring that the fields were properly cultivated and that crops were harvested and transported at the right time ...

[Van den Bosch summarized his administration as follows:]
1. During my administration peace and order have been re-established in Java. The rebels and their leader Diponegara and others have surrendered unconditionally to the government.
2. The continuation of peaceful conditions has been ensured by exiling Dipanegara and other rebellious and dangerous princes and chiefs. Furthermore, the debts incurred by kings and princes at both courts [i.e. Yogjakarta and Surakarta] have been taken care of. They are now paid a generous monthly allowance, which should provide for their needs very well.
3. The area under direct government rule in Java has been increased by 25 per cent in terms of territory as well as population. The following former princely territories have been added: Banjoemas, Bagelen, Madioen, and Kediri. This is of great financial importance to the government because in these areas the cultivation of

crops suitable for the European market can be considerably expanded.
4. The budget deficit, which for the last half-century has made the colony a financial burden to the mother country, has been transformed into a considerable surplus. In 1832 more than five million and in 1833 more than ten million guilders have been remitted [to Holland] ... and by the end of 1834 it can be safely assumed that a total of twenty-eight to thirty million guilders will have been transferred. This considerable surplus has been obtained without introducing new taxes and without increasing existing ones. On the contrary some of the more oppressive taxes have been removed and others have been reduced.
5. The production of coffee, sugar, and indigo has been expanded greatly because of the introduction of the new cultivation system.
6. The object of this system is to lighten the heavy burden of the land rent on the Javanese and to ensure that they will earn a larger or at least the same income without having to work harder. The system has also made it possible that, within a few years, other important products can be sent to the home market—products such as tea, cinnamon, tobacco, silk, and cochineal. Furthermore, the Javanese are paid a higher price for coffee than previously. And finally, the system has provided the government with the means for remitting large sums [to Holland] ... while the Netherlands has also gained supremacy in the colonial produce trade.
7. Trade in this island has risen considerably because of the expansion of production. Owing to the rise in price of certain products as well as the increase in production, exports today are almost double what they were in the years immediately prior to my arrival ... Profitable employment has been provided for Dutch shipping, which has more than doubled ...

J. van den Bosch, *Rapport over mijne verrichtingen in Indie gedurende de jaren 1830, 1831, 1832, and 1833*. (*Koninklijk Instituut voor de Taal-,Land,- en Volkenkunde van Nederlandsch-Indie, Bijdragen, Deel 7, 1864*) pp. 315,321,472-74.

2   J.C. Baud: Criticisms of van den Bosch and the Culture System in the Netherlands and the Indies, 1832

In the month of June [1832] all sorts of alarming rumours became current in the mother country about the probable results. Your Excellency's measures would have with respect to peace and order in the island of Java. There was talk about people leaving their lands in the Priangan regencies and Cheribon, and about a rebellious spirit in Bantam, and this was used to put your policies in a very unfavourable light. This was the first time that the government in the Netherlands began to fear that the new measures [i.e. the Culture System] would not last long, particularly as they would soon be bereft of Your Excellency's support in person [van den Bosch had requested permission to return home]. These particular letters from Java and the spirit in which the returning officials and officers spoke made this anxiety grow stronger and stronger; and when the letters of Your Excellency, particularly the one of 14 March 1831, no. 289/7 (Cabinet), not only spoke of the desire to be replaced speedily but also frankly recognized that there was fairly generally a spirit of discontent and opposition in the colony, the feeling of anxiety rose even higher ... In the month of September 1831 it also appeared fairly obvious that General de Kock [who was to succeed van den Bosch as governor-general] greatly doubted the expediency of the system introduced by Your Excellency ...

Your excellency has expressed the conviction that the party that is so hostile towards the new system will not let any opportunity pass by to overthrow or undermine it. I completely share this apprehension; I fear that every change of personnel in the administration will be the sign for a new struggle, and I expect during my short presence in Java many open and secret attacks. But if Lieutenant-General de Kock had taken over the government now, then without any doubt these attempts would have been made with even greater force, and the faction in question would undoubtedly have chosen the slogan "Now or never" in their machinations. The reason is that in the Indies also the General is considered to be hostile to the new system and a supporter of the so-called liberal ideas. Is it not better under these circumstances that his appointment be postponed until the new system has been consolidated more, and the tree known by its fruits?

It is true that this tree has already borne fruit, but this was not yet sufficiently known in July 1832 in Europe to reassure anyone with preconceived doubts, who can only judge the situation from a distance and on the authority of others. Private reports now sent from Java recognize that production has increased compared with former days, but they add that this production is bought at the cost of disproportionate sacrifices that cannot be sustained and by measures that sooner or later will disturb the peace of the island ...

On the other hand, it is true that the party in question is now remaining quiet, which seemingly indicates an improvement in the political situation. However, in my opinion this should only be ascribed to the experience they have gained that Your Excellency does not tolerate any opposition. It does not mean at all an improvement in public opinion. Sufficient proof for this can be found in the hereby-enclosed extracts from some private letters, which without breaking good faith I can only present to Your Excellency without mentioning names, although the writers are among *the most important officials and citizens* ...

Extracts from some letters from Java:

19 February 1831

Our Governor-General will soon realize that the forced cultivation of sugar and indigo, for which the poor Javanese labourer hardly receives anything, will cause rebellions in various parts of the island. This is already the case in Bantam from where the resident Smulders has sent the most alarming reports to the government, with the result that now in all haste an expedition has to be sent there on the ships *Rupel* and *Pollux*.

The emigration from the Cheribon region and the Priangan has been on such a large scale, solely because of the forced labour, that all the residents have now received a circular ordering them to drive back to Cheribon all people who have recently arrived in their residencies. It is easy to guess what the consequences of this will be after some time.

16 September 1831

The Governor-General never attends the meetings of the government any more. It is as if he has met the devil in Batavia. His Excellency is completely absorbed in sugar and indigo, which will never enable him to extricate himself from his difficulties. In Europe one seems to expect a great deal of profit from these great enterprises, which alas will probably go the same way as other speculations of this kind. If in some areas the indigo and sugar cultivation still brings some profit, this is snatched up by the sugar mills and the *Handelsmaatschappij* [Netherlands Trading Company, which monopolized colonial trade], while the people are being exploited and the government will have to bear losses in other areas. The cultivation is especially oppressive in the Residencies of Cheribon, Tegal, and the Priangan. In the latter the regents and the people are loudly complaining. Holmberg [the Resident], a weak man, is now bending as much under the yoke of the Governor as he formerly did under the yoke of his wife. The threat of being replaced if he does not strictly comply with the orders and desires of the Governor-General makes him keep his mouth shut and he refrains from warning about the consequences he must fear for the future.

Never before has there ruled in Java such a despot as the self-opiniated and stubborn J. van den Bosch. A ... who a few days ago returned from a trip, could relate many instances of his stubbornness and despotism and his system of cultivation. In the *Oosthoek* [eastern corner] of Java the people are leaving their villages because of the forced delivery of sugar cane, so that its cultivation will disappear again. The planters in the areas surrounding Batavia are about to be ruined because the Governor-General no longer allows *budjangs* [seasonal labour] to come from the Cheribon region because he needs them himself there.

I fear very much for the contractors, Loudon, Dennison and Sturler, because their sugar cane will everywhere be ripe and rotting before their European machinery will have arrived. But as none of them have much to lose and because of that have made such hazardous contracts, although hoping for great profits, it will probably be the poor natives again who will suffer most—they will be discouraged from ever planting sugar cane again. Only in Bantam and Japara can the cultivation of sugar succeed, because there the natives plant and mill the sugar cane themselves, and so can count with certainty on being recompensed for their labours, providing that this cultivation is profitable. However, in this residency one should not expect the progress promised.

The indigo crop has also been unsuccessful, because it was already ripe and too old before the factories were completed. The indigo planted on cleared virgin lands in the Priangan has now been abandoned and the natives are forced to plant indigo *on the rice fields*. Many rice-growers will be harmed because rice-planting does not begin everywhere at the same time, and the cultivation of coffee will be completely neglected, yes ruined. These measures, which have caused discontent among the chiefs as well as the common people, will completely dissipate the support given to us by the people of the Priangan regencies during the war in the principalities [i.e. the Dipanegara War, *see* document 37].

May God save us from a new rebellion.

6 November 1831

Our Governor-General may be clever and good, but His Excellency keeps these qualities very much hidden from us, because we never see him. And he only has contact with a number of old gentlemen, who in respect of their ability do not seem to be a happy choice. He can count his friends on his fingers. The army and all of the civil service, with the exception of van Sevenhoven [Director of Cultivation] and a few others whom I do not want to name, are completely averse to him ... He therefore stands completely alone and those who could be useful to him let him go his own way, and follow up his orders strictly, leaving him to account for the consequences. In short they have shelved all their ambitions. How matters will develop this way nobody understands, and perhaps least of all His Excellency. He just keeps consulting an uninformed person such as van Sevenhoven, a muddle-head such as van Lawick, and suchlike who give him lipservice ...

17 May 1832

Ostensibly the situation is quiet in the Cheribon region, but it simmers a great deal. Forced cultivation does not suit this country. The time of the old Company has passed and the Javanese have become so enlightened that they will not take things lying down for long ...

Baud aan van den Bosch. Aan boord van het schip Princes Marianne den 24 December 1832. No. 26 Partikulier en zeer Vertrouwelijk. in: J.J. Westendorp Boerma *Briefwisseling tussen J. van den Bosch en J.C. Baud, 1829-1832 en 1834-1836*. Tweede Deel. Brieven van Baud. (Historisch Genootschap, Werken, Derde Serie no. 81.), pp. 105-9, 116-122.

3 J. van den Bosch: Despatch to de Eerens, 30 April 1836

[After a brilliant military career, Major-General D.J. de Eerens was appointed governor-general of the Netherlands Indies, a position he held from 1834 to 1840.]

For the future it will be important to ensure that only known supporters of the present system of government in the Indies will be promoted to important positions. The existence of the State [the Netherlands] is so closely tied to its [the Culture System's] success that it could be thrown into the balance by private considerations. Preventive measures are even more necessary because there is a faction in the Indies, connected with a similar group here, that opposes the expressed directives of the King—also in matters not concerning the colonies—often using reports sent from the Indies. For example at the moment again there is one in circulation by Vitalis, a colonial official, about the indigo cultivation [document 4]. I only have it on hearsay, but if its contents are as claimed, it is shameful, and the activities of this official must in the future be watched ...

The opposition in the Indies and here is not planning to stop until it has succeeded in having a governor-general of its own choice appointed, that is, someone who will remit as little as possible [i.e. budget surpluses], who will give preferential treatment to local trade, who will ruin the *Handelsmaatschappij*, and who will make the mother country serviceable to the Indies, and not the Indies to the State. This objective, however, will not be easily achieved, as long as I may be honoured with the King's trust.

I must ask the special attention of Your Excellency for officials who are invested with the important position of resident. When these are suitable for their position and work diligently, the [forced] cultivation will succeed; but if they are unwilling or unsuited, everything will be inefficient. The only way to prevent this is to transfer or dismiss on compensating pay officials who do not live up to expectations. The Residents of Bantam, Tegal, Pekalongan, and Rembang seem to me to be bad appointments ...

Changing from persons to business, it is in the first place the coffee cultivation that must be emphasized and which in the interest of the government deserves Your Excellency's greatest attention. I venture to trust that when the trees which have now been planted bear fruit, the average production could amount to 100 million pounds. However, diligent care must be taken that this cultivation does not decline again and that every year one-twelfth of the trees must be replaced with great care.

The cultivation of sugar must be extended on government lands and by private interests to a limit of half a million *piculs* [1 *picul* = 61.7613 kilograms]. The present high prices cannot be expected to last. They have always been subject to heavy fluctuations. And the average price paid on delivery should not be higher than ten guilders—or at the highest twelve guilders.

Indigo is a precious product and deserves all the encouragement it can get. Production must be increased to one million pounds.

The cultivation of tea can become as important for Java as coffee production. However, it will still require a number of years before all difficulties are overcome. In the meantime it is advisable that tea should be planted in all suitable residencies. Very fertile lands must be selected for this purpose and up to one million bushes should be planted yearly. I repeat that good, fertile lands must be selected. I believe that these can be found particularly in Banjoemas and other new residencies.

The cultivation of cinnamon should also be encouraged as much as possible and should be increased similarly in all residencies. Both cinnamon and tea could become major products for our trade.

Cochineal, silk, and tobacco could become of minor importance—although I fear that they will never be major products.

I should be pleased if Your Excellency would request the Director of Cultivation to prepare a report showing the state of cultivation, its possible extension, and the most suitable means to be used. In addition to the projected quantities of coffee, sugar, and indigo, we should count on a production of two to three million pounds of tea, four to five hundred thousand pounds of cinnamon, and in proportion, twenty thousand pounds of cochineal, silk, and tobacco. Experience will teach us the appropriate increase in production that is needed. Such a report, accompanied by the submissions of Your Excellency and the government, would certainly be pleasing to the King.

The cultivation of rice especially deserves the care of the government, because it is of importance to the Javanese. Of particular importance is the construction of proper irrigation works. I am sure that this will always be a subject of the special attention of Your Excellency.

The financial situation of the colony is of no less importance to the [Netherlands] Government. It is certain that without the generous contributions of the Indies, the State would have been ruined and we would long ago have been forced to submit ourselves to the mercy of the opposition. But now we have been saved from our predicament and we can patiently wait until the time when we will be able on the basis of reasonable conditions to reach a final settlement. It is a matter of great anxiety that the financial situation of the Indies is of such importance, with so many important interests depending on it. Everything that may have a harmful effect on it causes serious fears here for the future, while every sign pointing to increasing prosperity brings great pleasure. Everything has now been arranged, and deviations from the accepted principles could only cause unpleasant impressions: *le mieux est l'ennemi du bien* [change is not always for the better]. Your Excellency then should stick exactly to the existing regulations ...

So far as trade is concerned, it is the intention of the King that as little as possible of local production will be sold in Java, but that instead as much as possible will be consigned to the *Handelsmaatschappij*. I must tell Your Excellency that, so far as I am concerned, I would like to leave some more leeway to private traders, but the *Handelsmaatschappij* strongly objects to this, arguing that imports by private traders would depress the market here, while it also considers that in the interests of our budding secondary industry it must be made difficult for foreigners to obtain return freights. It is known to Your Excellency how much we are opposed in this by foreigners and that we have been forced in their interest to levy duties on our own goods [this refers to pressure by the British Government]. That this causes a very unpleasant feeling, Your Excellency can certainly imagine. As a result the King feels strongly that no produce, unless it is absolutely necessary, should be sold. This is even more important since our own merchants often lower themselves to bring out English industrial goods and so act to the detriment of the common good. It is truly lamentable to see that for so many the quest for gain is of such preponderant importance, although they usually thereby rob themselves of the profits they could otherwise make.

I am having copper coins made here and I shall again send silver specie in order to diminish the necessity to sell produce. I realize very well that the position of Your Excellency will be made more difficult because of this and that the pressure of commercial houses in Java to sell produce by public auction will be very strong. Still the common good and the strong determination of the King in this matter do not allow for any deviations from the established rule. Only as much produce may be sold as is necessary to keep the funds in the Government Treasury to the agreed level, and absolutely no more. Also the tin from Bangka can from now on be remitted, because it is doing very well here.

So far as the governing of the natives is concerned, I have already given my views in the memorandum I left behind [*see* document 1], and I only wish to add this: I have always found it to be dangerous to take the lower classes of the people away from the influence of their chiefs, or to superimpose on these people a happiness that they do not understand. If it depended on us to make the Javanese happy, then no sacrifice would appear to me to be too large, but all our philanthropic dreams have only led them into popular uprisings and wars. Hundreds of thousands of people in Java have been slaughtered because we wanted to make them happy in accordance with our views. A sound knowledge of the Javanese character, economic life, and views is required before any good can be done in this respect, and I feel that I should advise Your Excellency to change as little as possible in the existing situation. They [the Javanese] cannot be protected enough against the Europeans and Chinese. It is not their chiefs, who are so often given a bad name but to whom the Javanese nevertheless remain faithful with unbreakable loyalty, who suppress them—at least not in their opinion—but the bloodsuckers I have just named, who, if not checked, torture them. Their activities should be carefully watched ...

Van den Bosch aan de Eerens, Geheim. Particulier. no. 2, in: F.C. Gerretson *en* W.Ph. Coolhaas *Particuliere Briefwisseling tussen J. van den Bosch en D.J. De Eerens 1834-1840*, (Historisch Genootschap, Werken, Derde Serie, no. 83) (Groningen: Wolters, 1960), pp. 47-54.

4   L. Vitalis: The system of forced cultivation in Java, 1851

The introduction of the new system of forced cultivation was announced in a circular explaining the principles, procedures, and purpose of the system. Immediately its opponents began to raise their objections. And it is very peculiar that all these opponents were paid government officials. Some complained: "We will no longer be Residents but farmers". And others said that anybody who sacrificed himself for the government deserved to be hanged ... These gentlemen did not hide their feelings from the regents. This caused a great deal of harm to the people because the regents, who preferred very much to be left alone and only carried out inspections when they had to accompany the Resident on tour, were very happy to see that their superiors harboured the same feelings. This is the reason why in some residencies where the Resident was opposed to the system, the poor peasants were forced for six years to carry out a great deal of useless work without receiving any payment. In some areas the people were pestered to plant sugar cane in soil that was unprepared. Elsewhere peasants were compelled to deliver to the Chinese mill-owner double the amount they were paid for ... In one residency ... the people were obliged to plant millions of coffee trees in soil that consisted of limestone and was completely infertile. When in 1837 I inspected this residency, I had to suggest stopping this cultivation, because after two thousand peasants had been forced to work for five years, some of whom had to walk twenty-eight miles to the plantations, the total harvest was only 3 *piculs*. So only thirty-six guilders were to be divided among all these labourers for five years of toil. In other places coffee trees had been planted on exhausted lands that had been abandoned by the population. In short, from Rembang to Pekalongan everything possible had been done to make the people discouraged and discontented.

In Cheribon, Tegal, and Pekalongan, the European authorities were up against the machinations of the regents, who saw with great reluctance that the powers they had been able to maintain secretly, to the detriment of the people, were diminishing daily as a result of the extension of the new system. They therefore constantly intrigued to make the people discontented, which in their view was the only way to make the government stop the cultivation of the new crops. So they selected for the cultivation of indigo all the rice fields that were close to the factories. The result was that the people of these villages moved away because they had no fields in which to plant rice for their own upkeep; and soon the only people left in the region were the chiefs.

As the regents supplied the residents with lists of the villages charged with producing the various crops, they took care to include all villages so that they checked out with the lists of the *controleurs*. But they excepted the richest villages from forced cultivation on the condition that these villages—which were divided among the regents, district heads and lesser chiefs, and relatives of the regents—would deliver people and horses for their own use. Those arrangements obviously put the other villages at a distinct disadvantage, because their task was now doubled. Also the regents took recourse to torture to compel the heads of these villages to supply more people for the plantations than was indicated on the lists. In this way, of course, the crops were not in good condition.

I was sent there to inspect the situation. I never warned the heads beforehand when I decided to go on tour. Once I unexpectedly arrived at a factory and the first thing I saw was ten old men—all heads and members of the village councils—whose thumbs had been fastened to a rope thrown over a tree branch so that these unfortunate men could hardly touch the ground with their toes. A few moments later the district head appeared and seeing himself caught in the act, excused himself by saying that he had acted on the orders of the Regent. These men were punished because they had not supplied enough from their respective villages for the forced cultivation. I investigated the matter and compared the number of labourers who were working in the plantations with those on the lists. To my astonishment I found that the villages whose heads were being punished supplied more people than they were obliged to, while many of the larger villages did not supply anybody at all ... In another district I found village heads lying completely naked on the ground with their arms bound and exposed to the sun. This was also done on the orders of the Regent ...

The system has worked very badly in the Priangan regencies. Nowhere else have the people been more vexed and suppressed. The government wanted to pay less for indigo in the Priangan because the people there do not pay tax. But I know of no other residency in Java where the burdens on the population are heavier than in the Priangan. It is true that they pay tax to their own heads instead of to the government. But this does not mean that they are better off. They have to pay one-fifth in kind of all [produce], ... of which one-tenth is for the regents and one-tenth for the priests. Furthermore, the people supply everything that the chiefs need for their *sedeka* [feasts] without any payment, and all services have to be performed without payment. Moreover they only receive 7 guilders for a *picul* of highland coffee of 225 pounds, while coffee-planters elsewhere receive 21.60 guilders for the same weight ...

The forced cultivation of indigo was introduced in the Priangan in 1830. And in 1835 I was charged with the inspection of the factories in this residency in order to determine whether the sorry state of affairs pictured by the Resident Holmberg de Beckfelt was not exaggerated ... The following extract from my report of 29 January 1835 is indicative of the situation of these poor peasants:

> Truly their situation is lamentable and really miserable. What else can one expect? On the roads as well as in the plantations one does not meet people but only walking skeletons, which drag themselves with great difficulty from one place to another, often dying in the process. The Regent of Sukapura told me that some of the labourers who work in the plantations are in such a state of exhaustion that they die almost immediately after they have eaten from the food which is given to them as an advance payment for the produce to be delivered later. If I had not witnessed this myself I would have been hesitant in reporting this ... These victims can even be found on the roads leading from Tasikmalaja, Garoet, Ardjawinangon, and Galo. One even passes them unnoticed! What then must be the fate of those who collapse on the desolate roads and paths? The Regent, when asked why he did not have the bodies buried, replied: "Every night these bodies are dragged away by the tigers." ...

The decrease in the production of indigo and rice has now become a question of great importance ... The suppression of the people began as early as 1836 because it was from that time onwards that the cultivation of export crops for the European market was pushed excessively ... Poverty has increased yearly and the number of people leaving their districts for other areas has constantly been growing ... In the regulation of 28 March 1834, no. 1, ... the government has set out how much labour was to be used for forced cultivation, i.e.:

"Four families are to be exclusively concerned with the cultivation of 1 *bouw* [1 *bouw* = 7096.5 square metres] of land. Two and one-tenth families per *bouw* are to be used for the harvesting of the crop, the delivery of firewood, the treatment and the transportation of the crops." These regulations were strictly adhered to ... until May 1836 when the Director of Plantations, Mr Elias, departed for Europe. From then until the appointment to this post of Mr Baud in 1842, the productin of export crops, in particular indigo, was increased excessively ... The pitiful results [in the residencies of Cheribon, Pekalongan, and Bagelen] were as follows:

> The people are overburdened with work, with the result that they are unable to take care of their own affairs and have no time to work the land and grow the crops needed for their own upkeep.
>
> The people have been forced to cede a larger share of their *sawahs* [wet rice cultivation] than is required by the government. The result is that they have to go without four-fifths of their rice land, which is absolutely necessary for their unkeep.
>
> The need to rest the land to maintain fertility has been neglected and at present the land is so exhausted that there are villages where the people are growing indigo, which yields no more than two guilders for a whole year's labour.

[Furthermore] the inhabitants of each district are bound to buy and take care of the upkeep of six draught horses as well as their harnesses, which are to be used by the residents, regents, and other officials on their tours of inspection. The funds necessary for the upkeep of these horses etc. are deducted from the amount due for produce delivered, as if the advantage these officials draw from the system of forced cultivation were not sufficient to buy the necessary horses. The government, blinded by the vast amount of produce delivered by these three residencies during the four years when production was pushed excessively, felt that it should reward these residents, who in fact had caused the greatest possible harm to the interests of the state ...

Immediately after the introduction of the new system large areas of land that previously were covered with forests or were not irrigated were made into *sawahs*. This was made possible by the river dams built to supply the sugar factories with water. During the western monsoon this water was not needed by the factories, and while the sugar cane was harvested, the water was used to irrigate the rice land through which the canals had been dug ... Previously various low-lying and marshy regions had not been suitable for agriculture. But after the surplus water from floods during the rainy season had been channelled there, a great deal of mud and other sediment was deposited so that large parts of these regions were recreated into fertile lands.

In many districts there was no river water to irrigate the *sawahs*, so the people could only grow *padi gendjang* [i.e. rice which ripens early—three and a half to four months after planting—but which yields considerably less than *padi dalem*, slow-growing rice which ripens five to six months after planting] ... The people therefore were entirely dependent on rainwater ... and every time the rains stopped early there were large losses in rice production. But since the setting-up of sugar factories in these areas the canals dug have supplied the necessary water for the lands and the people have been able to concentrate on the growing of *padi dalem*, at the same time being protected against losses caused ... by the early arrival of the dry season ...

The largest part of the *sawahs* on which sugar cane and indigo are now grown and which received an ample water supply was until 1836 planted with *padi dalem*. Only that part of the land—at the highest, one-quarter of the total *sawah* area of a village—on which sugar and indigo was to be grown was planted with *padi gendjang*. This was because an early harvest was necessary to get the land ready for the cultivation of crops destined for the European market.

These then are the causes of the great increase in rice lands and the abundant supply of rice that was brought onto the market until 1837 ... Even if the new system of cultivation had not been successful, it is evident ... that its immediate impact would have been beneficial to Java because of the great improvements and considerable increase in rice cultivation.

What then are the fateful circumstances that ... during a period of ten years have changed this state of prosperity into one of suppression and misery for the poor inhabitants of Java? One of the reasons is the desire of officials to increase the profits of the system and to gather a fortune within a few years. Another reason is the desire to gain the approbation of the government for the delivery of large quantities of produce and to be decorated for their good services ... From the moment that the Javanese were forced to grow sugar cane or indigo on one-third or even half of their *sawahs*, it was no longer possible for them to grow *padi dalem*. And it was from that time that the decline in the production of rice commenced. The situation became worse when in 1840 the less fertile lands—which since 1836 had only been rested every alternate year instead of four out of every five years—were completely exhausted ... and it is since then that the farmers have suffered double losses—because of the decline in both the yields of sugar and indigo *and* in rice production ... The exhaustion of the soil causes the farmers to lose more than half the produce they earlier obtained from the same area of land. They also lose, at least for a large part, the benefits of the second crops after the rice harvest, such as *ubis* [sweet potatoes], *kumbilis* [herb-like tubers], corn, peas, white beans, *palma christi* [castor-oil plants], water melons, and various kinds of vegetables, because they lack the time to take proper care of these plants.

It is terrible to think that the poor farmers do not only have to pay taxation on the land, which hardly yields any rice, but also on that part of the land on which they are forced to grow sugar and indigo and for which, in spite of all the work, they hardly get any payment; that the money to pay taxes must be taken from the sale of the little rice they have rather than being paid out of the proceeds from the produce delivered for the European market, as the government promised; that the taxes must be paid during the last six months of the year during which the rice costs only four to six guilders per *picul*, while in the next few months the farmers are forced to buy rice for their own upkeep for which they have to pay twice or three times as much; ... and that since the harvests of 1840 and 1841, rice prices in the countryside have risen to ten and fourteen guilders per *picul*! This is the price paid by Europeans who are living there. How much then must the needy Javanese pay, who live from day to day and at the highest buy a whole *kati* [1 *kati* = 625 grams] at once? It is terrible to see the bitter poverty in which farmers live during the western monsoon since the wages paid for forced cultivation are not sufficient to pay taxation. This is the reason why people are constantly on the move from one place to another and why the people are restless. This will not change until the government takes measures to eradicate the existing abuses and thus show the Javanese, who because of their good character fully deserve to be protected in their interests by a fatherly government, that the promise "the improvement of his future living conditions" has not been false ...

It is painful to admit that the situation of the Javanese is indeed so shocking that it is difficult to present a completely realistic picture. Fortunately, this disastrous situation does not exist generally: in many residencies of East Java, a few regions excepted, where the influence of the native heads is still too strong, the people are benefiting from the new system of cultivation. But for the indigo farmers of the Residencies of Cheribon and Bagelen and the sugar and indigo farmers of the Residency of Pekalongan this system has been until now *a source of suppression* that has *already lasted for sixteen years*.

In addition, the people have to obey the various demands of the regents, who are charged with executive power and who attempt to perpetuate the abuses of Asiatic rule. This would not have been possible if a European system of taxation had been introduced, one based on the principles of individual freedom and free disposal of the fruits of one's labour.

In addition the European administration compels the people to deliver materials under the pretext of the beautification of the cities, the improvement or construction of *pasanggrahans* [guest houses for officials], police posts on the major roads, postal stations (in one of the Javanese residencies there are buildings of that kind that have cost the people eight thousand guilders each!), and many other works ...

In addition account should be taken of all that is demanded from the Javanese in terms of "seignorial services", which are not officially limited ... [These services] are either paid for by reductions on wages ... or in money, or by their own labour, or by the delivery of building materials for which they do not get paid.

And finally there should be added to this the countless number of Chinese who have leased government road tolls and subject native farmers at almost every step at the road leading to the market-place to new extortions, so that often they lose half of their produce in this way. It should therefore be no surprise that the poor Javanese have no time to take care of their own households and farms. And one must agree that the fate of the Javanese, who are suppressed from all sides, is extremely miserable and that it is cruel that a government that gives itself the distinction of being a *fatherly administration* lets such abuses continue ...

It must come as a great surprise that in spite of the decline in rice production the land tax is increasing yearly! I have heard from a good source that in a certain district where in 1845 the tax amounted to about 42,000 guilders, this sum was increased in November 1846 by 17,000 guilders, or about 50 per cent ... What are the results of *over-taxation*? In the villages where there are enough people to cultivate all the *sawahs* ... the land tax is paid regularly, because the greatest desire of the Javanese is to possess *sawahs*, which provide him and his family with the necessities of life. The farmer therefore always takes care to pay his taxes in time, so that the village chief has no cause to refuse him his share in the coming harvest. But if the Resident makes up the assessment in November and not in July, as is laid down in the regulations, ... various compulsory measures are taken to force the taxpayers to pay the increased amount before the end of December. But as the taxpayers at that time have no money at their disposal and hardly have enough rice left for planting in the next year, it will be very difficult to get the necessary money together. Moreover the village chiefs, who are daily reminded by the district chiefs and the *controleur* about the arrears in taxation, immediately seize buffaloes, agricultural implements, or other goods belonging to the defaulters ...

A time is determined within which the money must be paid. The farmer asks to borrow the necessary money from his relatives. If he does not succeed then he pawns his best clothes to the Chinese, who only give him a third of the value and on top charge 3 to 4 per cent per month. It should be obvious that a Javanese can very seldom redeem the goods he has pawned during the rainy season, because he must then spend money for the cultivation of his land and he has to pay a very high price for the rice needed to feed himself and his family. In addition he may have to take on the upkeep of his parents. And the interst he has to pay during these four or five months might be as much as the value of the goods he has pawned. If the person who owes the tax only possesses buffaloes, they are sold for half their value or even less. On this point no grace is given, because if the village chief does not pay the due taxes, his legs will be clamped in a wooden block until everything that is owed by the whole village is paid. So everything is sold for whatever price it fetches. If, however, the assessment is made in July, the poor tax debtor will have the opportunity to find work in one factory or another and can in this way pay off one-sixth every month of the amount due. But otherwise he has to give up his only buffalo, which is so very necessary for the cultivation of his land and which he has only been able to buy after *five or six* years of work. If on the other hand he is able to sell his buffalo during the sugar cane harvest, a factory owner will pay twice as much for it. If the tax debtor has no property at all, his wife and children are treated as slaves until everything is paid. It is often the case that three-quarters of the villagers have no rice left in November. If then the tax assessment is made in November and is increased by two guilders per *bouw*, which is excessive but nevertheless happens, these compulsive measures are taken.

A certain village, which possesses thirty-one *sawahs* of the second class, paid in 1845 tax to the amount of 310 guilders, which is already very high for *sawahs* of that kind, but in 1846 the tax was increased by 125 guilders, or 4 guilders per *bouw*. How is it possible for the people to pay these taxes when they have not any rice left for their upkeep? This suppressive way of governing is also the reason why so many thieves are found in the rainy season ...

Irregular rains during the monsoon of 1844-45 caused the rice harvest to fail in a region ... known as the *granary of the Residency* [Cheribon]. Unfortunately, for the same reason, harvests were also bad in the other regions, so that help from other districts could not be expected. This is how the great famine came about in which a large number of people perished ... Many inhabitants of these districts had moved in time to somewhere else, particularly in Indramajoe ... Others had gone to the Priangan Regencies, where in the Regency of Bandoeng there is a large area of rice land. Others, however, who were either more attached to the land on which they were born, or who were less intelligent, sought their food in the forests and tried to satisfy their hunger with roots and wild fruits, from which hundreds died. All roads and paths were covered with bodies. These bodies, with their hands bound together, were dragged to the river by the inhabitants of the villages in which they fell and were thrown to the crocodiles. Large hordes of children, whose parents had died from hunger, wandered throughout the land to beg food from the various owners of sugar factories ... I know one of these factory-owners who for a considerable time daily fed about sixty of these unfortunate little ones. Often there were more. Their number increased daily. The new arrivals were wild-eyed and as thin as a skeleton. They were treated with particular care by this factory-owner. First they were given little food, but a few times a day, in order to restore the stomach, which was weakened by exhaustion. Twice a day they were given rice with some vegetables by the factory-owner himself. Mothers with children at their dried-out breasts threw themselves at his feet, beseeching him to take their children, whom they could not feed any longer. Another factory-owner ... spent a sum of five thousand guilders to help these unfortunate ones. Every morning he sent some trusted persons ... to take care of those unfortunate people who because of their weakness had not been able to find their way home. Every day these people found bodies of men, women, and children. Once they found two skeletons of children, who probably had been torn apart by jackals. The first of the factory-owners I mentioned was Mr van Toll and the other was Mr Leysius.

These dramas took place in *Java*, a land where Providence has given its most beautiful gifts to the plant kingdom. It is true that the government did send help to the people of these regions, but as always, *after the people had already been severely hit by famine ...* It is sad to have to admit that poor, hungry people who came in droves to beseech private people in the Residency of Cheribon for food did not dare to turn to the government officials. When they were asked why they did not go to the officials for help, the answer was: "*We fear them*"!

L. Vitalis, *De invoering, werking en gebreken van het stelsel van Kultures op Java* (Zaltbommel: Noman, 1851), pp. 1-5, 14-16, 21-22, 28-34, 40-42, 57-61, 82-86.

The impact of Liberalism on Dutch colonial policy, 1848-1900

Criticism of abuses and malpractices had reached Holland only sporadically during the heyday of the Culture System. It was only after the mid-1840s that pamphlets and newspaper reports began to appear in the Netherlands decrying the miserable lot of the Javanese. This criticism intensified during the 1850s when humanitarian colonial reformers were joined in their attack on the Culture System by doctrinaire Liberals in the Dutch Parliament as well as by a group of more pragmatic private bankers, industrialists, and traders, who had greatly profited by the system of van den Bosch, but who now wanted to invest their accumulated capital in private plantations and mining enterprises in the Indies. Although humanitarian interests played a role, most of the Dutch Liberals were just as interested as their conservative opponents in extracting the largest possible profits from the Indies, and argued that private enterprise unfettered by government interference was bound to create the best of all possible worlds for the Dutch and Indonesians alike.

One of the most prominent colonial reformers during the 1850s was Baron van Hoevell, a minister of the Dutch Reformed Church, and an ardent Liberal and humanitarian. In 1848 he had been involved in a demonstration in Batavia by disgruntled Europeans—mainly Eurasians—who had petitioned the King for freedom of the press, the establishment of secondary schools in the colony, and representation of the Indies in the Dutch Parliament. After strong pressure by the colonial authorities van Hoevell resigned from his church post and returned to the Netherlands, where soon afterwards he was elected to parliament. Van Hoevell in his parliamentary speeches stressed that both the rulers and the subjects in the colony would profit most if the colonial government abandoned outright exploitation and instead made its first duty the raising of economic and educational standards among the indigenous people (*see* document 5).

Even more incisive and damaging was the criticism of Eduard Douwes Dekker (*see* document 6), a former colonial official who, using the pseudonym "Multatuli" ("I have suffered a great deal"), published a novel in 1860 called *Max Havelaar*, in which the inhumanity and immorality of colonial rule in the Indies were vividly portrayed. *Max Havellar* caused a public outcry in the Netherlands that greatly aided the final onslaught on the Culture System by the Liberals, who by the early 1860s had gained sufficient strength in the Dutch Parliament to push through their colonial programme. The pressure of private planters in Java for a secure supply of land and labour was also growing, and when in 1863 Fransen van de Putte, a former planter from Java, became Minister of Colonies, the fate of the Culture System was sealed. Document 7 illustrates some of the arguments put forward by Liberal-inspired colonial officials, businessmen, and planters.

The forced cultivation of some crops was quickly abolished (pepper in 1862; cloves and nutmeg in 1863; indigo, tea, cinnamon, and cochineal in 1865; and tobacco in 1866). In 1870 it was decided to abolish the forced cultivation of sugar over a period of twelve years, but coffee, which was considered a necessary mainstay of government revenue, remained an exception and its forced cultivation was allowed to linger on in some areas as late as 1916.

The *Agrarische Wet* (Land Laws) of 1870 attempted to provide planters with security of land tenure, and at the same time to protect the interests and rights of the indigenous people. Virgin land could be rented from the government for a period of up to seventy-five years, but land owned by native villages or individuals could be rented only for shorter periods. No native-owned land could be sold to Europeans or other non-Indonesians. Indonesians could also obtain—if they so desired—European legal rights on their land as distinct from the provisions of the *adat* law (indigenous customary law). The supply of plantation labour was regulated by the *Koelie Ordonnantie* (Coolie Ordinance) of 1880, which laid down that contracts specifying the duration and conditions of employment were to be signed before a magistrate. By law the employer had to provide the workers with proper housing and medical care. In return the coolies were bound to the plantation for the duration of their contracts, unless they could show due cause in a court of law.

The earlier attempts by Daendels, Raffles, and the Commissioners-General at defeudalization, which had been abandoned during the Culture System, were now taken up again. And by the beginning of the twentieth century the Javanese regents and their subordinate officials—*priyayi*—had lost most of their feudal privileges and local independence and had been reduced to a corps of civil servants under the direct control of the Batavian Government.

Liberal colonial governments also established a rudimentary modern indigenous education system. Motivated by Liberal ideals as well as the growing demand for local—and therefore cheaper—Western-trained personnel by the rapidly expanding civil service and private enterprise, they enabled a wider section of Indonesians to receive some Western education. As a first step a number of native teachers' training colleges were set up in the 1850s, followed in 1867 by the establishment of a department of education. A government decree of 1863 opened all positions in the civil service to all citizens in the colony, irrespective of race or creed. Not to make this decree a dead letter, European primary schools were opened in the same year to Indonesians, although soon high school fees were levied to restrict entry as much as possible to upper-class Indonesian children. While the European Primary School Certificate gave automatic entry into the lower civil service positions, the European high schools, a number of which were also now established in Java, prepared students for the medium and higher echelon positions. In addition some special training institutions for Indonesians were set up. One such was the *Dokter-Djawa* School, originally a school for indigenous vaccinators, which by the 1870s had grown into a medical school; another was the *Hoofden Scholen*, to train the sons of native chiefs. From the early 1870s three-year elementary schools to cater for the education needs of the general indigenous population were established. In the period 1873-99 the teachers colleges were attended by 2356 students, of whom 907 graduated, while the *Dokter-Djawa* School was attended by 729 students, of whom 152 graduated in the period 1875-1904. In the period 1871-98 the number of elementary schools increased from 263 to 516, the number of boy students from 12,186 to 48,156, and the number of girls from 4420 to 8238.

The earlier years of the Liberal period showed a marked improvement in the native economic situation, but native prosperity diminished again after 1880 when planters were hit severely by a steep decline in prices for their produce on the world market and by an outbreak of disease in coffee and sugar. Native wages and the income received from land rented to plantations were sharply reduced. The spectacular rise in the native population during the second half of the nineteenth century was not matched by a proportional increase in the total income of the native sector of the economy, and in Java a situation of "shared poverty" arose, where the same product had to be shared by an ever-increasing number of people. To make matters worse, the indigenous people were forced to bear a disproportionately heavy tax burden.

Private European enterprise had forced the colonial government to spend vast sums of money to build railways and tramways, and to improve and expand roads, harbours, and irrigation works. And while the European plantation and mining concerns were the major beneficiaries of this, they refused to pay a proper share of the colony's tax bill, of which more than 80 per cent was passed on to the indigenous people. Similarly, the vast expenditure incurred at this time by the colonial government in effectively occupying the Outer Islands had to be paid for mainly by the Javanese, although most of the benefit went again to the European companies that had been pressing for the proper protection of their investments in the outlying areas.

The budget study by Heyting in the 1880s (republished by Boeke—*see* document 8), although incomplete, presents a sample of the economic plight of Javanese farmers. It also shows that the money economy had by no means replaced the traditional subsistence economy as yet.

By the end of the nineteenth century the colonial economy had severely stagnated (*see* document 9), and the colonial government itself was on the verge of bankruptcy because it had not the means to pay for the vast expenditure it had been forced to make. The considerable loss in government revenue caused by the abolition of the Culture System had not been balanced by the introduction of another efficient system of taxation. The Javanese were taxed to the hilt and carried a heavy debt burden, but the Europeans refused to pay more.

5   **W. R. van Hoevell: Parliamentary speech, 8 December 1851**

It has been said that we [the Liberals] want to change everything in Java, that we want to destroy the system of forced cultivation, and that we want to construct another system in its place. Gentlemen, I consider it my duty ... to repeat again straight out and as concisely and clearly as possible what I, and many others with me, desire with regard to the system of forced cultivation. I will therefore answer the following three questions:
1. What value has the forced system of cultivation?
2. Has this system served its purpose?
3. What changes have to be made immediately?

What value has the system of forced cultivation? I do not hesitate to say that in 1830—and before that—the system of forced cultivation, in the way it was conceived by General van den Bosch and not in the way it was executed, was perhaps the only possible and feasible means to make Java produce in a very short time for the European market ... It was found from experience that Java was lacking in something that was absolutely necessary to produce crops for the European market on the basis of free labour ... Why did the system of free labour produce only little coffee, sugar, and other crops for the European market? Because the necessary capital and knowledge were lacking. The Commissioner-General du Bus [1828] wanted to solve this problem by means of European colonization; he wanted private [Europeans] to bring capital and know-how to Java. But General van den Bosch was in a great hurry and suggested something else, which at that time perhaps was correct. He understood that because of the lack of enterprise and the prejudices existing in the fatherland at the time against investments in the Indies, the necessary capital and technicians would not be brought to Java. He tried to reach his goal by putting the government and its servants in the place of private capital and private entrepreneurs. What otherwise would have been achieved through free will, because of the stimulus of capital, was now achieved through orders and compulsion ... But how has the system of General van den Bosch worked in Java? All the descriptions given in this Chamber of the miserable situation of the Javanese population caused by the Culture System— all these pictures of famine, misery, pauperization, epidemics, depopulation—all this is true and not overdone. This, however, was not a *necessary* result of the system, but the blame should be put *on the way it was executed* ... But I also admit that there are reasons to declare that the system has at the same time rendered good service. I do not only want to point to the millions that have flowed into the Treasury and the large growth of our merchant navy; but I also want to stress that the interest of the mother country in the colony and the willingness to invest capital and know-how in the Indies have gradually but surely increased. I also want to point to the fact that in areas where the system has worked well, such as in Pasoeroean, Probolinggo, and some other districts, the people are indeed prosperous ...

Now I come to the question, has the Culture System, which was so excellent in its conception and in its intentions, but so disastrous in the way it was executed—has this system now served its purpose? Should it be demolished and destroyed immediately? My answer is: definitely no. But my reasons are different from those of the Member from Rotterdam (Mr Baud) [the major colonial expert of the Conservative faction]. Although wishing to return to the old system of freedom [of trade and labour], which would involve the introduction of liberal institutions, he argues against the abolition of the Culture System because it would lead to the destruction of trade and shipping, and to national bankruptcy ... I do not desire the continuation of the system on these grounds. I have other reasons. So far in this discussion the Culture System has been looked at mainly with regard to its effect on the Javanese and Javanese society. But there is still another consideration: the influence of the system and of the whole colonial monopoly position on the Treasury. I do not have to remind you ... [that it] has been calculated that it is just this monopoly system that causes great harm to the Treasury. That is to say, if this system did not exist and the government just restricted itself to its duties as sovereign and did not take part in production and trade—the Indies would bring yearly millions more into the Treasury. I do not want to say at all that I consider this argument to be correct. But it seems very probable to me, although I wish to leave the question undecided. I only wish to say that it would be worth while to investigate this question carefully. If [this argument were] right then the Member from Rotterdam would have no longer any cause to oppose the immediate abolition of the system. This is clear from what he said openly yesterday. Only the concern for the Treasury, and for our shipping and trade holds him back. But even if this argument is true, then I say no, we should not abandon the Culture System. This is so, gentlemen, because I have other reasons for wanting the Culture System to continue ...

Firstly, the Culture System, although it has brought more European industry and capital to Java, has still not realized by any means what it was meant to do in this respect ... Secondly, I do not want shocks; I do not want to cut down the tree, but I want to prune the dead branches and I want to give the tree a different shape. I do not want to ignore the fact that the system has existed in Java for more than twenty years. We are no longer in 1830. Those who would have voted against the system of General van den Bosch at that time should realize that in this last quarter of a century it has taken root, that it has effected a complete change in Java, a complete reformation—yes, I dare to say, a revolution of Javanese society. I do not want to experiment with the Javanese people, but I want to develop the people and their institutions gradually. That is why I desire that the system shall not be demolished and that is why I say that the system has still not achieved what it set out to do.

I am now coming to the question: what changes should be made immediately? First I will give a general answer. We must *work towards* a system of free labour and free production. But we must reach this goal not by *demolishing* the existing system of production, but *through* this system. This system must be developed in such a way, it must be given such a direction, that it finally brings us to a situation of complete general freedom of production and labour in Java.

Mr Baud has pressed the government for an investigation. What kind of investigation? An investigation to determine the authenticity of the misery that has been reported here and the role played by the Culture System in this? Gentlemen, I want more than such a general investigation. I believe that the time has come, or rather that it is long overdue, to *take action*. I want action. What kind of action? ...

Firstly, the Culture System must be freed from the excesses and abuses that have caused and are still causing so much misery ... Secondly, the Culture System must be used as a means to achieve a system of free production and labour ... I shall give a few examples of measures ... which it appears to me must be taken *immediately* ...

In the *first* place, gentlemen, the percentages paid to officials on the amount of produce delivered must be abolished. The resulting *auri sacra fames* [sacred lust for gold] has been the cause of the deplorable excesses in many places. This evil, or rather the cause of so much evil, must be taken away immediately. If the salaries of officials are not sufficient, then they should be increased. But to recompense them for every *picul* of sugar or coffee, for every pound of indigo that they deliver through the Javanese to the government—and to give greater rewards in proportion to the increase in these *piculs* and pounds—that is an immoral stimulus, a temptation to which the government may not expose its officials ...

A *second* measure I suggest should be taken is to appoint more European officials in the *Binnenlands Bestuur* [Local Government Service], so that it will be easier and more effective to control the native officials.

A *third* measure I would like to suggest is to improve the salaries of *native* officials. Gentlemen, there are native officials who have to carry out important duties and who are charged with the administration of districts in which fifty to sixty thousand people are living and who are paid forty, fifty, or sixty guilders per month. It is impossible for them to live on this, and so you force them to abuse their authority and enrich themselves at the cost of the people. Also they share at present in the percentages awarded on produce delivered. In this case, I say take these percentages away from them and instead give them an ample salary that does not bring them into temptation, yes, even forces them, to take from the Javanese what you withold from them.

A *fourth* measure that should be taken is to treat benevolently people who report the existence of corruptive practices. So far, those who brought abuses to light ... were regarded as enemies of the Culture System, as opponents, as dangerous people ...

And *finally* I want publicity. I desire that everything that happens in Java should no longer be kept quiet but made public. I want this large factory of a few million souls who have been made to work by force to be brought into the limelight. If five, six, or seven years ago publicity had been given to the false reports made here about Java—about the actions of officials high and low, and the failures and mistakes—then I am sure that because of public knowledge many of the misfortunes that we now deplore could have been prevented ...

The second objective is that the Culture System should no longer be considered as a normal situation that is to remain, but as a means to achieve a system of freedom of production and labour in Java. I shall restrict myself to suggesting three measures to reach this objective.

The *first* measure is to help and encourage the development of private initiative in Java in the interest of land reclamation, agriculture, and plantation industry. Last year I directed the attention of the Minister of Colonies to the large tracts of virgin land in Java that only wait to be cultivated. Among other things I also pointed out to him a large area in the Priangan regencies. Soon after this happened a few persons contacted the Minister of Colonies for permission to have this land either on a rental basis or by straight-out sale to develop by their own industry and capital ...

A *second* measure I would like to see is that within the workings of the Culture System the government should delegate as much as possible to private initiative ... As an example, ... when the new sugar contracts are awarded, I want the needs of the factories to be no longer met by the government but by private entrepreneurs. There will not be any difficulties as long as the people are not overburdened by seignorial services. If you want some evidence for this, then you should read the work of Mr Bosch. At least I was struck by the following passage from this writer:

> A few years ago I was visiting a sugar contractor who, with the exception of the cane, had to provide everything himself without any help from the government administration. This is evidence that the Indies Government considers that such an enterprise is quite feasible. This man was very discontented and incensed about the local officials who refused to help him with anything and left him to fend for himself. He had difficulties with everything: he could not get lime, bricks, timber, or people, at least not as many or as easily as he wanted. Recently, when the factory was working and flourishing, I asked him how the business was going and if all the difficulties had been overcome and forgotten. As soon as the surrounding population was aware of an ensured market for its produce, everything—timber, lime, bricks, etc.—was delivered in abundance and there was no shortage of labour ...

The owners of sugar factories should be given the free disposal of their produce, and in this way the government will be able to gradually withdraw from the trading sector ... When the sugar-millers have the free disposal of their product, and no longer receive advance payments, they will learn to be more dependent on their own powers. And it will be easier for them to make the transition to another system where without the interference of the government they will make contracts with the people regarding the planting of the crops ...

The *third* measure I have in mind, which I should have mentioned first, perhaps, because in many ways it is the most important one, concerns the education of the Javanese. There is a close connection between the Culture System, that is the Culture System as a transition measure to free labour and production, and the education of the Javanese. It is said, and perhaps in some ways not unjustly: "You cannot give the Javanese the free disposal of the fruits of their labour because they let themselves be fooled; they fall into the hands of the Chinese; they are children and they cannot be in charge of their own goods." If this is true, and if this is one of the reasons why the Culture System is to remain for the time being, then educate the Javanese; give them a sound primary education, develop the people to a higher civilization, and the evil that now still necessitates the Culture System will gradually disappear ...

W. R. van Hoevell, *baron, Parlementaire Redevoeringen over Koloniale belangen*. (Zaltbommel, Noman, 1862), Eerste Deel, 1849-53, pp. 181-91; Tweede Deel, 1854-56, pp. 5, 10-11, 18-21.

6 Multatuli: Max Havelaar, 1860

[*In the following selection Multatuli describes the perniciousness of the system of indirect colonial rule under which the regents and their subordinate officials were allowed to exploit the people.*]

It is not unusual at all for regents with an income of two or three hundred thousand guilders a year to be in financial difficulties. The main reason for this is the truly princely carelessness with which they squander their income, their negligence in supervising their subordinates, their mania for buying things, and especially the advantage often taken of these weaknesses by Europeans.

The revenue of the Javanese chiefs are four fold. Firstly, a fixed monthly salary. Secondly, a specific sum as compensation for rights transferred to the Dutch Government. Thirdly, a bonus as a percentage of the quantity yielded by his Regency of products such as coffee, sugar, indigo, cinnamon, etc. And finally, the arbitrary use of the labour and property of his subjects.

The last two sources of revenue require some explanation. The Javanese is naturally a farmer. The land on which he is born, promises much for little work, and lures him to this, and, above all, he is devoted heart and soul to the cultivation of his rice fields, in which he accordingly shows particular skill. He ... goes with his father to the field at a very early age, to assist him with ploughing and digging of dams and channels for the irrigation of his land. He counts his years by harvests, he determines time and season by the colour of his standing crop, he feels at home among the comrades who cut the paddy with him, he selects his wife from the girls of the *desa* who at eve, to the sound of merry singing, pound the rice to remove the husk ... Possession of a team of buffaloes to draw his plough is his ideal ... In short, rice is to the Javanese what the grape is to the wine-growers along the Rhine and in the south of France.

But foreigners came from the West, who made themselves lords of his land. They wanted to benefit from the fertility of the soil, and ordered him to devote part of his labour and time to growing other products which would yield greater profit in the markets of Europe. To make the common man comply, only a very simple device sufficed. He obeys his chiefs; so it was only necessary to win over those chiefs by promising them a proportion of the proceeds ... And the scheme succeeded completely.

Considering the immense quantity of Javanese products marketed in the Netherlands, the effectiveness of this policy is obvious, even though one cannot consider it noble. For if anyone were to ask whether the grower receives a reward proportionate to the yields, the answer must be in the negative. The government compels him to produce on *his* land what pleases *it*; it punishes him when he sells this crop to anyone else but *it*; and *it* fixes the price it pays him. The cost of transport to Europe, through a privileged trading company, is high. The money given to the chiefs to encourage them increases the purchase price even further, and ... as, after all, the entire business *must* yield a profit, it can be made in no other way than by paying the Javanese just *enough* to keep him from starving otherwise the productive capacity of the nation would decline. The European officials are also paid a bonus in proportion to the production.

So the poor Javanese is driven forward by the whip of a dual authority; he is often taken away from his rice fields to work elsewhere; and famine often occurs as a result. But ... happily flutter the flags at Batavia, Semarang, Soerabaya, Pasaroean, Besoeki, Probolinggo, Pachitan, Chilachap, of the ships which are being loaded with the crops that make Holland rich!

Famine? In rich, fertile, blessed Java—*famine*? Yes, reader. Only a few years ago, whole districts died of starvation. Mothers offered their children for sale to obtain food. Mothers ate their children ...

But then the Motherland stepped in. In the council-chambers of the parliament in Holland there was dissatisfaction, and the Governor-General of that day was forced to issue instructions that in future the output of the so-called *European-market products* was not to be driven to the point of causing famine.

I realise I have been bitter. But what would you think of me, if I could write about such things *without* bitterness?

It now remains for me to discuss the last and major source of revenue of the native chiefs: their arbitrary disposal of the persons and property of their subjects.

Accordingly to the idea generally held in almost all of Asia the subject, with all he possesses, belongs to the prince. The descendants or relatives of the former princes gladly make use of the ignorance of the people, who do not clearly understand that their *Tommongong* or *Adhipatti* or *Pangerang* [noble titles] is now a *paid official* who has sold his own rights and theirs for a fixed income, and that therefore the poorly paid labour in coffee plantation or sugar cane field has taken the place of the taxes which were formerly exacted from the peasants by their lords. So, it is quite normal for hundreds of families to be summoned from a great distance to work, *without payment*, on fields that belong to the Regent. Nothing is more normal than to supply, unpaid for, food for the Regent's court. And if the horse, the buffalo, the daughter, the wife of the common man find favour in the Regent's sight, it would be unheard-of for the possessor to refuse to give up the desired object unconditionally.

There are regents who make only moderate use of such arbitrary powers, and only exact from the humble what is absolutely necessary to support their rank. Others go a little further. But nowhere is this illegal abuse altogether absent. And undoubtedly it is difficult, if not impossible, to eradicate such an abuse *entirely*, because it is deeply rooted in the very nature of the people who suffer by it. The Javanese is generous, particularly if it is a question of proving his attachment to his chief, to the descendant of those his forefathers obeyed. He would even consider to be lacking in the respect due to his hereditary lord if he entered the *kraton* [palace] without bringing gifts. These presents are admittedly often of such small value that to refuse them would be tantamount to humiliating the giver; and so, often this custom amounts to no more than the homage of a child, who seeks to express his love for his father by offering a small present, than be conceived as a tribute to tyrannical despotism.

But ... in this way the existence of a *charming custom* makes it difficult to abolish an *abuse*.

This is realised by the government; and when you read the official laws and instructions and advice for the officials one would applaud the humanity they appear to be motivated by. Everywhere the European who holds authority in the interior is told that one of his most sacred duties is to protect the population against their own docility and the rapacity of their chiefs. And, as though it were not sufficient to prescribe this obligation *in general*, the *Assistant Residents*, when assuming administration of a Division, are bound to take a *separate oath* to the effect that they will consider this paternal care of the population as a primary responsibility.

This is surely a noble vocation. To stand for justice, to protect the lowly against the high, to defend the weak against the strong, to demand the return of the poor man's goods from the grasp of the noble robber ... is it not enough to make a man's heart glow with joy, the thought of being called to so glorious a task? And if at times the officials in Java should be dissatisfied with his position or his reward, let him turn his gaze to the sublime duty resting upon him—to the supreme enjoyment which the fulfilment of *such* a duty brings with it; and he will desire no other reward.

But ... that duty is not easy. First of all, he has to decide precisely where *Custom* has grown into abuse. And ... where abuse *does exist*, where robbery or tyranny *has* been indeed practised, the victims themselves are only too often accomplices, either from excessive submissiveness, or from fear, or from lack of confidence in the will or power of the person appointed to protect them. It is common knowledge that the *European* official may be transferred at any moment to another post, while the *Regent, the powerful Regent*, remains. Moreover, there are so many ways of appropriating the possessions of a poor, ignorant man. If a *mantri* [lower native official] tells him that the *Regent* would like his horse, the animal is soon after to be found in the Regent's stables; but this does not necessarily prove that the Regent does not intend to pay a high price for it ... some time. If hundreds of people are working in a chief's fields without payment, it by no means follows that this is being done for his benefit. May it not have been his object to make the harvest over to them, from the purely philanthropic calculation that his land was better situated and more fertile than theirs, and so would reward their labour more liberally?

And again, where is the European official to find witnesses with the courage to make a statement against their ruler, the dreaded Regent? And, were the official to risk a charge *without being able to prove it*, what would become of the relationship of an *older brother* who would then have impugned his *younger brother*'s honour without good cause? What would become of the good opinion of the government, which gives the official bread for his service but would deny him that bread, dismiss him as incapable, if he should lightly suspect or accuse of wrongdoing one so highly placed as a Tommongong, Adhipatti, or Pangerang?

No, no, the official's duty is not an easy one! This is already evident from the fact that everyone knows that every native chief oversteps the limit of permissible use of the labour and property of his subjects, ... that all Assistant Residents take the oath to combat this ... and that nevertheless it is only very rarely that a Regent is charged with tyranny or misuse of power ...

Multatuli, *Max Havelaar of de koffieveilingen der Nederlandsche Handel-Maatschappij*, (Rotterdam: Donker, 1958), pp 62-6.

7   Deliberations by the learned society Indisch Genootschap about the Culture System, 1866

Mr Feist: When it is said that people are compelled to work in Java, then this is true with respect to some regions, but by no means to all. I have travelled throughout the whole of the island and therefore have been in the position to familiarize myself with local conditions everywhere. But I must declare that in various regions I found that people were not compelled to labour, and that the people were planting crops of their own free will and because of that were enjoying great prosperity. Undoubtedly the Javanese have acquired this willingness to work from the Culture System, which has taught them to work and which has now brought them to a stage where they fit into another system.

However, the system of free labour does not show favourable results everywhere, because the fact that the seignorial services have not been abolished prevents the Javanese from controlling their property and time. Without the abolition of the seignorial services a system of free cultivation will not be possible. However, I have experienced myself that even at this uncertain stage, much can be achieved with the help of the Javanese, providing they are paid a decent wage. When I took over the factory, which I now own, it produced 30 *piculs*. Within a few years I had doubled this production and increased it even to 70 *piculs*, while I believe that a target of 80 *piculs* is by no means impossible. The people are quite willing to work for a decent wage. But this is not the case everywhere and it is therefore necessary that the Javanese be given security of their property and the free disposal of their time. The Javanese will only work voluntarily if they are free men ... Finally, I wish to say, that in so far as I have understood Mr Millard [a previous speaker], he has only highlighted the bad aspects of the Culture System, but has ignored its good effects. He says that it has not taught the Javanese to work. I disagree. And I am of the opinion that the Culture System, during its thirty years of operation, has shown the Javanese the advantages of work, or at least has made them used to the idea of regular work ...

Mr van Swieten: How can one say that the Culture System has created a willingness to work among the population? The supporters of this system maintain that compulsion is still necessary to make the Javanese work. After a period of thirty years the Culture System should have been either able to inculcate a willingness to work and, if so, compulsion is now no longer necessary, or it has not done so and it is clear that the Culture System has not achieved this objective. Mr Feist says: the people are now working of their own free will, compulsion no longer exists. If that is so, the maintenance of the Culture System is no longer necessary. However, the *Indische Weekblad van het Recht* [the *Indies Legal Weekly*] reports that in 1864 the police records show that still about half a million *rotan* [bamboo stick] strokes were meted out. And there are eyewitness reports about the practice of binding unwilling workers and smearing their faces with dung. Surely such measures can hardly be expected to increase the willingness to work.

Mr de Serriere: Two years after the introduction of the Culture System Mr Tobias [Director of Cultivation] told Count van den Bosch: "On the way from Soemedang to Cheribon I saw twenty-five natives lying in stocks in the gruelling sun. Probably this was done to invite them to work".

Mr Feist: It is very well possible that these things did happen, but it is just because of them that the population was taught to work. When an obstreperous boy does not carry out what he is told to do, he should be punished and forced to obey.

Mr de Serriere: Why is it then that for the construction of the Indies railways more people offered themselves than were needed, and many had to be sent away?

Mr Feist: Perhaps the influence of the residents could have helped somewhat ...

Mr Schill: ... I want to say a few words about an article by Mr F. J. Kock of Enschede, entitled "The crisis of the cotton industry in Twenthe", which appears in the latest issue of the periodical the *Economist*. This article traces how the cotton industry has developed in Twenthe [eastern part of the Netherlands] since 1861 and how this industry is trying with great energy to compete successfully with foreigners, particularly the British, and to establish itself solidly. But not unjustifiably the question is posed: what are we going to do with the increasing production? Will this not become too large? Will sufficient outlets be found? ... However, I want to direct your attention more specifically to the following sentences:

> Our markets in Java are restricted! But would they be or remain so restricted if this market was opened up more to private enterprise, and the government no longer remained the exclusive plantation entrepreneur and its agent, the *Nederlandsche Handelsmaatschappij*, the supreme merchant? It is well known that whoever is in control of exports also controls imports, but in Java exports are almost totally controlled by a single body. A free, brisk, and strong private trade cannot develop, therefore,

with the fatal result that our cotton industry can hardly find an exporter for its produce and is forced to take care of this matter itself to a large extent.

This outcry from our industry against the existing system in Java pleases me somewhat. After all, when an industry which developed, if not totally, but at least to a large extent, because of protective measures that were an outflow from the system of management in Java and its concomitant trading monopoly, agitates against this system on the grounds that it obstructs its progress, then surely we have come very close to recognizing that this system is harmful and untenable ... the plans for reform which van den Bosch brought with him to Java had no other purpose than to exploit the people of Java, to attract large sums of money to the state by means of their land and labour.

The real intentions of this plan were initially disguised by nice-sounding declarations that the only objective one had in mind was the interests of the Javanese; the truth of the matter was hidden under a beautiful official style of writing ...

Mr Sandenberg Matthiessen: Gentlemen! It is only a few months since I left Java. It is sometimes said that a person who has been back for some time in the mother country forgets much, yes, often too much about what he has seen, heard, experienced, suffered and, particularly, enjoyed in the far-away East ...

However, in this struggle about colonial affairs, there is one fact, one point of departure, which is agreed to by everybody, whatever his political colour, and that is that the present situation in the Netherlands Indies is in many aspects distressing and is getting more wretched from day to day. Officials, industrialists, merchants, all agree with this. Even the government has said unashamedly in 1865 that it has taken into consideration that there is a need to establish principles on the basis of which agricultural and industrial enterprises can be founded in the Netherlands Indies. This confession is deplorable after a rule of centuries in [the Indies], from which particularly during the last thirty-five years millions have been gained. This is not only a deplorable confession but also at the same time a condemnation of all previous [colonial] administrations, because this uncertainty is neither caused by the condition of the soil nor the lack of labour. There are no natural barriers present in the Indies that can obstruct its growth, prosperity, and happiness. In fact the government points out the cause itself: until now a principled policy for agricultural and industrial development has been lacking. So until now there has been misgovernment, and despite many official decisions there has been a complete indecisiveness, which also elucidates other matters that otherwise would be difficult to explain.

Java is a producer of rice, which is the most important staple food for the Javanese. But why have there been shortages from time to time? Why has there been famine from time to time? The reason is that Java is still only partly brought into cultivation, because of a lack of a proper [development] policy.

Java produces coffee, which is the most important source of income for the *batig slot*. But why then are there indeed grounds for fearing that the yearly coffee harvests will decline. Again the reason is the lack of a proper policy.

Java produces sugar. Has the contract [government contract with private entrepreneurs] system been bad? If so, why was it not abandoned after the expiration of the contracts? If it was successful, why has it not been expanded during the last fifteen years? Again, the reason is a lack of a proper policy.

The stationary production of all sorts of agricultural crops, abuses, corruption, extortion, contradictory official circulars—all these things are the result of the lack of guiding principles.

But in addition to this first [indisputable] fact, we have, God be praised, a second one; that is, that the Indies is capable of a tremendous development providing it is governed logically and consequently. The Conservatives say: give us power, and there will not be enough ships available to transport the crops we shall produce through the extension of the compulsory system after we have cleansed it of abuses. The Liberals say: give us full power and the indirect advantages that will result from private cultivation, and industry will make the earlier budget surpluses look rather insignificant. So there is general agreement about the feasibility of development, but there is controversy *as to the method*.

It is certainly difficult from a constitutional point of view to answer the question as to how colonies and conquered territories should be governed. However, in the case of colonial policy there surely must be in the first place an objective, which is to be achieved by reasonable and fair means. If the latter is not complied with, either the objective is not achieved or it is achieved only temporarily. You all know that England from time to time gives self-government to some of its colonies, which means that the retention of the colonies is not the most important principle of British colonial policy. You also know that England has wanted to keep British India under its complete control. And it has achieved this objective, although an enormous use of power has been necessary to suppress a very threatening rebellion and in order to achieve this objective it has had to expand its army and navy to a hitherto unknown extent. You also know that England sets great store by the advantages flowing from the relationship between the mother country and the colony, but that it does not demand budget surpluses created by systems of compulsory cultivation.

It is thus obvious that our colonial policy, which rejects the idea of self-government of the colonies and which is not only concerned to retain them for their own sake but also wants to use them for the benefit of the Treasury and to balance the home budgets, must be based on very different principles from the British colonial policy.

On the other hand, one surely realizes immediately that our colonial objectives are abnormal, and cannot be sustained for long. It is an abnormal state of affairs when such a small and weak State as the Netherlands should eventually rule over large parts of the East; and it would be equally abnormal that any conquered territory anywhere in this world should let itself be used continuously to send millions to the mother country while it had to go without the necessary things that could be produced by these millions.

In my view, then, the best colonial policy for the Netherlands would be one that dares to look the future squarely in the face, and tries as much as possible to replace abnormal conditions by natural ones, and which tries to take all rightful causes for rebellion away as much as possible. In the meantime the sources of income for trade and shipping should have been made permanent by the time our possessions are partly or totally lost.

The first time I went back to Europe after a ten-year stay in the Netherlands Indies was in 1859. At that time there was still general enthusiasm in Java. Sugar factories were being sold for fabulous sums, tobacco plantations shot like mushrooms out of the ground, and new commercial houses established themselves in the provincial capitals, concluding contracts with great abandon. There was an *appearance* of prosperity! Soon after I returned in 1860 there was a rapid turnover in bankruptcies; and finally plantations, after having swallowed up tons of gold, were either abandoned or sold for ludicrously cheap prices; the commercial firms had to write off capital sums from their books; the sugar-planters were plagued by the government, which introduced all sorts of foolish legal requirements or refused payments it was legally due to make. In one word, when a few months ago I left again, there was a general depression—a crisis among the officials, because they really did not know any more how to act; a depression in trade, because one could not offer collateral any more for money already borrowed or still to be borrowed; depression among the industrialists, because anybody who already headed a business looked with anxiety at the future, while anybody who wanted to start up something would walk from one office to another without being able to borrow money ... There was no money.

And now what are the causes of all this?

The prosperity of Java is solely dependent on agriculture. The farmer needs a *de facto right to his land, and freedom of labour and investment.* None of these conditions is at present in existence in Java. Present day Java is similar to Europe in the Middle Ages, although there are a few trimmings of Western civilization. There are French chefs and dressmakers, but a European cannot buy or rent even a small piece of land; there are modern carriages, but the price of rice fluctuates heavily because there are insufficient means of transport and no interior roads; there are telegraph poles ... but it has been admitted that the ownership of the land in which these poles are placed is unsure; there are steam-driven printing presses, but there is also the possibility of being exiled; there are missionaries and the beginnings of education, but the opium monopoly is maintained.

I have said that in the first place the farmer needs a de facto right to his land. It is unnecessary to argue here that property rights are the only stimulus for the cultivation and improvement of the soil, and to engage in useful experiments. Landowners are gradually beginning to form the class in society that has the greatest interest in the maintenance of peace and order. Moreover cultivated properties will soon form one of the most fertile sources of income for the State, because of land tax, death duties, and transfer duties. But what the government has completely lost sight of is the fact that it would be of great importance, in the event of foreign occupation, for a part of Java to be the private property of Dutch capitalists.

I will not concern myself with the question whether land rights in Java are based on Mohammedan law or on a mixture of Islamic and Hindu laws; or whether the sovereign owns the land, as Raffles declared in his land-rent regulations; or whether Mohammedan law should have been taken as the basis for the Culture System. All I want to point out is the fact that the government has always considered itself as the owner of the land, and on this ground has levied land rent and has introduced the Culture System. The government should be consistent. It should not on the basis of its property rights dispose arbitrarily of the land of the Javanese. On the other hand it should not act like a coy young girl and begin to doubt the validity of this right as soon as European industrialists want to develop this land.

The second requirement is free labour, which at the moment is entirely absent in Java. Just to illustrate this problem, let us for a moment make an imaginary trip through Java.

On our arrival by steamship in Soerabaja, hundreds of prows rush out towards us as soon as the smoke is visible, competing to bring us ashore. On shore we see carriages for hire and there is a great deal of loading and unloading of goods and every business is able to attract a sufficient number of workmen. Then we arrive on our front verandah, where all necessities of life are held up to us for sale. You will ask: but surely this is free labour? And I will reply: there are no seignorial services in the capital cities, where the natives are not dependent on the native chiefs and have few obligations, so they can dispose freely of their labour without any obstructions.

The next day we travel into the country. The morning is cool and the shadow of the tamarind trees is pleasant. We travel fast and on the river we see people strenuously pushing their prows upstream; we pass market-places where people are teeming like an ants-nest, buying and selling products. Thus we must also admit that to some extent also in the countryside there is freedom of labour.

Then our carriage is halted because the road is under repair. We are surprised how slowly and lazily the work is being carried out. And we are told: it is because of the seignorial services—that man who is working there does not receive any payment. Whether he works hard or slowly does not matter because he goes home at the same hour. If he is diligent, the lazy ones get upset.

We continue our journey and arrive at a sugar factory. We are received with great hospitality. The rooms are made ready and the table is set. And after having made a visit to the factory, we ask the owner: "How is it going at present?" He replies: "Fairly well, except for the trouble with cart drivers and coolies. Imagine, sir, months before the milling season I gave cash credit to a hundred cart-drivers, of 80, 100 to 120 guilders, but what do they do? Only some of them come back. Some say that their animals have died. Others had no animals or carts when I made a contract with them. Others again have received cash advances from two or three factory owners. In the early days, when there was a strong and just government we could get as many coolies as we wanted."

The next day I will bring you to a tobacco plantation where the natives have been planting more and better every year. The crop has increased from 48 to 70, from 70 to 180, from 180 to 37,000 pounds. I will bring you to various plantations and enterprises and daily you will see great differences and you will continually change your mind. The cause of this is taxation in terms of labour, the seignorial services. Wherever there is forced labour the same inadequacies occur. The slavery of the West Indies, the seignorial services of Egypt, the serfdom of Russia, and the corvee of the Middle Ages, teach us that the labourers become lazy and uninterested because there is no stimulation to work hard, while furthermore effective supervision is impossible. Everybody in the *desa* [indigenous village] who has some influence, who delivers chickens, eggs, and women to the chief, is exempted from seignorial services, which makes the task even harder for those who are not exempted. Moreover, the *desa* is not asked how much manpower it can supply to carry out a certain task, but the chief is just ordered to have the work performed with whatever manpower he can muster, and if he does not comply he will be fired ...

These seignorial services have had the following threefold result, which at first glance would appear to support the contention of the old-time colonials that the Javanese are still unsuited for free labour:
1. The soil of Java is still to a large extent uncultivated, while in some areas the villages are overpopulated.
2. The Javanese are too lazy or too indifferent to cultivate their own village lands.
3. The sugar factory-owners cannot depend on a continuous supply of labour, irrespective of what wages they offer.

When the two requirements, de facto control over land and freedom of labour, are lacking, there is no capital available. And even if it was available it could not be used. At the moment there is no capital in Java for the simple reason that there is no economic stability. Let us hope then that soon the legislator will take away the obstructions that stand in the way of free enterprise ... and that soon the time will come that the Netherlands capitalists will prefer the ownership of fertile lands in Java to Turkish and Austrian shares ...

Indisch Genootschap. *Beraadslaging over het Gouvernements-Kultuurstelsel op Java ook in verband met het wetsontwerp tot regeling der grondslagen voor de vestiging van ondernemingen van landbouw en nijverheid in Nederlandsh Indie* (The Hague: Nijhoff, 1866), pp 278-83; 307; 334-39.

8 J. H. Boeke: Budget studies in Koetoardjo, 1886 and 1888

1. Tjowikromo of Bendo (Koetoardjo) in 1886

Tjowikromo is a farmer living in the *desa* Bendo, district of Kemiri of the county of Koetoardjo. His landholdings consist of 200 r^2 of *sawah*, 20 r^2 of *tegalan* [non-irrigated fields], and a yard of 147 r^2 [r = roede = 3.767 metres]. He has to pay 6.62 guilders in land rent and 1 guilders in head tax. Moreover, 77 times during the year he was required to perform seignorial services for the government and 110 times he had to perform community services for the village.

The family of Tjowikromo consists of his wife, his mother-in-law, and three small children. There is no opportunity in the *desa* of Bendo to earn extra income on [Western] enterprises. As an additional business Tjowikromo sells *djawet*, a refreshing drink, which provides him with extra income for six months of the year. For a few months of the year his wife weaves coverlets. But it is not possible to determine exactly how much monthly profit is made by [these extra activities], because in the case of the weaving it is not known how much yarn was left at the end of the period of investigation, while the *djawet* business was already in operation before the investigation, and the ingredients were apparently not paid for immediately—at least expenditure on these ingredients is still mentioned some months after sales have stopped ...

If running costs and sales receipts are balanced, the weaving made a profit of 1.18 guilders and the *djawet* business 7.41 guilders; in order to obtain the latter Tjowikromo had to put in 429 hours.

The budget gives the impression that Tjowikromo is still rather clumsy in dealing with the demands of the money economy. The attempts to balance money expenditure and income are rather haphazard and ad hoc and depend solely on sometimes burdensome loans. These loans are the highest entry for net income and they are necessary as soon as something unexpected occurs. The smaller income gained from the sale of crops produced on the *tegalan* and the yard is usually immediately spent—at least in part—on day-to-day living ... money expenditure for this purpose is not shown in detail but is grouped under the heading expenditure of extraordinary income. In other words money income is still considered as a windfall and it is insufficiently realized that this brings with it in terms of expenditure a rather pressing demand for money. During no less than 196 days of the year there was no money income nor expenditure, but during this period apparently no money is kept for unexpected expenditure and when this occurs credit has to be obtained. The study does not yet present a complete picture of Tjowikromo's credit needs. In August he still had to buy 3 *piculs* of rice by means of renting out 100 r^2 of *sawah* during the western monsoon, while for a loan in October of 120 *duiten* [brass coin] he had to surrender 20 r^2 of *tegalan* in the wet season. The sale of 1 *picul* of rice in May, the cheap season, for 288 *duiten*, was caused by extreme necessity, similar to the sale of crops produced in the yard ...

It is clear how heavy the impact of taxation in money is on this household. Each payment necessitated one or other ad hoc rescue measure, with the result that, at the end of the year investigated, the Tjowikromo family had to face the future with an increased debt of 733 *duiten* and an encumbrance on 120 r^2 of its land.

"Arminius" [pseudonym for H. G. Heyting] states that Tjowikromo is representative of the average villager in the low lands ...

Expenditure

	cents	%
Food	991	33.5
Fire and light	171	5.8
Clothing	320	10.7
House and furniture	—	—

Sickness		150	5.1
Education		—	—
Feasts		416	14.0
Transport		—	—
Taxes		914	30.9
	Total	2962	
Running expenditure of farm, etc.		2784	
	Total	5746	
Repayment of debt		541	
	Total	6287	

Expenditure in more detail

Number of transactions		cents		%
Food				
rice		234		23.6
accessory dishes		192		19.4
salt		88		8.8
meat and fish		194		19.6
	Total	708	Total	71.4
tea, sugar, and sweets		214		21.6
tobacco and *sirih* [betel nut]		69		7.4
	Total	991		

Fire and light: Under this heading both kerosene and peanut oil are included. The latter, of course, could also be used as food.

Taxes

Land rent		795
Head tax		119

Running expenditure

Agriculture		235
Cost of yarn		462
Cost of *djawet* ingredients		2087
	Total	2784

Income

Number and kind of transactions		cents
1 sale of rice		288
32 sale of other crops		1258
4 sale of woven goods		580
50 sale of *djawet*		2828
3 wages		78
1 gift		14
	Total	5046
	Loans	1274
	Total	6320

2. Sodrono of Kalimenagwetan (Koetoardjo) in 1886

The Sodrono family consists of husband, wife, and five children of unknown age. Sodrono is a farmer and has the use of 100 r² of *sawah* and 50 r² of *tegalan* as "communal" property; and he individually owns 120 r² of orchard and a yard of 100 r². He has to pay 5.36 guilders in land rent (the yard, which is smaller than ¼ *bouw*, is free of land rent) and 1 guilder as head tax. In order to pay these taxes of 6.36 guilders Sodrono put aside 6 guilders (720 *duiten*), which he had made in 1885 from the sale of a calf; the remainder (144 *duiten*) was saved bit by bit.

Sodrono is a cautious person and is careful with his money. He did not suffer from any unexpected adversities and was able to live through the year without having to take up a loan.

But in this instance also, money is still considered as something superimposed from the outside, which although it causes him some anxiety still does not form an integral part of his daily life. During no less than 242 days of the year under investigation not a single monetary transaction took place. For the remaining days there appear 123 entries for expenditure and 108 entires for income, which were as follows:

Expenditure	No. of entries	Income	No. of entries
Taxes	3	Wages	3
Housing and materials	3	Crops from the yard	75
Food	105	Chickens	11
Buying of crops	5	*Tegalan* produce	16
Transport	3	*Sawah* produce	3
Clothing	3	Total	108
Feasts	1		
Total	123		

Considering the similarity in the number of entries and the total income and expenditure, which—with the subtraction of the 720 *duiten* saved for taxation—amounted to 2223 *duiten* and 2188 *duiten* respectively, one gains the impression that every time money comes in it is immediately matched by a similar amount of expenditure. This is expressly confirmed by the monthly statistics. So the Sodrono family considers money income exclusively as a means to buy extras, which if the money was not there would simply not be bought. This does not mean in the least that these needs, which can only be satisfied occasionally, are far above the immediate necessities of life. This should be clear from the unfortunately incomplete list of "purchases of groceries" supplied by Arminius:

	duiten
Kerosene	215
Salt	192
Sirih	108
Smoking needs	89
Trasi [prawn paste]	81
Tempe [soya bean cake]	70
Buffalo meat	28
Coconut oil	10
Fish	4

3. Wongsowikromo of Kalioerip (Koetoardjo) in 1888

The Wongsowikromo family consists of the husband, wife, mother-in-law, and three small children. Kalioerip is a small mountain *desa* and the land is only of medium quality. Wongsowikromo has individual heritable property rights to 30 r^2 of *sawah*, 20 r^2 of orchard, 50 r^2 of *tegalan*, and a yard of 60 r^2, for which he has to pay 0.88 guilders in land tax and 1 guilder in head tax. Moreover he was required seventy-eight times (at an average of five hours) to cultivate coffee for the government and had to perform village services seventy-two times (at an average of eleven hours). Because of sickness and feast days he was unable to work during eighty-four days. Following an agreement with the government forester, Wongsowikromo—like others in his village—has planted *djati* [mahogany-like] trees and therefore has obtained the right to plant dry crops such as chili and peanuts between those trees.

The same remarks that were made about the management of money by Sodrono apply to Wongsowikromo.

On 265 days of the year no monetary transactions took place, although Wongsowikromo is partly dependent for his rice needs on the market. Income and expenditure of money usually coincide on the same day. This, however, does not mean in the least that in the meantime Wongsowikromo has no money in hand. Heyting noted what amount of money Wongsowikromo had in hand at the end of each day. The findings were as follows:

days	duiten
71	—
4	1
59	2
7	9
37	10—20
17	20—40
14	40—60
141	60—100
9	100—200
7	200 and more

It appears from this that Wongsowikromo has in general protected himself against unforeseen expenses, although perhaps rather lightly.

	Expenditure		Income	
		cents		cents
Food		2465		
Kerosene		23		
Clothing		411		
House		—		
Feasts		66		
Sickness		75		
Taxes		225		
	Total	3265		
Running costs		579		
	Total	3844		

Expenditure in more detail

Food

Rice	1647	66.8
Corn	14	0.6
Cassava	94	3.8
Accessory dishes	149	6.1
Salt	250	10.1
Sugar	17	0.6
Meat and fish	138	5.6
Tobacco and *sirih*	156	6.4
Total	2465	

Clothing

Hat	28
Sarong	200
Handkerchief	12
White cotton	36
Pants	30
Children's jacket	45
Dyeing black of man's jacket	60
Total	411

Running costs

Purchase of seedlings and tools	64
Purchase of yarn	455
Wages helper	60
Total	579

From the tegalan

Ketela [cassava]	160
Bananas	116
Kapok	23
Indigo	5

From the orchard

Various fruits	374

From the yard

Coconuts	203
Bamboo	24
Cucumber	26

From the djati forest

Chilis	85
Egg plant	7
Peanuts	291
Timber	270
Alang-alang [long grass]	721
Other grass	18
Coffee	222
Sheep	203
Woven goods	105
Total	2853
taxation refund	81
Total	2934

J. H. Boeke, *Inlandse Budgetten* (*Koloniale Studien*, 1926), pp. 322-31.

9   J. Homan van der Heide: Economic studies and criticisms, 1901

The statistics point ... to a negligable increase in arable land, an insignificant rise in rice production, and a considerable increase in rice imports. The logical conclusion must be that, with a rapid increase in population, Java is suffering from an ever-increasing shortage of rice. The only important improvement has occurred in the planting of crops other than rice. But this has had no significant impact on the buying power of the people. This is obvious from the exports of copra, wet indigo, kapok, cotton, cassava flour, oils, and native tobacco (the only agricultural produce exported by the indigenous population), the average value of which amounted to 4.3 million guilders in 1884-88, 5.3 million guilders in 1884-98, and 4.7 million guilders in 1894-98 ...

Cattle stocks have not risen in proportion to the population. The number of cattle per thousand inhabitants has decreased from 238 in 1885 to 225 in 1895 (later figures are not available), while ... in 1889-93 on the average 540,000 hides were exported as compared with 442,000 in 1894-98 ... The statistics do not only show an ever-growing shortage of rice in Java, but also that in general the prosperity of the native population has seriously declined in the period 1885-96 ... [It is then argued that rice production has not kept up with the population increase.]

The difference is not *small*, but very *large*, because in the period 1885-96 there was a 25 per cent increase in population, while the amount of arable land increased only by 6.2 per cent and the plantings of rice only by 3.43 per cent ... The population has increased four times more than the area of arable land and seven times more than the plantings of rice. There was no increase at all in rice production. [The reason for this is that] the newly reclaimed areas are generally inferior, while ever-larger areas of the best soil are being used for the cultivation of sugar. So it is not surprising that a small increase in rice-planting is not followed by an increase in production ... The progress made by the sugar industry was compensated for by the fall in wages and the increase in population. The progress of private coffee, tea, and quinine production did not equal the fall in the production of government coffee, not the speak of the fall in wages and the population increase. Tobacco production increased by 8.5 per cent, the population by 25 per cent. The available quantity of rice per capita of population fell from 1.9 *piculs* per annum to 1.58 *piculs*. The average export surplus for the whole of the Netherlands Indies declined from 56.7 million guilders in 1885-90 to 43.4 million guilders in 1891-96, while the overseas debt increased.

Imports of cotton goods, which are considered a particularly suitable gauge of the buying power of the indigenous population, increased by 14 per cent and that of yarns by 9.5 per cent ... As, almost exclusively, imported clothing materials are used in Java, it is evident from the import statistics of textiles, yarns, and clothing that the whole of the population spends per capita 1.25 guilders per annum and that this already small amount is still decreasing.

The total revenue of the land rent has declined. The same is the case with the slaughtering tax, trade tax, and the opium monopoly. The average per capita assessment of the trade tax declined from 2.51 guilders in 1885 to 1.73 guilders in 1896. The salt monopoly yielded 18 per cent more as against a population increase of 25 per cent. It appears from the amount of salt consumed that the consumption of salt per capita decreased in that proportion. Only the revenue from the rent on pawn shops surpassed the population increase considerably. This special tax on poverty and decline realized 40 per cent more ... The total taxation revenue, ... most of which is paid by the native population of Java, ... decreased by almost 2 million guilders in 1885-96 ...

The years 1885-90 must because of the general depression and the decline in prices ... be viewed as particularly unfavourable, with the result that the imports by private persons into Java declined on the average from 104 million guilders in 1883-84 to 78.8 million guilders in 1885-87.

The years 1891-96, however, have shown strong progress almost everywhere in Europe, America, Asia, and Australia ... [But in Java] there was not only a deterioration in the economic situation of the people in the period 1885-96, but also in the years 1897-98 there was no progress to be noticed, although there were many favourable factors present ...

The rice crop in these years [i.e. 1897-98] was successful: in 1897 it was 2.5 million *piculs* and in 1898 4 million *piculs* more than the average ... The output of sugar also rose markedly, but this gain was more than compensated for by a fall in coffee production. While sugar production rose between 1896 and 1898 by approximately 3 million *piculs* at a value of 20 million guilders, the export of coffee fell by one-half or upwards of 20 million guilders. In 1896 the people earned 5 million guilders from the forced cultivation of coffee for the government and in 1898, owing to a fall in production, they only earned 2.1 million guilders. Also the people's income from private coffee cultivation has diminished markedly as a result of a fall in production ...

During the years 1896-98 the government as well as private companies have constructed a large number of public works, such as railways and tramways (in 1897 and 1898 15.8 million guilders were spent on the building of railways and 16.2 million guilders on the construction of tramways), river and other water works (e.g. 8 million guilders were spent on the irrigation works in the Solo Valley), and gas and electrical installations, which provided an extra source of income for the people. In spite of all this it must be concluded from a comparison of imports during 1897-98 and 1891-96 that there was no increase in economic prosperity, as can be seen from the following table of imports of the various articles, which are mainly for the consumption of the native population.

Imports into Java and Madoera

	Average 1891—96	Average 1897—98	% increase 1897—98	% decrease 1897—98
Cotton (guilders)	29,447,000	29,092,000	—	.20
Woollens (guilders)	1,869,000	1,348,000	—	28.00

Fish (1893—96: kg)	29,682,000	30,528,000	2.80	—
Net imports of rice (*piculs*)	1,040,000	1,307,000	25.50	—
Earthenware	1,447,000	1,262,000	—	12.75
Ironware	4,244,000	4,526,000	6.60	—
Total imports by private persons	106,573,000	108,261,000	1.60	—

The conclusion that must be drawn from the imports situation must also be drawn from that of the revenue from taxation, which is almost totally borne by the indigenous population. This should be clear from the following table:

Revenue from some taxes in Java and Madoera (million guilders)

	1896	1897	1898
Slaughtering tax	1.31	1.30	1.32
Gambling tax	0.19	0.18	0.19
Trade tax	2.35	2.36	2.35
Land rent	17.13	16.96	17.44
Rents on opium	12.15	12.16	11.64
Opium monopoly	2.05	2.02	1.88
Tax on carriages	0.25	0.24	0.28
Salt monopoly	7.37	7.45	7.84
Tax on pawnshops	1.09	1.09	1.14
Head tax	3.10	3.14	3.18
Total	46.99	46.90	47.26

The increase in revenue in 1898 from land rent and the salt monopoly must be the result of the favourable rice harvest, while the increase in head tax and the tax on pawnshops is the result respectively of the population increase and the pauperization of the people. The opium monopoly shows a considerable decrease in revenue. The increase in the total revenue from these taxes during the years 1896-98 amounted to only 2,750,000 guilders or 0.6 per cent, while the population during these two years increased by about 4 per cent. The average per capita assessment of the trade tax decreased again from 1.73 guilders in 1896 to 1.64 guilders in 1898. It should further be mentioned that the total export of goods on account of the private sector has on the average fallen from 135 million guilders in 1891-96 to 129.5 million guilders in 1897-98. The export surplus has therefore declined from 28.4 million guilders in 1891-96 to 21.2 million guilders in 1897-98. At the same time the overseas debt of Java has considerably increased because of the capital invested in new railways and tramways ... and new agricultural and other enterprises.

During the last few years a great deal has been written about a decline in the prosperity of the indigenous population ... The *Verslag van de Kamer van Koophandel* [Report of the Chamber of Commerce] of Semarang of 1898 mentions ... "a decrease in the buying power of the people". The *Verslag van de Kamer van Koophandel* of Batavia for the year 1899 reads: "In general the market remained depressed during the whole of the year because of an oversupply. Total sales were less than in 1897" ... The Assistant Resident H. E. B. Schmalhousen ... wrote in 1899 ... "To put it mildly, in many regions of Java the economic situation does not improve. Wages have fallen to the lowest minimum and the reclamation of land cannot keep pace with the population increase. The livestock is declining qualitatively and quantitatively because of a lack of grazing grounds. And although these facts are not mentioned in the Colonial Reports, they are nevertheless true ... " The Assistant Resident P. J. F. van Heutz wrote ... in 1900:

> During the past century the Netherlands has succeeded in reducing to complete poverty a very diligent and cultured people, which is endowed with a great capacity for development, in a land that may be called an ideal example of tropical fertility. The poverty of the Javanese is so abject that it deserves to become proverbial. It does not matter how much one tries to imagine the greatest possible poverty, that of the Javanese will always be greater. While formerly ornaments and other luxury articles could be found among the people, today they only exist in their imagination. Gold and silver have become unknown metals, except for the silver which has to be sacrificed to the *fiscus* [taxation] and they have been replaced by tin, and galvanized iron. The pawn shops, with their usurious interest charges, where everything that can be spared and also much that cannot is piled up, yield so little that this source of income is also threatening to dry up ...

Even the *Amsterdams Handelsblad*, [*Amsterdam Trading Post*], which is usually so unperturbed and optimistic and which is such a great admirer of the Netherlands Liberal colonial policy, concludes its discussion about the economic situation of Java thus: "Our total impression is the following: the situation on the whole has remained practically stationary. In some areas small gains are noticeable and in others regression ... And although one cannot agree with the pessimists that prosperity is declining, the last word on this subject has not yet been spoken. One can rightly expect from the Netherlands Government in Java that it will do everything possible to increase this prosperity"

J. Homan van der Heide, *Economische Studien en Critieken met betrekking tot Java* (Batavia: Kolff, 1901), pp. 128-29, 111, 130-36.

The Ethical Policy, 1901-42

The Liberal colonial policy was strongly criticized from the early 1880s onwards by a growing number of Dutch politicians and journalists, foremost among whom were the leaders of the Neo-Calvinist and Catholic parties, who condemned Dutch colonial policy as unjust and unchristian. They were supported by the Dutch Socialists, still comparatively few in number at this time, and by a small group of Radical Liberals who had broken with the rigid beliefs of doctrinaire Liberalism. One of the most prominent spokesmen of the last group was P. Brooshooft, a journalist who had lived in the Indies for a considerable time and who through his vivid writings, brought the plight of the Javanese to the attention of a wide section of the Dutch public (*see* document 10).

In 1901 a Calvinist-Catholic coalition came to power in The Hague and announced that a new approach would be taken in colonial management. A new colonial policy was introduced, usually called the "Ethical" Policy, which can be seen as a Dutch version of the "white man's burden". The outstanding feature of the new policy was the official abandonment of exploitation and direct state intervention in the economic sphere in order to improve the economic position of the indigenous population. Indigenous education was boosted considerably and a beginning was made with administrative and political decentralization, culminating in 1918 with the opening of the *Volksraad* (People's Council), a type of colonial proto-parliament.

ECONOMIC POLICY

The nature of the Ethical native welfare programme is well illustrated by the slogan "irrigation, emigration, and education", used by the prominent colonial reformer van Deventer, who in 1899 in an article called "*Een Eereschuld*" ("A Debt of Honour") had demanded that at least an amount of 187 million guilders, i.e. 151 million guilders remitted as budget surpluses since 1867, and 36 million guilders paid in interest and repayments of the colony's debt since 1877, should be restituted to the Indies. Van Deventer also demanded that the Netherlands should take over the whole of the Indies debt, amounting to 100 million guilders, leaving "a debt of honour" to the Indies of 67 million guilders, to be used for economic development projects.

By 1900 the majority of Dutch politicians, including the conservatives representing metropolitan trading and industrial interests, which had become worried about the serious decline in indigenous buying power, had become convinced that *laissez-faire* colonial policy had run aground and that speedy and effective measures should be taken to improve the colonial economy and finances.

The seriousness of the situation was highlighted in a number of government-sponsored reports that appeared in 1904; and in the same year the Dutch Parliament approved a proposition that the Netherlands take over the responsibility for the repayment and interest charges of the floating debt of the indies, which amounted to forty million guilders. This grant-in-aid, which was a watered-down version of van Deventer's earlier demand, was to be used to finance a programme to raise native agricultural productivity by the expansion of irrigation, the introduction of agricultural extension services, better rural credit facilities, and the emigration of Javanese farmers from overpopulated areas to other Indonesian islands such as Sumatra and Sulawesi, where land was still in plentiful supply.

Another and far more detailed investigation into the economic condition of the Javanese people was carried out in 1904-5, the results of which were summarized by Hasselman in 1914. They show (*see* document 11) that the decline in native prosperity in Java was perhaps not as widespread as had originally been feared, although it should be kept in mind that owing to the often fairly primitive methods used, the results of the survey cannot always be considered conclusive.

In the period 1900—1940 more than 270 million guilders were spent on irrigation works, resulting in an increase of the total wet rice area from 2.7 million hectares to 3.4 million hectares. And, although a spectacular result in itself, it was immediately absorbed by the continued rapid increase in population. The population of Java, which stood at 29.9 million in 1905, reached 40.9 million in 1930 and 48 million in 1940, while the average size of native landholdings fell from 1.2 hectares in 1922 to 0.9 hectares in 1938.

Far less effective than irrigation were the efforts of agricultural extension officers, who by means of demonstration fields and other types of in-training tried to induce farmers to use fertilizers, better seeds, and more efficient implements. Progress was only very slow owing to the strong cultural resistance and the general indifference of farmers to these new-fangled foreign measures. The introduction of new food crops and commercial crops, and the construction of fish ponds to improve the villagers' diet, proved to be somewhat more succsssful.

A great deal of attention was also given by the colonial government to the problem of rural indebtedness and the evil of usury. Pawn shops, which were the normal source of credit for Indonesians, had been a government monopoly sincs 1814, but the practice of farming out these shops, mainly to Chinese, had resulted in a great deal of usury and other malpractices highly detrimental to the indigenous people. In order to stop these abuses the colonial government took over the running of pawn shops itself in 1900. In addition other sources of credit were created, such as the *desa lumbung* (village rice banks), where people could borrow rice until the next harvest at rates of interest ranging from 20 to 25 per cent, while the traditional money-lending rates would often be as high as 50 per cent. From the profits of these rice banks, village banks were set up to take care of the need for cash credit. By 1930 six thousand rice banks and an equal number of village banks had been founded.

The least successful measures were the attempts by the colonial government to induce Javanese farmers to migrate to other islands of the Archipelago. The first organized attempt in this direction was made in 1905 when, as an experiment, an agricultural colony was set up in the Lampungs (South Sumatra), which by 1930 numbered thirty thousand people. Efforts to settle Javanese farmers in southeast Borneo and Celebes (Sulawesi) met with failure. The situation improved somewhat during the 1930s when as a result of more skilful propaganda, better selection methods, and more extensive preparatory work in the areas of settlement, more farmers could be induced to leave. In the years 1936, 1937, 1938, 1939, and 1940 respectively, 13,152, 19,152, 32,259, 45,339, and 50,622 Javanese emigrated, followed by another 47,095 in the first three months of 1941.

Obviously the Ethical programme of indigenous economic development, which was almost entirely concerned with raising agricultural productivity, was unable to solve Java's basic economic problems. The Dutch apparently had no serious intention of introducing drastic changes in the colonial economic structure by such means as large-scale industrialization. Admittedly, the importance of industrialization had been stressed by a number of Ethical reformers from the beginning of the century. But the various investigations that were held and the plans proposed came to nothing simply because they militated against the interests of the imperial economy as a whole. In particular the large-scale plantation and mining combines in the colony, which wielded great power in the

Dutch Parliament, were strongly opposed to industrialization, which would have tended to increase the demand for labour and therefore its price. This would have been damaging to these concerns, which for their profits were largely dependent on cheap land and the lowest possible coolie wages. Moreover industrialists in Holland, as well as Dutch labour, were unwilling to be priced out of the Indonesian market, which was one of the most important outlets for Dutch industrial produce such as textiles and machinery.

From the end of World War I a number of Dutch politicians, mainly Socialists, together with various economists, strongly criticized the Ethical Policy for failing to raise the indigenous standard of living. And although the claims of some politicians that millions of people were starving in Java were certainly overstated, it is clear from various investigations held at this time that the people of Java were by no means better off and perhaps even worse off than they had been in 1900. Document 12, which is taken from an economic survey by Huender, published in 1921, certainly points this way. And a number of budget studies conducted in various parts of Java by the economist Boeke clearly show that the standard of living of the indigenous population was generally still very low and that the money economy had still not very deeply penetrated into the villages (*see* document 13).

The economic problem in Java was severely aggravated by the economic depression of the 1930s. In particular the Western export sector was hard hit. The acreage under export crops was drastically reduced and, of a total of 250 sugar factories in Java, nearly 200 stopped operating, with the result that thousands of coolies were sacked and were forced to return to the already overcrowded villages. There were, however, some compensating factors: the land vacated by Western plantations could now be used for food production; and it was during the 1930s that the colonial government finally took the industrialization of Java more firmly in hand. One important reason for this change was the growing fear that Japan would price European firms completely out of the colonial market. The colonial government tried to create a more favourable climate for industrial investment by introducing import restrictions and regulations ensuring a balanced industrial growth. Subsequently, a number of foreign companies established factories in Java, producing rubber tyres, textiles, bicycles, paints, beer, soap, and margarine. The number of indigenous small-scale industrial enterprises also increased markedly during the Depression and the number of workers in the industrial sector (excluding cottage industries) rose from 1.5 million in 1929 to 2.8 million in 1939, while in the same period the proportion of the national income produced by industrial enterprises rose from 4.7 per cent to 10.4 per cent.

This rise in industrial output—although significant—was not sufficient to absorb the surplus labour force in rural Java. Most redundant workers had to fall back on the village economy, where they were given a share of the steadily decreasing communal pie. Those workers who had been able to find employment on plantations or in factories were probably not much better off than the unemployed or under-employed peasantry. Wages were very low and, as is shown by the Coolie Budget Investigation of 1939-40 (*see* document 14), with the exception of those in West Java many Javanese workers were suffering from malnutrition. In judging the efforts of the Dutch to solve Java's economic plight it is obvious that they gave—as is usual with colonial governments—too little and too late. All that perhaps can be said is that by using stop-gap measures the Dutch colonial government managed to keep an even keel.

10 P. Brooshooft: The Ethical direction in colonial policy, 1901

It is a peculiar phenomenon that during the last 150 years or so, and in particular in our time, ethical sunrays are breaking through the darkest clouds of egoism. By ethical I mean here the opposite of selfish, because almost all attempts at moral improvement must involve the submission of one's own self. These [ethical] aspirations grow stronger in all fields in line with the increase in unashamed selfishness. There are increases in the means of destruction as well as genuine and half-genuine peace manifestations; there is shameless war as well as loud protest; shameless speculation on the stock exchange as well as genuine disinterestedness; immoral literature as well as books full of beautiful wisdom; exhausting living as well as propaganda for better health; barren religion in the Churches as well as vital humanism; scraping individualism as well as levelling Socialism ... where shall I end this summary of all the contrasts between present-day egoism and altruism? ...

When I speak about ethical colonial policy, I certainly do not mean the policy of loud political advertisement that exploits the so-called love of the Javanese for entirely different purposes. Repeated government statements that the well-being of the Javanese and their grateful acceptance of our rule are the main guideline can only cause vexation if at the same time nothing tangible is done to increase the real happiness of the Javanese. I even want to warn emphatically against a theatrical policy that makes us fulfil our duties towards the Indies on the cheap; that makes us self-satisfied when we give ten thousand or so of the richest natives ... the opportunity to put a few guilders in the savings bank; or that makes us believe that we bring the poor man better justice when we pay the highest judicial officials 1400 guilders per month instead of 1000. We should also not become sentimental and not play for effect with such catch-phrases as "the beautiful Insulinde", "belts of emeralds", or "warm hearts for a good and honest brown brother", who is certainly not better or more honest than the average human being, and that is putting it mildly.

What should motivate us to carry out our obligations in the Indies is the best of human inclinations: the feeling for justice, the feeling that we should give the best we have got to the Javanese who have been subjugated by us against their will, the noble-minded impulse of the stronger one to treat the weaker one justly. And I find it pleasing to be able to point to growing signs here and there of this sense of justice. This is true of political parties as well as of individuals ... The Anti-Revolutionary Party wrote in Article 18 of its general platform: "that the selfishness of our policy to exploit the colonies for the benefit of the state or the private entrepreneur must be replaced by a policy of *moral obligation* ... The Radical, Liberal-Democratic, and Socialist parties have subscribed far more strongly to the ethical principle in their colonial programmes. Only the Catholic Party, although wishing to see the Javanese prosperous, still would like the Netherlands to profit from them. In any case it means that also for the brown man the most desirable objective on earth should be the prospect of romping about in a Catholic heaven and so it [the Catholic party] has left its only generous-hearted Indies expert, Des Amorie van der Hoeven, standing alone in his camel hair shirt crying out in the wilderness ...

Considering the heavy burdens we put on the natives, the question spontaneously arises: what are we *doing* for them? The answer can be short and clear: we are pushing them into an abyss. We are pushing them into that same quagmire of misery in which millions in Western society are submerged to their necks. Men who have nothing else than their labour to sell are exploited by the capitalists, who hold the power. I want to prove this first of all with regard to the major source of income for the natives: agriculture. Not only in Java but in the whole of the world the soil is the source of all prosperity ... The important question thus in determining the prosperity of a people is: how much do they participate in the profits that are taken out of the *soil*?

It is extremely shameful for our government that as long as we are ruling in Java, the Javanese have hardly drawn any income worth mentioning from their own fertile soil. The greatest profits regularly ended up in the hands of foreigners. The natives had to yield the largest and best part of their crop to the ruler, first as compulsive deliveries during the time of the Company, and later through forced labour under the Culture System. Until 1870 the State held on unscrupulously to this monopoly of easy profits, and the European private entrepreneur was not allowed to compete in the agricultural field. Then a change occurred. But unfortunately it was not the Ethical faction, with its desire to do justice to the Javanese, that turned the scales in the decision to abandon the exploitation by the State, but it was the arrogant demand of Western capital, which sought new employment for the riches it had already gathered [in the colony]. A system should have been set up which, out of a sense of justice towards the Javanese, would have ensured them the largest share of the profits drawn from the Javanese soil, which now were abandoned by the government. But the opposite occurred. In order to favour the Netherlands traders, industrialists and fortune-hunters, the richest plantation industries—sugar, indigo, tobacco, and partly also coffee—were transferred into the hands of Netherlands capitalists. One section of the coffee plantations that still provided a nice profit were retained by the government and the Javanese continued to work under almost the same unfavourable conditions. And with respect to the less fertile lands, one thought that the interests of the Javanese were best served by forcing *freedom* of action on them for which they were not ripe ... good coffee lands were leased on a long-term basis to private European entrepreneurs and land-lease ordinances were issued in order to lure the lands of the Javanese into the hands of European sugar, indigo, and tobacco planters. Seemingly these ordinances were also intended to prevent abuses ... and some of these regulations were well meant, but everybody understood that through the influence of European capital on the native chiefs they were evaded in all sorts of ways ...

In any case the final result was that the agricultural land of the Indies, with the exception of what was absolutely necessary for the growing of food for the natives, was as legally as possible given into the hands of European and Chinese planters, while the natives could be hired by the foreigners to work on these lands for daily wages. But among these numerous and often-revised government regulations there were none that ensured the Javanese reasonable wages for the work performed. This, it was argued, would have been improper interference in private labour agreements.

But while helping to alienate the agricultural land, [the government] did little if anything at all in the way of introducing measures to improve the ancient Javanese cultivation of rice ... and make it more profitable. So little has been done in extending irrigation that, according to the calculations of the irrigation expert Homan van der Heide, out of the 2,700,000 *bouws* that are suitable for irrigation, only 300,000 *bouws* are fully irrigated, while 2,400,000 *bouws* are still waiting to be irrigated or improved ... And for whatever irrigation works that have been constructed, the Javanese have been made to pay more than enough because of the seignorial services demanded during the construction and the increase in land tax during or after completion.

The government has also done nothing to improve rice production in other ways, such as the granting of premiums or loans to introduce better ploughs or hoes (the hand hoe is still the main tool), to improve preparation of the rice (this is still done by hand with a pounder on a block), or to introduce better fertilizers ... Now the government is to experiment with ... "demonstration fields", where the Javanese will be taught to work along more scientific lines. But as long as the government fails to give temporary financial help, the poor Javanese will not be able to pay for the tools and fertilizers needed for more intensive cultivation. It must also be mentioned here ... that in addition to lack of money and the stubborn attachment to tradition, the land tax is an important reason why the Javanese cannot improve their productivity. They know that every increase in production will be followed by an increase in this tax, which is already pressing so heavily on them.

So far as the granting of loans for native agriculture is concerned, the slow wheels of government are finally beginning to turn after various officials have for years pointed to the great need for this in connection with the fatal evil of usury. It has charged the former Assistant Resident of Poerwokerto, Mr de Wolff van Westerrode, who has greatly distinguishsd himself in this field by setting up a savings bank and agricultural credit bank in his area, with investigating the best ways and means of creating state institutions for agricultural credit. There is no doubt that Mr. Wolff will acquit himself excellently of his task, but whether his proposals will result in anything is another question. To delegate a matter to a commission has too often been in the Indies a pretext ... to abstain from real action.

The government has also done nothing to improve the cattle stocks of the natives, and it has not even got decent statistics ...

In short, there is nothing to be seen of the "benefits" which Minister Cremer [Liberal] ... has said repeatedly will make the Javanese love our rule. [This is so at least] with respect to ... rice cultivation. And one *bouw* of *sawah* still produces only 25 to 30 *piculs* of rice (there are some of 50 or 60 *piculs*, but also of 10 *piculs* and less), which—taking the average high price of two guilders—will fetch fifty to sixty guilders. The average land-holding (communal or individual) is 1 to 1½ *bouws* and this will steadily decrease because of the steep rise in population. The income from second crops per *bouw* can be put on the average at twenty-five guilders. So one can calculate the income earned from Java's fertile soil by five-eighths of the people who have the most ancient rights to the land and whose profession is agriculture. Not counting bad harvests or other misfortunes, the average yearly income of the Javanese farmer can at the highest be put at one hundred guilders.

[The Javanese] are also unable to earn more from their land by renting it to private European industry or by working on the plantations. Rents paid by the factory-owners for land are based on the productivity of this land when it is cultivated by the Javanese themselves. In the eastern regions, such as Soerabaja, Pasoeroean, Probolinggo, and Besoeki, the highest prices are paid, ranging from 100 to 150 guilders per *bouw*. But after all, the soil there is the best and is properly irrigated, etc., and everything including rice and other victuals is much more expensive, so that the native himself makes higher profits when he cultivates the land, but at the same time pays more for his upkeep. In Kediri, Madoera, and Central Java the rents paid for land are 20 guilders per *bouw* and even less. So [land rents] are about the same as the income earned when the land is cultivated by the farmers themselves. But even if this was much higher, it would not be to the advantage of the villager. This is because the private European plantation industry that has developed so strongly since 1870 is especially pernicious in that it takes away the land from the small man and gives him money in its place.

A good rice harvest provides the Javanese with food for almost the whole year. If there is a shortage in the last few months, they can fall back on the second crops, and so these families ... can look after themselves fairly well during the whole year. The rice is carefully stored in a *loemboeng* [little shed], but money on the otner hand slips through the fingers of the Javanese like water and it seduces him because of a primitive and childlike love of pleasure. So if a representative of a sugar mill or indigo factory (who are almost always supported by the village heads) comes and asks to rent his land, the tinkling sound of the guilders is too attractive for him to refuse the offer. This is especially so during the period when the land tax needs paying, because otherwise he might have to seek work a long distance away or pawn or sell something. But the small amount of money is soon dissipated on small feasts such as weddings, births, and deaths, at which he likes to be extravagant; or it is spent on sweets or debauchery (gambling, opium, dancing girls), things he would otherwise not have indulged in. But he has lost his land for sixteen months. And the month of May, during which bushels of ripened rice flood the village and warm the hearts of old and young, brings him neither joy nor food. If there is a little money left, he will be able to buy some rice, but soon food will be lacking ... Instead of calmly working in the *sawah* with the safe feeling that there is food for him and his family in the *loemboeng*, he now has to earn a few nickels for his upkeep by working in the cane-fields or in factories where the work is unpleasant, severely regulated and controlled. As a result he and his family become discontented. If he falls sick, there is no money or food at all. If he has a weak character, he becomes wanton and debauched. The work in the factory only lasts for part of the year and a time of pressing need, of pawning and getting into debt, will arrive in any case. And when the capitalist again knocks on his door in order to lease his land again for two years ... if necessary by evading the regulations, pressed as he is from all sides he will snap up the chance. In the meantime he cultivates his *sawah* again, but he is not the same man anymore. He now has worries, debts, and bad habits. People who profit from such a situation, such us gamblers, usurers, prostitutes, and sly opium sellers, have established themselves around the factories. And many of [the peasants] go from bad to worse. And the end comes when they have to sell their cattle, their house and land. The *gogol* [landed villager] then becomes an *orang menoempang* [labourer without land rights]. Village life has been demoralized and the villagers have been made unhappy.

Such are the consequences of the influx of European capital, which is considered by the majority of Netherlanders as of such great benefit to the natives, so that an influential party like the Liberal Union dares to preface its colonial platform with the words "the development of private industry". Learned economists usually summarize the benefits of this private European industry in this one sentence: "it brings so many hundreds of thousands of guilders among the population". But they do not mention or they do not know about the psychological destruction of the simple villagers. And then what does it actually mean, "to bring thousands of guilders among the people"? In fact it is no more than a grandiose generalization which does not say anything about the remuneration of the individual ... After all, the question that matters is not how much the total wage bill of a factory is, but how much each worker in this factory earns. And also here ... the answer is very unsatisfactory. Excluding the situation in East Java where, as we said before, the standard of living and therefore of wages is higher, normal coolie labour in the sugar and indigo plantations in the largest part of Java brings twenty cents for a twelve-hour day. Labourers during the planting season who work on a contract basis can earn more, but the work is heavy and demoralization lessens the energy—most of these coolies do not earn more than twenty cents per day. Labourers in the factory, depending on their particular task, earn from twenty to twenty-five cents, while women and children earn fifteen cents for twelve hours. Moreover, far fewer workers are needed than in earlier years because of the increase in the use of machinery, and other technical improvements.

The owners in Europe, usually directors of large concerns, are solely interested in large profits or dividends, and they literally put the thumbscrews on the managers to economize as much as possible on wages and all other expenditure. There is for example the scandalous situation where coolie wages, which were lowered because of the sugar crisis (price decline) in 1883 by an average of five cents per day, have not been increased again, although the sugar industry ... now shows great profits ... The owners, however, keep their money boxes as tightly closed as the deaf ear they turn to the voice of justice ...

My conclusion is that our policy with respect to native *agriculture* pushes the villagers slowly but surely into the same swamp of moral and physical misery into which the disinherited masses of Western society have sunk. These are at present struggling against the heartless suppressors and attempt to push themselves out of their misery. Once they are out, a bloody struggle will come about which will end an era of great misery. In the Indies this is only just beginning. And only later centuries will judge the period when a people was robbed of its land and was made the slave of insatiable fortune-hunters.

But people will ask: "What should we have done then?" The answer is very simple. The State, which now in Western society will have to wage a heavy struggle in order to obtain the power to make the people economically happy and *really* free (i.e. to ensure for the *community* a decent existence under reasonable working conditions), did have such power in the Indies and should not have abandoned it. It was the narrow-minded bourgeois spirit, not a high-thinking mind, that in 1870 attempted to repair the wrongs of the Culture System by letting the European capitalists loose on the natives. All these laws [i.e. Land Laws of 1870-71] were not the result of a nobility of mind, of a sense of justice, but flowed from an easy-going compliance with the slogans of the day. The *miserliness* should have been taken out of state supervision, but this supervision itself, which is so necessary for the naive Indies people, should have been retained. Instead of private enterprises state enterprises should have been set up ... which should be run by trained, honest, and properly controlled personnel. Land and labour should be hired from the people as is done now by the private firms, but without the present abuses ... and with a system of payment which suits the character of the Javanese better, that is, in small instalments. *All* should participate in a certain part of the profits, and another part of the profits should be kept in reserve for times of bad harvests and price declines.

It is a fallacy to argue that the State in this way would take on too big a risk. The hundreds of millions gained by private firms from coffee and sugar cultivation prove that the Treasury, when it is strictly just to the natives, can cope in all unfavourable periods, if only a sensible system of financial reserves is set up.

It is also a fairy tale that good state managers cannot lead an enterprise as well as good company officials. It is certainly true that to regulate all this in detail would have cost a great deal of time and effort. But were we not obliged—after hundreds of years of injustice—to do our utmost and to investigate in the greatest possible detail what the people really needed? ... Truly, the [Culture] System should not have disappeared, but it should have been turned into a blessing for the people. An iron fist would have been necessary ... to protect the small man against the voracious greed of the private capitalists.

But now the damage is almost irreparable. The exploitation of the Indies by private firms is difficult to stop. It is not possible to take away the rights of all these factory-owners and long-lease owners and little can be done to force them to give the native the greatest possible share of the profits made from his birth-land. But I still say: push things *as much as possible* in this direction. Use part of the debt of honour, which is to be paid by the Netherlands to the Indies, to set up state agricultural enterprises, especially sugar factories ... Hundreds of young men, who now are desperately trying to find a way to earn their livelihood, could find work there ... The model state factory would also push up the wages in private enterprise. This well-ordered system is the only way for the native to obtain a proper share of the richness of his land. At the same time the cultivation of rice should be developed by means of education, state loans, and the establishment of credit banks.

But I know that all this will not happen. The iron wall of a false sense of freedom, which rules our times, stands between me and the power of the State. I shall be pushed aside with such big words as "reaction", "return to obsolete systems". Still I wanted to say how I see the situation. And history shall prove me correct.

Not only in the field of agriculture but also in many other areas is the policy towards the Indies strongly capitalistic in character. I am referring here to the tendency to favour and to spare the rich and powerful, and on the other hand to take everything from the poor man and to neglect his interests. Mr van Kol [Socialist] was completely correct when in Article 1 of his "programme" he called the exploitation of the Indies *capitalistic* ... Not one European ... pays as the native does—25 per cent of his income [in taxation]. The principle of hitting the poor harder than the rich, which caused the great revolution of the eighteenth century and which now is generally condemned in European public finance, is still practised in the Indies year in and year out. And not one of the theoretical economists who run the Netherlands Government ... has even thought of protesting against this.

But in most other government decisions and deeds the capitalistic nature of policy is visible. For example it was strongly evident in the Mining Law of Minister Cremer ... A few years ago great enthusiasm was awakened in the Indies—as in almost the whole of the world—in mining exploration ... It became therefore necessary to revise the mining legislation, and this was a good opportunity to obtain new sources of revenue for the Treasury, which had been depleted by the loss of the surplus budgets, the Atjeh war [serious colonial war in North Sumatra], and the loss of profits from the Culture System. Large-scale exploration by the State and, where the prospects were good, exploitation by the State, were the proper way to make the treasures of the Indies soil serve the general interest ... But this capitalist Minister *par excellence* ... continued the policy of favouring the most powerful industrial entrepreneurs ... When the profits had to flow again into the pockets of private businessmen, one could have expected that the Minister by means of progressive taxation could have channelled at least an important part of these *very high* profits into the Treasury ... The fact is, however, ... that Mr Cremer asked, in addition to a straight tax of eighteen cents per *bouw* (which was rightly kept low in order not to hit too hard the entrepreneur who had not been successful), for a tax of 2 per cent on gross profits, which after strong opposition from the Chamber was finally increased to 4 per cent ... These very wealthy mining capitalists of the future ... will, thanks to Minister Cremer, be able to spend their millions again in Europe without having ceded to the Indies community a reasonable part of the treasures dug from the Indies soil ...

The government is also failing ... to properly ensure that contract labourers in the plantations and mining enterprises in the Outer Islands are decently treated ... the fact that more and more Javanese are prepared to do this (whole groups of them together with their wives and children can be seen sitting on the foredeck of almost every steamer leaving for the Outer Islands) is certainly one of the most obvious proofs of the growing poverty of these people, who are so strongly attached to the land of their birth. This alone is enough to make the departing labourers unhappy. But disease, dying far away from the village of the forefathers, the disappointment of the expectation of earning enough in the foreign land to return home, the loss of wife or children, and their own physical suffering or bad treatment, make this emigration a veritable martyrdom for its numerous victims.

The government is of the opinion that it did enough when in 1880 it issued *paper* legislation to regulate the contracts to be concluded with the labourers: money advances, working hours, the kind of work to be performed, the duration of the contract, etc. (the well-known *Coolie Ordinances*). These contracts had to be *registered* before the local government official in the place of arrival.

As always there is again here the *apparent* care for the small man, while in fact he is not *really* helped. There is hardly any inspection to see whether the stipulations of the contract are adhered to and whether the people are treated humanely and honestly. [Inspection] is one of the normal duties of assistant residents or *controleurs*, who sometimes reside in district *centra* [centres of district administration by the government] or coastal cities far away from the plantations. Moreover they are often acting in line with government thinking, which is concerned to cause industrial enterprises as little trouble as possible. And so they mainly restrict their interference to the punishment or pursuit of runaway coolies ... or of one or other manager who has become too notorious because of the murder or maltreatment of coolies. Specially appointed and paid labour inspectors ... such as exist in the Netherlands and who regularly supervise working conditions, nutrition, housing, hospitals, and the treatment of labourers in general, are unheard of.

The facts prove that such supervision is urgently necessary. I will not use as evidence ... the various cases of serious maltreatment and the legal prosecution of managers and foremen that have occurred on the east coast of Sumatra. I consider these as "sensational", as *ce qu'on voit* [the obviously visible], while what really matters is *ce qu'on ne voit pas* [the invisible], that is, the daily suffering and hardships of coolie life, which for one reason or another do not draw the public attention ... I heard some details about this from a credible person who is in charge of such a plantation and who has seen the situation with his own eyes ...

> After a tiring journey the group of coolies has finally arrived. The travelling passes are collected and a helpful *mandoer* [overseer] shows them their communal quarters. The building is made of bamboo and is not built on stumps as is usual in this region, but rests straight on the ground. Everything has to be done in there: cooking, sleeping, and eating. Everything is closed off and there is no ventilation. The coolies are obliged to buy rice from the plantation. Meat they do not get. As they are days walking away from a populated area they are also unable to visit a *waroeng* [little store] to feast on a piece of *ikan* [fish]. There are chickens, but they are only for the manager and his staff. After all, where is the coolie who has 2.50 guilders to buy a chicken from some *hadji* [usurer] trader? On payday the people get very little money in their hands, because the administrators take care to get the advance payments back as quickly as possible. And then there is the *hadji mandoer* [moneylender] from whom the coolie has borrowed money, who is waiting grinning at the door to get his money back immediately with the necessary interest. The manager does not care about all this and looks on laughing at these fellows who with puzzled faces and empty-handed return to work!

It happens daily that people get sick, often because of hunger, the lack of nutritious food, or exhaustion. This does not worry the administrator. If they are sick they still have to work until they collapse. The man starts to work again and in fact collapses a few moments later. My spokesman saw one lying down in his stuffy, dirty, smelly living quarters, dying without anybody taking any notice. The people look thin and emaciated. And they do their work listlessly from morning to night. And sorry will be the man who pauses for a moment to sit on a fallen tree to smoke a cigarette. The *mandoer* has been given special instructions to make good use of his stick, which he, however, does only very seldom use and only when the *toean besar* [manager] is in the neighbourhood. If he does nothing in such a case, the *toean* himself will use his horsewhip ... When my spokesman reported to the administrator that a coolie was lying in one of the huts with fever and suffering from convulsions, the answer was: "Oh, let this bastard get ... I can get ten other ones in his place." [This administrator] loudly laughed when my spokesman proposed the construction of special bamboo quarters for the sick. This manager was a German. And he also dismissed the idea of setting up a store where dried meat could be sold with the words: "Surely they are not servant girls!"

Only compulsory action by the State can force ... the greedy plantation-owners to act in a more humane way. And only after an *independent* corps of officials charged with the inspection of labour has been established will it be possible, in my view, to ensure better treatment of the coolies in the Outer Islands ... Our investigation as to what we have done or are doing for the natives ... has unfortunately but of necessity become an almost continuous accusation against the Netherlands colonial policy. It has also been a continuous demonstration of the principle of selling the small and poor man short and favouring the rich and powerful ...

Where must the money come from to do all these things? ... There is no money to be found even for the most urgent measures ... This is not surprising! Imagine that in the Netherlands heavy taxes had been levied for half a century ... and that on the other hand no canals had been dug for seagoing vessels; that rivers had not been made navigable; that Amsterdam and Rotterdam could not be reached safely from the sea and that these cities could not be reached from Germany by river; that yearly floods ravaged large parts of the country; that there was only one central railway line and few side tracks and some privately run tram lines; and that the security of private property left much to be desired. Imagine also the considerable budget surpluses that resulted from this neglect of public interest and the heavy taxation being usurped every year by a power that argued that it possessed a historical right to rob the Netherlands of about 800 million guilders in capital and interest. What financial and productive power would our fatherland still possess under these circumstances? ...

After the introduction of the Culture System many millions flowed into the Netherlands Treasury. Ten of millions were shown on the Indies budget as contributions to the Netherlands finances. And by not allowing expenditure on even the most urgent matters in the Indies, many more millions were left, which under the name of "budget surplus" were transferred to the Netherlands. The financial expert Mr N.P. van den Berg has calculated that the Indies in this way has remitted 764 million guilders between 1831 and 1877 in capital and low interest to the mother country. This is after the debts to the Netherlands have been subtracted.

Any people, even if not burdened by an exhausting Atjeh war, would after such a regime be completely emaciated and would be unable to lift itself out of this poverty without help from outside. So it cannot be doubted that in order to cure the Indies of this far-advanced decay, the Netherlands must redress the injustice that has been done and restore a part of the millions that have been taken away from the Indies. The present [colonial] budgets are always closed with a deficit (only in 1901 was a balanced budget obtained because of the rise in the price of tin) ... and the most pressing needs cannot be filled; the capacity of the people to pay is exhausted more and more through heavier taxation ...

It does honour to Mr van Deventer that, while we other writers have only been complaining for years about the injustices done, he has had the moral courage to demand squarely in his article "A Debt of Honour" that the Netherlands should return part of the millions from which it has benefited.

As the starting-point he took the Accountability Law of 1867 ... With this "law for the regulation of the administration and accountability of the finances of the Netherlands Indies" ... the principle of the strict separation of colonial finances from those of the mother country was introduced, and as it was even more clearly put in hhe almost unanimous decision of the Second Chamber ... of 1898, that after that law "the mother country as well as the Indies *have to provide for their own expenditures*". Nevertheless, still another 151 million guilders in Indies budget surpluses were remitted between 1867 and 1877. But when in 1883 the Indies because of this new bloodletting had to stop its payments, the mother country did not come around to give back part or all of these 151 million guilders. It *lent* the Indies 45.5 million guilders against a considerable interest, and this game was repeated in 1898 when 55 miplion guilders were lent, so that since 1883 the Indies have already paid about 50 million in repayments and interest on these two loans. So also after 1867 the completely unreasonable system was followed by which the Indies and Netherlands finances were considered as one, as long as the Indies showed a budget surplus. But they were separated again as soon as the Indies ran into deficits and needed help from the Netherlands. Restitution must now be paid for this injustice ...

The 151 million directly remitted, together with the 50 million-odd sent as repayments and interest, make together about 200 million guilders. And this is the amount which, according to Mr van Deventer, must be repaid as a debt of honour by the Netherlands to the Indies. The first hundred million should be used to transfer the accountability for the loans of 1883 and 1898 from the Indies to the Netherlands. The other hundred million should be given by the Netherlands to the colony in order to provide for urgently felt needs ... An initial capital of a hundred million, spent on projects to increase production, would get us quite a distance in restoring the prosperity of the Indies. So the situation is not desperate if one only has the courage to use the proper medicine. However, developments during the last few days do not look very hopeful. During the recent parliamentary elections the Indies hardly counted more than a rotten apple in a greengrocer's shop. And the elections resulted in the coming to power of a clerical Cabinet and a clerical majority. Little is to be expected by the Indies from the Catholic section and although the Anti-Revolutionary Party (Neo-Calvinist) ... has declared in its programme that we no longer may only profit from the Indies and that the policy of *exploitation* must be replaced by one of *guardianship* and *moral obligations* ... there is little to be seen of this beautiful declaration of principles in its recent *action* programme. This contains three demands in terms of colonial policy:

1. Native Christians should not be left subject to the Mohammedan law.
2. The *Christianization* of the Indies should be furthered.
3. The poisoning of the people through opium should be stopped.

Does such a programme, which is almost entirely religious, not make a mockery of the great poverty of the people and of the urgent need for numerous measures that have to be taken to protect the Indies against a continuing decay?

Truly, if during the next few years the pauperised natives are being drugged with the privilege of becoming Christians, then I hope that Dr Abraham Kuyper [leader of the Neo-Calvinists]—who is so full of love for his Netherlands *small people*, for the baker, the small shopkeeper, who after all also demand from their worldly government first of all *worldly* benefits—then I hope that this Christian leader will be able to justify this gross deceit of the poor Javanese before the God of the Christians ...

P. Brooshooft, *De Ethische Koers in de Koloniale Politiek* (Amsterdam: De Bussy, 1901), pp. 3-5, 28-31, 54-62.

11 C.J. Hasselman: General survey of the results of the investigation into economic prosperity in Java and Madura, held in 1904-5

Population statistics: in judging these figures, account must be taken of the incompleteness of the various regional returns and the unreliability of many figures because of defective and inexact enumerations in earlier years. However, it is certain that [in the period 1880-1905] the population of Java ... has steadily increased and that in the ten-year period 1895-1905 the population has grown from around twenty million to twenty-three and a half million, or by more than three and a half million people.

Although there has been a steady increase in population almost everywhere, in some districts there was a temporary decline resulting from epidemics, bad harvests, natural disasters, etc. (Bantam, Limbangan, 1880-85); (Grobongan, 1898-1902); (Soerabaja, 1890-95). Usually these temporary declines were followed by an equally speedy increase. Exceptional increases have been noticed here and there as a result of immigration. The various reasons for immigration were: the advantages offered by private industry, better living conditions, improvements in the means of communication, etc. Emigration takes place on a permanent basis (because of repeated bad harvests, epidemics, overpopulation, shortage of land), and also on a temporary basis (disasters, cattle pest, the tiger plague; sometimes also because of forced cultivation or other government measures). The extent of emigration was nowhere such that it resulted in a noticeable decrease in population.

Overpopulation exists only in a few regions. It can be said to exist in districts where the number of landless peasants is very large and where there is practically no opportunity to gain a sufficient income outside agriculture (Magelang, Temanggoeng, Poerworedjo, Blitar), or where the harvests are inadequate (Keboemen, a part of Madoera, Berbek) ... It appears that in Java there are per 1000 individuals 448 children, 480 adults, and 72 people who are fifty years and above. There are 1045 females against 1000 males. The number of births is around 50-60 per 1000 inhabitants. The yearly population increase in the period 1870-1905 was about 17.6 per thousand. The population density in 1907 was 225 per square kilometre. The *average* increase amounts to at least 8.5 per cent every five years, so that the population doubles itself every forty-two years ...

Nutrition: as a rule two meals are taken each day, one at noon and the other around sundown. The staple food is rice or rice mixed with corn, or cassava and other roots, meat, fish, and side dishes. In a number of districts breakfast is taken, consisting of tubers or other titbits, which are consumed sometimes together with tea or coffee.

Except for an increase in the use of meat and fish in some districts, no important improvements in the diet were noticed. In fact almost everywhere nutrition was considered sufficient. Often the food intake temporarily decreases during the last months before the rice harvest, when food becomes scarce and more expensive ... On the whole, more fish is eaten than meat. In a number of regions meat is only eaten on feast days. In twenty-four districts or parts of them an increase in meat consumption was reported. In seven districts meat consumption decreased mainly because of an increase in the use of fish, while in the remaining areas meat consumption remained the same ...

The consumption of salt rose in all areas, with the exception of Soerabaja. The consumption of salt is dependent on various factors such as economic conditions (there was a decrease in consumption during the disastrous years 1901 and 1902, followed later again by an increase); the production and consumption of clandestine salt; weather conditions; police surveillance, etc. The general increase in salt consumption is attributable mainly to the population increase, the increase in the number of salt stores, and the introduction of salt bricks ...

Housing: in the main centra as well as in the countryside of almost the whole of Java and Madoera, some improvement in housing can be observed ... This was caused by ... the fall in prices of materials, greater prosperity, the influence of government officials, greater needs, the imitation of non-natives, the greater proficiency of tradesmen, the fear of theft and fires, immigration, and other local factors ... In one district (Temanggoeng) some decline was reported, and in some others the situation remained the same (Demak, Grobongan, Rembang, Probolinggo) ... The care and upkeep of house yards also improved in many districts, mainly as a result of greater pressure by government officials ... In fifteen districts the situation in this respect remained the same. In general the Sundanese take more interest in the upkeep of their houses and yards than the Javanese or the Madurese. This is partly because of the greater proficiency of the former in bamboo construction, but also perhaps because they do not indulge in opium-smoking. In a large number of districts an increase was reported in the number of brick houses and the use of roof tiles. Where this was not the case it was attributed to the lack of usable materials, fear of earthquakes, sometimes the cost of felling trees, and the obligation to obtain a licence. Generally, the increase in the use of tiles and galvanized roofing is greater than that of building bricks.

In Keboemen the superstitious belief is held that the chances of dying are greater in houses with tiled roofs ...

Housing timber is either bought (from other villagers, in the markets, or from private timber yards) or acquired by cutting trees on one's own land, on land to be reclaimed, or in the government forests. Often it is also stolen from the forests ... There has been an improvement almost everywhere in furniture and household utensils and the ordinary villager makes use more and more of tables, chairs, cupboards, beds, plates, cups, glasses, and kerosene lamps, although they are usually rough and of inferior quality. In the houses of some traders more interest is taken in wall decorations. Of course there are many local differences. But in general the Sundanese have in this respect been quicker in taking over European customs than the Javanese or Madurese ...

Public health: this is considered satisfactory in almost all districts. In some regions the situation is unsatisfactory because of the existence of stagnant pools and swamps (South Priangan, Tjilatjap, Djember, Panaroekan, Banjoewangi); recurrent floods (Demak, Keboemen, Besoeki, Bangil); lack of water for bathing, drinking, and cleaning; newly reclaimed land; or the planting of *sawahs* with east monsoon rice. In the various coastal areas health conditions are not good because of the influence of coral reefs and fish ponds ... So far as medical care is concerned, natives prefer to be treated by native *doekoen* [soothsayers] with native medicines rather than by European doctors or *dokters-djawa* [native doctors]. The number of native doctors is sufficient to cope with the people's demand for medical help. Moreover in some places use is made of the services of missionaries. The reasons for the people's unwillingness to call for official medical help are distrust of European medical treatment and medicines, as well as fatalism, stupidity, and poverty, and partly also the long distances that have to be travelled to visit a doctor ...

According to some reports the *dokters-djawa* only seldom visit the villages and they are generally considered by the people as too far removed socially. The respect of the natives for the European medical profession does not appear to have increased, because one of the official functions of doctors and *dokters-djawa* is to check and treat prostitutes, which makes doctors servants of the police in the eyes of the people. Finally, European medicines are often incorrectly applied by the native chiefs, and the *doekoen*, of course, make capital out of this ...

In most districts there are no qualified midwives and of those who are available only little use is made. Many natives take offence at women in childbirth being treated by Europeans. Still, some officials are of the opinion that greater use would be made of qualified midwives if more were available.

It can be concluded from an investigation in the district of Serang that the number of deaths of women in childbirth and of stillbirths is about the same among the native population as in Europe, where qualified medical help is available everywhere. Some are of the opinion that the use of *doekoen* must be preferred to the services of European midwives. Others argue that the population must be persuaded—if necessary by force—to take recourse to European midwives ...

In almost all district *centra* there is a hospital for natives. Furthermore, in various places there are missionary hospitals and hospitals for diseased prostitutes. The extension of old hospitals and the building of new ones is considered necessary in some districts. Almost everywhere the natives show an aversion to government hospitals, mostly because of the unusual food and treatment, often also because of prejudice or unfamiliarity. For the better-situated these establishments are not comfortable enough. Other objections are: the restriction on personal freedom, the lack of homeliness and being away from the family, the fear of dying without the observance of the ritual precepts, the presence of prostitutes, distrust of European medicine, fear of operations, etc. According to some reports, this general aversion is steadily declining and much is dependent on the tact of the doctors in question. Missionary hospitals, which are usually better equipped and better run, appear to be less objectionable to the natives, although these hospitals are not everywhere immediately successful.

Another objection against government hospitals is apparently that *red rice* is used, which is also given to prisoners. According to Dr van Buuren (Kediri) the situation in almost all government hospitals in the countryside leaves much to be desired with respect to equipment as well as treatment ... The policlinics (which are usually situated in the districh *centra*) are reported to be catching on well in twenty-nine districts, and are unsatisfactorily or not at all attended in thirty-one districts ... The question whether the population is suffering from chronic diseases that seriously affect the capacity to work (malaria, syphilis, eye diseases, leg sores, leprosy, beri-beri, etc.) received negative replies in forty-three districts, and more or less affirmative replies in fourteen districts, while no replies ... were received from seventeen districts ...

The reports from the district administrations are not always identical with those from the medical practitioners. For example, the district of Rembang gave a negative reply to the chronic diseases question and the civilian doctor gave an affirmative reply. Malaria and syphilis do have an important impact in many regions; the same is true of eye diseases, as for instance in Serang where in some families people regularly become blind by the time they are forty-five to fifty years old ... In this respect there are important differences between Europeans and natives, because the latter, although suffering from ghastly leg wounds or a far-advanced stage of consumption, continue to work so that their output suffers little or not at all ... According to Dr van Buuren the most common diseases are eye diseases, malaria, syphilitic leg sores, consumption, and cancer. "They spread slowly but surely, while absolutely nothing is being done about them" ...

During the last twenty to thirty years there have been few large-scale epidemics, though mention must be made of the fever and cholera epidemics in 1901 and 1902. Only in one district were cases of beri-beri reported ...

The agragrian situation: communally held property is not found at all in the regions of Bantam, Batavia, the Priangan regencies (with one exception), Madoera and Besoeki, and Old-Probolinggo. Communal lands that are periodically divided are found, although not in the same measure everywhere, in thirty-three districts of Central Java, Soerabaja, and Pasoeroean. The Culture System appears to have resulted in an increase in communal property. Little use has been made of the opportunity provided since 1885 to convert communal property into personal inheritable property. Instead a tendency has developed to periodically divide communal property into permanent shares. Shareholders are all members of the village community, who possess a house and yard and are able and willing to pay land rent and to render the seignorial and village services that rest on the land. Owners of hereditary, individually owned lands, which are larger than the communal share, are sometimes not allowed to share in the communal lands ... It is generally accepted that 1 *bouw* of *sawah* land or 2 *bouws* of *tegal* [*tegalan*] land are needed for the upkeep of a peasant's family ... In thirteen districts the portions of land were considered too small, and in twenty-nine districts they were considered satisfactory, more than satisfactory, or too large. In some districts a tendency was noticed to cut up the land shares in order to reduce the impact of the seignorial services, or because of the increase in the number of partners, or the unwillingness to emigrate. Here and there the number of partners is restricted to stop the frittering-away of land.

In some districts shareholders have to take turns and are allotted parcels of land once every two, three, four, or six years. In other areas the size of the allotment remains the same and only the user changes. *Sawah* shares that have become free are in the case of death allotted to the heir or his replacement or to one of the oldest inhabitants (hereditary owner) who still has no share, or to a newcomer. Sometimes the vacant shares are divided among the other shareholders or rented to the highest bidder or sold on account of the remaining partners. In some districts prospective shareholders must live in a village for at least three years before they are eligible to share in the land.

The question whether abuses have crept in over the allocation of vacant shares has been answered in the affirmative in some areas. The abuses consist of the allocation of vacant shares by the village head to his own relatives or members of the village council; allocation to the highest bidder; allocation without consulting the other partners; the bribing of the village head ...; the renting of whole complexes for the benefit of the village council; and the selling of shares. Mention must also be made of the "*dadal* right", i.e. the right to take away shares because of the refusal to pay taxes and to render seignorial and village services ... Although in the majority of districts where the system of periodical allotment is practised people are not interested in a more permanent form of land ownership, there nevertheless has been an evolution in this direction ... in some other districts the system of periodical division ... has been replaced partly or totally by communal landownership on the basis of permanent shares. The causes that obstruct this evolution are the uneven fertility of the land, the conservatism of the people, the influence of chiefs and officials, and the renting of lands to sugar factories. Favourable factors are the desire to increase productivity and to prevent the corruptive practices of village government. Also the influence of native and European government officials must be mentioned here ...

On land that is permanently owned (individual ownership and communal ownership on the basis of permanent shares) ... the area of land needed for the upkeep of a family varies from 1/1 *bouw* (Poerbolinggo, Grobongan) to 3 *bouws* (Limbangan). The availability of land is considered unsatisfactory in twenty-nine districts or parts thereof, and is considered satisfactory or too great in seventy-three districts or parts thereof ... The frittering-away of permanently owned land occurs as the result of inheritance, gifts, or marriages, and also because of sales or pawning. The cutting-up of land is impeded, however, by the taxes resting on the land, which are only bearable when the property is large enough to ensure a profit. As a result sometimes only one of the heirs takes over the property, while the others are paid an indemnity. Sometimes the land is cultivated each year in turn by the heirs, or it is sold and the money is divided.

The accumulation of land in a few hands mostly occurs as a result of sales on the basis of the right to buy the property again, or pawning, sometimes also renting, but seldom by straight-out sales ... The accumulation of land by people from outside the village is checked in some areas by the regulation that they must have a replacement to render services and pay taxation in the villages where they own land.

Against this there is the practice in some regions that a person is only obliged to pay taxes and render services once, irrespective of how many land shares he owns. This, of course, can further the agglomeration of land.

Large landowners are to be found mostly in the Priangan regencies and in a few districts of Ngawi and Djombang. The single ownership of many small parcels of land occurs in Bantam and various districts of Central and East Java ...

The question how long there will be sufficient agrarian land available can only be answered properly after an exact local investigation has been held by experts who are able to take into account all the factors involved ... According to the reports from the districts—in so far as they are reliable in this question—the extension of agricultural land is still possible in thirty-eight districts and not possible in thirty-eight other districts. In most districts it is felt that cheap agricultural credit is the first prerequisite for farmers wishing to start on new reclamations ...

Thrift: the natives are generally not thrifty. The Madurese and Tenggerese, however, show a greater inclination to save than the Javanese. Also women as a rule are more thrifty than men ... Account should be taken, however, of the fact that many do not save in terms of money, but invest in land, cattle, jewelery, boats, nets, etc. Money-saving (because of the introduction of better credit facilities) appears to be slowly on the increase, although not always in a productive manner. In some regions there is still the custom of keeping money in earthenware pots or bamboo cases. Sometimes money is saved for a certain feast or for a rest. An increase in the desire to save was reported in twenty districts or sections thereof and a decline in eight districts. Favourable factors mentioned included plans to reclaim land, the [Mecca] pilgrimage, increasing economic development and security, a better insight into one's own interests, the growing influence of government officials, and the impact of credit services. Unfavourable factors were the growing needs resulting from the expansion of European plantations, the greater opportunity to buy things, improvements in communications etc. ... Capital formation still occurs very seldom among the native population. And although in various districts of the Priangan, in Bantam, and in Pasoeroean, and in some regional and district *centra* there are to be found large landowners, traders, chiefs, and other persons who possess considerable capital, in proportion to the total population their number is very small. The capital is again not always held in money but in land, cattle, houses, or rice. It should also not be forgotten that yearly a considerable amount of money is leaving Java on account of the pilgrimage to Mecca. At a conservative estimate the number of pilgrims could be put at six thousand per annum and if each spends about 400 to 500 guilders, then savings of two and a half to three million guilders are spent annually by the native population ...

Money-lending: although the lending of money against interest is forbidden by Islam, most natives gladly lend out money under different pretexts such as sales, pawning, pre-payment, sale with the right of buying back, etc. And although few natives are professional usurers, it is still true that in the village a great deal of money is lent out against usurious interest. The lending conditions vary in accordance with circumstances and the profession of the lender ... Usually collateral is demanded to half the value of money advanced. The interest varies from 32 to 100 per cent, and sometimes from 200 to 400 per cent per annum ...

Whatever the form of the loan, the borrower usually ends up losing his possessions, because he is unable to repay or rebuy. Farmers usually start by borrowing from other villagers in order to be able to cultivate their *sawahs*. Repayment is usually in the form of rice. Later, in the months of scarcity before the harvest, an advance is taken on the crop. Furthermore, often I.O.U.s are signed without any understanding of their content and the final result is the alienation of land to the money-lenders ... Especially in West Java, but also in other places, this system of usury leads to the accumulation of land in a few hands ... It appears that, in the Priangan regencies, of the more than 6000 *bouws* of land on which money was borrowed, only 970 *bouws* or 15 per cent were returned to the borrowers. In a district of the region of Bandoeng there are forty-one landowners who together possess more than 2000 *bouws* of *sawahs* or an average 53 *bouws* per head ...

It is considered impossible to obtain a reasonably accurate estimate of the state of usury. Such an estimate was attempted in the Priangan regencies, where the data were gathered by a native official who was disguised as a pedlar. It appeared that in that region alone there were 434 known usurers, who had a combined annual turnover of 2,300,000 guilders and 3400 *piculs* of rice. More than 9000 *bouws* of land were appropriated by them ... European and foreign Oriental money-lenders [i.e. mainly Chinese] demand in the same way as native money-lenders the highest interest rates from the poorest section of the people. It often happens that pedlars and visitors to the markets who borrow 1 guilder in the morning must repay 1.05 guilders in the evening—or twenty-four hours later. It also sometimes happens that a borrower who is unable to fulfil his obligations is only charged with the repayment of the accumulated interest. If the borrower later happens to fall on better times he is again charged, because the interest keeps accumulating.

There was a case in East Java where in this way a borrower was required to pay interest of 520 per cent per annum. The district court dismissed this claim as contravening good public order and morality. The claimant acquiesced in this decision ...

The influence of cultural factors on native economic welfare: the general feeling of native officials, traders, and other private persons who were consulted is that the Javanese masses are indeed lazy. This is evident from, or is the result of, the love of pleasure-seeking; of shyness; of weakness of character; or of the lack of courage, insight, self-confidence, and perseverance. Others attribute to the Javanese in addition a lack of forethought and co-operation, a lack of independence, sense of duty, self-control, and trust in his own opinion; or they point to his desire for popularity and prestige, his little interest in saving, the fact that he is quickly satisfied and has only small needs, and his intellectual and material backwardness. Some are of the opinion that the Javanese are not aware, or sufficiently so, of the state of decay in which they live. The reasons forwarded for this decay are despotism, the caste system, class privileges, the usurpations and avarice of the chiefs, the autocracy of the village heads, inequality before the law, and the *hormat* system [i.e. the customary acts of submission and reverence which the common people were due to perform with respect to the indigenous nobility and other officials]. Other natives seek the cause for the unsatisfactory situation of the people in the existing religious beliefs and the *adat*, and also in inadequate education and the competition of other races.

Most of the natives who have been consulted are of the opinion that the government and its officials must take the initiative in introducing measures to improve the situation. Some are going very far in this and demand that the government use compulsory methods also in those matters where it hitherto has abstained from any direct interference. Other measures that have been recommended are: sound education at home, education that is character-building and available to all classes of indigenous society; lectures and publications; education in the technical, agricultural, and literary fields and in cottage industries; the development of religious feeling and a religious doctrine which activates people; the emancipation of women; the restriction of polygamy; and the further simplification of the *hormat* system; easier communication between European and native officials; the abolition of hereditary government and despotism; and an equal and just law for all. Other desires were that regions with sufficient irrigation should be closed for the [European] sugar industry; that irrigation and credit facilities be extended; that the development of native plantations and mining enterprises be encouraged, and that practical information be given to the people about trading and co-operatives ...

Early marriages and polygamy: it is customary almost everywhere to marry off children early. The unmarried state is considered by the people as something improper, abnormal, and unnatural. Moreover many parents wish to see their family increase quickly in order to ensure that they are taken care of in their old age. Other causes for early marriages mentioned are: the desire not to leave the children behind uncared for; the shame which many feel about having an adult unmarried daughter at home; the interest of good morals; the desire to receive the customary presents for the wedding-feast; and the conservatism of the Javanese, who in this respect still adhere strictly to the *adat*.

In Serang (Bantam) the natives argue that it is highly dangerous to have an adolescent virgin or a young widow in the house, because they cause more trouble than a herd of buffaloes. It is also preferred to have young men marry early for reasons of morality and to familiarize them early with responsibilities.

The age at which children are married varies for girls from seven to fifteen years and for boys from fourteen to eighteen or twenty years. Sometimes marriage is only a formality and the partners go and live together when they reach marriageable age. But also sometimes (for example in parts of Bantam) girls from seven to ten years old are completely surrendered to their husbands. Dowries are usually small and in some regions amount to only five guilders, and sometimes even less. Previous consultations about the mutual feelings of the prospective marriage partners occur more frequently among the better-situated families and the nobility than among the poorer sections of the population.

The better-situated families often have their children married early, for example at their eighth year, in order to profit in this way from their situation of prosperity and arrange a better marriage than later, when perhaps this prosperity might have declined ... It was felt in some districts that early marriages were decreasing, particularly among officials and the nobility. In most districts, however, it was reported that the situation in this respect has remained the same or that there was an increase in early marriages. Important factors in this respect are, of course, the struggle for existence, educational development, and the gradual penetration of Western ideas.

What has been said so far is only applicable to first marriages. Far less trouble is taken over later marriages and the interference of parents—if it is there at all—is much less. It can be taken for granted that early marriages often result in divorce and the taking of a second wife.

Polygamy is fairly common among the natives. Many believe that having more than one wife is pleasing to one or other god. Other factors involved are: sensuality, the barrenness of the first wife, a surplus of women, or where the first wife has been forced on a man, who might take the wife of his own choice later. Polygamy occurs most in Serang (Bantam), in the Priangan regencies, Cheribon, Pemalang, Batang, Keboemen, Soemenap, Pamekasan, and Bondowoso, and the incidence is of course greater among the better-situated than among the poorer classes. Polygamy is decreasing among native officials, while village heads usually have two wives. The general impression is that polygamy is decreasing rather than increasing. The factors at work here are a growing feeling of their own worth by women, the struggle for existence, and yet also an increase in the standard of living. And although the number of divorces is decreasing here and there, especially among the higher classes, marriage ties among the lower classes are still far from being solid ...

The term *the urge to squander money*: this means ... for example, the custom of spending a great deal of money on various religious and other *slametans* [feasts] given on the occasion of marriage, circumcision, the commemoration of death, etc. Money squandering is considered to have increased in fifteen districts, while in all other (sixty-three) districts it remained the same or was decreasing. Increases were noticed especially in West Java with respect to the use of fireworks in the *poeasa* (fasting) month, while here and there a greater degree of ostentation was noticed at harvest festivals and at weddings ... The extent of *gambling*, which mostly occurs secretly, is difficult to estimate. Also in this respect it is felt that only in eighteen districts or sub-districts ... was there an increase, while in fifty-nine districts—or by far the most—the situation was reported as stationary or on the decline ...

The use of opium: it can in general be concluded that there has been a fair decrease in the use of opium after the institution of the government opium monopoly ... and that the usage of opium is generally dependent on economic conditions ... This conclusion is not supported by the Colonial Reports, which show that the use of opium in Java has increased from 735,000 *thails* [1 thail = 0.05409 kilograms] in 1904 to 870,000 *thails* in 1912 in spite of the closing-down of a considerable number of shops and dens ...

The consumption of opium is of old the largest in Central Java, in particular in Kediri. In West Java there is hardly any smoking of opium ... In Kediri (and elsewhere) a decrease was noticeable in years of economic depression such as 1901, 1902, and 1903. But when the situation improved in 1904 there was again an increase in the use of opium. Also in Malang the use of opium is very much dependent on the success of the coffee harvest. Little has been reported about the influence of opium-smoking on general prosperity. It was stated in Grobongan that opium-smoking causes the people in times of economic decline to become quickly exhausted and collapse. In Pati it was felt that the provision of better medical facilities would result in a decline in the use of opium, because many natives with chronic diseases start to smoke opium ...

Conclusion: although the area of arable land exerts an important influence on the general level of economic welfare, other factors also play an important role. Such factors include the nature and fertility of the land; climatic conditions; the incidence of crop failures; the situation with regard to irrigation; cattle stocks; the opportunity to transport produce and earn extra income; and also the personal disposition of the people (diligence, energy, money-wasting, desire to save, etc.).

Considerably varying answers were received to the question whether prosperity was greater in areas where land was available in sufficient or abundant quantities than in areas with little or insufficient land. Almost everything depends here on local conditions ...

The same factors are also of primary importance in judging the question whether the ordinary landowner has the means at his disposal to provide for the needs of his family. In by far the majority of districts one was of the opinion that this question was to be answered in the positive. Negative answers were given with regard to parts of the population in the districts of Anjer, Buitenzorg [Bogor], Poerwokerto, Poerbolinggo, Tjilatjap, Pati, Poerworedjo, Toeban, Sidoardjo, Lamongan, Toeloengagoeng, Besoeki, Pasoeroean, and Probolinggo ...

The poor villagers, whether they are farmers, landless labourers, small traders, or tradesmen, provide for their upkeep by additional work such as coolie labour, peddling, the sale of grass, firewood, and forest produce, and by getting employment in one of the various [Western] plantations. The respectable people among them are usually able to provide sufficiently for their own needs and those of their families.

So far as the general standard of living of the natives in Java is concerned, there are indications that the way of life is becoming more costly. One can point to the increasing consumption of various imported goods, while also from the state of clothing, housing, and nutrition it can be concluded that an increase in the standard of living has taken place. The village women no longer wear ornaments in the form of a rolled-up coconut leaf, but jewelery made of nickel or Berlin silver. *Sajur* [vegetables] are no longer eaten from native-made earthenware but from Delft plates. The native tailor is now equipped with a Singer sewing machine and is able to deliver within an hour a coat and *katok* [short pants]. At festive meals one is no longer content with rice and various sorts of fish and meat, but European canned vegetables are also served, and the tins of Huntley and Palmers can be found in the remotest villages. The flint and tinder have been replaced by matches, and the use of soap is on the increase. Tables, chairs, kerosene lamps, spoons and forks, etc., which formerly were only used by the *prijaji* or the better-off are now also found in the houses of many villagers ...

This increase in the standard of living is a fairly general phenomenon in Java. Only in four districts or sub-districts was a decline in the standard of living reported (Koeningan, Bodja, Wonosobo, and Magetan), while in six other districts (Cheribon, Madjalenka, Pemalang, Patjitan, Rembang, and Grissee) the situation was reported to have remained stationary. In all the other sixty-six districts an increase in the standard of living was clearly evident.

This increase is mainly attributed to the decline in price of many articles of daily use, the increase in imports, and improvements in communications ... Decreases in the standard of living were attributed to the cutting-up of land into small pieces or the disappearance of one or other plantation industry, which has not been replaced by something else.

It is difficult to find a categorical answer to the question how much the general economic prosperity is influenced by the increase in the standard of living. Against the damage suffered by the native industry from imports of European goods can be put the greater inclination to work that will result from the desire to satisfy the new demands, and the spirit of enterprise that will be stimulated by the contact with other more energetic elements ...

The general impression given by the reports from the districts—taking into account the circumstances under which, after all, the investigation was held—is that economic prosperity has declined in thirteen districts or parts thereof, and that it has increased in thirty-two districts or parts thereof. In the other districts the situation has remained the same ...

The regions where a decline in economic prosperity is considered to have taken place are situated mainly in the Residenceis of Banjoemas and Kedoe and also in some districts such as Krawang, Batang, Kendal, Toeban, Djombang, Panaroekan, and the district centre of Madioen ...

C.J. Hasselman, *Algemeen Overzicht van de uitkomsten van het Welvaart-Onderzoek gehouden op Java an Madoera in 1904-5* ('s-Gravenhage: Nijhoff, 1914), pp. 12-14, 21-22, 285-94 (including footnotes 4, p. 285; 2, p. 288; 2, p. 289; 1,2, p. 291; 1, p. 292; and 1,2, p. 294), 318-23 (including footnotes 1, p. 319; 2, p. 320; and 1, p. 322), 343-48 (including footnotes, 1,2, p. 343; and 1,2, p. 347), 360-61.

12 W. Huender: Survey of the economic conditions of the indigenous people of Java and Madura, 1921

The ... calculation of the Regent of Serang that a family needs 18.43 guilders per month or 221.16 guilders per year to have the same solid nourishment as is provided to state prisoners is, despite its local nature, a welcome piece of recent information. It should hardly be necessary to repeat that the foundations ... on which these sorts of calculations are based are always shaky.

It was calculated that the Sundanese, Javanese, or Madurese farmer gains yearly 103 guilders from his land and 30 guilders from his yard, if he possesses one. Almost all his available time and that of his family is needed for the cultivation and upkeep of his land and yard. So, if he is able to earn something extra, it can never be very much. Perhaps the hard-working family may have the opportunity to earn some additional income by helping others with planting or harvesting, labouring, cottage industry, trade, or keeping cattle or chickens. How much additional income would such a family be able to earn? According to ... data obtained in 1903 from sixty-four families in the Residency of Semarang ... the average yearly earnings per family were upwards of 17.50 guilders. This figure, which was only valid for a small part of the Javanese population and which is now comparatively dated, may now on a rough estimate well be increased to 25 guilders for the whole of Java and Madoera ... According to this estimate the average annual income of the Javanese peasant would be $103 + 30 + 25 = 158$ guilders. In Central Java this should also be the normal income of those who hold the land on the basis of hereditary tenure, while in large parts of West Java it will be less and in East Java more, although not significantly ...

Although at a guess three-fifths of the indigenous population of Java and Madoera are exclusively engaged in agriculture, there are still two-fifths who earn their living in an entirely different way. There are few people who live entirely from grazing stock or trading. And with a few exceptions such as a Javanese batik establishment in the principalities which has a yearly turnover of 700,000 guilders and a profit of 50,000 guilders, industries that provide the main source of livelihood are almost entirely in the hands of Europeans, Chinese, or Arabs.

It has been calculated or assumed ... that all those who are engaged in activities other than agriculture are earning the same as coolies in Western enterprises ... According to the Colonial Report of 1920 the daily wages of a coolie in a factory or plantation vary from thirty to fifty-four cents. Taking the regional averages, then, the average daily wage for the whole of Java and Madoera would almost stand at forty cents. Assuming that a coolie in a Western enterprise stays away from work only on Sundays—although in reality absenteeism is often considerably higher—the total annual income should be upwards of 125 guilders. Adding the extra earnings of a coolie's family, which are roughly 45 guilders, the two-fifths of the Indonesian people who have no land rights will have an annual average income of 170 guilders.

Based on these averages, the total average annual income of the whole of the population will be ... 161 guilders. Comparing this figure with the calculation of Heyting (50.15 guilders [in 1885 and 1889], Sollewijn Gelpke (110 guilders [in 1901]), van Deventer (80 and 100 guilders [in 1904 and 1913]), and Steinmetz (122 guilders [in 1912]), a significant increase appears to have occurred ...

Has the rise in income kept pace with the rise in living costs? The *Report of the commission to legally determine minimum wages of labourers in Java and Madoera* of 1920 estimates the daily living expenditure at 1.25 to 1.40 guilders or 450 to 560 guilders per year for a coolie family that still has some extra income from land, and at 1.40 to 1.70 guilders or 505 to 630 guilders per annum for families that draw their income from land. Taking the calculations (221.16 guilders) of the Regent of Serang as a basis, one would be inclined to answer the question in the negative in the case of coolie families. The situation is somewhat different for farmers. The needs of peasants are usually small and their living standard low. At least the more orderly families will try to retain the largest possible share of the products they have grown for their own consumption. If the total harvest from *sawahs* and *tegalans* is stored, the value of which has been estimated at an average 103 guilders, then such a family, if it lives frugally, will perhaps be able to feed itself. In such a case a family will have at its disposal a sum of 158 minus 103 guilders, that is, 55 guilders, in cash, which will have to last for a whole year to pay for clothing, the upkeep of the house and furniture, etc., but also—and not least—to pay taxes ... Peasant families then, whose net income was estimated by van Deventer in 1904 at thirty-nine guilders, should be able to make ends meet. Price rises, however, of various items of produce, in particular rice, are not necessarily an advantage. An increase in the price of rice means usually that [farmers] now consume a quantity of produce that brings a higher price on the open market. Furthermore, the rise in prices of other goods that have to be bought with the cash balance of fifty-five guilders acts as a disadvantage.

Thus the conclusion must be that Indonesian peasant families can live on their incomes in the same way as in 1904. The fact that their average annual income has risen from 80 guilders to 158 guilders, i.e. by 97.5 per cent, is only meaningful in terms of their net cash income, which has only increased from 39 to 55 guilders per annum.

This is insufficient to compensate for the rise in the cost of living.

So the situation of these peasant families has either remained the same or has deteriorated, but in no case, even with a rise in income of 97.5 per cent, has it improved. It has been argued that in contrast probably to coolie households, peasant families in Java and Madoera with a reasonable amount of land at their disposal must be able to make ends meet if they do not sell their crops but keep them in storage. However, such a family must not be hit by accidents such as diseases, bad harvests, floods, fire, or theft. One wonders how many families there are in such a fortunate position. The smallest misfortune, the least miscalculation, will upset the family budget and force the head of the family forever into the grip of the moneylender. In such a case the produce must usually be sold after the harvest for low prices in order to satisfy the demands of the moneylender. To finance the upkeep of his family, the land-owning peasant either gets himself ever more deeply into debt or hires himself out as a labourer ...

Underlying the Western measures taken in Java during the last fifty years to increase the prosperity of the people, there almost always was the assumption that the Indonesian was motivated primarily by economic considerations and that out of enlightened self-interest he would react to new stimuli. This assumption has been proved wrong at various times ... There are ties of a non-economic nature that caused the people to stick to the existing situation, and to remain immune to economic stimuli. The people also feel—probably instinctively—whether a new measure will endanger the existing social fabric or not. Moreover there is the fact that people in the tropics, such as the Sundanese, the Javanese, and the Madurese, usually act in ways called lazy and indolent by Westerners. Sometimes this is attributed to the native system of production, which is designed to produce only as much as is needed by a certain group of people, and sometimes the reason is the impact of climatic conditions. This lessens the living requirements of the people, and increases the means to satisfy these needs without too much effort; it also has a repressive effect on the social needs, i.e. those needs that do not flow from the personal desires of the individual but are in accordance with the general rules of society.

Thus it must be the task of the Western measures to create, if possible, individual and social needs and stimuli, and to try to change the mentality of the Oriental. There is ample evidence that the people ... are far from "lazy" when it comes to matters they consider important and useful. As long as this interest (be it rightly or wrongly) is lacking, attempts by the government to compel the people will have no effect. And yet this is how things were tackled after 1830 when, owing to his lack of interest in producing for the world market, it was concluded that the Javanese would only work under compulsion. Later the same mentality often persisted and matters such as credit facilities and co-operatives on a Western basis were often pushed too hastily. Obviously these difficulties and disappointments can only be prevented when the government is aware of the real feelings and desires of the Indonesians.

Self-expression and auto-activity are the only way to ensure the welfare programme a chance of success eventually. It is well known, however, how in Java and Madoera things were really done; how a village even today is often forced to agree to and to act in accordance with the wishes of the *controleur* ... In spite of all these difficulties one can think of many government measures that will be of economic benefit to the people. The heavy pressure of direct taxes should be alleviated, tariffs on imports should be lowered, [the people]should be given the free disposal of their labour, and seignorial services should be abolished in areas where people can work for wages. More roads, railways, and irrigation works should be constructed; the harm done [to the native economy] by the Western sector of the economy should be ameliorated, and ample amounts of currency should be circulated. Such measures must be of benefit to Indonesians, even though their ideas are different from ours and the stimuli and needs that characterize Westerners are lacking ...

The available statistics are often not very exact, and in many respects the situation in various regions of Java and Madoera is not comparable. This makes it very difficult to present a picture of the economic conditions of the indigenous population that is realistic in all details, and to make a reliable comparison between the present and the past. Yet a few general conclusions can be made and these can be summarized as follows.

The main field of economic activity in Java and Madoera is still what it has been since time immemorial: agriculture. The proportion of farmers to non-farmers has changed since 1905 in favour of the latter. Both sections of the population, however, show a considerable increase. The acreage of land in use by the people was sufficiently increased to cope with the population increase, partly because of the employment of Indonesians in the industrial sector. The number of irrigated *sawahs*—which consist of first-grade land—increased considerably, unless this increase is caused by the inclusion of lands cultivated in earlier times but not registered. The average land yields, however, remained stationary or decreased a little. It is doubtful whether cattle stocks have kept up with the population increase. If they did, this increase was attributable mainly to the eastern residencies where the number of cattle increased to such an extent as to compensate for the regression ... elsewhere in Java. In any case the number and quality of horses is declining. This does not seem to be caused by the extension of railways and tramways. The fishing industry only provides a precarious and moderate income. Indigenous industry has nowhere developed strongly, and is usually very small. The Indonesians have for the most part been pushed out from the trading and shipping sector by the Chinese, Arabs, and Europeans. An Indonesian middle class that could act as the backbone of society is lacking. The few large indigenous landowners or capitalists do not form an integral part of the total indigenous economy.

All this would not be so important if only the many Western plantations provided the population with compensating benefits. But this is not the case. The sugar industry is disadvantegeous to Indonesians who have land rights; and the wages it pays to Indonesian workers are, if sufficient to live on, certainly "minimum wages". The cultivation of indigo is dying out. Tobacco cultivation provides considerable advantages to a part of the population in the principalities, Pasoeroean, and Besoeki, although abuses are not entirely absent there. The other, often more recently established, plantation enterprises pay very low wages. And even if wage increases have occurred or are taking place, there is still the question whether these rises are keeping up with increases in price of the people's necessities of life.

On the other hand, it must not be forgotten that the Western plantations as a whole provide the population with more advantages than would have come its way if these enterprises had not been established in Java ... While the average yearly income of Indonesians in the whole of Java and Madoera amounts to about 161 guilders, there are strong deviations in various parts of both islands. From this yearly income the Treasury takes an average 13.50 guilders or 8.3 per cent in money taxes. If services rendered in labour and land are shown in money terms, the amount of taxation increases to 22.50 guilders or 13.2 per cent of the total income ... Such data have led to very divergent conclusions. Hasselman [see document 11] concluded in 1914 that "the prosperity of Java was increasing rather than declining". Van Kol writes in his book *The Netherlands-Indies in the States-General*, which was published in 1911, about "emaciated regions", "a destitute colony", "physical decline of people and cattle", and he was hardly less pessimistic in the First Chamber of Parliament of 17 March 1921 ... Whether the assertion in 1902 about a "decline" in the economic conditions of the people of Java was correct or fictitious can not be answered because of the lack of ... comparative material from the end of the nineteenth century.

The taxes paid by the people do not show a healthy natural increase. This must be attributed to the fact that there has been no improvement in economic conditions. Land rent ... amounted to 17,700,000 guilders in the first years after 1883 and in the period 1917-20 to about 21,500,000 guilders. Moreover part of this increase is due to the registration of land which earlier were secretly cultivated. The old trades tax to be paid by Indonesians, which in 1920 was amalgamated with the general income tax, yielded in 1880 in Java and Madoera 1,860,000 guilders, even less in the period 1908-13, and in the years 1914-18 an average of upwards of 2,000,000 guilders ...

It is disquieting that taxation is not increasing more. Stagnation, considering the considerable population increase means in this instance regression. On the other hand it is impossible to maintain that the indigenous population is not taxed heavily enough. Taking account of the low capacity of the people to pay the contrary is rather the case; and present plans to have the people pay even more (for example by increasing the head tax and the land rent) can only make one shudder. In fact the most difficult and pressing problem in Java and Madoera is that, while the people have been taxed to the utmost limit and are "minimum sufferers", apparently the various government measures taken to improve the situation have not been effective. The people themselves, however much they might have been "awakened" in their thinking and feelings, have shown so far very little economic initiative of their own. All that is noticeable here and there is action for higher wages. On the other hand it should be realized that the government, which was forced to run in on a large backlog within a short time, has only been able to realize its plans in part. And so, for example, measures relating to public security, education, public health, and the improvement of Indonesian agriculture and industry, are as yet only in the beginning stage. It also seems as if various measures taken during the last fifteen years are gradually beginning to show results. However, the lack of an Indonesian middle class ... remains alarming.

The final conclusion then must be: the Indonesians of Java and Madoera earn more than previously and, comparatively speaking, they pay less taxation than before. But because of the rise in prices of essential goods they enjoy little benefit from this situation, because they are left with too little cash in hand to pay for their upkeep. Government help to improve their economic situation is necessary and must especially be directed at stimulating and reinforcing their economic initiative and desire for economic independence.

W. Huender, *Overzicht van den economischen toestand der inheemsche bevolking van Java en Madoera* ('Gravenhage: Nijhoff, 1921), pp. 138-42, 204-7, 243-47.

13 J.H. Boeke: Budget studies in various parts of Java, 1924-25

1. Samin of Tjiterep (North Banten)

Samin is forty-three years old and lives in the *desa* Tjiterep, heading a family of seven adults. His wife is thirty-nine years old. He has two sons of twenty-six and twenty-four years, a daughter of twenty-one years. Then there is his son-in-law of twenty-five years and his father of sixty-five years.

Except for a yard of ½ *bouw* on which the house is situated, the family has no land of its own. However, it share-crops 2 *bouw* of *sawah salah mangsa* (to be cultivated during the eastern monsoon) and 3½ *bouw* of *sawah darat* (which depends on normal rainfall). Half of the yard has been planted with cucumber. Furthermore, the men work as coolies; fruit is sold and a cart is rented out. The family owns four horses, two buffaloes, and two sheep, and has contracted a debt of 42.50 guilders. In terms of *desa* services each man has to carry out guard duty once per week and has to work on the road and irrigation ditches once per month. During the year investigated (September 1924 to August 1925), the four horses died in February and March and both sheep in May. In November a grandson was born, while in June the grandfather died. These events did not involve any monetary transactions. The family suffered a great deal of sickness (in total twelve months). There was a good harvest.

Because of the great variety of work the family earns a money income throughout the whole of the year. The most prosperous months are August, September, and October. In August the men earned 44.40 guilders in coolie wages. During September and October a profit of 12.85 guilders was made of the sale of *sawoh* [fruit] and 14.40 guilders on renting out the cart. There was another 7 guilders in coolie wages in October and 12.50 guilders was made from the sale of rice. So in October Samin was able to buy a new buffalo for 58.50 guilders. In contrast June and July were rather bleak months with a money income of only 7.40 guilders and 5.20 guilders for coolie work. Only between August and November and February and March was it necessary to buy rice.

Despite all the adversity, this family was able to manage. In December 1924 ten guilders were spent on a *slametan* [feast], probably in connection with the birth of the grandson.

Expenditure			Income	
	guilders	%		guilders
Food	131.15	76.2	Sale of rice	38.00
Fire and light	8.51	4.9	Sale of *atap*/bamboo	5.00

	guilders	%		guilders
Clothing	13.02	7.5	Sale of fruit	33.50
House and furniture	3.00	1.7	Rent of cart	31.90
Sickness	2.85	1.7	Coolie wages	153.58
Education	—	—	Sale of other produce	3.45
Feasts	10.81	6.3	Total	265.43
Transport	—	—		
Taxes	3.00	1.7		
Running costs	33.97			
Purchase buffalo	58.50			
Total	264.81			

Expenditure in more detail

	guilders	%		guilders
Rice	60.66	46.3	Timber	0.05
Corn, cassava, peanuts	4.01	3.0	Matches	2.60
			Kerosene	5.86
Sweets and accessory dishes	10.28	7.8	Total	8.51
			Head tax	3.00
Salt	6.15	4.7	Planting costs	3.00
Sugar	4.71	3.6	Seedlings	6.50
Cooking oil	2.90	2.2	Fertilizer	0.45
Fish and meat	24.69	18.9	Sawoh	19.55
Coffee, tea, etc.	0.57	0.4	Other	4.47
Tobacco and *sirih*	17.16	13.1	Total	33.97
Total	131.13			

2. Nadi of Madjalaja (Central Priangan)

Nadi, who is forty-five years old, is a small trader (called *dagang blantikan* in this area) and lives in the *desa* Madjalaja (district of Bandoeng). He does not own any land but only a house built of timber with a tiled roof. For the year of investigation (running from July 1924 to June 1925) he did not pay any taxes.

His family consisted of his wife, a son of fifteen years and a granddaughter of three years. Nothing extraordinary happened during the year.

The Nadi family did not contract any loans and the income from the little business, into which there was an average daily investment in goods of 1.83 guilders, steadily came in every day. The normal items of food such as rice (31 cents), salt (1.5 cents), fish (5.5 cents), firewood (4.5 cents), and tobacco and *sirth* (2 cents), were bought and paid for daily. Every two, three or four days kerosene was bought at an average of 3 cents per time.

The small business made a profit of 178.50 guilders, which was sufficient to keep the family in food, fuel, and lighting for the whole year. The running capital totalled from 2.50 to 3 guilders; only once (9 October) were purchases made to the value of 9 guilders; and only once, on 12 July, of 4 guilders. The capital was kept so small because of the daily balancing between expenditure and income.

Expenditure			Income	
	guilders	%		guilders
Food	150.05	80.8	Income from business	830.94
Fire and light	19.65	10.6		
Transport	4.10	2.2	Wages for wife	6.75
Rent for yard	11.99	6.4	Wages other members of family	32.66
Taxes	—	—		
Running costs	652.44		Gift	10.41
Total	838.23		Total	880.76

Expenditure in more detail				
	guilders	%		guilders
Rice	113.13	75.4	Firewood	14.79
Salt	4.50	3.0	Kerosene	4.86
Sugar	0.21	0.1	Total	19.65
Oil	0.43	0.3	Purchase of goods	640.15
Meat and fish	18.01	12.0	Other	12.29
Total	136.28	90.8	Total	652.44
Tea, etc.	6.19	4.1		
Tobacco and *sirih*	7.58	5.1		
Total	150.05			

3. Moernasan of Bandjaran (Central Priangan)

Moernasan of the *desa* Bandjaran, district of Bandoeng, is forty-five years old and lives in his own yard in his own house, which has a tiled roof. His family in addition to his wife consists of an elder sister and her mother and two grandchildren, nine and six years old. The eldest one attends the local vernacular primary school. Moernasan is a farmer and owns 332 r^2 *sawah* classed from fourth to sixth grade and 2.124 *bouw* dry land classed from third to sixth grade. On the *sawah* he cultivates rice mainly for his own consumption; on the *tegalan* he cultivates cassava and second crops such as chilis etc., mainly for commercial purposes. There are various fruit trees in his yard and some bamboo. The female members of his family make bamboo rice cookers, baskets, and other kitchen utensils. Furthermore, he owns three chickens and twenty-four chicks. Two *menoempang* [landless villagers] have built houses in the yard; they do not pay him any rent but probably help him on the farm.

At the beginning of the year under investigation (July 1924) Moernasan has a loan from the district bank of 50 guilders which has to be repaid as a lump sum. He does this in September and has to pay 55.25 guilders, which was made possible because he had received a lump sum of 65 guilders for the sale of produce from his *tegalan*. In the next month (October) he again borrows 50 guilders from the district bank (it is not possible to determine from the account what he has used this loan for).

No unusual expenditure is shown during the next few months and whenever the sale of produce from *sawah*, *tegalan*, or yard or of the bamboo wickerwork was not sufficient to cover the normal household expenses, small loans were made by other villagers (between 1 and 5 guilders), which were paid back later in the year. Although there is a large number of sales recorded of produce from the yard and *tegalan*, and from the wickerwork (there were 82, 61, and 62 entries respectively), the amounts of money involved were always small. So in some months (May, July, and August) monetary income is only around 6 guilders, and although expenditure in these months is adapted as much a possible to the level of income, these attempts are not always successful. Moreover the cost of living for this family of four adults is rather low. Rather conspicuously, under none of the categories of this group are there daily entries. The entries for meat and fish and for drinks, respectively numbering 280 and 288, are the most frequent ones. Still, with the exception of meat and fish and rice, none of the categories shows an average expenditure higher than 5.5 cents per entry; most entries, including those for fuel and lighting, are not higher than 3 cents. Rice was only bought during seven months (September-January, March and April—in September and January to a value of about 2.50 guilders, in December and March for about 10 guilders, and in the other months for a little less than 5 guilders.

So far as taxation is concerned, it should be noticed that in the year investigated Moernasan has not paid any of the land rent he is due to pay for his *sawah*—2.25 guilders—and his *tegalan*—2.77 guilders. Also the head tax amounting to 3.87 guilders has not been completely paid.

Income is considerably higher than expenditure.

Expenditure			Income	
	guilders	%		guilders
Food	101.15	63.5	*Sawah* produce	33.75
Fire and light	4.38	2.7	*Tegalan* produce	188.32

Clothing, etc.	31.41	19.8	Yard produce		22.88
House and furniture	4.49	2.8	Eggs, etc.		2.14
Sickness	0.21	0.1	Wickerwork		17.84
Education	5.05	3.2	Various		0.10
Feasts	3.85	2.4		Total	265.03
Transport	—	—		Loans	76.20
Taxes	8.69	5.5		Total	341.23
Total	159.23				
Running costs	25.90				
Repayment loans	85.40				
Total	270.53				

Expenditure in more detail

Rice	39.81	39.3	Matches		0.18
Corn, cassava, peanuts	3.00	3.0	Kerosene		4.20
				Total	4.38
Accessory dishes and sweets	9.70	9.6	House		0.10
			Furniture		2.50
Salt	2.52	2.5	Other		1.89
Sugar	2.98	2.9		Total	4.49
Oil	4.68	4.6	Head tax		3.54
Meat and fish	30.21	30.1	Buying off village service		5.15
Total	92.90				
Tea, etc.	5.30	5.2		Total	8.69
Tobacco and *sirih*	2.90	2.8	Tools		2.40
	99.10		Wages		18.99
			Seed		1.00
			Fertilizer		1.17
			Other		2.33
				Total	25.89

4. Pa Tasnjan of Kalibakoeng (Tegal)

Pa Tasnjan is forty-five years old and lives in the *desa* Kalibakoeng in the district of Slawi, a mountainous area in the area of Tegal. He possesses three building plots. On one of these, measuring 34 r², his house is situated; it has a tiled roof and brick pillars. The second plot, measuring 62 r², is inhabited by two *pondoks* [landless peasants] who only have houses made of bamboo with *atap* [split bamboo] roofs. The third plot measures 16 r² and has a house similar to his own that he has put at the disposal of a younger brother. In addition Pa Tasnjan owns a *tegalan* classed as fifth grade and measuring 274 r². He has to pay 1.35 quilders land rent for his total holdings.

The family of Pa Tasnjan consists of his wife, his daughter of about twenty years, and his younger brother, about twenty-two years old. So there are four adults. Cassava is cultivated on the *tegalan* and between the rows watermelons are grown. In the yards there are a few coconut trees and other fruit trees and four clusters of bamboo.

In February 1925 Pa Tasnjan borrowed 60 guilders from the district bank, apparently offering his land as collateral ...

There were only forty-one entries for money income, of which thirteen were concerned with loans and gifts. Only during 184 days of the year of the year (18 August 1924 to July 1925) was money spent, but during 131 of these days the total amount of money spent was below 10 cents ... The days when larger sums were spent coincide without exception with the receipt of money income, which was spend immediately or within a few days, ususally on food and kerosene. In the case of larger earnings the money was also used to take coconut trees out of pawn; the buying of bamboo chairs (7 guilders); repayment of debts (2.34 guilders); the purchase of jewelery (19 guilders) and clothing (4.10 guilders); and the payment of divorce costs (2 guilders). The final account of the monetary transactions of the Tasnjan family is as follows:

Expenditure		**Income**	
	guilders		guilders
Normal expenditure	48.05	Normal income	59.87
Taking out of pawn	2.32	Loan district bank	60.00
Repayment debt	20.36	Total	119.87
Divorce costs	2.00		
Taking out of pawn of coconut trees	3.00		
Purchase bamboo chairs	7.00		
Total	82.73		

The fact that income was also increased by the sale of chickens (25 guilders), which of course reduced the money-earning capacity of the family, and the fact that no taxation was paid during the year do not have to be taken account of because they are compensated for by an increase in the value of the family's property in the form of jewels (19 guilders) and bamboo chairs (7 guilders).

In summary it must be concluded that this particular family can only be said not to have declined economically if at the end of the year (1 August 1925) it still had about forty guilders in hand of the loan contracted the previous February with the district bank. If, as is probably the case, this is not so then the particular loan has not been financially beneficial to the Tasnjan family—this is apart from the difficult problem of saving up the sixty guilders plus interest in adverse economic conditions ...

5. Pa Nawijah of Bedji (Pemalang)

Pa Nawijah is fifty years old and lives in the *desa* Bedji, in the district of Pemalang. His family in addition to his wife comprises a son of twenty-five years and his wife, a son of twenty years, and two girls of ten and six years: so there are five adults and two children.

Pa Nawijah himself works on his yard of 62 r^2, which also contains his house, and on 1 bouw of *sawah*, which is his communal share. The eldest son drives the *dogcar* [horsedrawn carriage], which is hired out for passenger transport. The second son is not permanently employed and was married during the course of the year.

Pa Nawijah has to pay the following taxes:

	guilders
Land rent for the *sawah*	15.18
Land rent for the yard	0.88
Water rights	1.00
Income tax	3.12
Head tax	3.70
Total	23.88

From the income figures it is clear that the family tries to earn money in all sorts of ways, but the major income-earner is the *dogcar* business. This was started in June 1924 when a *dogcar* and two horses were bought from a Chinese for 400 guilders; 150 guilders were to be paid down and the rest was to be paid off in monthly instalments of 10 guilders. However, Pa Nawijah was not able to get together these 150 guilders completely and so he obtained a loan from the district bank for 50 guilders to be paid back in monthly instalments of 5 guilders.

In the beginning everything went well but in December the trouble started when one of the horses became sick and the *dogcar* could only be taken out every two days. As a result income fell from 50 guilders to 25 guilders. Then an amount of 42.50 guilders was borrowed from the pawn shop to pay off the full debt to the Chinese. During January the earnings from the *dogcar* fell to 20 guilders and at the end of that month again an amount of 45 guilders was borrowed from the pawn shop. Foreseeing more deficits, Pa Nawijah decides to pay the last two instalments to the district bank at once in order to obtain further credit. On 3 March ¼ *bouw sawah* was sold in *tebasan* [i.e. with the rice crop on it] for 22 guilders, and 10.13 guilders was paid to the bank. Seventeen days later he had a new loan from the bank of 50 guilders.

The *poeasa* [fasting] month arrived with its extra expenditure and feasting. New clothing had to be bought (10 guilders); a *slametan* had to be given (2.44 guilders); pawned goods had to be retrieved

(24.80 guilders); and horse rigging had to be renewed (2 guilders). The horses were worked as much as possible every day. To have more cash in hand, P. Nawijah rented out ¼ *bouw* of *sawah* for 15 guilders, and some jewelery was pawned for 11 guilders. During May the *dogcar* was working every day, although income was declining, but in June the horses were sick again. On 10 June one horse was sold for 14 guilders and the income from the *dogcar* business fell to 13 guilders. In July it climbed to 20 guilders, but this amount was still too small because the feed for one horse already cost almost 10 guilders ...

Looking at it superficially, the Nawijah family seems to have done well economically, because net income surpasses expenditure by 110 guilders. However, if it is taken into account that the capital investment producing the major part of this income has strongly declined in value and therefore the opportunity to earn future income is very much diminished, our final conclusion must be different.

Expenditure			Income	
	guilders	%		guilders
Food	93.35	67.9	Sale of *djahe* [ginger]	9.70
Fire and light	19.16	14.0	Sale of leaves	0.04
Clothing	12.70	9.2	Sale of fruit, bamboo	7.90
House and furniture	3.75	2.7	Sale of chickens	1.25
Sickness	1.20	0.9	Sale of eggs	0.40
Feasts	3.95	2.9	*Tebasan* ¼ *sawah*	22.00
Transport	0.20	0.1	Renting ¼ *sawah*	15.00
Income tax	3.12	2.3	Dogcar business	408.45
Total	137.43		Wages	4.00
Running costs	216.74		Total	468.74
Total	354.17		Sale of horse	14.00
			Pawns retrieved	20.00
			Total	502.74

Expenditure in more detail				
Rice	13.60	14.5	Matches	1.98
Soup vegetables	6.42	6.8	Kerosene	17.18
Accessory dishes	11.73	12.5	Total	19.16
Salt	6.05	6.5	House	2.95
Sugar	9.74	10.4	Furniture	0.80
Oil	3.08	3.3	Total	3.75
Meat and fish	16.27	17.7		
Total	66.89	71.7	*Running costs* horse:	
Tea, etc.	12.07	12.9		
Tobacco and *sirih*	14.39	15.4	Shoeing	5.54
Total	93.35		Feed	196.30

Medicine	0.70
Upkeep dogcar	9.90
Wages	3.60
Purchase of one chicken	0.70
Total	216.74

6. Tamin of Ledok (Pekalongan)

Tamin lives in the *desa* Ledok, which is close to Pekalongan. He is a shoemaker, twenty-five years old, married but childless. As a shoemaker he has a fairly regular income. He did not spend anything on housing and furniture during the whole year, while he only spent 0.10 guilders on clothing and 0.15 guilders on transport. During the year the only extra expenses were for a *slametan* in November, costing 20.04 guilders but which netted 10 guilders, and in March 1925 for sickness of his wife (7.50 guilders). Otherwise his expenditure was for food, fuel, and lighting and, considering the smallness of the family, consisting only of two adults, costs varied little, moving between 14 and 18 guilders, with the exception of the month of June 1925 when economy measures brought down expenditure to 10.13 guilders.

In this case all conditions seem to be present to prevent the need for credit. Still the family is continuously involved in credit transactions, mainly for the purpose of balancing the budget, as is clear from the following table:

Month	Income without loans	Expenditure without loans	Loans	Repayments
	guilders	guilders	guilders	guilders
July 1924	8.95	9.45	—	1.00
August	15.25	14.76	7.00	6.00
September	16.15	14.08	—	—
October	20.25	16.52	10.00	12.32
November	22.25	34.47	18.40	12.50
December	19.65	18.28	2.50	2.50
January 1925	15.00	16.42	5.00	4.50
February	16.00	17.15	6.00	5.00
March	16.70	28.14	10.00	—
April	25.40	18.29	—	7.00
May	13.35	17.41	6.25	—
June	9.75	10.13	1.50	2.00
	Total 198.70	Total 215.10	Total 66.65	Total 52.82

Tamin's credit transactions are harmful to him because expenditure exceeds income by 16.40 guilders and at the end of the year he is burdened with an extra debt of 13.83 guilders ...

7. Wardi of Pontjol (Pekalongan)

Wardi lives in the *desa* of Pontjol near Pekalongan and works in a batik enterprise as *koelie ngetjap* [printer] earning 1 guilder per day, which is paid to him every day. His wife is a batik-maker but seldom works as such. They have one son of sixteen years, who still lazes about receiving daily spending money from 5 to 10 cents (which totals 23.04 guilders per year and is shown in the budget under accessory dishes).

Wardi owns a simple house on a plot of 27 r^2. The *atap* roof, when in need of repairs, is fixed by his father, and so no expenditure is shown on the budget for housing. He is to pay 0.60 guilders land rent, 2.60 guilders head tax and 3.60 guilders income tax. However, in the period under investigation (July 1924 to June 1925), he does not pay any tax with the exception of 1.50 guilders as *pitrah* [gift at the end of the fast].

Wardi's situation is the opposite to Tamin's (see previous budget) in that he is evidently able to save up for extraordinary expenses, and only has to borrow in exceptional circumstances. Apparently he does not like borrowing. On 15 July he pawned a *kain* [batik cloth] for 1.50 guilders, but afterwards felt that he would rather sell a table for 3.50 guilders; he retrieved the *kain* for 1.53 guilders. These transactions cost him two days in wages, as he stayed away from work. In July and August he repaid 4.10 guilders in private loans. But he borrowed no more during the rest of the year ... At the end of the year Wardi had a deficit of 8 guilders ...

8. Kasanmoestari of Pagergoenoeng (Magelang)

Kasanmoestari is fifty-five years old and lives in the *desa* Pagergoenoeng, sub-district of Grabag, district of Magelang. He owns 94 r^2 of *sawah* on which rice is cultivated and on the best part of his *tegalan* (34 r^2) he grows various sorts of vegetables; another *tegalan* of 268 r^2 is used for grassland, while 12 r^2 is planted with bamboo. He has two houses with a yard measuring 114 r^2. He has to pay 1.11 guilders in land rent.

His family consists of his wife, a son of seventeen years, who helps his father, and two daughters of ten and fourteen years, of whom the elder cuts grass and the younger is not yet permanently employed. He owns three cows.

Pagergoenoeng is a mountain *desa* where people own a great many cattle, mainly used to produce fertilizer. The *desa* is situated about 4 *paal* [approximately 4 miles] from the large market in Grabag. There are no Western plantations in the region where extra money can be earned. The *desa* itself has a market that is not of great importance.

The Kasanmoestari family obtains most of its food from its own land. In the months of October and November 3.95 guilders and 1.26 guilders were spent to purchase cassava, corn, and rice. In the same months sums of 1 guilder and 3.20 guilders were spent on repairs to the house, which caused a considerable drain on cash. Kasanmoestari borrowed 10.50 guilders privately, which covered the small financial deficits during the remainder of the year. He was able to satisfy normal money demands by periodical sales of agricultural produce ...

Expenditure			Income	
	guilders	%		guilders
Food	20.93	47.3	*Sawah* produce	31.88
Fire and lighting	4.85	11.0	Yard produce	11.80
Clothing and jewellery	3.20	7.2	Preparation of produce	1.05
House and furniture	4.69	10.6	Sale of chickens and eggs	0.85
Sickness	—	—	Total	45.58
Education	—	—	Loan	10.50
Feasts	5.97	13.6	Total	56.08
Transport	—	—		
Taxes	4.56	10.3		
Total	44.20			
Running costs	0.83			
Repayments loan	0.50			
Total	45.53			

Expenditure in more detail				
	guilders	%		guilders
Rice	0.92	4.4	Matches	0.96
Corn, cassava, peanuts	2.58	12.3	Kerosene	3.89
			Total	4.85
Accessory dishes, sweets	7.60	36.2	Land rent	1.11
Salt	1.48	7.1	Head tax	2.20
Sugar	1.66	8.0	*Zakat* [religious tax]	1.25
Oil	1.16	5.6	Total	4.56
Meat and fish	2.43	11.6		
Total	17.85	85.2		

Tea, etc.	1.54	7.4
Tobacco and *sirih*	1.54	7.4
Total	20.93	

9. Hadji Abdoelgapoer of Kalipoetjoeng (Blitar)

Hadji Abdoelgapoer is about fifty years old and lives in the *desa* Kalipoetjoeng in the district of Blitar. He is a farmer and sugar-grower; runs a horse cab business and repair shop; lets houses and rents out furniture; and also runs the village lighting system. He holds 3 *bouw* of communal *sawah*, 14 *bouw* of *tegalan*, ten houses, eighteen cows, fourteen horses, seven cabs, and a steel sugar cane crusher. Furthermore, he has rented 1 *bouw tegal* for two years.

Hadji Abdoelgapoer is a village patriarch. His family, in addition to his wife, comprises fifteen children, grandchildren, and relatives; of these six are adults (fifteen to thirty years) and nine are children (three to thirteen years). In addition he employs seven young fellows as cab drivers. He has to pay 57 guilders in income tax and 65 guilders in land rent.

In June and July 1925 he planted 6 *bouw* of *tegalan* with sugar cane, and in November 1924 made a share-cropping arrangement for 6 *bouw* of corn. During the year investigated he harvested 6 *bouw* of sugar cane, but 3 *bouw* of corn had failed.

His stock increased by two calves, one cow, and two horses (the latter having been bought respectively for 190 and 80 guilders). Furthermore he took 160 coconut trees as collateral at 2.50 guilders per tree, and he installed a petrol pump for 108 guilders. Including the income gained from property added during the year, Hadji Abdoelgapoer considers that during the year investigated he has become 1070 guilders richer in earthly goods. The following table of income and expenditure shows a surplus of 59.75 guilders, which resulted from the following transactions:

	guilders
Paid more into the district bank than borrowed	204.20
Paid out more to private individuals than borrowed	215.75
Bought more land than he sold	360.00
Took land out of pawn	280.00
Took goods out of pawn	100.00
Total	1159.75

It is interesting, considering the size of the family, that the expenditure on food does not differ very much from that of the common villager. Finally it must be admitted that Hadji Abdoelgapoer was unwilling to give complete and detailed information about his income and expenditure ...

10. Pa Marsidin of Patemon (Pamekasan)

Pa Marsidin is fifty years old and lives in the *desa* Patemon situated in the city of Pamekasan in the middle of a number of smithies. The station of the Madoera tram is situated in this *desa*, from where most of the drivers of hire cabs originate.

The family of Pa Marsidin consists of his wife and a daughter. He is himself already too old to work and his wife sells *rudjak* [spiced fruit salad garnished with chili], the ingredients for which are bought by the daughter in the market. Their house, constructed of timber with a tiled roof, stands on the land of a relative. Pa Marsidin does not own any cattle and he does not have to pay any taxes. During the whole year nothing is spent on clothing, the house or furniture, sickness, feasts, or transport. The family does not borrow money.

Money comes in every day and is spent every day ... The daily expenditure on ingredients is never higher than 0.50 guilders and with this capital, plus the labour of both women, the family's income is produced; this averages 0.22 guilders per day. Even this amount is not totally used by these three adults. They live on an average of 0.18 guilders per day: 5 cents for rice, 4 to 4.5 cents for corn, 2 cents for additional food, 1 cent for salt, 2 cents for tobacco or *sirih*, 2 cents for firewood and 1 cent for kerosene, and they probably eat the remainder of the *rudjak* ...

11. Soerodiastro of Kraton (Madioen)

Soerodiastro is *tjarik* [clerk] of the *desa* of Kraton in the sub-district of Maospati in the district of Madioen. His family in addition to his wife consists of a son of eighteen years, a daughter of eight years, and two grandchildren of thirteen and eleven years. The son helps on the farm, while the grandchildren tend the stock.

Soerodiastro holds 4 *bouw* ex officio and shares 2 *bouw* of *sawah*. He has let 3½ *bouw* to the sugar factory and on the remaining 2½ *bouw* he has planted rice (2 *bouw*) and cassava (½ *bouw*). His yard measures a *bouw* and contains his house, a kitchen, a rice barn, and a cow shed. Furthermore, coconuts, cassava, rice, and *pisang* [banana] are cultivated in the yard.

Soerodiastro has to pay 29 guilders in land rent. His income is fairly regula:. His *sawah* produces income during ten months (no income in February and April), the largest amount being in August (62 guilders) and the lowest in October (0.75 guilders), and in the other months it fluctuates between 7.75 guilders (September) and 23 guilders (June). In February he makes 17 guilders out of produce from the yard, in March 1 guilder and in July 3 guilders. As a committee member of the *desa* bank he is paid between 1 and 1.30 guilders per week, while his job as *tjarik* also brings in money regularly, the largest amount in April (15.50 guilders) ... In October the sugar factory pays him 120 guilders for land rented.

The Soerodiastro family only has to spend little on food. In March 1925, 16.25 guilders were spent on food and 5.13 guilders on fuel and kerosene. In the other months food expenditure did not rise above 5 guilders, while in June only 2.55 guilders were spent and in November a minimum of 1.52 guilders. In the other months, with the exception of March, only around 1.70 guilders were spent on fuel and kerosene. Purchases of rice occur only in March, and of corn, peanuts, and cassava only between January and April. Only accessory food dishes are bought almost daily, while kerosene is bought every second day.

Here again is a case where credit is used solely as a means to balance temporary deficits and to pay off loans, especially those given by the district bank. During the year there are two entries in the budget for repayments to the district bank amounting respectively to 37.63 and 37.30 guilders. In order to meet the first payment a loan of 20 guilders is obtained from the *desa* bank and a loan of 10 guilders from the pawn shop. For the second payment 45 guilders are borrowed from the pawn shop.

Soerodiastro apparently likes parties; and the way he handles money can also be gauged from the expenditure on jewelry. The family is still largely living in a self-sufficient economy, although, comparatively speaking, it also has an ample money income.

In November Soerodiastro received 40 guilders as a debt payment, so he also shares his abundance with others.

Expenditure			**Income**	
	guilders	%		guilders
Food	49.09	12.9	*Sawah* produce	181.50
Fire and light	23.30	6.1	Yard produce	21.00
Clothing	56.35	14.8	Land rented out	
House	16.00	4.2	to factory	129.00
Sickness	1.50	0.4	Wages *desa* bank	58.21
Feasts	197.25	51.8	Wages *tjarik*	51.32
Taxes	37.20	9.8	Total	441.03
Total	380.69			
Running costs	59.90			
Total	440.59			

Expenditure in more detail

	guilders	%			guilders
Rice	7.50	15.3	Clothing		30.30
Corn, cassava,			Jewellery		26.05
peanuts	4.59	9.4		Total	56.35
Accessory dishes	16.29	33.2	*Landrent*		34.00
Salt	3.35	6.8	Other		2.60
Sugar	2.56	5.2	*Pitrah*		0.60
Oil	2.37	4.8		Total	37.20
Meat and fish	2.84	5.8			
Total	39.50				
Firewood	3.34				
Matches	1.50				
Kerosene	18.37				
Total	23.21				

12. Soemominhat of Poerworedjo (Madioen)

Soemominhat of the *desa* Poerworedjo (sub-district of Oeterna in the district of Madioen) is a share-cropper of 2 *bouw* of *sawah* on which rice is cultivated in the western monsoon, with second crops in the eastern monsoon.

Soemominhat does not have his own yard but lives on one owned by a relative. He is also allowed to sell the produce grown in the yard and therefore has to pay land rent to the amount of 1.51 guilders. He also has to pay land rent of 1.59 guilders on the particular part of the *sawah* he is cultivating. His family comprises his wife, who from time to time earns some money selling native medicines, and four children aged fifteen, thirteen, seven, and one. The eldest daughter works whenever possible, earning a daily wage of 10 to 25 cents. In October she worked in the sugar factory for fifteen cents per day, which can be considered a normal wage.

There is a regular income from the *sawah* and the yard during most of the year; rice is sold in April and June, peanuts in March, and cassava in September and November ...

Although Soemominhat has his own rice, this commodity is regularly bought from January to September. In April 80 cents worth of cassava is purchased. In May 2.50 guilders worth of corn is bought, partly instead of rice (3 guilders). In August cassava is purchased (4 guilders), partly in addition to and partly to replace rice (4 guilders), while in October corn and cassava are the only staple foods; during November and December only cassava is used (5 and 6 guilders). Only during these three months when cassava is the main staple food are accessory food dishes bought. Salt and kerosene are bought monthly ...

The family makes ends meet without the regular use of credit. Only once, in November, were goods (worth 25 guilders) retrieved from the pawn shop, but no money was borrowed during the year.

One of the children goes to school at a cost of 0.25 cents per month.

The Soemominhat family is an example of a hard-working farmer's household that manages its finances carefully.

13. Kasanredjo of Sidomoeljo (Madioen)

Kasanredjo lives in the *desa* of Sidomoeljo in the sub-district of Tjaroeban, district of Madioen. His family comprises in addition to his wife five children from 1 to 9 years old. The eldest goes to school (costs 0.10 per month); the second tends the buffaloes. The youngest three are daughters. In June 1925 another son was born.

Kasanredjo only has the disposal of a yard of 223 r^2 and a communal share in a *sawah* of 200 r^2, for which he has to pay 0.70 guilders and 4.29 guilders respectively in land rent. However, in addition he has rented 1 *bouw* 84 r^2 of *sawah* on the condition that he will pay the 12.31 guilders of land rent incumbent on this land. On his yard there are situated his house, a kitchen, a rice barn, and a shed for his buffalo and one calf. There is a small village bank which issues loans to be paid back within a week and *selapan* loans (of which a quarter has to be repaid every thirty-five days). Both husband and wife are members of this bank and make use of both kinds of loan provision. The wife, however, stops borrowing after the birth of her son, which is an occasion for relatives and friends to present gifts worth 28.50 guilders and which causes Kasanredjo to spend extra money for sweets, etc. Also in the following months more money is spent on sweets and cakes.

From the statement of income and expenditure one would conclude that the Kasanredjo family has lived above its means. Expenditure exceeds money income by 50 to 60 guilders—although the farm is well managed.

The solution to this anomaly is to be found in the incompleteness of the income statistics. Kasanredjo's wife in fact received an inheritance from her father's estate, which during the year was paid to her bit by bit by her brother (who lives in another *desa*). Kasanredjo did not record this income, perhaps because he was frightened that the village head or other excessively interested parties might hear about it. The inheritance amounted to 90-100 guilders, which in the year of investigation was not yet completely handed over.

Expenditure			Income	
	guilders	%		guilders
Food	41.08	2.5	Rice	41.64
Fire and light	11.91	7.3	Green beans	26.60
Clothing	33.47	20.4	Coconuts	3.45
House and furniture	22.34	13.6	Cassava	4.83
Sickness	2.40	1.4	Tobacco	2.65
Education	1.20	0.7	Various	7.07
Feasts	31.10	19.0	Tamarind	0.80
Transport	0.50	0.3	*Sirih*	1.20
Taxation	20.05	12.3	Gifts	28.50
Total	164.05		Total	116.74
Running costs	3.20		Loans	50.00
Loan repayments	59.00		Total	166.74
Total	226.25			

Expenditure in more detail

	guilders	%		guilders
Corn	1.06	2.6	Firewood	1.50
Cassava, rice peanuts	0.28	0.6	Matches	1.35
			Kerosene	9.06
Accessory dishes	14.64	35.7	Total	11.91
Salt and chilis	2.70	6.6	Clothes	31.67
Oil	2.05	5.0	Jewellery	1.80
Meat and fish	2.10	5.1	Total	33.47
Total	22.83		House	19.75
Sirih and tobacco	1.14	2.7	Furniture	1.30
Tea and sugar, etc.	17.11	41.7	Crockery	1.29
Total	41.08		Total	22.34
			Land rent	17.30
			Head tax	2.75
			Total	20.05

J. H. Boeke, *Inlandse Budgetten* (*Koloniale Studien*, 1926), pp. 272-321.

14 L. H. Huizenga: Some results of the Coolie Budget Investigations, 1939-40

The families were divided according to the nature of their major occupation (usually determined by the occupation of the head of the family) into four groups, i.e.: 1. Plantation workers. 2. Factory workers. 3. Foremen and tradesmen. 4. Farmers.

The number of families investigated

Category of family	Living on the plantation	Living away from the plantation	Total
Plantation labourers	319	696	1015
Factory labourers	105	148	253
Top workers	128	159	287
Farmers	—	390	390
Total	552	1393	1945

The average size of the family, in the case of plantation, factory, and top labourers who lived on the plantation, was 3.70, 4.07, and 4.52 persons respectively. For those living away, the figures were 4.85, 5.02, and 5.50, and for the farmers 5.26 ...

Of the three categories of labourer investigated, 30, 40, and 50 per cent respectively lived in houses provided by the plantations. Only in a few cases were they required to pay rent for this. The wage-earning families not living in plantation houses lived, in 90 per cent of the cases, in their own homes. In the case of the farmers this percentage stood at 98. The families which did not live in their own houses lived mostly in houses owned by relatives and did not have to pay rent. Of the remaining eighteen families that lived in houses owned by strangers, only seven paid house rent ...

The size of the houses varied a great deal locally. In general the families living on the plantations had less living space than those living outside. Particularly small was the living space of families housed in communal living quarters found on various plantations. The top labourers had by far the largest houses, while the factory labourers usually had somewhat more spacious houses than the plantation workers. The farmers' houses were on the average almost as large as those of the top labourers, although account must be taken of the fact that especially in the farmers' houses, space has to be set aside for storing agricultural implements and crops ... In general the plantation houses were more solidly built and better kept up than those outside. Among the latter the houses of the top labourers made the best impression, while the houses of the plantation labourers had the worst appearance. A higher percentage of the houses of top labourers had brick walls and tile floors, and few of them had *atap* roofs. With respect to furniture and utensils, there was a sharp division between the top labourers and the other categories, including the farmers ... Finally it must be mentioned that in particular those plantations that had to accommodate the whole or part of their workforce had taken certain social and hygienic measures for the benefit of the workers ...

The number of landowners among the families living in plantation houses was very small, although they usually had the right to cultivate their plots in the plantation quarters. Most of the out-living wage-earners owned some land, which in most cases consisted of *sawah* and yard or only a yard. With the exception of one family, all the farmers owned land, either *sawah* plus *tegalan* or *sawah* plus yard ...

The average size of landholdings did not differ very much for the three categories of wage-earners, ranging from 0.28 to 0.30 hectares. There were strong local variations in this average. The same was the case with farmers, who per family owned almost five times as much land [as the labourers]. The largest landowners were in West Java, the smallest in Central Java. In the heavily populated *sawah* regions of Central and East Java the average landholdings of farmers varied between 0.5 to 0.9 hectares. It must also be mentioned that the yards of the farmers were on an average about twice as large as those of the wage-earning families ... The upkeep of the yards and *tegalans* was almost always done by the owners themselves; in the *sawah*, however, this was by no means always the case. In addition to letting *sawahs* (mainly to sugar and tobacco plantations), share-cropping occurred a great deal in Central Java, the latter mainly in the case of top labourers. It was striking that in Central Java—not taking account of the letting of land to plantations—the farmers did not cultivate one-fifth of their land themselves. On the other hand some again rented more land or went in for share-cropping ...

The cultivation of the yards showed considerable local differences. The most intense cultivation was in Central Java and the least intensive in West Java. Moreover as a whole the greatest care for upkeep was shown in Central Java. The majority of trees planted in Central and East Java were coconut trees ...

The ownership of stock varied greatly from area to area. The farmers on an average owned a great deal more stock than the wage-earning families. Cattle were used exclusively for transport. The number of animals depended very closely on the size of the property, the particular kind of *sawah*, and the intensity of cultivation. The families living on the plantations usually only owned some chickens, with the top labourers owning more of them ...

The average size of the monthly income per family was in the case of plantation, factory, and top labourers living on the plantation 881, 1158, and 2334 cents respectively and for those living out, 520, 829, and 1798 respectively ... The farmers had an average income of 677 cents, the size of the income depending fairly closely on the size and quality of the land owned ...

The income and expenditure on consumable items of both plantation worker families and farmers' families in general balanced each other, while factory workers and non-resident top workers spent 10 per cent less on consumable items than their income, and resident top workers 40 per cent less. This indicates that saving occurred only in the higher income families ...

From the fact that many families during the period of investigation either spent money before they had received any income or spent more than they earned, it can be ascertained that as a rule they kept some money in reserve. In the case of more than 90 per cent of the resident plantation labourers' and factory workers' families, monetary income consisted of wages provided by the plantations, while in the case of the other categories this percentage varied between 60 and 80 per cent ... The most important category of other monetary income was in the form of loans, which depended in size on the amount of plantation wages received, and particularly in the case of top labourers fairly large sums were involved. Furthermore, loans were considerably more important among the non-resident groups than among the resident families. About 50 per cent of the monetary income of the farmers' families came from the sale of agricultural produce and the letting of land, while next in importance was income from commerce and loans, the latter being at least equally, if not more, important to the farmers than to the non-resident plantation and factory workers.

Among the wage-earning families money expenditure was for more than 85 per cent concerned with consumable goods and the repayment of debts. While among the resident groups the repayment of debts, especially among the plantation and factory workers, was much larger than expenditure on consumable goods, among the non-residents expenditure on consumable goods was on the average somewhat larger. Expenditure on consumable goods and repayment of debts accounted together for 80 per cent of the total money outlay of the farmers' group, with the expenditure on the former being more than five times as much as on the latter. So repayment of debts is by no means as prominent among farmers as among wage-earning families, because ... the buying of consumable goods on credit is far less customary among farmers. ...

The total expenditure of the resident categories of wage-earner families was respectively 883, 1048, and 1697 cents and of the non-residents respectively 549, 762, and 1612 cents per family per month: in per capita terms respectively 8.0, 8.5, and 12.5 cents and 3.8, 5.1, and 9.5 cents per day ... The farmers with an average expenditure of 666 cents per month per family or 4.3 cents per capita per day spent slightly more on consumable goods than the non-resident plantation workers. The families in West Java spent by far the most on consumable goods, while those in Central Java spent the least ...

The consumable items were partly bought and partly obtained in kind from their own enterprises or in other ways. As was to be expected, the provision in kind was most prominent among the non-resident families, in particular the farmers, who obtained 41 per cent of the value of their consumption in this way, while this percentage was much lower among the non-resident wage-earners, decreasing to 22 per cent for the plantation workers and 7 per cent for the top labourers. The value of goods obtained in kind by the three groups of resident workers varied from 3 to 6 per cent of total consumption. Of the total value of consumable goods purchased, one-third was paid in cash by the resident plantation and factory workers' families, one-half by the non-resident plantation and factory workers' families, three-fifths by both categories of top workers, and five-sixths by the farmers. There was considerable local difference in this respect, with people in West Java buying proportionally a great deal more on credit than in Central Java ...

Composition of Expenditure on Consumable Goods
(% of total expenditure)

Major Items	Resident			Non-Resident			Farmers
	Plantation workers	Factory workers	Top workers	Plantation workers	Factory workers	Top workers	
Food	73	73	59	75	72	58	71
Fire, light, water	7	6	8	8	9	8	9
Clothing	1	1	2	1	1	4	2
Luxuries [mainly smoking needs]	8	9	8	6	7	7	5
Various [mainly slame-tans]	5	5	15	8	8	16	10

The volume of the total quantity of food consumed rose in relation to an increase in welfare. However, this increase was by no means as sharp as in the case of the total expenditure on food. From the statistics of the individual cases investigated it appeared that ... among the most prosperous groups the quantity of food in unprepared form was seldom higher than 800 to 1000 grams per day.

Rice accounted for the largest share of the quantity of food consumed. In the case of the resident groups, which on the average consumed about the same quantity per head per day (400 to 450 grams), rice accounted for a little more than half of the volume of the total quantity of food, while the out-living groups used a little less than half. This proportion decreased slightly with an increase in prosperity. Furthermore, there were considerable regional differences. For example, in West Java, where on an average 500 to 600 grams of rice were consumed per head per day, this proportion could increase to between 85 and 90 per cent. In East Java, however, it could fall to between 5 and 10 percent (25 to 75 grams per head per day), because there rice was being replaced by corn, the proportion of which rose to between 50 and 55 per cent (225 to 275 grams per head per day). Both among the resident and non-resident groups in East Java the consumption of corn fell in relation to an increase in prosperity while the consumption of rice rose relatively sharply ... Fresh cassava was consumed everywhere in Java, but in particularly large quantities in Central and East Java (150 to 250 grams per head per day), while the average consumption in these areas of the plantation workers' families was many times larger than that of factory workers and top workers. The latter groups usually bought cassava in fermented form or in the form of sweets. The consumption of dried cassava was localized and the average quantity consumed varied from 50 to 100 grams per head per day, falling rapidly in relation to increased prosperity.

With respect to the other food items specified in the budget, it should be mentioned that, proportionally speaking, the consumption of granulated sugar, soya bean curd, coconut oil, and coffee showed the greatest rise in relation to upward changes in the income of all groups. Among the non-resident groups, particularly where the differences in prosperity were largest, relatively sharp increases occurred. Less pronounced were increases in the consumption of brown sugar and soya bean cake, while such articles as salt were hardly affected by fluctuations in income ...

The calorific value of the food consumed inclusive of festive food amounted to about 2000 calories per head per day for the resident wage-earning families and the non-resident top workers, while for the other three categories this average was considerably lower (1300 to 1400 calories). There were considerable local differences, in particular in the case of the non-resident plantation workers' families ... In West Java the average of all cases investigated lay above 1700 calories, while in Central and East Java they were all below 1600 calories. The lowest figures were obtained in Central Java where in some cases the food consumed by plantation workers' families did not even amount to 900 calories per head per day. The farmers' families there were not much better off, although the land in the regions concerned was fertile, irrigated, and cultivated during the whole of the year. However, there was a population density of more than 800 per square kilometre. In general the calorific value of food per head per day rose—although at a gradually decreasing rate—in line with an increase in expenditure on consumable goods, that is, providing that this expenditure did not surpass roughly 10 guilders per month per family (about 7 cents per head per day). After that calorific value remained more or less stationary around 2000. Cereals—in particular rice—provided by far the most calories, i.e. from 70 to 80 per cent of the total. This percentage decreased with an increase of prosperity among both the resident and non-resident groups ...

The average percentage of consumption of albuminoids per head per day varied between 50 and 60 grams for the resident wage-earning families and the non-resident top labourers, while for the other categories this percentage was between 30 and 40 grams. For the last three categories about 10 per cent of this (3 to 4 grams) was of animal origin, while for the resident plantation and factory workers' families and the non-resident top labourers this percentage was more than 15 per cent (8 to 9 grams). There were wide local variations in the average consumption of albuminoids, with the variation in animal albuminoids being proportionally much larger than for vegetable albuminoids. The total albuminoid consumption was smallest among the non-resident plantation labourers' families on the two sugar plantations in Central Java, which were twice investigated and where the total food consumed did not even contain 900 calories per head per day. During the first investigation the average consumption of albuminoids was a little below and during the second investigation a little more than 20 grams per head per day, of which 10 per cent were of animal origin. The highest consumption was found in West Java where, with the exception of one farmer's family, none of the five families investigated in each category consumed less than 45 grams per head per day, with four out of twenty cases even consuming more than 65 grams per day. In families that spent more than 10 to 12.50 guilders per month (7 to 9 cents per head per day), the average per capita consumption of vegetable albuminoids usually did not increase, while the consumption of animal albuminoids often still did, in line with an increase in total consumption.

Cereals were the most important source of albuminoids, accounting for 55 to 70 per cent of the total, although their importance in this respect was not as great as in the provision of calories ...

The average consumption of fats per head per day varied among the resident groups from 21 to 36 grams and among the non-resident groups from 14 to 38 grams. All categories consumed more when prosperity increased. The averages showed considerable local variations, which proportionally were most pronounced among the non-resident plantation workers' families (3 to 24 grams) and least among the non-resident top workers' families (24 to 55 grams). People in West Java, generally speaking, consumed far less fat per head per day than those in Central and East Java. As in the case of animal albuminoids, the average consumption of fats per head per day continued to increase after total expenditure on consumable goods had reached 10 to 12.50 guilders per family per month. However, as the quantity of fats consumed at the same level of total outlay on consumable goods showed great local variations, the local rates of increase often varied greatly.

Among all the family categories investigated, more than 80 per cent of the fats consumed came from rice, corn, coconuts, and coconut oil. Both among the resident and non-resident categories the proportion of coconut oil used rose with an increase in prosperity, while the consumphion of rice and corn fell ...

The consumption of carbohydrates by the three resident categories of wage-earning family amounted to about 400 grams; in the case of the non-resident top labourers' families it was at least 350 grams, and in the remaining three other non-resident groups 250 to 275 grams ...

The consumption of vitamin A by the resident categories varied from 1500 to 3500 *I.E.* [*Internationale Eenheid*, International Units], and by the non-residents from 1900 to 3000 *I.E.* ... There were considerable local variations, with a relatively low consumption by the non-resident plantation workers' and farmers' families in West Java ... which did not rise above 1000 *I.E.* per head per day, and in five cases ... not even above 500 *I.E.* Although such low figures were also found in Central and East Java, on the whole the average daily consumption of vitamin A per head was much larger, and in East Java it amounted often to more than 5000 *I.E.* ... There did not appear to be any connection between the total expenditure on consumable goods and the quantity of vitamin A consumed.

Vegetables were by far the largest source of vitamin A, followed at a considerable distance by fruit, both categories of food accounting for 90 per cent of the total amount of vitamin A consumed. Among the non-residents the relative importance of vegetables as a source of vitamin A decreased while prosperity increased ...

The average consumption of vitamin B1 per head per day by the three resident categories and the non-resident top labourers amounted to between 270 and 300 *I.E.* while the remaining three non-resident groups consumed 185 to 205 *I.E.* ...

L. H. Huizenga, *Het Koeliebudgetonderzoek op Java in 1939-40* (Ph.D. thesis, Wageningen, 1958), pp. 255-77.

Political and administrative decentralization

The existing government apparatus at the beginning of the twentieth century—which was highly centralized and autocratic—could no longer cope with the vastly changed conditions in the Indies. The central government was not only confronted with the gigantic task of administering a newly acquired and vast island empire, but also colonial officers were required under the terms of the Ethical Policy to interfere far more frequently and drastically in native affairs than previously.

In order to relieve the *Binnenlands Bestuur* (Department of Regional and Local Administration) from some of its burden, new "technical" departments such as Agriculture, Public Works, and *Volkscrediet* (the People's Credit Service) were set up: these were better equipped to implement the Ethical welfare programme.

To meet the growing pressure of Europeans for a greater say in the running of the colony's affairs the Decentralization Law of 1903 expressly stated that some measure of self-government would be granted through the creation of municipal councils and regional councils. In fact, however, only a slight measure of autonomy was conceded to these councils, which only had jurisdiction over roads, public works, and parks and gardens, while important matters such as police, public health, and education remained under the control of the central government. The first municipal councils were established at Batavia, Meester Cornelis (Jatinegara), and Bandung in 1905. The first regional council was established in 1909 in the important tobacco-growing area of East Sumatra. By 1918 there were thirty-two municipal councils and twenty-five regional councils.

In 1914 de Graaff, a former director of *Binnenlands Bestuur*, who had been appointed by parliament as a special commissioner for decentralization, submitted a voluminous report on administrative reform in the colony. He proposed that the Indies should be divided into twelve large *gouvernementen* (administrative units) to be headed by a governor and supported by their own finances. Furthermore, de Graaff planned to increase the efficiency of the European colonial administrative corps by reducing its numbers, increasing salaries, and by better selection and training procedures. The native administrative corps—the *Inlands Bestuur*—was to be given more responsibility, better training, and higher salaries. Finally, the regional councils, which had been found to work unsatisfactorily, were to be replaced by regency councils.

De Graaff's scheme, however, was rejected by parliament, where since 1913 a Liberal coalition had held a majority. Among others, van Deventer complained that de Graaff had ignored the instruction of parliament to seek a reorganization on the basis of self-government and he dismissed the *gouvernementen* of de Graaff as *"ambtenaarsstaten"* ("bureaucratic states").

The ruling Liberal coalition was far more concerned with accommodating to some extent the growing pressure of Indonesian nationalists at this time for a greater degree of participation in government. In 1916 the Liberal Minister of Colonies submitted a proposal to parliament for the establishment of a *Koloniale Raad* (Colonial Council), which was to have a multi-racial membership and advisory powers. This was approved by parliament, and the council, called the *Volksraad* (People's Council) was officially instituted in May 1918 by the progressive Governor-General van Limburg Stirum. Members of the *Volksraad*, who enjoyed full parliamentary privileges and immunities, were to be partly elected and partly appointed. The *Volksraad*, which could be consulted on all matters of state by the colonial government, was responsible for the preparation of the annual budget in conjunction with the Governor-General, although final approval still rested with the Dutch Parliament.

Any hopes the Dutch might have held about pacifying radical nationalists by instituting the *Volksraad* were dispelled almost immediately after the opening of the first session when *Sarekat Islam* leaders such as Tjokroaminoto severely criticized the colonial system. Again during the second session of the *Volksraad* on 14 November 1918 radical Indonesian members strongly condemned the colonial government for distinctly favouring the interests of European capital, and rebuked Europeans in general for their attitude of racial superiority towards Indonesians. While these speeches could obviously only accentuate the existing feelings of uneasiness in the colony, European fears about an impending revolution in the Indies were raised to a hysterical pitch when rumours reached the colony about a *coup d'etat* in the Netherlands led by the Socialist leader Troelstra (*see* document 15:1). Communist-influenced European soldiers and sailors in the Indies held demonstrations and the Indonesian Communist leader Darsono incited Indonesians to follow the Russian example. In the *Volksraad* on 16 November the Dutch Socialist Member Cramer pledged his full support for the Indonesian nationalist cause and on his instigation the *Radicale Concentratie*, a front of radical Indonesian and European members, was formed.

The immediate reaction of Governor-General van Limburg Stirum was that the *Volksraad* would have to be transformed into a full parliament in case the Socialists came to power in Holland. And on 18 November he stated in the *Volksraad* that he envisaged important political changes in the colony and a transfer of responsibility from the colonial government to the *Volksraad*, the extent of which could as yet not be fully determined. On 2 December van Limburg Stirum informed the *Volksraad* that a commission would be established to advise on constitutional reforms (*see* document 15: 2, 3).

The Socialist *coup* in Holland fizzled out. And the Dutch Government—which after the elections of May 1918 had again come into the hands of the rightist parties—as well as the vast majority of Europeans in the Indies, were highly critical of van Limburg Stirum's handling of the situation and of what they termed rash and irresponsible promises of Indonesian self-government (*see* document 16). The time of the more progressive colonial reformers, who were sympathetic to the Indonesian nationalist cause, was clearly running out; moreover many Europeans who previously had been "ethically" inclined now began to get second thoughts when confronted with the rapid and turbulent tide of radical Indonesian nationalism. By 1921 van Limburg Stirum and his small band of trusted advisers had been replaced by a group of more conservative and reactionary men who exchanged the earlier policy of *rapproachement* to Indonesian nationalism with one of stark repression. Many colonial Dutchmen and conservative politicians in Holland were apparently convinced that only a small segment of the top layer of indigenous society had been infected by the disease of "Communism" and that in any case the nationalist leadership did not truly represent the voice of the Indonesian masses. This reactionary spirit is well portrayed in the private letters of the progressive Creutzberg, who became vice-president of the *Raad van Indie* (Council of the Indies) in 1924, and de Graeff, a more liberal-minded governor-general (1926-31). (*See* document 17.)

In the period 1918-40, when various conservative coalitions remained in power in the Netherlands, the most influential figure in colonial affairs was Colijn, one of the leaders of the *Anti-Revolutionaire Partij* (Neo-Calvinists), and a colonial diehard. Colijn had a colourful and successful career. After having gained a medal for valour as a young lieutenant in the Lombok campaign (1894), he was appointed adjutant to General van Heutz, the conqueror of Atjeh, and became adviser on the reorganization of colonial government and administration during van Heutz's term as governor-general. In 1909 he entered the Dutch Parliament and served as Minister for War from 1911 to 1913. From 1914 to 1922 he was a director of the Royal Dutch Shell group. And after ending his formal business career he entered politics again in 1922, serving almost continuously in Cabinet posts—including the prime ministership and the ministry of colonies.

While Colijn agreed with the general condemnation of earlier liberal-minded colonial statesmen for having been too weak in dealing with Indonesian nationalists, his criticism was far more fundamental. In his pamphlet *Staatkundige Hervormingen in Nederlandsch-Indie* (*Constitutional Reforms in the Netherlands Indies*), published in 1918, he argued that indigenous political development should start off at the grass roots level and that the establishment of the *Volksraad* had been entirely premature, as this institution had no roots in the people. Colijn also dismissed as unrealistic the attempts to superimpose on the Indies a modern unitary state on the European model. He argued that, considering the vast differences in cultural, economic, and social development within and between the various Indonesian islands, the only proper solution would be the establishment of a federation (*see* document 18). While, as his critics pointed out (*see* document 19), Colijn's ideas might, ideally speaking, have been correct, they were unrealistic because of the radical turn the Indonesian nationalist movement had taken. Any idea of federation would be rejected by radical Indonesian nationalists—and with some justification—as an attempt by the Dutch to postpone Indonesian independence to the far-distant future.

However, the *Herzieningscommissie* (Commission for Constitutional Reform), which had been instituted by van Limburg Stirum in 1918, in its report of 1921 rejected Colijn's proposals and advocated the creation of a unitary government with wide powers in internal affairs, although it did not press for full self-government. The commission also recommended that suffrage should be extended to all Netherlands subjects irrespective of race, providing that they complied with certain standards of education and economic prosperity.

The Minister for Colonies, de Graaff, dismissed the commission's proposals as "*studeerkamerwerk*" ("an academic exercise") and argued that the most urgent need was for administrative decentralization. And although, owing to the strong pressure of progressive opinion in the Dutch Parliament, the Netherlands *Grondwetherziening* (Constitutional Reforms) of 1922 laid down that in principle the Indies should be allowed to take care of their internal affairs as much as possible, and the name "colony" was officially abandoned, in practice very little notice was taken in the actual reform measures introduced by de Graaff in 1925. Admittedly the *Volksraad* was given co-legislative power and in 1929 Indonesians were granted a majority of seats, but without the introduction of the principle of ministerial responsibility to the *Volksraad* these measures were largely meaningless, as the final power still lay with the Dutch Parliament.

De Graaff, taking advantage of the swing towards conservatism in Dutch politics, managed to have his earlier proposals for administrative reform accepted by parliament, and Java was now divided into a number of semi-autonomous provinces, regency councils, and municipal councils. The Outer Islands were also divided into provinces, but administrative and political decentralization at the lower level was—unlike in Java—to be based on *adatgemeenschappen* (ethnic group communities). This was much closer in line with Colijn's ideas than the administrative decentralization of Java based on the Dutch model.

Although Colijn and his followers did not deny that Indonesia should eventually be granted independence, they saw this as a far-off prospect. Only after the Netherlands had completed its difficult and slow-grinding task of bringing the Indies to a sufficiently high level of modern civilization would the colony be allowed to go on its own.

For the remainder of their rule, then, the Dutch stubbornly refused to give in to the demands of Indonesian nationalists for self-government or independence. From the mid-1930s onwards, when the threat posed by Japan began to loom ever more ominously on the horizon, the pressure of Indonesian nationalists for political concessions began to be intensified. Influenced perhaps by American promises of independence made in the Philippines, a number of Indonesian *Volksraad* members, led by Sutardjo, presented a petition to the Dutch Queen, requesting that an imperial conference be held at which the question of self-government would be discussed and a definite timetable for its achievement determined (*see* document 20). It was more than two years before the colonial rulers deigned to give their negative reply, arguing that Indonesians were not yet ripe for independence (*see* document 21). Similar arguments were used to dismiss the agitation for a full parliament in the Indies led by the G.A.P.I. (a federation of Indonesian nationalist organizations) in the period 1939-41. (*See* document 22; for *G.A.P.I. see also* documents 69-71.)

The only "concession" made to Indonesian political demands was the declaration by the Dutch Queen in a radio speech on 10 May 1941 that an imperial conference would be held after the conclusion of the war; but by then, as it turned out, the initiative in political matters was by no means any longer solely in the hands of the Dutch

15 Promises of political reforms in the Indies, 1918

1. Telegram of the Minister of Colonies (Idenburg) to the Governor-General (van Limburg Stirum), 15 November 1918

[No. 411] Widespread nervousness caused by Troelstra's speeches socialist meeting Rotterdam repeated Tuesday in chamber urging immediate transfer Government to socialists following German example to realize women suffrage, abolition senate, eight hour day, and other social reforms, stop This pointing to intended co-operation socialists with anarchists. Ruys [prime minister] declared government, though prepared expedite decision and support reasonable reform proposals provided no departure from legal procedure will resist all violence and attempts overthrow constitutional powers, this declaration was followed by general movement all quarters to resolutely resist revolutionary movement which would endanger food supply and is not countenanced by majority people. Yesterday nervousness considerably allayed. Troelstra declared no intention use violence.

2. Telegram of the Governor-General (van Limburg Stirum) to the Minister of Colonies (Idenburg), 19 November 1918

[No. 462] Referring to your four-eleven I had statement made in *Volksraad* yesterday declaring new course imposed by recent world events for Holland also determinative for Indian government policy which more question of accelerated pace than change of course stop Close co-operation with *Volksraad* requested concerning food provision comma advance of social prosperity and necessary reforms in shortest possible time stop Government firmly resolved maintain order stop Renewed endeavours of Sneevliet [Communist leader] to lame organs public authority compel government expel him stop Announced institution committee investigate conditions sugar industry, quickest enforcement new military penal code, catering soldiers entirely at government's expense, rapid amelioration barrack conditions.

3. Letter of the Governor-General (van Limburg Stirum) to the Minister of Colonies (Idenburg), 1 December 1918

The telegrams about the revolution in Germany caused a great sensation here on 11 November. Everybody asked themselves what the consequences would be for our country and I myself was compelled to consider what attitude the Indies Government should take in case the revolution would cross over to the Netherlands. My greatest worry was the possibility of mutiny of the navy, which almost certainly would have been imitated everywhere else. I therefore consulted Admiral Bron, who was unable to prophesy what effect the hoisting of the red flag would have on the people here. We agreed that the ships should be dispersed and that in case things went wrong the commanders should impress upon their crews what consequences a mutiny of the navy could have for the wives and children of their compatriots. It seemed to me that the loyalty of the Menadonese, Ambonese, and native soldiers did not have to be doubted ...

I had decided that in case of the overthrow of the legal authority in the Netherlands, the Indies Government should continue its activities, ignore possible telegrams, and consider a revolutionary government as temporary until possible laws and regulations would arrive by mail. However, in that case an appeal would have to be made to the *Volksraad* to co-operate with the government and to take over temporarily the controlling power now exercised by the Minister of Colonies and the parliament. It seemed unthinkable that I would transfer authority to a local follower of the *Bolsjewiks* such as Baars, Sneevliet, or Coster, who probably would have been appointed from Holland if their friend Wijnkoop [leader of the Dutch Communists] had taken over the government.

Although I suppressed the most disquieting telegrams from Reuter and the Melbourne agency Orient about the happenings in Holland, a strong red wind was nevertheless blowing in the Indies, which for example did not leave the Advocate-General [G. W. Uhlenbeck] unmoved, as he told me. And its influence was so strong that even one of the most highly respected High Court judges demanded that a parliament should be established immediately in the Indies. Your Excellency will realize then what far-reaching desiderata were being put up by others. On the whole people were highly agitated and very nervous ... and wild rumours were circulating about the Queen having abdicated and that I was being replaced. The telegrams I had released about Toelstra's speech appeared ominous to many.

On 16 November the *S.D.A.P.* [Socialist] *Volksraad* Member Cramer made a speech ... and an agreement was reached for co-operation between his party, the *S.D.V.* [Communists] and the natives, inclusive of the *Budi Utomo* [nationalist organization]. The Resident of Batavia sent the head superintendent of police to me with disquieting reports about conspiracies ...

All this made me decide on 16.11 to intervene in the deliberations of the *Volksraad* and to make a declaration indicating that the government was not blind to what was happening ... I invited the President of the High Court [J. H. Carpentier Alting], whom I have learned to appreciate highly for his knowledge and his activities ... for a discussion on 19 November about the preparation of the reforms which, according to the majority of authoritative public opinion in the Indies, were considered necessary. He agreed with me that the most effective thing to do would be to institute a commission, which he would be prepared to head in addition to his many other duties. I felt that his appointment would also guarantee to Her Majesty's Government that a thoughtful approach would be taken. After repeated discussions also about the composition of the Commission, its mandate was formulated as follows: to advise the government regarding proposals which are to be made to the supreme government concerning the desirability of a revision of the principles of the government structure of the Netherlands Indies and the changes which accordingly must be made in the Constitutional Regulations and other ordinances ...

Your Excellency's telegram of 20 November, from which it was clear that the revolutionary movement had misfired, caused a general feeling of relief and there was a great feeling of gratitude for the averting of such a calamity. Tens of thousands of people signed the address of homage to the Queen, including sailors and soldiers, but the native members of the so-called Concentration [Radical Concentration] desisted. Tjipto [Mangunkusumo] acts as a real guttersnipe these days and reasonable discussion with him is impossible; Tjokro [Tjokroaminoto] is as untrustworthy as ever; and Dwidjosewojo [moderate nationalist] is unstable ...

S. L. van der Wal, *De Volksraad en de Staatkundige Ontwikkeling in Nederlands-Indie. Een bronnenpublicatie.* (Groningen: Wolters, 1964), Eerste Stuk. pp. 256-58.

16 Conservative reaction in the Netherlands

1. Letter of the Minister of Colonies (Idenburg) to the Governor-General (van Limburg Stirum), 11 December 1918

From your telegrams—and from press reports ... I have noticed that the current situation in Europe has also had a great impact on the Indies. And looking at it superficially I would say "too much". I would not be surprised that agitators have played an important role and that the situation has been greatly misrepresented. Certainly the whole world is moving into what one likes to call a "democratic" direction. But surely there are differences in the degree of urgency ... I am convinced that in the Indies we must avoid giving in to fashionable delusions, not only because this cannot be right theoretically, but also on practical grounds, because this must lead to chaos in the Indies. What is happening in Western countries lives more or less in the people and is a product of centuries of historical development. Neither the history nor the development of the Indies took place along these lines, and even if it did it has been very weak and incomplete. An uncritical adoption of Western ideals—or do I have to say slogans?—does not achieve what is aimed at in the West (where it has a certain right to exist), but the result will be an oligarchy of the worst kind, that is, of incapable people. We must be firmly opposed to this. If the participation of the people is wanted, this should not be restricted to a few, but this right should be given to many and not in matters which are only understood by a few, but in matters on which they can give a judgement, more or less. I am of the opinion therefore that the democratic development of the Indies must be channelled through the village councils and the regency councils, which must gradually be given greater responsibilities and allowed to influence provincial government as well as the *Volksraad*, if this is wanted. But I believe that it is a wrong policy to press already for an extension of the powers of the *Volksraad* ...

It was with interest that I noticed from your telegram that you have set up a commission for political reforms. My first impression was that such a commission should have been instituted in this country ... But on reflection I understood that your commission is meant as a type of lightning conductor and as such—apart from disadvantages—can have advantages.

If there is still an opportunity, perhaps the Commission for the Revision of the Constitution [instituted on 20 December 1918] will take account of the work of your commission, although I doubt very much whether the Netherlands Government will be prepared to make proposals at this stage which in fact would surrender the whole of the Indies to a small group of intellectuals and semi-intellectuals, who so far have shown very little evidence of altruism and a willingness to sacrifice themselves for the general benefit.

Of course ministerial "responsibility" to the *Volksraad* is out of the question; at least I refuse to co-operate in this. First of all "responsible" ministers can only be considered in the provinces—after the provincial councils have first been established and are working well, and then only carefully and gradually. These [provincial councils] are even considered necessary in British India, and consider how much further British India has advanced in this field, and how much greater its right is to participate in government through the sacrifices of at least some of its people in the war ...

S. L. van der Wal, *De Volksraad* pp. 261-62.

2. Private letter of A.C.D. de Graeff to the Governor-General (van Limburg Stirum), 17 February 1919

The day before yesterday I visited Mr Idenburg for two hours, and I am still very much impressed by our interview, which I will try to relate to you as fully as possible and without disguising anything. Mr Idenburg informed me that the feeling here in this country has *generally* turned against you. This is so in Amsterdam in the first place and in general among the "capitalists" ... The ruling tone in the Chamber has also turned against you. The Social Democrats are on your side, the attitude of the Liberal-Democrats is still uncertain, but *all* the other parties in the Chamber and all persons outside the Chamber who interest themselves in the Indies were angry about the fact that the government declaration of November was made without consulting the Home Government and the Chamber, as well as about the declaration itself. You know how Idenburg himself thinks about the matter from his Cabinet letter, which he read out to me. The Minister finds it a pity that you have gone so far without his foreknowledge, *not in the least* because he considers himself by-passed as a Minister—this is not his nature and he understands very well that no time was to be lost in the November days—but because also to your later explanation he cannot responsibly give his support.

He literally told me that there were few matters about which he had such a definite opinion ... as his conviction that a parliament with responsible government powers would during the first twenty-five to thirty years be disastrous for the Indies and would lead to the total loss of the colonies. He wants to leave the *Volksraad* as it is and does not want to give this body any participatory powers ... because this means responsibility. He would rather abandon the *Volksraad* again than push this institution prematurely into the foreground ... The Indies are politically still completely unripe: an Indies *people* which could be represented in a parliament does not exist. Even in British India one does not dare to introduce responsible government yet, etc., etc.

I must tell you honestly that I was aghast to hear "my" Idenburg speak in so reactionary a manner, and again I felt that Idenburg, with all his excellent qualities, is quickly influenced by others and will unconsciously present their thoughts as his own. This is not Idenburg who is talking—who while he was Governor-General repeatedly pressed the Minister to give the *Volksraad* at least co-legislative powers—but here speaks Colijn, who rules over everybody and everything; Fock, the disappointed eternal candidate for the office of Governor-General; Moresco [Secretary-General of the Department of Colonies] (the composer of the Cabinet letter in question), who is the aggrieved candidate for the vice-presidency [of the Council of the Indies], and many others.

I have talked long and earnestly with Mr Idenburg and I have explained my position to him ... I have argued that I cannot judge whether the circumstances during November were such that a declaration like yours was unavoidable, but that I immediately accepted that this was so. I said that I completely agreed that the heterogeneous masses called the people of the Indies are not politically ripe and that therefore the establishment of a parliament would be premature and wrong in principle. [I said] that such a parliament would probably be very one-sided and would be composed of strongly leftist elements; that the Indies Government would be caused a great deal of trouble and that the relationship with the Home Government would be threatened, etc., etc. But [I also stressed] that *nevertheless* it was my strong conviction that it would be out of the question to ignore any longer the ever-louder-sounding demands for parliamentary representation; and that we cannot wait for "political ripeness", and that *now* people in the Indies will no longer be put off with village, provincial, and regency councils only. [I argued] that in short a parliament and responsible government can no longer be postponed *ad calendas Graecas* [indefinitely] and that one must bite into the sour apple whether one wants to or not and hope for the best, because otherwise the Indies will come close to revolution.

I believe that my argument made some impression and will have some effect, although it is such a pity that Idenburg has already bound himself to so many others. Furthermore, it would have been better if your declaration could have been avoided but, as it has been given now, its disavowal by the Minister and the Chamber will cause such deep disappointment and will increase the accumulated grievances so much that it will hasten along the fearful process.

There are also some brighter aspects. Idenburg is worried on two counts that you will ask to be called back: firstly, because he has the highest appreciation and respect for your person, your gifts of character and intelligence, your earnestness, diligence, and dedication, etc. ... I know that you do not like to hear such praises about yourself, but I must tell you about them. They were so well meant and they were said without any reserve by a person for whose integrity I can vouch completely ... And secondly, he is anxious because your abdication *now* would be immediately connected with the action that the capitalists have started against you. The *general opinion* will be that you, who rose up for the hungry Javanese, had to capitulate to the exploiting Dutch capitalists ... This connection would be fatal.

So I promised Idenburg to tell you that it is his fervent wish that you should remain and that a way should be found that makes this possible without forcing you or him to abandon any of your responsibility. I cannot judge whether this is possible. Much will depend on the discussions in the Chamber ... Idenburg promised me that he himself will explain his point of view in such a way that the existence of a serious difference of opinion on this vital point will remain hidden as much as possible. He will avoid giving any decision on the question when a parliament will be instituted; he will emphasize the lower councils and warmly advocate their blessings, and he will even mention the possible institution of a parliament to crown the completion of the political detutelization process ... I do not have to tell you *how* much I am impressed by all this. I symphatize so much with you about the disappointments you have to suffer in your endeavours, with which I am also sympathetic, and I have the feeling that if the reactionaries win, untold harm will be done. But I also sympathize with Idenburg, who is a democrat at heart and yet misses—physically and mentally tired as he is—the strength to row against the reactionary current ... I also realize, now that I have taken your side, that I have in all probability lost all chance of becoming your successor. I do not really have to tell you that I have no regrets for myself, but I am sorry for the Indies in so far as now a person will be selected who does not understand the spirit of the time, who is a conservative, if not a reactionary ... I pray you, do not make any hasty decisions. The Minister desires nothing more than that you remain and he seriously intends to make things as easy as possible for you. The world is moving so fast that although we have no immediate result at present we will be more successful next time.

S. L. van der Wal, *De Volksraad* pp. 298-303.

3. Private letter of the Vice-President of the Council of the Indies (Creutzberg) to the Dutch Ambassador in Berlin (van Limburg Stirum), January 1924

I would gain a great deal more satisfaction from my new position if I could persuade my colleagues to accept a somewhat different view about the best way to govern the Indies. I am sceptical about this, however, and I fear that we are confronted here by a *Zeitgeist* [spirit of the times] that is much stronger than we are. Most of the prominent leaders are in this regard no different from the masses and they are incapable of differentiating. They are completely caught by the very understandable spirit of reaction that pervades various European countries, and this prevents them from realizing that the situation in the Indies must be viewed in a different perspective from that of the mother country. There are a considerable number of leading figures in the administration here who perhaps in Holland would be excellent administrators, but who have not the slightest understanding of the situation in which a colonial government is finding itself! The most irksome impressions of this I gained in and around the Ministry of Colonies. It seems to me that this is largely a question of fashion. One is considered to sin against the *bon ton* if one does not express oneself as coldly and cynically as possible about everything that appears in the Indies as a new and impetuous life. I am absolutely convinced that it is far more the "tone" of our present regime than specific legislative and administrative matters ... that sets the young people of the Indies—and I fear irrevocably—against the Netherlands. The embitterment in more or less intellectual native circles, especially among the students in the Netherlands, is taking on alarming proportions ...

Algemeen Rijksarchief. *Mr. K. F. Creutzberg aan van Limburg Stirum, Januari, 1924*, Archief Mr. J. P. Graaf van Limburg Stirum, collectie no. 114, no. 60.

17 Conservative reaction in Indonesia

Private letter of the Governor-General (de Graeff) to the Dutch Ambassador in Berlin (van Limburg Stirum), 26 October 1927

Now and then I am indeed greatly tempted to leave. I am very deeply disappointed in the rationality, the common sense and the sense of idealism of the people surrounding me. I am standing practically alone and the few supporters I do have are no match for the uncivilized din created by the *whole* of the European public and almost the *whole* of the European press ... I do not get the necessary support from the Minister, who lacks the power of a strong conviction and is not sufficiently able to control the running of affairs. Furthermore, he attempts to satisfy both sides, and tactics like this in a crisis of the kind we are living through now are untenable and pernicious. Treub [Conservative Member of Parliament], van Aalst [Director of the *Nederlandse Handelsmaatschappij*], *cum suis*, supported by the *Algemeen Handelsblad* [conservative newspaper], are setting the tone in Amsterdam. This is done here by Trip [Director of the Java Bank], supported by *Het Nieuws van de Dag*, the *Soerabajasch Handelsblad* [conservative newspapers], and gradually also the other newspapers, which have realized that they cannot keep alive when their own opinions differ from those of their readers. In my own surroundings I am supported by Creutzberg [Vice-President of the Council of the Indies], Gobee [Adviser for Native Affairs], the Advocate-General, Dr Kraemer [Linguist of the Bible Society]; a few heads of the regional administration (Couvreur of Makasaar,

Tideman of Palembang, Hardeman of Soerabaja, and perhaps a few more); a few heads of departments, in so far as they are interested in general policy, such as Hardeman (Education and Religion), Rutgers (Agriculture), and Rutgers (Justice), but that is about all. In the *Volksraad* I am supported by the left wing of the European group but often in a manner which sometimes brings to my lips the expression "beware of your friends".

I wonder whether you can realize how depressing such a position can be? I have come here, averse to all "politics" and with the purest of intentions, in order to create an atmosphere of mutual trust and cordial co-operation around the government. But the result is that one side calls me a traitor of my country, while the other side is becoming continually more convinced that, no matter how good the intentions of the government may be, it is no use supporting it because the Europeans have clearly shown their true colours and have made it known that thinking natives do not exist, that all of them are inferior beings who should be greatly mistrusted, and that the watchword should be "to keep them down" (the words of Trip). Things that a year ago would have been greatly appreciated by the native side now leave them more and more cold. *That* is the worst of the situation. Trip *cum suis* cannot talk about anything else than "the maintenance of the Netherlands authority", but it baffles me how they can emphasize this while at the same time they are undermining every day the representative of that authority in all sorts of ways, directly and indirectly, in season and out of season. Moreover I am even more handicapped by the fierceness of the campaign against me. And whenever I take a decision I ask myself involuntarily how it *might* be explained and what venom could be extracted from it. It is inexcusable to me that the President of the Java Bank even takes the opportunity of a farewell dinner to the departing vice-admiral to make a political speech which was definitely intended as an attack on government policy, and which was warmly applauded and appeared with great headlines in all the papers the next day. It is inexcusable to me that, on the initiative of Trip, a petition has been circulated among the public against the present draft law [proposal to have a native majority in the *Volksraad*] and that this petition was sent to all the departmental heads, the heads of the Services, the heads of regional administration, etc., with the request to circulate it among their personnel.

I have attempted *rapprochements* in all directions, and over and over again I have earnestly attempted to show my good intentions. The result is that I, who have so little aggressiveness in my personal make-up and am basically humble, have widened the gap so much that the possibility of bridging it is further away than ever. I have asked myself, of course, whether and how far I am guilty myself. But

I can declare with my hand on my heart that although I might perhaps be guilty because of a too naive and too unpolitical trust in humanity, the blame must be put on the other side. After the riots of November and January [Communist-inspired rebellions in West Java and Minangkabau] and the resulting fear among the European community, daily stirred up by the press, it has let itself be ruled so much by racial instinct, racial superiority, and racial hatred that all proportion has been lost sight of, and there is no place any more for quiet reasoning. I have to fight against sentiment, and that is a completely hopeless struggle. The situation is simply abhorrent; and the fate of the Indies, of the land and people which I care for above all, fills me with the greatest anxiety when I see how passionately white and brown are confronting each other, how action has bred reaction ...

S. L. van der Wal, *De Volksraad* ... pp. 28-29.

H. Colijn: On political Reforms, 1918

The same institutions that can be democratic for a people at a certain stage of development can become an instrument of repression and can cause a loss of freedom for a people with a different background ... [Colijn then argues that before the arrival of the Dutch there was no Indies state in existence and that whatever political unity there was in the twentieth century was the result of Dutch polices.]

This historical fact, that we Netherlanders are the rulers and the people of the Indies are the subjects, is the only realistic basis on which political reforms must be built so that serious mistakes can be avoided ... In the last few years a number of people who have the interests of the Indies at heart strongly deny this fact ... They are actually ashamed about the fact that we are the ruling power. So far as the past is concerned they certainly have a point, but they also feel that our present and future policy must be based on completely different premises, that is, on the principle of *association* [of all the races], which in the future will result in a complete *fusion* ... It should be easy for the politically educated reader to recognize that the basic premise underlying this ideal is the denial or underestimation of the primeval fact that there are differences between individuals and races ... It is an attempt to apply the revolutionary idea of equality to the field of ethnology. This is very significant because it is identical to the idea of neutrality in the field of religion ... [Although agreeing that the indigenous people in the past had often been wronged, Colijn argued that colonialism was a necessary evil. Colonialism in his view was historically inevitable and nations resulted from the interaction of cultures either indirectly or by the occupation of a weaker nation by a more powerful and more highly developed nation.]

The latter method always appears to be the most effective one. From the antithesis between the ruler and the ruled there evolves—historically speaking—the antithesis between prince and people, and government and subjects. This is characteristic of political development everywhere. Thus the course of historical development is such that the original sharp antithesis between ruler and ruled is an impetus for the latter to work towards gradually replacing the ruler. When this process is fully completed and the differences between the government and the governed have completely disappeared in a full democracy, then also the motive underlying political development will have disappeared and the danger of disintegration will be imminent, resulting eventually in another colonial situation. This explanation I found necessary to make it clear that in political life the antithesis between ruler and ruled is in no way unnatural and that therefore our acceptance of the historically grown relationship between the Netherlands and the Indies is in itself no reason for shame; the accusation of being reactionary is not at all justified *providing the ruler is fully aware of his vocation* ... Colijn compared the relationship between the Netherlands and the Indies with that of father and son].

When the son is growing up, inevitably the moment will arrive when he feels he should assert his own individuality ... the moment will arrive—to use a popular phrase—when he will ask for the front door key. This will happen—and is in fact happening—in the Indies ... Even at this stage all kinds of unripe elements demand rights which they are not yet capable of exercising. They loudly demand that the Netherlands should relinquish its rule. But does a good father immediately give in to such demands by children? It would be the easiest way out and he would save himself a great deal of trouble and abuse, also from outsiders. However, it is the father who is most conscious of his vocation who does not give in so easily, because he realizes that his resistance will be of very great importance in the character-building of the child. He realizes that the child, because his ideas are in conflict with his father's, must learn to test his personality and character so that he will be able to distinguish between what is capricious and undisciplined and what is part of his true personality. So far as education towards political independence is concerned, a similar relationship exists between the Netherlands and the Indies. However, we tend too much to give in out of weakness to the often unjustified demands of small groups asserting themselves as the voice of the young Indies. In this way one certainly avoids being branded as a reactionary, and one might even get a short vote of thanks from the democratic side.

However, abdication would not in any way whatsoever be in the *real* interests of developing an Indies democracy. This can only develop normally and strongly as a result of the *balancing power* provided by Netherlands rule. Nothing therefore would be more pernicious than that the belief in our vocation—under the influence of ideas of association—should weaken prematurely ...

[Colijn criticized the fact that Ethical politicians had concentrated too much on setting up autonomous units of government while they neglected the need for the decentralization of executive power. According to Colijn administrative decentralization and the granting of autonomy were interconnected because decentralisation was] ... a means to educate towards autonomy, because just as somebody who has learned to obey is at the same time taught how to give orders, somebody who has learned to execute faithfully the rules made by others is trained at the same time to make rules himself. As a result administrative decentralization is always followed by autonomy ...

[However, reforms so far were based rather mistakenly on] ... the type of modern, unitarian, parliamentary state which exists in the Netherlands, with its simple division into realm, province, and municipalities, which is apparently accepted by the designers as the optimum for all times and all nations, including the Netherlands Indies ... [A case in point, according to Colijn, was the *Volksraad*, which was introduced too hastily. The Indies were not yet ripe for a system of full parliamentary government with ministerial responsibility, so that all the present *Volksraad* could do was to subject the colonial government to constant criticism.] After all in democratic countries the minister is free—when the opposition is becoming unreasonable—to resign and to force the opposition to take over the government itself. He can say, as it were: If you can do it so much better, then do it yourself and we will have a turn at controlling you ...

The Indies Government has been denied this normal means of defence against the *Volksraad*. There are two reasons for this. In the first place, even the sharpest criticism does not guarantee that the opposition, when it has finally succeeded in toppling the government, has the will and the capacity to govern ... This is of course, even more true of men who have never had the opportunity to gain practical experience in government. In the second place, in the Indies the opposition between the government and popular representation will coincide more and more with racial division. Therefore, if at some time Dutch bureaucratic rule will have to cede power to a nationalist opposition, the return of the old government will be out of the question and it will mean the end of Dutch rule, not only in Java but in all our other possessions. The *Volksraad* in its present form is in a position to indulge in *unrestricted* and irresponsible criticism, the consequences of which it will never have to bear. One has created in the form of a merely advisory body an institution which possesses *more* power than a modern parliament ... [Colijn criticized the attempts to create a unitary state, without first having started to democratize local and regional government. He also pointed to the great cultural and ethnic diversity of the Indies, which necessitated the gradual construction of a federal system of government at the regional, provincial, and finally at the national level. This had produced:] the political dogmatism that, instead of trying to build self-government in the Indies on what has historically grown, has tried to create an Indies state out of nothing ... It should be immediately obvious that in instituting the *Volksraad* the all-important condition that autonomy must be built up *from below* has been completely neglected. The roof has been constructed before the supporting walls ...

[The most important advantage of a federal structure, according to Colijn was that it avoided direct confrontation about imperial matters between the Dutch Government and the various democratic institutions in the Indies. Moreover a system of direct elections could be more easily introduced at the provincial level than in the case of the *Volksraad*, because the] complete, or at least relatively greater, ethnological homogeneity of the provinces ... would exclude or certainly very much diminish the danger of one nation dominating the other through the *Volksraad* ... A federal organization opens up the possibility for each territory to develop at its own pace. It will be possible, for example, for a completely autonomous Java to be represented solely by natives in the Federal Council, while at the same time the deputies from Sumatra—because it is still in a stage of transformation—will be partly elected and partly appointed native members. Then again the deputation from New Guinea, because it is still completely underdeveloped, would have to consist entirely of officials of the autocratic Netherlands Government. Finally, while in a unitarian state it is certain that the various nationalities—in the absence of a positive community of interests—will unite themselves into a common front against the foreign ruler, this will be avoided in a Netherlands-controlled federation. In such a federal structure the Dutch Government will be able to retain for a long time to come its moral role of disinterested arbiter in the ever-sharpening struggle for national and economic dominance between the various territories. Dutch power will only remain as long as it is considered indispensable ...

H. Colijn, *Staatkundige Hervormingen in Nederlandsch-Indie* (Kampen: 1918), pp. 6, 8-10, 18-19, 23-24, 30, 35-36.

19 Commentaries on the views of Colijn

1. The Vice-President of the Council of the Indies (de Graeff) to the Governor-General (van Limburg Stirum), 15 April 1918

You can be sure of two things: firstly, that there will be pressure to make the electoral system for the *Volksraad* more democratic; and secondly, that there will be pressure to change the *Volksraad* from an advisory body into a co-legislative institution. This is *inescapable*; we may be able to temporize a little, but that is all. It is simply unthinkable that people might be appeased by local institutions, which they are to accept as their parliaments, when they have already been given a taste of a central representative body. Colijn has always been right in arguing that one should have started off with those local parliaments and built up to a central parliament. However, Colijn has not been able to understand that one should have started with those local parliaments twenty years ago and that *now* the central parliament can no longer be postponed. He became wise after the event when the course of events could no longer be changed.

I would also consider it *fatal* for the *government* not to present the *Volksraad* with a perspective [of future political development] *now*. Otherwise the gentlemen will take care of this matter themselves. There is no doubt about it ...

S. L. van der Wal, *De Volksraad* ... p. 225.

2. Despatch of the Governor-General (van Limburg Stirum) to the Minister of Colonies (Pleyte), 14 July 1918

According to the telegrams, the moment is now coming near when our working relationship will be ended. And I really do not have to say again how sorry I am, because I will lose out with this change of portfolios. It is also by no means certain that I will be able to work together with a minister from the Anti-Revolutionary Party. Colijn will certainly gain great influence ... he just does not realize that it is impossible now to change course again, and I certainly would not agree to it. I am also wondering whether in Holland they are sufficiently aware of the views and aspirations gaining momentum here in the Indies and whether they will agree with the view that it is necessary to steer the *Volksraad* in the direction I am aiming at ...

S. L. van der Wal, *De Volksraad* ... p. 236.

3. Despatch of the Minister of Colonies (Idenburg) to the Governor-General (van Limburg Stirum), 8 October 1918

Immediately on taking over the Department of Colonies I was forced to take up a position concerning the Bill submitted to the Second Chamber by my predecessor to change the Constitutional Regulations of the Netherlands Indies and to reform the principles of colonial government. Although I cannot agree with a number of important and even fundamental points developed in the explanatory submission accompanying this Bill, in order to avoid any misunderstandings I would rather not withdraw it, but I intend at the appropriate time to amend it to the extent that it will be more in line with my present views, which differ somewhat from my earlier submissions. [Minister Pleyte's Bill envisaged the establishment in Java of autonomous regencies in which administrative and legislative power would rest in fully elected councils and not in the centrally controlled bureaucracy. Idenburg had initially agreed with this.]

I have been reflecting more deeply on this indeed highly important matter, and I have also taken note of the recently published *Report on Indian Constitutional Reforms* by the English Minister for India and the Governor-General of India [i.e. the Montagu and Chelmsford report] and I have studied the sagacious writings of Mr Ritseman van Eck [basically similar to Colijn's] and the excellent booklet of Mr H. Colijn, Member of the First Chamber, entitled *Staatkundige Hervormingen in Ned. Indie* [*Political Reforms in the Netherlands Indies*]. And I have become convinced that an effective reform of our government in the Indies can only be based on the following two fundamental principles: firstly, *there must be a separation between the organs of actual popular government, autonomous government, and the government of the foreign, leading, Netherlands power*. This fundamental idea of Mr Ritseman van Eck, which is also warmly supported by Mr Colijn, I consider correct and very useful if implemented.

Secondly, it must be kept in mind that *the gradual evolution of the Indies State* must occur in line with what Mr Colijn terms the *federalist idea*. As we are now engaged in trying to reform the government of the Indies, we must keep in mind that also with respect to the future Netherlands Indies the following words of that British India Report (p. 277) do apply, i.e. that it must become "a sisterhood of states, self-governing in all matters of purely local or provincial interest."

S. L. van der Wal, *De Volksraad*, pp. 248-49.

4. Telegram of the Governor-General (van Limburg Stirum) to the Minister of Colonies (Idenburg), 14 October 1918

[No. 405] In order to dissipate misapprehensions of those who confuse self-government with independence and feeling of uneasiness as to future existing among Europeans I think desirable statement in *Volksraad* placing in foreground indissolubility ties uniting Holland and India, further on lines of your 360 adding that ultimate goal you sketched can only be attained when electorate sufficiently developed intellect and character to hold their representatives to account and that above self-government bodies will ever be maintained for whole archipelago central government in which native population will gradually have greater share and which will be responsible to Indian peoples in manner to be determined later. Please telegraph before end month whether you concur.

S. L. van der Wal, *De Volksraad* ... , p. 253.

5. Telegram of the Minister of Colonies (Idenburg) to the Governor-General (van Limburg Stirum), 16 October 1918

[No. 371] Entirely concurring views expressed your 405 I would only add granting responsible government must also depend on experience gained and skill acquired by elected representatives in managing public affairs in local bodies.

S. L. van der Wal, *De Volksraad*, p. 253.

20   The Petition Sutardjo

Letter of the President of the Volksraad (W. H. van Helsdingen) to the First and Second Chambers of the States-General, 1 October 1936

The *Volksraad*, making use of its competent power ... granted in Article 68 of the Indies Constitutional Regulations, has decided at its meeting of 29 September 1936 to request Her Majesty the Queen as well as the States-General to promote the calling of a conference of representatives of the Netherlands and the Netherlands Indies. This conference should on the basis of the equality [of the partners] construct a plan for the granting of an independent status to the Netherlands Indies within the limits of Article 1 of the Constitution and by means of gradual reforms and in a period of time within

142 / Colonialism

which the conference considers the realization of this ideal possible ... This decision of the *Volksraad* resulted from a proposal made by six of its members, Messrs Soetardjo, also called Kartohadikoesoemo, Dr G. S. S. J. Ratu Langie, I. J. Kasimo, Landjoemin gelar Datoek Toemenggoeng, Mr Ko Kwat Tiong and Said Abdoellah bin Salim Alatas ...

S. L. van der Wal, *De Volksraad*, pp. 220-21.

21 Reply to Sutardjo

Despatch of the Governor-General (Stachouwer) to the Minister of Colonies (Welter), 14 September 1938

I was requested in a letter from the Minister of 11 November 1936 ... to give my views as to how the Queen should be advised [with respect to the Petition Sutardjo] ... I had this ministerial despatch handed to the previous Government Representative for General Affairs in the *Volksraad* [Mr Peekema] ... who in his note of 27 January 1937 came to the conclusion that the petition in its present form and in the way it came about "is a somewhat crude summons to speedily grant self-government to the Indies along certain definite lines", which certainly cannot be agreed to unconditionally, but which on the other hand can also not be dismissed with a shrug of the shoulder.

"There is a lack of systematic thinking and guiding principles in the Indies Constitutional Regulations; and there is a great deal of uncertainty about where this country is going, in what way and in what tempo." This, together with the desire for a greater degree of self-government, which lives in many different forms in the Indies society, makes it, in the opinion of Mr Peekema, desirable to set up a government commission, which has also been recommended by Mr C. C. van Helsdingen during the debates in the *Volksraad* about the petition Sutardjo.

This commission should be charged with "indicating the lines along which the gradual political development of the Netherlands Indies is to take place ... "

Also the previous Adviser for Native Affairs [Gobee] ... was, according to his letter of 25 March 1937, ... of the opinion "that to further a quiet development of political relations in this country it is required that—taking into account the opinions of the inhabitants of the kingdom—guidelines should be established for the development of the political relations between the Netherlands and the Indies in the future".

Differing on this point from Mr Peekema, he was of the opinion, however, that for political reasons it would not be advisable to dismiss the idea of calling a conference of representatives of the Netherlands and the Netherlands Indies. Its task could still be very restricted and the working-out in detail of the principles indicated by [the conference] could be left to the government commission.

The previous Director of Education and Religious Affairs [Dr De Kat Angelino] ... concluded first of all in his secret letter of 5 May 1937 ... that the existing constitutional order rules out the granting of the petition. The requested conference of Netherlands and Netherlands Indies representatives chosen on the basis of equal rights, which, as is obvious from the petition, should be able to take binding decisions with regard to changes in the Constitution and the Indies Constitutional Regulations, is unconstitutional.

In contrast to these advisers, Dr De Kat Angelino dismissed the usefulness even of a possible programme of measures to regulate the development towards political independence of the Netherlands Indies, either within a definite period or not. All political influence that can be exerted by the Indies people on the policies of the central government without affecting the ultimate responsibility of the Netherlands nation for these policies has already been granted to the representatives of the Indies citizens in the *Volksraad*. Any further political emancipation means a transfer of power by the central government, i.e. the responsibility of the Indies Government to the Netherlands nation is shifted to the people of the Netherlands Indies, and therefore in his opinion the government must dismiss in principle the idea of a programme of political reforms. In his view the further political emancipation of the Indies can and may—if the Netherlands sees its duty as a leader correctly—only be the culmination of a many-sided, and completely social, development. In his opinion the Indies Government can say with the fullest conviction that it does not know any uncertainty, that it works towards the emancipation of society, that it welcomes all parties to participate, and that every step forward in this work automatically brings political emancipation nearer.

Although completely opposing the petition, Dr De Kat Angelino nevertheless ... considers it a fact of great political importance. He is of the opinion that the *Volksraad* should be told why the petition cannot be granted, while at the same time the government should make it clear that it is fully prepared to have an exchange of views about the further development of the political relationship between the Netherlands and the Indies.

He argues that the problem of the relationship between the

Netherlands and the Indies should not be seen solely in terms of the independence of the Indies, but that a system must be constructed for the whole of the kingdom, in which the various parts of this complexity of states will be able to lead their own lives as healthily as possible and in accordance with their own natural dispositions, while at the same time they will mutually co-operate and form a kingdom that is united and as strong as possible. So he advocates the establishment of an authority, which he calls the Imperial Council, that should have the task of advising the Crown about matters of importance to the empire as a whole ...

I finally had these submissions ... sent to *De Raad van Nederlands-Indie* [the Council of the Netherlands Indies], which in its detailed and sound advice of 25 November 1937 ... came to the following conclusions:

1. The granting of the Petition Soetardjo is in the first instance not possible because in the way it is worded it is incompatible with the existing constitutional law.
2. Completely ignoring this point, the granting of the petition is, however, also undesirable for political reasons. It is true that an expression such as "an independent status within the limits of Article 1 of the Constitution" leaves room for a great variety of interpretations. But the so-called dominion status which the proposers of the petition have in mind ... is a form of organization for which the Indies community—considering the stage of political development it has reached—cannot yet bear the responsibility.
3. It follows from 1 and 2 that a conference, the purpose of which is neither considered desirable nor possible, should not be advocated by the government.
4. Administrative reforms [i.e. establishment of autonomous provinces] that are now being implemented should be continued energetically. At the same time the delegation of autonomous power to the lower administrative units and a regulation of the financial relationship between the central government and these lower administrative units should be pushed through as far as possible. This means a considerable increase in the participation of the Indies community and its institutions in their own affairs, but it still leaves untouched the extremely important areas for which a greater and better assured participation of the Netherlands Indies is necessary.
5. This greater participation cannot for the time being be achieved by changing clauses of the Constitution or the Indies Constitutional Regulations ... because then the as yet indispensable principal powers of the Home Government would be abandoned. But [this greater participation] can be achieved in practice when

these ... powers are carefully handled and when full account is taken of the needs and demands of the Indies and also as far as possible of the views of the Indies.
6. In accepting the so-called technical revision of the Indies Constitutional Regulations, which has already been designed by the Department of Colonies, it is possible to show the participatory powers that already have been granted to the Netherlands Indies to their fuller advantage. [This technical revision was concerned to enable the Standing Committee of the *Volksraad* to deal with auxiliary budgets, draft legislation, and other government regulations, when the *Volksraad* was not in session.]
7. It would be useful to carry this revision further by changing Article 91 of the Indies Constitutional Regulations and by putting forward the times fixed for the discussion of the main budget. [Article 91 stipulated that matters dealing with international relations and international law were to be dealt with by the Governor-General. In practice this meant that in "mixed" cases such as opium legislation, trade regulations, and production restrictions, the *Volksraad* was not heard. Another grievance was that the *Volksraad* was asked to discuss the budget too early, i.e. about eighteen months before its implementation.]
8. It is necessary for the Indies Government to again explain and defend openly in the *Volksraad* this state of affairs, because only in this way will it be possible to keep within reasonable bounds the dissatisfaction about the attitude of the Home Government towards the Netherlands Indies that has been repeatedly shown and that can also be expected to occur periodically in the future. On the other hand [the Indies Government] must be diligent to the utmost in carrying out measures such as a large-scale administrative reorganization that will give the citizens a greater say in their own affairs. And the possibilities under the existing legislation of having a say in matters of imperial importance, which also touch on Indies interests, must be fully utilized.

As Your Excellency will have seen from this very concise survey, the considerations of the advisers are in general concerned with two aspects, i.e. the formal side, and the material or rather the political importance of the petition ...

I also recognize the political importance of this petition in so far as in my opinion it is widely believed that these regions are quickly outgrowing their constitutional framework. The European part of the population is in particular concerned about the influence the Home Government is allowed to exert on the activities of the Indies Government. The part of the indigenous population that rises to the discussion of political problems and that has desires such as were expressed by Mr Soetardjo is driving towards something far more fundamental, ... the realization of the ideal of bringing the control over these regions completely into indigenous hands. I agree fully that this striving is a political reality, the dynamic power of which is destined to increase. It would be a mistake to ignore the numerous examples provided by history and not to attach any importance to the desire for self-determination of awakening colonial peoples.

The Netherlands Government, however, has not failed to take notice of the signs of the times nor has it neglected to give the indigenous people a part in the central and local administration. Surveying what has been done during the last twenty years in the political field and what is still on the agenda for the near future, and taking into account the intellectual and material state of this society, there is no justification for concluding that political rights are not granted quickly enough. Furthermore, we are working diligently and energetically—as far as economic and financial conditions permit—towards the intellectual and material development of the indigenous people, in order to bring closer to fulfilment the conditions that are indispensable for the granting of further political rights to the people. It would be superfluous to go into further details about the matter in this despatch. The Council of the Netherlands Indies and Mr De Kat Angelino have in their submissions commented on the same ideas. And I agree fully with the latter where he underlines the great political importance of the much-discussed "ripeness" ...

On the one hand it can be admitted that in spite of what has been and is being done, there remains a strong and natural pressure to obtain more extensive political powers, and this pressure is a factor to be taken into account. On the other hand, there is the condition that for the time being we must hold to the present situation. This admission therefore should not be taken to mean that we should try to satisfy [indigenous demands] to some extent now, and construct, as the conference is supposed to do, a programme for the distant future, which pretends to indicate stages that are to be gradually realized as well as the tempo in which these goals are to be reached. The uncertainty about the future, the uncertainty especially about the course of the intellectual and economic development of the people, which is dependent on so many unforeseen, indeed uncontrollable circumstances, excludes at once the possibility of creating something realistic. If the government, ignoring the reality of the matter, should nevertheless wish to co-operate in designing the desired programme in order to open up a perspective—however little value it may itself attach to it—then I am completely convinced that it would not cause any satisfaction, not even temporarily. I do not share the hope apparently cherished by Messrs Peekema and Gobee that in this way it [the government] would profit from a desire to co-operate and would give a more happy direction to the indigenous movement. Such a programme would in this society not bring clarity and direction but commotion and confusion among the intellectuals, who in political affairs are still primitive thinkers. [Such a programme] would certainly be shouted down as inadequate and it could easily be attacked because of the numerous hypotheses on which it would of necessity have to be based. I instructed [government spokesmen] to be purposely reserved and to dismiss discussions about vague possibilities in the future during the general political debates of last year. In my opinion the government can easily say too much in these matters and it would serve her well in its dealings with the *Volksraad* and political movements to direct attention to concrete things ...

To call a conference as is wanted by the petition or to set up a commission as is desired ... by Mr C. C. van Helsdingen would give the unfavourable impression that government policy is uncertain. It would also create expectations that something new and great was to happen. This again would cause a great deal of loud commotion, while the final result of it all would be negative, or a programme would be worked out that would embarrass the government ...

I also wish to record here that the idea of Mr De Kat Angelino to set up an imperial council should in my view not be recommended. I find it difficult to see how such a body can be properly fitted into the political structure, nor can I see its usefulness, while I can not imagine how a satisfactory membership of this body can be composed. Mr De Kat Angelino wants to give a considerable number of seats to the political parties, which probably would have to be promised an important say in order to get the idea of such an institution accepted. But I fear that this would immediately pull down the quality of the council in view of the lack of expertise ...

S. L. van der Wal, *De Volksraad*, pp. 382-90.

22 Rejection of an Indonesian parliament

Despatch of the Minister of Colonies (Welter) to the Queen, 13 February 1941

The *Gaboengan Politiek Indonesia* is a federation of a number of indigenous political associations that are very much nationalistically inclined. [The *G.A.P.I.*] has already earlier propagandized the idea of instituting a full parliament in the Netherlands Indies, to which the government would owe political responsibility ... During the deliberations in the States-General about the Indies budget for 1941, which took place during March 1940, the aspirations of this association were the subject of a great deal of discussion. There was almost unanimous agreement with the view held by the undersigned, that we are confronted here with a premature slogan which does not fit in the course of gradual political development of the Netherlands Indies. This is so, because this slogan demands the immediate realization of something that is in fact the finish of a democratic evolution of the government system. Such a final stage, when a full Parliament to which the government is responsible will be instituted, is in its own good time only thinkable when such a structure is founded on a society that has advanced intellectually to the stage where it can support it.

It would not be objectionable in itself if a leftist-oriented political federation such as the *G.A.P.I.* nevertheless continued to work for the implementation of its political slogan. What makes the activities of this group objectionable, however,—and the Governor-General is apparently driving at this when he calls this action "improper"—is that it seemingly attempts to take advantage of the difficult situation the Kingdom of the Netherlands finds itself in, and to suggest that such large-scale political reforms are needed just now in order to strengthen the "moral resistance" of the Indies population. The suggestion is then apparently that in the event of these reforms not being effected, the population would not be found prepared or able to bear the trials of the war and the separation from the mother country with the required calmness and firmness.

The only proper attitude is to dismiss such a political action. It does not need saying that on the other hand the traditional policy towards the Indies must be continued, and that one should continue to work towards the gradual preparation of the Netherlands Indies for self-government within the context of the kingdom. One must add that because of the present circumstances there can be no question of political and constitutional reforms, which would necessitate a change in the Constitution or the Indies Constitutional Regulations ...

Finally, with regard to the telegram of the Secretariat of the *G.A.P.I.*, this does not in the opinion of the undersigned need any answer or other treatment. The undersigned would therefore respectfully suggest to Your Majesty that the papers concerned should be deposited.

S. L. van der Wal, *De Volksraad*, pp. 570-72.

23 Declaration of the Netherlands Government in exile in London, 27 January 1942

The present political structure of the Kingdom of the Netherlands, as well as the internal relations between the mother country and the overseas territories, are based on the Constitution of 1922 and the resulting Constitutional Regulations of the Netherlands Indies, Surinam, and Curacao. Since 1922 the intellectual and material development of these overseas territories, especially of the Netherlands Indies, has shown some marked advances. As a result of this, special attention has been directed in the representative institutions in the motherland and the Indies as well as outside to constitutional measures for the further emancipation of the overseas territories within the framework of the kingdom.

While the occupation of the mother country has lamed the political life there, the situation is different in the overseas territories. In spite of the fact that the ties with the mother country were broken, these territories under the leadership of their governors have shown an excellent bearing and strength of mind and have given proof in these times of their capacity to stand on their own feet. This has stimulated the process of intellectual and political awakening in ever broader layers of the population.

In order to give direction to this respectable striving for a relationship between the various parts of the kingdom that is in harmony with these changed circumstances, on 10 May 1941 Her Majesty Queen Wilhelmina announced in a radio speech that after the war an imperial conference would be called.

S. L. van der Wal, *De Volksraad* ... pp. 670-71.

EDUCATION POLICY

The provision of modern education facilities for the indigenous population, on which a rather hesitant start had been made during the second half of the nineteenth century, received a considerable boost under the aegis of the Ethical Policy.

Around the turn of the century a larger number of Dutchmen—both in the colony and at home—had begun to believe implicitly in the value of education, which in the typically liberal philosophical atmosphere of the time was considered to provide an effective cure for the inherent evils in indigenous society and as an absolutely necessary condition for indigenous economic progress. A typical example of this reasoning is provided by the writings of Habbema, Inspector of Education during the first decade of this century (*see* document 24).

Even more idealistic, but no less genuine, was a smaller group of Dutch colonial reformers, of whom Snouck Hurgronje, the noted Islamic expert and Adviser for Native Affairs, was probably the most brilliant representative. He believed that only by giving in readily and at the right time to the growing demand for Western education, particularly on the part of the Indonesian upper classes, could the Kingdom of the Netherlands retain the Indies. They argued that in associating the leading Indonesian classes with Dutch culture and by granting them an ever-increasing share in the running of colonial affairs and government they would tie them inextricably, spiritually, intellectually, and politically, to the ruling classes in the Netherlands. And when this process of association had finally run its course there would have come about the beautiful ideal of a Kingdom of the Netherlands consisting of two autonomous parts: one in north-western Europe and the Other in South-east Asia (*see* document 25).

Another more prosaic, but nevertheless powerful, argument for allowing larger numbers of Western-educated Indonesians into the more responsible positions in the colonial public service was the consideration that Indonesians, because of their lower standing of living, could be paid considerably less than the expensive expatriate Dutchmen (*see* document 26).

A considerable controversy, however, arose as to what kind of educational programme should be introduced; and in particular, such questions as what minimum standard of education was to be provided, and whether in all native schools Dutch was to be used as a medium of instruction, caused a great deal of altercation in official and educational circles. Some educationalists and politicians, such as the Minister for Colonies, Fock, who strongly believed in the rapid industrialization of Java, wanted a frontal attack: he advocated that primary schools with a technically based curriculum should be made available to all Javanese as quickly as possible and irrespective of the cost involved (*see* document 27:1). The majority of officials, however, including Governor-General van Heutz and Snouck Hurgronje (*see* document 27:2), were strongly opposed to Fock's plan on the grounds that it would result in a vast waste of public money and might even create a discontented and politically dangerous intellectual proletariat. The general European opinion was that the government should only provide education when a certain section of the indigenous population expressed a need for it. And assuming that the vast majority of Indonesians, who were still agrarian-based, did not have such a need because they did not express it, it was felt that only the simplest possible education was necessary for the indigenous masses, on whom the Dutch language, modern science, and history would be completely lost.

It was Governor-General van Heutz who hit on the ingenious idea of the communal village school, which after 1907 became the standard elementary school for the vast majority of Indonesians. The village school was in many ways a typical Dutch treat in that this three-year school, providing reading and writing in the vernacular and simple arithmetic, had to be built and paid for (and have the teachers' salaries provided) by the villagers themselves on a voluntary basis. Only in very exceptional cases would the government be prepared to grant a very limited subsidy to villages. In addition so-called Second Class Vernacular Schools were established, providing a somewhat more extensive curriculum primarily for lower-class Indonesians who were no longer rurally based. Vernacular Continuation Schools were set up for the brighter pupils who had passed through the village schools.

Between 1900 and 1942 there was gradually established a dual system of education: a vernacular one that did not reach beyond the primary level; and a Dutch-language system reaching from primary school to university.

The vernacular system, which was primarily designed to eradicate illiteracy, only progressed very slowly. And the argument advanced by van Heutz in establishing the village schools, that people only appreciate something when they have to pay for it, might perhaps have been applicable to the generally thrifty citizens of the Netherlands. But to the vast majority of Indonesian villagers these new-fangled institutions were of very limited appeal; and it soon became apparent that if van Heutz's instruction about a voluntary communal effort was adhered to, hardly any schools would arise. Officials therefore began to put pressure on the villagers, with the result that in many areas the village school came to be widely considered as another form of taxation, another curse of Allah superimposed upon them by the colonial government (*see* document 28:1).

Only after the early 1920s, when the colonial government decided to grant more liberal subsidies to village schools, did the situation begin to improve; it was, however, to deteriorate again during the Great Depression of the 1930s when funds for vernacular education were also severely curtailed. By 1940 the number of village schools had risen to the extent that they could accommodate a little over 40 per cent of Indonesian children in the six to nine age group. The average literacy rate was, however, by this time probably still below 10 per cent (*see* document 30). And whatever gains the colonial government had been able to make in eradicating illiteracy were almost immediately absorbed by the continuous rapid increase in population.

In addition to the apparent unwillingness of the colonial government to allot sufficient funds to allow a rapid increase in the number of vernacular schools, there were a number of other important factors which adversely affected the literacy programme. For example, vernacular schools were basically intended to produce literate farmers and workers, but the vast majority of lower-class Indonesian parents could not see any value in sending their children to school unless this would help them to advance themselves on the traditional socio-economic value scale, that is, to obtain white-collar jobs. Another factor was that the vernacular school did not sufficiently fit in with the rhythm of rural life, and holidays, for example, did not take any account of harvesting seasons, when children were urgently needed on the farms, of days of religious observance, or of other feast days. Some Dutch educationalists (*see* document 29) also criticized the curriculum of vernacular schools as too intellectualistic and claimed that, in order to prepare pupils better for the rural life they were supposed to return to, the idea of the "work school" of the Montessori and Froebel type would be more suitable. They said that the curriculum was too Western-oriented and should be changed to take much greater account of local cultural patterns. And although some attempts were made during the 1920s and 1930s to follow up these criticisms, the indigenous population in general remained uninterested in the vernacular schools, and the high rate of absenteeism and premature leaving continued, which of course reduced the efficiency of the vernacular system even more.

In contrast, the Dutch-language schools system expanded very rapidly during the first two decades of the twentieth century. And in addition to various types of primary schools catering for specific population groups (European Primary Schools, Dutch-Native Schools, Dutch-Chinese Schools, and Dutch-Arab Schools), three-year secondary schools (*M.U.L.O.*) and five to six-year secondary schools (*H.B.S.*, *A.M.S.*, Lyceum) were established. The *M.U.L.O.* gave entry to various tertiary institutions for study in Agriculture, Medicine, Dentistry, Law, Education, Veterinary Science, and Engineering—institutions somewhat akin to Australian institutions of advanced education. The five to six-year secondary schools gave access to university. Between 1919 and 1941 the following faculties were established in Indonesia: Engineering, Law, Medicine, Public Administration, and Arts. There were also a number of Indonesians studying at universities in the Netherlands.

Entry into the Dutch-language schools was restricted to Europeans, Eurasians, and children of upper-class or well-to-do Indonesian or other non-European parents. The high school fees introduced to reinforce this rule did not seem to have deterred a considerable number of lower-class Indonesian parents from sending their children to Dutch-language schools. A government investigation held in 1926 found that out of a sample of 52,600 children in Dutch-

Native Schools 66 per cent did not comply with the social and economic entry norms originally laid down.

This obvious predilection of Indonesians for entry into Dutch-language schools was not caused solely by a thirst for Western knowledge for its own sake, but also because a Dutch school certificate opened up the possibility of a position in the colonial civil service, which carried the highest degree of social prestige in the Javanese world.

By the mid-1920s, however, the production of Indonesian Dutch-language school graduates was surpassing the number of vacancies in the civil service and an enquiry held in 1924 found that in Batavia 16.5 per cent of the estimated ten thousand Dutch-speaking Indonesians were unable to find clerical work of any description and preferred to stay unemployed rather than accept manual work. This unemployment problem was viewed with considerable alarm by a large section of Europeans in the colony, a number of whom came to believe that a relationship existed between this "intellectual proletariat" and the radicalization of the Indonesian Nationalist Movement that was occurring at this time. And although an official investigation held in 1926 (*see* document 58) concluded that no valid correlation could be established, this did not deter a growing number of critics of the Ethical education policy from persisting in their belief and demanding a slowing-down in the expansion of Dutch-language schools (*see* document 31). One of the most prominent critics was Meyer Ranneft, an important colonial official and spokesman in the *Volksraad* of the sizeable group of Dutchmen who considered the Indies as their permanent homeland (the *blijvers*) as opposed to those Dutchmen who returned to Holland after their tour of duty had been completed (the *trekkers*). (*See* document 32.)

As a result the colonial government instituted in 1926 the Dutch-Native Schools Commission, which after a series of important sociological investigations concluded in 1929 that the Dutch-language school system suffered from two basic defects. Firstly, it failed to satisfy the actual educational needs of society, because more graduates were being produced than could be absorbed by the economy. For example, it had been found that in 1928 about a quarter of Dutch-speaking Indonesians employed in the civil service and by European industry held positions in which Dutch primary school qualifications were not necessary. Moreover in the school year 1928-29 as many as 9120 Dutch-speaking Indonesians were graduating, while there were only 3900 new openings. And although the Commission pointed out that it did not subscribe to the current opinion that there was a special relationship between Dutch-language education and the incidence of Communism, it nevertheless believed that the "overproduction" of Dutch-speaking

Indonesians was an important contributory cause of the widespread discontent in indigenous society.

The second basic defect of the system was its inefficiency, caused by the fact that large numbers of pupils left school before the completion of their courses. It was found that only 40.9 per cent of students entering the first year of the Dutch-Native Schools managed to obtain the final diploma. This wastage was caused partly by the difficulty of the teaching programme and partly by the high cost of Dutch-language education, which lower-class parents often could not sustain for the whole period.

The main solution to these problems suggested by the Commission was to severely curtail the influx of students into these schools by restricting entry—as had been originally intended—solely to children from upper-class Indonesian milieux.

Realization of the deep and widespread political discontent that a curtailment in Dutch-language education would undoubtedly cause in the Indonesian community initially restrained the colonial government from taking any drastic action (*see* document 33). However, a fortuitous opportunity to act on the suggestions of the Commission was soon presented to the colonial government by the advent of the Great Depression of the 1930s, which enabled it to slash savagely the funds for Dutch-language schools ostensibly on the basis of budgetary considerations alone (*see* document 34:2).

Not to be thwarted, Indonesians began to set up their own private Dutch-language schools, which spread so rapidly that by 1937 they had surpassed the number of government schools in terms of students. Attempts by the colonial government in 1932 to stop the growth of these "*Wilde Scholen*" caused such a furore in the whole of the indigenous world that the government finally was forced to withdraw the proposed legislation from the *Volksraad*. Again the realization that the Dutch-language school issue was highly sensitive politically prevented the colonial government from continuing its policy of curtailment after 1936 when the worst of the Depression had passed; and as a result a rapid expansion of these schools took place again until the end of Dutch rule.

The dual nature of the Dutch colonial education system came under severe attack from a number of progressive Dutch educationalists, who in particular criticized the "*concordantie*" principle, i.e. the insistence on keeping the Dutch-language schools in Indonesia on a strict par in terms of standards and curricula with their counterparts in Holland, which was considered to be wasteful and contrary to the real educational needs of indigenous society. A typical representative of this school of thought was Albert de la Court, the politically progressive former Director of the Teacher's College in Bandung (*see* document 35).

24 J. Habbema: The political and economic importance of education for the native people, 1904

Many still doubt the wisdom of providing the native masses with education. The desirability of education for upper-class children is recognized, but not for children of the ordinary villager. It is often argued that education should not be provided for all children not only because they do not need it but also because it will make them averse to manual labour. Boys who have been to school do not want to go back behind the plough but aspire to a "position" and as the number of positions is limited the result will be the creation of an intellectual proletariat. This could cause the government a great deal of trouble because disappointment followed by discontentment can lead to all sorts of excesses. And in particular among dissatisfied intellectuals will criminal and other bad elements be found.

But the best way in fact to counteract the formation and expansion of an intellectual proletariat and to reduce any other disadvantages of native education to a minimum is to spread the idea of education ... as widely as possible among all classes.

But what is the situation at present?

A Javanese boy who has successfully completed a course in a primary school and has obtained his final certificate ... fancies himself to be quite somebody and this is understandable, considering that in Java and Madoera, with a population of about thirty million people, only about a thousand pupils per year are able to obtain such a certificate.

It is not surprising then that these boys develop pretensions and consider themselves too good to walk behind a plough again.

In fact the vast majority of them succeed in getting a position in private enterprise as *mandoer* [foreman] or clerk in the village, the regional government service, the Surveyor-General's department, the railways, the post office, etc ...

As soon as the majority of the people have been educated, the prestige of being an educated man will be reduced ... And the demand for positions will become so great that the graduates from native schools will be forced to find other employment, in agriculture or in a trade.

I do not deny that probably the number of "troublesome" natives will increase with the spreading of education, but against this there is the considerable advantage that the influence of fanatics and other individuals who are hostile to authority will diminish in line with the degree of intellectual development of the people, who will no longer allow themselves to be so easily aroused and incited as "the stupid masses" by the first rebel-rouser that comes along.

It can also be assumed that it will as a rule be far more difficult for the chiefs, Chinese, and Arabs to fool and exploit an educated native than a villager who still remains in a state of complete ignorance.

Finally, education can play an important role in eradicating superstition ... which still presses as a heavy yoke on the native people and seriously obstructs the people's freedom of action. The people are allowed to work only at certain times ... and things have to be done in certain ways otherwise there will be conflict with Dewi Seri, Gendroewos, Poentianaks, and all kinds of other spirits and spooks. A great deal of time and money is lost because of superstition. One only needs to refer here to the time-consuming stalk-by-stalk harvesting of rice, which is interspersed by the necessary *slametans* and *sedekahs* [feasts and prayers] in memory of deceased relatives. One only needs to think of the money wasted on *doekoens* [soothsayers] and the exorcising of devils ...

Lately, the question whether the natives are lazy or not has been often discussed, and opinions differ very widely—ranging from not lazy to very lazy.

It seems to me that, if given a sufficiently strong stimulus to work, the natives are no lazier than Europeans. One must remember that in the Indies the enervating climate makes working, particularly on the land much more burdensome than in Europe; and in the tropics less effort is required to provide for one's daily needs than in a more moderate climate, where so much more is needed in the way of clothing, lighting, and fuel alone ...

So in my view the natives are not lazy, but they are very careless and thoughtless about the future. The main reason for this is that they do not use their brains, because they have not been taught to do so ... In our own society carelessness is often found in uneducated people who live from day to day and who worry very little about their future and that of their families. When money is plentiful, most of it is wasted. This is also true of the natives. When they have money, they cannot wait until it has been spent on finery and sweets. They never think about saving, and in the event of the least adversity, sickness, or crop failure, there is no money to see them through the bad days. The result is poverty ...

How then can education be a means to combat this native thoughtlessness and so indirectly lead to an improvement in native economic conditions? ... It will be mainly through the civic virtues inculcated at school, that is, when the teachers perform their task properly. Orderliness, neatness, diligence, a sense of duty and obedience, are just as much taught at school as reading and writing, and it is just those and other civic virtues that are lacking in native children, because they are usually badly brought up by their own families ...

J. Habbema, *Onderwijs politiek en economisch belang van onderwijs aan de bevolking van Nederlandsch-Indie* (*Indische Gids*, 1904), pp. 995-98.

25 C. Snouck Hurgronje: The ideal of association, 1911

It is not enough, however, just to take measures designed to prevent the population from becoming discontented or rebellious and in this way secure our rule. Our objective should not be the hitherto so highly praised peacefulness, but movement. Our rule will have to justify itself on the basis of lifting the natives up to a higher level of civilization in line with their innate capacities. Education and training are the means to achieve this objective. Even in countries with a much older Islamic culture than in our archipelago we see education successfully at work in liberating Mohammedans from some of the medieval rubbish that they have carried in their train far too long. Admittedly the *system* that has historically evolved does not lend itself to deep-going reforms, neither through the modernization of the law nor through the popularization of mysticism; but the *Muslim society* nevertheless proceeds in the direction of modern culture, going outside the system and silently ignoring what it does not dare to touch. This is what is happening in Turkey, Egypt, and Syria.

Our task as educators and tutors of the East Indian Mohammedans is made easier by a number of factors which in other countries do not exist, or only to a lesser degree. One such is the relatively short period of time the Islamic system has been in force here. As a result many aspects of life have been left untouched, which facilitates the adoption of new cultural ideas, as long as we abstain from attacking the religious content. The centuries-old custom of the natives, particularly in Java, to come to terms with very different races and civilizations, has saved them from the narrowmindedness that results from isolation. It would be difficult to find anywhere in this world a people more willing to obey its chiefs than the Javanese, and it would be equally difficult to find foreign-dominated indigenous administrators who are more willing than the Javanese aristocracy to act according to the advice given by foreign government officials.

Particularly with respect to the education of their children, the native officials are not only wont to ask the advice of European officials but they also follow up this advice with an almost moving trust. In the early days they were usually advised to give their sons a fairly simple education, because it was argued that the knowledge needed by Europeans to get on in life would be useless to them in their rather limited field of work. Even this sort of advice was obediently followed up although many, thrusting their tonges in their cheeks, thought differently in private.

Since the change that has occurred in European opinion about the intellectual capacity of the natives and perhaps also even about their moral fibre, providing they have received a proper education, it has become apparent that there is a strong desire among the Javanese upper classes to familiarize themselves completely with modern civilization, so much in fact that soon the facilities provided by the government will not be able to cope with this demand ...

What other colonial powers are trying to force upon their subjects with great difficulty—i.e. an education that prepares them to participate in their own way in the life of their rulers—is in fact being clamoured for by the indigenous population in Java and parts of the Outer Possessions. Would it not be terribly shameful for our colonial administration to leave this intellectual gold mine unexploited, just like a person who has obtained a concession but has no capital and keeps his business ostensibly alive until a more energetic syndicate will take it over from him?

But what has all this actually to do with the Islam question confronting the Netherlands? In fact, everything. The only real solution to this problem is to be found in the association of the Mohammedan subjects of the Netherlands state with the Netherlanders. If this succeeds, the Islam problem will no longer exist, because there will have been created a cultural unity between the subjects of the Netherlands Queen on the shores of the North Sea and those of *Insulinde* [i.e. Indonesia], which will obliterate the importance of religious differences in the political and social sense. If [association] is not successful, the Indonesians, because of their inevitably increasing intellectual development, will of necessity be drawn ever further away from us, as others will take over the leadership from us.

Experience teaches us that we cannot expect the government to achieve this solution alone or in the first place. And although it does not lack the necessary sympathy in this matter, it actually lacks the will to move. The reasons for this we may as well leave aside, because after all the government is a rather cumbersome body that usually can only be moved by rude shocks ... There is, however, still another way which with less noise, although perhaps less quickly, can achieve the objective ... : that is the irresistible pressure that is usually exerted on the government by public opinion.

So large sections of the Netherlands people have first to become convinced that the association of the civilization of the native population of the Indies Archipelego with ours must be effected; that the present intellectual movement of the higher classes of native society urgently requires us to further this association; and that there is *periculum in mora* [danger in delay]. And we must go further than just words and become actively involved. We must be willing to make sacrifices both in terms of money and time. If it is left solely to the government there is a great danger that, owing to its innate irresolution, it may be taken by surprise in the end, when the correct moment to take and maintain control of the movement would have irrevocably passed.

So far the realization that we are dealing with an urgent popular need is only to be found in a fairly small group of people here [i.e. in the Netherlands]; and in fact the only ones who apparently are fully aware are the active supporters of the [Christian] missions. Or, rather: they are striving for an association of a much higher order than the one we have just mentioned, that is, a unity, if it could be achieved, which would take away all the obstructions to the unity of civilization and national consciousness of the eastern and western parts of the Kingdom of the Netherlands—if such a thing is possible!

However, the great admiration with which we view the sacrificing labour of the missionaries, and our great appreciation of the liberality of the many people in the mother country who support these efforts, should not make us forget how limited are the chances of success for the Christian missions in countries which have been touched by the spirit of Islam. The more sensible missionaries have no illusions about this, although this does not stop them from giving up. Under no circumstances should our people and government even consider the possibility of delegating the implementation of the ideal of association to the Christian missions, while neglecting the movement in the native world that is at present gaining momentum and that provides such a very favourable opportunity.

The existence of this movement points undoubtedly to the practicability of the realization of a beautiful political and national idea, that is, the creation of a Netherlands nation consisting of two parts widely separated geographically but spiritually closely united, one in north-west Europe and the other in South-east Asia. This is not a Utopian ideal, but is is an objective which the people and government of the Netherlands would reproach themselves about for ever if they did not grasp it in time, letting the present opportune moment pass by without taking any action. In this case the following quotation from Goethe is entirely applicable: "*Was du ererbt von deinen vatern hast, erwirb es, um es zu besitzen*". ["What you have inherited from your fathers, you must gain again in order to possess it."] Our inheritance in this case consists of the beautiful and rich tributary regions held by us until now by force. But if this claim is to withstand the stormy pressures of the times, we must now follow the material annexation by a spiritual one.

In order to avoid disappointment and confusion we must become fully aware of the limitations within which this spiritual annexation is possible. However important religion may be in the life of our people and state, even in this small Western country of the Netherlands it is not what holds us together. Our unity is rooted in more general cultural ideas, to the formation of which Christianity has undoubtedly contributed a great deal, but under the aegis of which not only Christians but the members of a great variety of religions, including Jews and freethinkers, have equal rights to the accommodation of their particular views. This unity is so great that they would oppose with all their strength, even at the cost of sacrificing their life and goods, any attempts to force them to take on another nationality or to become subject to another government. So it is logical therefore that neither our government nor our people can mount a propaganda campaign for the purpose of trying to convert the Mohammedan natives to a [different] religion, however large the number of its adherents here. An attempt *to undermine the fundaments* of the Islamic system, which partly rules and would like to completely rule the life of the natives, may only be made by a religious association, church, or missionary society. The state may only make sure that nobody is obstructed in his freedom of action.

However, it is allowable and not out of place in this particular case to stage a campaign for the purpose of annexing the natives to our state and nationality more firmly than hitherto has been the case. After all, for centuries they have been devoid of their own independent political power or national life; and we, who took away from them what they may have had in this respect, promising to respect their religious institutions, therefore accepted the moral obligation to educate them so that they could participate in *our* political and cultural life. They themselves are now dismissing whatever pretexts there may be for postponing the fulfilment of this duty, because of their own continuously growing pressure for this spiritual annexation. Here it is by no means sufficiently realized how strong this pressure in fact is. It is not only the native offficials and ... aristocracy who in the first place want their children to learn Dutch, and after that to gain as much as possible of the knowledge that is opened up by this language; even the number of Mohammedan religious teachers is increasing who entrust the education and training of their sons to European control rather than having them trained in Islamic scholastic knowledge. One is repeatedly told by natives in Java that the patronage of *pesantrens* [Islamic centres of learning] is strongly declining and that everybody is nowadays bent on attending *school*. The fear expressed in earlier days in pious circles that such a *rapprochement* to Dutch culture would endanger the faith inherited from the forefathers is being more and more replaced by the conviction that is possible to remain true to the old religious concepts and customs without continuing to live in the old ignorance, from which the best possible way to be extricated is to entrust oneself completely to the training in the European school, and even, if circumstances permit, also to education in an European family. This trust is not unconditional when the native is forced because of lack of space or financial reasons to send his children to a Christian school, *where children are obliged to attend lectures on religion*. The fact that many are prepared to take this in their stride is certainly strong proof of how deeply the need for education is felt. It would be dangerous to draw any other conclusions. [Forced religious instruction] is very much felt to be objectionable, and the fact that of necessity many remain silent should not tempt us to hope that subsidized Christian schools of this kind would be a suitable means to satisfy the enormous demand of natives in Java for European education.

It is true that, owing to the religious tolerance of the vast majority of the Javanese aristocracy, which borders on indifference, as well as the fact that the lower classes of the people have been used for centuries to dealing with people of different races and religions, the missions here do not experience the degree of difficulty that in many other Muslim countries obstructs them. On the other hand, the majority of the Mohammedan religious teachers, although generally used to restricting themselves within their own narrow field, are stimulated into reaction by the vigorous activity of the missions. They consider this attempt to convert the Mohammedans to Christianity as part of a European plan to rob the natives of what Allah has destined for them in the other world, after first having taking away already so many of their earthly possessions. If the government forces people who desire Western-style education to publicly subsidize schools *in which Christian religious instruction is imposed on the pupils*, then one can undoubtedly expect strong opposition to be mounted against the idea of association. This would either stop the *rapprochement* to our culture or would at least result in a strong demand that if schools with a specifically religious basis were to be subsidized, the natives should be allowed to express their preference, which would be for subsidized schools on the basis of Islam ...

Let me stress it again: the strong desire to be incorporated in our cultural life, which has been apparent in the native society during the last quarter of a century, *has occurred entirely without any reference to religion*. We should rejoice that the natives have not been held back by the system of Islam, which actually is opposed to such an association, from striving for such a *rapprochement* as is also so desirable to us ...

With respect to the conviction that our people have the urgent obligation to satisfy the ever-pressing demand of more intellectually developed Javanese and Malays for better education, the objection is sometimes raised that in this way only the upper layers of the people are reached, while the infinitely larger masses of common people remain untouched. And it is further argued that because of this a hitherto unknown cleavage will come about in the level of civilization of the aristocracy and the masses, which threatens to break the natural links between them.

It would undoubtedly make our task more successful if we could start from all directions at once, providing one knew the correct methods and had sufficient means at one's disposal to lift by means of effective education the mass of small Javanese peasants simultaneously to a higher intellectual level and to draw the Javanese aristocracy as closely as possible within our own spiritual atmosphere. However, this is beyond our power if only because the psychology of the common man poses for the moment too many insoluble riddles. And since we lack the proper data to make a correct diagnosis, the prescribed cure could well turn out to be completely wrong. With every attempt we make in the present circumstances to bring the villagers to a higher level of civilization, we run the great danger of superimposing something on them that they do not want, while at the same time we cannot be sure at all that such a thing is in fact suitable for them.

I do not hold any great hopes for the recently established village schools. They probably will not do any harm, but even the greatest optimist could not possibly consider these institutions as a gigantic step forward in the direction of association. I would rather see important experiments of this kind postponed until the time when we can make use of a considerable number of highly trained Javanese who can combine Western wisdom with Eastern experience. They would also be less likely to err than we in determining how the small-scale farmers of their own people could be induced to participate in the present-day economic life within the limits imposed upon them by nature.

Surely one prefers to start a project at a point that shows the greatest possibility of success; and one can be sufficiently sure of success if one starts with the Javanese upper classes ...

No less urgent than the speedy multiplication of facilities by which natives can obtain the higher training desired by them is the need for the government to revise its practice of job delegation in the public service in such a way that all the work that can be done by the modern educated indigenes is in fact also entrusted to them. The present situation should no longer be maintained where the young natives who have come to the fore as the best products of the new policy are considered by the departmental chiefs as phantasms, which after a great deal of hesitation are pushed into some forgotten corner where one can no longer be disquieted by their countenance. Surely these people do not come falling out of the sky like meteors. Their arrival could have been expected for years and there is no excuse at all for being unprepared. The Indies Government must keep hammering on the door of the Department of Interior Administration and the Department of Education until they have satisfactorily solved these various interrelated problems ...

Fainthearted critics have often tried to put the fear of God into the supporters of association by prophesying that if this policy is continued it will eventually have disastrous consequences, and that an unbalanced and rebellious class of natives will be created, having lost contact with their own society without fitting into another social system.

Such objections have always been uttered in the past when a particular group of people tried to push itself out of a way of life that had become too narrow for it. However, such objections have never been able to stop this craving for enlightenment once awakened. We have also experienced political and social changes that did not occur as peacefully and gradually as had been intended. In these ventures to unknown heights there are always some participants who make thoughtless, giddy jumps, which cause some moments of general confusion. We expect that this will also occur in the East Indies, and those prophets we just mentioned will be ready to point out triumphantly that their sombre divinations have been fulfilled. We only hope that because of the exceptionally peaceful nature of the natives things will not get too far out of hand, and that under wise direction equilibrium will be soon restored.

However, we must by no means think that we are still at the crossroads in the history of the development of the Indonesians and that the decision whether to go to the right or the left is dependent on the will of our government. The process has begun without having been elicited by the government or the people of the Netherlands; in fact it has occurred despite unofficial obstructions. It is no longer a question whether those sections of the people of the Archipelago who are most open to higher development will surpass us in the intellectual field or not; the only question we can raise is whether the further growth of this movement that has begun so forcefully will occur with our co-operation and under our guidance, or whether it will happen despite our opposition and under the direction of others, who would soon appear on the scene. It seems to me that the answer to this question could hardly be the subject of a prolonged discussion ...

We have viewed here the consequences of the adopted policy of association from the restricted vantage point of Islamic policy. But we may certainly add that it also provides the solution in so many other aspects of the problem to the future relationship between the people of the Indies Archipelago and us. Also from a general political point of view it is extremely important for us not to wait until, surprised by events, we have to make concessions to the natives, concessions which at present we still give to them voluntarily and in a form we consider the most suitable.

Dr van Hoevell many years ago desired that the Netherlands should try to overcome the disturbances in the interior of Java not by the building of material fortresses but rather fortresses of gratitude in the hearts of the Javanese. Such idealism is too noble and beautiful to be realistic. A people is never thankful even for the greatest benefactions superimposed by foreigners. However, if on the other hand by means of association, which is desired by both sides, the stage is reached where both the Javanese and the Netherlands have achieved the greatest possible common intellectual ground, then there will be no need to speak about gratitude to foreigners because what was foreign will have become part of oneself; there will be only Eastern and Western Netherlanders, who politically and nationally form a unity, irrespective of the difference in race.

What then could possibly obstruct the realization of this ideal? The differences in skin colour or background? From how many countries of Europe and Asia do many of the present Netherlanders originate, and what is more untrue and conceited than the line in our national anthem, "free from foreign stains"? The mixing of our blood with that of the Indonesian race has already been occurring to such an extent for centuries that all shades between white and black in skin colour are represented among Netherlanders.

What then about too great a distance in civilization and philosophy of life? The upper classes among the natives would like nothing better than to reduce this gap to the minimum. Their students, who live with us at Leiden, Delft, and Amsterdam, are spiritually much closer to you and me than whole classes of our own people and sailors. However, such a strong spiritual unity is never responsible for tying a whole people together. A common past is the thing that holds together what is variegated; this applies to the various classes of our people, and it applies also for our people as a whole with respect to Indonesia, although the realization of this unity has not yet penetrated all strata of our nation.

Islam and Christianity can in the practical national life tolerate each other quite well, as long as the Pan-Islamic idea is set aside... So far as tolerance is concerned many of us could learn a great deal from the majority of natives.

As a student I once attended a lecture by Ernest Renan on the question, "What actually constitutes a nation". The answer was in the main as follows: the really constituting element of a nation is neither race nor skin colour, nor language, nor religion, nor natural frontiers, but it is "le desir d'etre ensemble" [the desire to be together]. And although this phrase does by no means explain it completely, it undoubtedly contains part of the truth. We know the feeling that despite differences in origin, sphere of life, and level of civilization, and notwithstanding all the political and religious dissension, when it comes to the point, we all want to remain together as Netherlanders. So now we have the situation where the most noble representatives of a large group of peoples, who already for a long time have been under our political control, urgently beg to be adopted ... into our national family. Let us extend our hands to them, and let us transform into positive deeds this mutual desire to live together as one nation, "le desir d'etre ensemble", so as to show that our small nation has never forgotten to perform great deeds!

C. Snouck Hurgronje, *Nederland en de Islam* (Leiden: Brill, 1911), pp. 79-88.

26 J. W. T. Cohen-Stuart: The Indonesiation of the Colonial service, 1907

It is of great importance for the continuation of our rule that we should bind the people to us, partly by letting them participate as much as possible in government administration and partly by letting them feel our rule as little as possible. Both these objectives can be achieved most effectively if we restrict ourselves as much as possible to a supervising role and leave the task of governing wherever possible to the natives themselves. In this way also the mistakes that are made will not be blamed so much on us as on their own countrymen ... The appointment of native officials instead of European ones wherever feasible will also greatly decrease the burden on the budget ... A European type of administration is too expensive for a country like the Indies ... Obviously a rich country like the Netherlands with a population six times smaller can easily afford a larger budget than the Indies, which is a poor country. But a serious inconsistency has crept into the Indies budget, which has to provide for a European administration that is twice as expensive as that in the Netherlands. The first thing to be done is to change this situation, if we want to be in a position to provide properly for the unmet needs of the Indies. And this can only be done by gradually replacing European officials by native ones, who will be paid at a lower rate based on the lower standard of living of the people ...

J. W. T. Cohen-Stuart, "*Oprichting van Inlandsche Rechtscholen*", (*Indische Gids* 1907, pp. 1332-33.

27 Controversy on mass education

1. D. Fock: On mass technical education, 1905

We must go in the direction of technical education ... I do not want a slow and gradual development ... I envisage a large-scale organization. I realize that this will cost money, but this expenditure is in fact an investment. Only practical education can advance the population economically. The cost should not be considered unbearable, and most of the money can be found by borrowing. This is a matter which cannot and must not be postponed any longer. A slow and gradual expansion will achieve nothing ...

S. L. van der Wal, *"Het Onderwijs Beleid in Nederlandsch Indie 1900-1940—een bronnenpublicatie"* (Groningen: Wolters, 1963), p. 45, note 1.

2. C. Snouck Hurgronje: On the fallacy of mass education, 1905

Supposing that it was desirable to industralize a large sector of the Javanese economy, it would still not be possible to achieve this because the native population itself has not the slightest interest in the matter. I say it again. The European educator is only able to guide development. He cannot create something out of nothing ... Let us suppose that the foreign doctor, in spite of this completely impassive attitude of the patient, is not only able to give a correct diagnosis but also an effective remedy—risky suppositions to make. The result will be that these people, after having completed their training, will ask the government for suitable employment, because their own society can neither use nor pay for such highly trained workers. The state, which created these superfluous tradesmen and industrial workers, will not be able to back down from its obligation to keep them alive ... Saving banks and credit institutions, emigration, and technical training, if superimposed from above ... do not bring the Javanese one step closer to prosperity ...

S. L. van der Wal, *"Het Onderwijs ... "*, pp. 49-50.

3. J. B. van Heutz: On Fock's plans, 1907

Two possibilities were open to me: either to carry out blindly what the ill-informed Minister wanted, which would have cost the Treasury approximately 100 million guilders per annum; or I could have discreetly gone my own way still leaving him [i.e. Fock] the honour of being progressive in education. I have chosen the second path and I have restricted the expansion of *Tweede Klasse Scholen* [more advanced vernacular schools] as much as possible ... And, more realistically, I have immediately set up village schools which only receive temporary government support and which—at an annual outlay of one million guilders—will achieve just as much in the way of reading, writing, and arithmetic as the far too expensive *Tweede Klasse Scholen* of the Minister. The latter are only useful for the comparatively small group of people who are entirely removed from the village sphere ...

S. L. van der Wal, *Het Onderwijs* ..., p. 123.

28 Obstacles to vernacular education

1. J. H. Gunning: On the progress of village schools, 1919

In some parts of the Priangan [West Java], on the west coast of Sumatra and Korintji [West Sumatra] there seems to exist a great deal of interest in village schools. But everywhere else ... the founding and upkeep of village schools depend on the pressure of the native heads, which varies from "gentle persuasion" to outright force ... Perhaps initially one has fallen for the illusion that villagers were already influenced by the new spirit that animates the "awakening East". After all it is easy to believe in what one hopes for ... But when it became clear that in the village the situation had remained almost unchanged, it was obvious that the activity of the government officers would be construed into a command from above ... The natives know indeed that it pays them to obey the government ...

J. H. Gunning, *Koloniaal Onderwijs Congres, 1919. Praeadviezen*, p. 105

2. C. O. van der Plas: On forceful methods in education, 1919

In Madoera I once saw a small group of crying children who, undergoing a form of punishment, sat in front of the house of the *Assistent Wedono* [lower indigenous official]. They were stamped all over in ink with *"Je Maintiendrai"* [motto on the coat of arms of the Dutch royal house], because they had been guilty of not attending school ...

C. O. van der Plas, *Koloniaal Onderwijs Congres, 1919. Praeadviezen*, p. 212.

29 P. Post: The need to adapt village schools to local demands and culture, 1927

In the beginning the school is determined by society ... When the school has finally been completely accepted it will be possible to introduce very carefully new elements. Only then and not earlier will the school begin to influence its surroundings ... At present the village school has not been adapted to [local conditions] and is therefore not accepted ... [Post argued that, for example, school times should be changed to suit village life].

The village school, however primitive it is, is something new. It is different from the *pesantren*, which is a haven for everybody in the district. In harvest time, when many migrate elsewhere to work, the *pesantren* opens its doors widely for everybody ... The village school is not a centre, except in those very few places where the teacher has a strong personality. After one o'clock it is dead until half past seven the next morning. If only this school could have been built in such a way that it could become an extension, an enrichment, of village life. In Javanese districts, for example, this could be done by building the school in the form of a *pendopo* [pavilion-like building]. Why should the children of a people that lives with its whole soul in nature be confined in such a sombre, windowless space? In this climate a roof is all that is needed. Classrooms could be separated by bamboo partitions, which would be as efficient as the present thin walls in the village schools. Behind the *pendopo* there should be the *dalem*, the house of the teacher. In the East there have never been schools as we know them. The *asramas* [dormitories], the *pesantrens*, are the homes of the pupils, or at least the teachers live there ... The *pendopo* would be suitable for meetings in the evening, where the contact with the family or rather the *desa* [village] can be better established than in the houses of the parents ...

If it was possible to have elementary religious instruction, then the school would undoubtedly rise very much in stature. This religious education would have to be in accordance with the wishes of the respective parents in the villages, which—and here there is a great difference between these people and Europeans—hardly differ in rural areas ... An investigation among six hundred families in Batavia ... showed that all of them, without exception, wanted religious instruction ... Why then should this unhealthy and very miserly idea of a school without religious instruction be maintained any longer ... ?

P. Post, "*Advies van den Onderwijsraad aan den Directeur van Onderwijs en Eeredienst over de verhooging van de maatschappelijke en karaktervormende waarden van het Inlandsch Lager Onderwijs* ... 17 October 1927, no. 345" (Publicaties van het Bureau van den Onderwijsraad VII, Weltevreden, 1929), Bijlage F.

30 The indigenous literacy rate—from the 1930 Census

Geographical Distribution of Literacy 1930

	%
Menado (Northern Sulawesi)	21.9
Moluccas	14.5
South and East Borneo	5.3
Timor	5.1
West Borneo	5.0
Sulawesi	4.2
Bali and Lombok	3.2
Sumatra	10.7
Java and Madura	5.5
Outer Islands	8.7
Netherlands Indies	6.4

Literacy in Urban Areas 1930

	%
Makassar	12.7
Bandjermasin	10.0
Medan	23.5
Padang	28.9
Palembang	13.2
Batavia	11.9
Semarang	12.1
Surabaja	12.2
Bandung	23.6

The Growth of Literacy between 1920 and 1930

	1920 %	1930 %	Increase %
Java and Madura			
Males:			
Adults	6.5	11.4	4.9
Children	3.2	7.6	4.4
Females:			
Adults	0.5	1.3	0.8
Children	0.6	1.6	1.0
Outer Islands			
Males:			
Adults	12.6	17.2	4.6
Children	6.2	8.3	2.1

Females:			
Adults	3.3	4.6	1.3
Children	1.7	2.9	1.2
Netherlands Indies	3.9	6.4	2.5

Volkstelling 1930, Deel V, Hoofdstuk VII, 83, Deel VIII, Hoofdstuk IX, p. 31.

31 The Resident of Besuki: Education and radical nationalism, 1924

In a prosperous country with an economically healthy peasant class Communism will find it difficult to get a hold and extremist political agitation will be the exception.

The government will have to take upon itself the difficult task of achieving this objective by means of a complexity of measures, which naturally should be concerned in the first place with native agriculture, the major means of existence of the population.

There can hardly be any doubt that the productive capacity of native agriculture can be improved to a considerable extent.

So far the farmers have made very little use of the comprehensive government aid scheme, partly because of the conservatism inherent in the peasantry and partly because this scheme did not go far enough.

For years funds that should have been earmarked for agriculture were diverted to education owing to the growing pressure of the natives for more and better schools. Education is after all considered in native society at its present stage of development as a panacea for all evils, and it is too often lost sight of that the graduates of the rather sophisticated primary schools have to fall back on a society that lacks the capital needed to make these intellectuals productive.

Periods when the arts, sciences, and educational institutions are flourishing usually coincide with or are preceded by periods of great economic development, which create a big demand for intellectually trained people in all sorts of fields. The situation in the Indies, however, is rather different. The structure of colonial society is more complicated as, in addition to the indigenous population, which is lacking in capital, there is an economically strong group of foreigners. And it is in fact this foreign capital that has caused the expansion of education in its present form. As soon as the demand of this comparatively small sector for intellectually trained personnel is satisfied, the system will gradually but surely get into a jam.

It is therefore becoming more and more obvious that it is necessary to take more immediate measures to increase prosperity and to create a national indigenous capital. In order to restore the threatening imbalance, for a number of years in the future more funds should be allocated to the Department of Agriculture than to the Department of Education. The government lacks the means to expand energetically in all directions at once ...

The present political situation in Java is the result of a *natural drive for development* by a resistance movement which, although it has been unable to remain free from foreign influences, would also without these influences have come about, though perhaps under another name, with the same extremist and Communist tendencies. So it is a movement that has *not* been instigated and sustained from the *outside*, but has its origin in *internal* conditions. The realization of this fact is very important because it indicates at the same time what kind of measures should be taken in opposing this resistance movement. While measures of a political nature would be sufficient to deal with a resistance movement that has come about as a result of outside influences, a resistance that is rooted in the country itself can only be combated by improving local conditions ...

The indigenous education policy that has been pursued in the Indies for a considerable number of years now has resulted in the establishment of a number of educational institutions which yearly produce a large number of people trained for a particular job or profession. However, when they return to their own social milieu they will have difficulty in finding employment because the people are not wealthy enough to afford their services and to sustain them properly in their particular professions or trades. Not all of these graduates can be absorbed by the civil service or the large plantation concerns, because the number of vacancies is limited. Still, every year hundreds of graduates from primary schools and *M.U.L.O.* schools—tradesmen, doctors, and now also engineering graduates, and within a few years Masters of Law—will have to be found jobs. The government and private industry will soon no longer be able to employ all new graduates. And it is also very doubtful if this problem can be solved by attracting foreign capital, as it is by no means certain that French, English, German, American, or Japanese companies will be willing to employ *native* doctors, engineering graduates, and Masters of Law, not to mention the graduates of the primary schools and *M.U.L.O.* schools who every year enter full life by the hundreds. The result will be the creation of an intellectual proletariat which, unable to find work, will be an easy target for agitation, embittered as it must be about a government that, having provided the opportunity to obtain qualifications for advancement, has at the same time failed to provide possibilities for employment ...

Koloniaal Archief, *Resident van Besoeki aan den Gouverneur-Generaal, 7 November, 1924. No. 60/geheim. Mailrapport 70x/25. Geheim Kabinet Verbaal 29 Mei 1928 H9.*

32 J. Meyer Ranneft: Speech on education and radical nationalism, 1927

Although I am a layman in the field of education, I still venture to participate in this debate on the grounds of my deep conviction that in the final analysis education is only a means to an end—and that it may never be more than that and become an end in itself. After all the interests and needs of society come first and about them I want to say a few words now. Society in the Indies, which the government is at present forcing to develop rapidly by means of education, has two important characteristics. Firstly, this society ... is one of sharp contrasts; it is ... a conglomeration in a labile state of equilibrium. Secondly, the country is poor, and there is an enormous difference in per capital national income between us and Holland—not to speak of America. When we examine the results of our education system, we see that they fall short just on these two important points. Are the discontent and the contrasts heightened by education? Is education a contributary factor in making these [socio-economic] contrasts so sharp that the country could disintegrate? Do not misunderstand me ... I realize that education brings development, a greater sense of self-importance, nationalism. I realize this and appreciate this. I also realize that just because of this a struggle will come about ... which may bring progress ... If I did not realize this I would not stand here before you and fight.

However, in spite of all this there is still the threat of dangerous excesses. I can appreciate struggle ... but not murder. I can appreciate nationalism, but not the extreme form which is called Communism, with its tactics of terror and force ... Mr Moelia [moderate Indonesian nationalist] said yesterday in his important speech ... that the impact of education in this respect is not of primary importance ... I also believe that this is so, but that does not mean that although of secondary importance this impact should not deserve our fullest attention. It is in Japan [cited by nationalists as a country with a progressive education policy] that the government keeps a constant watch to ensure that education shall not produce the dangers and excesses I have just mentioned. Do such dangers also exist in this country? If so, to what extent? This I do not know, and that is why I am asking for an investigation in order to get some clarity in this matter. In any case there are surely some indications that these dangers in fact exist ...

Let us for example consider the age of the Communists who have been transported to Digul [concentration camp in West New Guinea]. We see that more than 80 per cent of them are young men, who were educated during the last twelve years [see document 58]. At the same time we must consider that the large expansion of the Dutch-Native Schools began in 1914. Is there a connection between these two facts?

We must also keep in mind the large number of boys who could not cope with the programme and had to leave school before the completion of the course. There is something wrong with this almost institutionalized failure rate, which particularly in the case of the Dutch-Native Schools is very high. I have calculated that within ten years between twenty and thirty thousand people will wander around Java who have not been able to complete their schooling and therefore will be disappointed ...

I must admit that I am sorry that we have already sacrificed so much to the spirit of the times, even to the extent that we have already established a Faculty of Law and that in a little while we will also have a Faculty of Medicine. While in themselves they are excellent institutions, we must ask ourselves in the first place whether we will be able to pay for them and secondly whether they actually fit into the framework of the existing stage of development in this country. The opportunities to receive tertiary education elsewhere, that is, in the mother country, appear quite adequate ... Those Ethical, socially committed people [who advocated a continued expansion of Dutch-language education] are certainly idealistic. And although I also feel somewhat Ethical and socially committed, I wish to add immediately that I always look at these matters rather soberly and always want to stay within the realm of reality and possibility. And if it is not possible, then I desist.

But people here want to persist in the manner of *"apres moi le deluge"* ["after me comes the deluge"] and everything will be all right. No ... but everything will not be all right. A father at a certain moment says: my sons must have a brilliant education, they must go to university; and everything the father owns he spends on this education, but when he cannot sustain it he has to send his sons into the world with uncompleted degrees and half-cocked ideas. This is the great danger in the strong pressure for more education. And the situation will become steadily more dangerous when in future budgets more money will be allocated to education, unless, as we hope, more people will object to this and put up a strong opposition.

In my view education is not the panacea that will improve the lot of this people. Intellectualism has already taken too strong a hold here. It is not that I am against the intellectual development of everybody, but if we look at the countries where education has been more practical in nature and has been restricted to what is actually needed by society, then we see that the results of education are much better than here, where education is still solely directed at the gathering of ever more knowledge. This increased knowledge is good in itself but it should also be practically useful.

And we must ask ourselves whether we are on the right track with our education in so far as the demands of the economy are concerned. Education should be of benefit to the economy in that it should strengthen business life by producing native employees who can handle any type of job in industry, commerce, and shipping in the same way as is now done by Europeans. However, in this area a great deal is still left to be desired at this moment ... because we are on the wrong track, from which we must turn away as soon as possible. Therefore, we must relate education to practical life and adapt to the economic needs of this country.

Mr Stokvis [Socialist Member of the *Volksraad*]: Cheap labour!

Volksraad. Handelingen, 22 Juni 1927, pp. 305-8.

33 Suroso: Speech on the right of Indonesians to receive Dutch-language education, 1927

The great interest shown recently by Europeans in native education leaves me with a feeling of suspicion rather than gratitude ... In this interest I can only see the danger that the education system for the native people will be disorganized and that its expansion will be halted ... Furthermore it has been suggested that an education policy should be introduced that is based on the needs of the economy. The advocates of such a policy are correct, the only purpose of education in their eyes being to train employees, in thinking that the results of education should be judged by the number of graduates produced. It is therefore not surprising that these voices were only heard for the first time after the Communist danger had started to threaten this country. For is it not true that many consider the existence of unemployment as the cause of this danger ... ?

The Netherlands Indies is now being drawn into the world economy. Its population does not only consist of indigenous people, but also of an ever-increasing number of foreigners, who consider Indonesia as their fatherland. If these population groups are allowed to receive a better education ... then it is no more than just that the government should bring the indigenous population to the same level of development as the other population groups, so that it may take a worthy place in the world economy and can cope better with the struggle for life. So, if every European or Chinese child is given the opportunity to receive elementary education in the European primary school or Dutch-Chinese School, then every indigenous child must also be given this opportunity ... The fact that European society is in a better economic position than the other groups is due in the first place to the education the European receives ... The level of development in a society is thus to a certain extent dependent on the level of education the people receive. That this could well result in an intellectual revolution, because society is living through a period of intellectual overproduction, is unavoidable. But are the inventions in all kinds of scientific fields in Europe not the result of this kind of overproduction? Overproduction and unemployment actually stimulate every individual to find a way out, to carve out a new means of existence. Therefore this phenomenon ... if it exists at all, causes me no anxiety, but it rather encourages me ...

Volksraad. *Handelingen*, 22 June 1927, pp. 310-11.

34 The Depression and education

1. Despatch of the Minister of Colonies (Colijn) to the Governor-General (De Jonghe), 10 October 1930

It should be clear by now even to the greatest optimists that we are not dealing with a short-term economic disruption ... This is a general collapse which will severely affect the world economy for years to come ...

I do not have to emphasize to Your Excellency that I am very much aware of the very great importance which in many ways is attached to a steady expansion of all types of education facilities. Nevertheless, I cannot close my eyes to the precarious financial state of the country, which decidedly does not permit an expansion of education at the present rate ...

Koloniaal Archief. *Minister van Kolonien aan den Gouverneur Generaal, 10 October, 1930. Verbaal 10 October 1930 no. 23/754.*

2. Despatch of the Governor-General (De Jonghe) to the Minister of Colonies (Colijn), September 1932

Before the beginning of the economic depression, when there was no possibility of economizing on the present scale, it was clear—also because of the investigations of the Dutch-Native Schools Commission—that during the preceding years unintended or unforeseen outgrowths had appeared in the education system ... which necessitated a drastic reorganization in the provision of education. This especially applied to Dutch-language education which, because of the unsystematic expansion of Dutch-Native Schools and also because of subsidy legislation that was too liberal and difficult to control, soon came to be disproportionate to the capacity of the Indies Treasury and the socio-economic need for Dutch-speaking personnel. It was thus obvious that the government, when it was forced by the Depression to severely curtail education, *had to* grasp this opportunity to introduce reforms at the same time. To a certain extent it is fortunate that compelling external causes instigated this action; without this stimulus the purging process would have taken much longer and the opposition would have been even stronger and tougher. But it *had to come* ...

S. L. van der Wal '*Onderwijs* ... ' pp. 562-63.

35 J. F. H. A. de la Court: A postscript on the principle of concordantie, 1945

The fact that the education system was too expensive and too top-heavy was caused primarily by the insistence on *concordantie*, i.e. the requirement that education in the Indies should be equal to that in the Netherlands not only in terms of standards but in everything else ... Thus this Amsterdam standard has pushed more advanced education to such a level that a far too large proportion of the education budget was devoured, while the social effect of this education remained far below expectations. This was so in the first place because the capacity of the Indies society to absorb graduates was inadequate ... causing discontent and disappointment, and secondly because only a few Indonesian parents could afford to pay for this long-extended schooling ...

Dutch-language education dislocated society and was not adapted to the needs of the country. It stimulated the desire to reach a higher salary scale rather than the desire to serve the country and the people. It sometimes offered material advantages, but it did not create idealism ...

J. F. H. A. de la Court, *Paedagogische Richtlijnen voor Indonesie* (Deventer: 1945), pp. 69-70.

Part II
Nationalism

Anti-colonial movements in the nineteenth century

Nationalism in the sense of resistance to foreign rule existed in Indonesia during the whole period of the Dutch presence. In the Dutch East India Company era, when the foreign impact on traditional civilization was slight, armed uprisings against the colonial power were sporadic. In Java, where the power of the Company was centred, the people as a whole tolerated the usurpers with sullen resignation, firmly believing that the wheel of history was bound to turn in the foreseeable future. But during the nineteenth century, when Dutch influence was felt more deeply and by widening circles, the reaction of the Javanese changed and armed uprisings occurred with increasing frequency as the century progressed. In the period 1840-75 there were only six years in which Java was free from anti-colonial rebellions or disturbances.

Most of these uprisings showed distinct millenarian tendencies. The leaders were usually *guru ngelmu* (mystics), or *kiyayi* (Islamic teachers), who were reputedly endowed with magical powers and presented themselves to the peasantry as the *Ratu Adil*, the long-expected Messiah, who would drive out the Dutch and establish a kingdom on traditional lines in which happiness, justice, and prosperity would prevail. The concept of the *Ratu Adil* is contained in the various prophecies that were current in Java from the end of the eighteenth century. The best known were those attributed to Jojobojo, an eleventh century ruler of the kingdom of Kediri in East Java. With the growing impact of Islam on Java during the nineteenth century, the Muslim concept of the *Mahdi*, the just ruler who would appear and abolish corruption and injustice, often becomes intertwined with the traditional Javanese prophecies. This is clear from the version of the Jojobojo prophecies published by the Dutch scholar Wiselius in 1872 (*see* document 36).

Most of these nineteenth century rebellions were ill co-ordinated, localized, and badly planned affairs, which could be easily suppressed by the colonial power.

An important exception was the Java War (1825-30), a fierce guerilla struggle led by the Javanese prince Dipanegara, which resulted in tens of thousands of casualties and economic destruction on a vast scale.

The major underlying cause of the war was economic. The principality of Yogjakarta, where hostilities broke out, had a long record of stubborn though unsuccessful anti-colonial resistance during which it had lost a great deal of its territory to the Dutch. This meant that the class of noble administrators and other courtiers surrounding the sultan in his *kraton* (palace complex), who were customarily not recompensed for their services in money but were given the use of land and the seignorial services to be rendered by the peasantry living on it, now had to be content with ever-decreasing parcels of land. This reduction in the standard of living naturally accentuated the already strong anti-colonial feeling of the nobility. However, in order to forego as little as possible of the grandiose style of living they were accustomed to, the nobility through their *bekel* (stewards) tried to extract as much as possible from the peasantry, which was already overburdened by a host of other taxes, including the extortionate dues levied at the numerous toll-gates, usually farmed out to the Chinese.

When after 1816 a number of private European planters arrived in the principalities of Central Java offering large sums as advance payment for the use of land and the services of the peasants living on it (in order to grow crops for export), it is not surprising that their requests were readily granted by the Javanese nobles. But when Governor-General van der Capellen, a genuine liberal and humanitarian, arrived in the principalities for a State visit, he was horrified to see these European planters living like feudal rulers lording it over the indigenous peasantry; and in 1823 with one stroke of the pen he forbade the renting of lands to Europeans. The Javanese nobility, although they were given their lands back, were now in a serious financial impasse, not only because their income was lowered, but particularly because they were required to reimburse the European planters for the advance payments, which in typical fashion had long since been dissipated, and the various improvements such as roads and irrigation works.

The ensuing discontent and hate engendered among the nobility against the Dutch, together with the great suffering of the peasantry, only needed the determined action of a respected leader to spark off a general resistance movement. This leadership was provided by Dipanegara, who held various grudges against the Dutch and was on bad terms with the immediate entourage of the ruling sultan. He strongly resented having been by-passed for the throne and, living as a recluse and mystic of the more orthodox Islamic kind, he severely criticized the immoral life at the court and the close relationship of the sultan and some of his advisers with the Dutch, the unbelievers.

Various intrigues by his enemies at the court as well as a number of affronts by the Dutch Resident Smissaert finally drove Dipanegara into open rebellion and to proclaiming himself the *Ratu Adil* and Sultan of all Java; large numbers of the nobility and the vast majority of the peasants thronged to join his forces. Document 37 contains excerpts from a manuscript about the outbreak of the war written by a Javanese nobleman who fought on the side of the Dutch.

It was also during the nineteenth century that the Dutch began to extend their effective control over the whole of the Archipelago via their "pacification policy". In some areas, such as Minangkabau (West Sumatra) and Atjeh (North Sumatra), this resulted in protracted and bloody struggles.

In Minangkabau the Dutch in 1821 interfered in a civil war fought between the *Padri*, fanatical Muslim reformers, and the chiefs. Minangkabau was a matriarchical society with a strongly democratic tradition and political organization, which, like so many other areas of Indonesia, had adopted and adapted Islam on its own terms, effecting a synthesis between the Islamic law and the *adat* (traditional customary law). When at the beginning of the nineteenth century a number of pilgrims returned from Mecca, where they had been imbued by the puritanical Wahabi doctrine, and tried to introduce by force similar reforms that were directed mainly at the power of the *adat* chiefs, a civil war broke out. By 1821, however, the *Padri* had occupied most of the country and introduced their system of theocratic rule. The Dutch, who were unaware of this, fell for the story told by emissaries from the *adat* party requesting military aid against the hated *Padri*, who, they claimed, could be easily defeated within a few weeks. In return the Dutch were promised the overlordship of Minangkabau, an area known for its coffee production and gold mining. Instead of weeks it took the colonial forces until 1837, when the last major *Padri* leader, Tuanku Imam Bondjol, was finally defeated. Document 38 contains excerpts from the memoirs of Tuanku Imam Bondjol.

Even longer and more devastating in terms of life and resources was the war against Atjeh (1873-1903), a sultanate at the northern tip of Sumatra, which until then had stubbornly defied any attempts by Europeans to obtain a foothold in its territory.

The piracy practised by the Achinese; the demands for protection of European plantations in the east-coast sultanates of Langkat, Deli and Asahan, which were claimed by the Achinese; and the fear that other imperial powers such as Germany, Italy, or the U.S.A. might establish themselves in the area finally caused the Dutch, with the blessing of the British, to send an expedition to Atjeh in 1873— an expedition that was promptly defeated. Other expeditions, although more successful in open combat, were unable to bring the

Achinese, who resorted to guerilla tactics, under complete Dutch control. Even less successful were a naval blockade, the establishment of a concentrated defence line around the capital, Kotaradja, and occasional attempts by the colonial government to bring the Achinese to heel by negotiations. Military bungling and official indecisiveness made the war drag on for decades, costing the colonial Treasury millions of guilders.

It was not until the acceptance by the colonial government of the advice of Snouck Hurgronje, the noted scholar of Islam who was the first European to make a thorough study of Atjeh and its civilization, that Achinese resistance finally began to crumble. Snouck was the first to point out that three parties were contending for supremacy in Atjeh: a small and unimportant group centred around the sultan, the *ulebalang* (the traditional nobility), and the *ulama*, Islamic religious teachers. The *ulama* were according to Snouck Hurgronje, the soul of the anti-Dutch resistance. They had a strong religious as well as political hold over the common people, who generally felt exploited by the *ulebalang*, and they exhorted the Achinese to fulfil their duties as Muslims and wage a *perang sabil* (holy war) against the *kafir* (unbeliever) invaders. Many *hikajat* (tracts) about the holy war were circulating around Atjeh as a kind of war propaganda (excerpts from one of them are shown in document 39). Snouck argued that sitting behind a stationary defence line was useless and that if in particular the *ulama* led bands were relentlessly pursued until they were either annihilated or surrendered, the war would soon be over.

However, it was not until the end of the century that his plan was officially adopted. Its execution was put in the hands of General van Heutz, a fire-eating though capable field commander, who with his mobile columns was able to stamp out open resistance, bringing an uneasy peace to Atjeh until the outbreak of war with Japan in 1942.

Undoubtedly these nineteenth century uprisings and resistance movements form an important chapter in the history of the struggle waged by the various peoples of the Archipelago to retain or regain their freedom. But to classify them as early examples of Indonesian nationalism seems unhistorical. The concept of Indonesia was as yet unknown to the people concerned, who on the whole were interested solely in defending their particular region or sultanate and in protecting and reinforcing their own traditional civilization.

In Java the threat posed by the West to traditional civilization was met in a negative fashion, by ignoring it, by harking back to the past, and by transcending the problem by encouraging the latent popular expectation about the impending arrival of a golden age.

Indonesian nationalism in the sense of the desire to create a nation-state out of the vast agglomeration of ethnic, cultural, and geographical entities constituting the Netherlands Indies, is a comparatively recent phenomenon, dating from the early decades of the twentieth century.

36 J.A.B. Wiselius: The prophecies of Jobobojo, 1872

At that time there was no king who was more powerful than Djojobojo. He had two residences, one at Daha and the other at Kediri. From there he ruled the people that lived to the east and the west. He was feared by everybody, because he was well known for his greatness, power, and strength in war. All were impressed by his knowledge and obeyed his commands. Even more important, Djojobojo was an incarnation of Bhattara Wishnu, and no king anywhere dared to oppose him. His bearing commanded respect and reverence; he lived quietly as a recluse and never forgot to take account of God in his actions. He greatly desired a son, who finally was born to him ... Around this time Djojobojo was visited in his palace by a priest from Ngroem. He was a priest-king named Sultan Moelana Ali Samsoedjen who ... because of his knowledge of the supernatural, but even more because of his Arabic origin, caused King Djojobojo to treat him respectfully and reverently.

After the necessary formalities had been concluded, Samsoedjen began the conversation, saying: "Well, King Djojobojo, I have come here to familiarize you with the teachings of the Kitab Moesaran, in which it is revealed that your descendants who will remain unbelievers will still reign over Djaha for another three generations. After that your Kingdom will disappear and be succeeded by another.

Djojobojo kissed the feet of the priest-king, his teacher, after which Samsoedjen left.

About a month after the departure of the priest, Djojobojo invited his son Pagedongan to climb Mount Pandan with him to visit a Buddhist teacher and recluse called Soehita, who lived on the summit. He went on this journey equipped with all the gifts which the new religion [i.e. Islam] could give him. After Samsoedjen departed the King had been instructed in the Islamic religion [by] ... a priest from Ngroem. He also had been instructed in the science of the obscure, so that gradually he did not only know what had happened before the world was created, but also what was still to happen with regard to the kings who were to follow in the future and their actions. He could also prophesy about these future kingdoms, using symbols and allegories. All these qualities of the King helped to bring the country to prosperity. The inhabitants hardly needed to work. His army was the most powerful in all of Java. The great esteem in which the King was held continuously increased so that everybody feared him, because he knew about all the actions of the people on earth.

When Djojobojo and his son reached the top of Mount Pandan, the *pandita* [the Buddhist teacher] came out to welcome them and, on recognizing the King, he invited them to sit down ... The teacher called for a female servant (a nun), who soon appeared carrying food. She brought a tray with seven different dishes ... The food consisted of: 1. a dish of *djoewadah* (small cake made of rice flour, sugar, and coconut milk); 2. a basket of *koenir* (tumeric); 3. a dish of white onions; 4. a large pepper with *seroeni* flowers; 5. a large pepper with *melati* (jasmine) flowers; 6. various types of *kadjar* (herbal plant); 7. a basket of dry rice. Ki Hadjar. [the teacher] kneeled before the King and informed him that the meal was ready.

As soon as Djojobojo saw the food he became very incensed; he pulled out his dagger and killed the teacher and his servant. The pupils who witnessed this from afar were struck with fear and fled. Pagedongan, seeing what his father had done, wanted to say something, but fear prevented him from doing so.

Now Sri Boepatih Djojobojo came down from the mountain with his son and entered his *kraton*. He sat down and his son kneeled before him and asked his father why he had killed the teacher.

His father replied: "If this teacher had remained alive, he would have stopped the course of events. Also he has sinned against my teacher Sultan Moelana Ali Samsoedjen, because he made his secret public. Moelana Ali instructed me in the secrets of the book Moesaran after I had promised him not to speak about these matters in the island of Java ... "

After that, Djojobojo began to explain future events in connection with the seven dishes of food ...

"The seven dishes put in front of me by the teacher mean that seven eras will come in which seven kingdoms will succeed each other. After me another two generations will rule in Java. Then four kingdoms will arise, but my kingdom will not be among them because it will be erased from the world of states. I myself will depart from here and nobody will know my abode, because I will be contained in the soul of my teacher Sultan Moelana Ali, whose descendants will later be recognized as kings of Java.

"The first four kingdoms will be Djengala, Kediri, Singasari, and Ngoerawan. They will be very prosperous and justice will prevail. But because of vendettas and internecine wars they will later be depopulated. This era will be known as Narpati. After one hundred years another era will begin, called Kala Wisesa. The King will reside at Padjadjaran and his reign will be called Teteken. There will be no war or injustice in the era. After one hundred years this blessed reign will end. A war will break out between relatives of the King about the succession to the throne. And all of them will be destroyed. Those in power will struggle continuously. There will be discord about the possession of land and the people must pay their taxes in gold. This is so because Ki Hadjar offered me *koenir*.

"When the last King of Padjadjaran has died another era will begin, called Srikala or Sangkala. The King is Praboe Brawidjaja ... he will reside at Madjalenka [Modjopahit] and the era of the government of this Nalendra Sangradja Pati will be called Nandoer Pati. The people will have to pay taxation in the form of money, because I was offered *djoewadah* on Mount Padjan by Ki Hadjar. After one hundred years this kingdom will be destroyed and another one of scented *glagah* [a reed like sugar cane] will come up [Demak]. The era will be known as Kala Wisaja. This will be a period of trouble. A change of religion will take place and the people will stop praying to the deities and there will be general prosperity. The King will be called Kipata Kala Wisesa and his reign will be called Adiati. He will be a just and pious prince who belongs to the order of *walis* or priests. He himself will give religious instruction and will found the holy faith. And everybody will respect him. The people in his lands [from Demak to Giri] will pay taxation in money, and also in silver and gold. This will be so because on the mountain I was offered *melati* flowers.

"After sixty-four years this kingdom will disappear and the era called Kala Djongga will begin in which the kingdom of Padjang will rise. The prince will be just and pious but he will not be succeeded by his children. The people will pay taxation in the form of money and clothing, because I was offered various kinds of *kadjar*.

"After thirty-five years Padjang will be replaced by the kingdom of Mataram, which inaugurates the era called Kala Sekti or Kala Sekti Doepara. Prince Praboe Njakra Buwana Senopati will be the first king. He is a descendant from priests and he will therefore gather all priests and soothsayers around him to dispense justice. This king is the wheel of the earth and his reign will inaugurate a time of prosperity in Java. War will make the kingdom powerful and women and treasures will be obtained as tribute. The king will be rich and feared by the people. Also the people will be rich and will therefore be able to pay heavy taxes. Taxation will be paid in reals [realen], because Ki Hadjar placed a plate with white onions in front of me. Another three generations will rule after him. Then after one hundred years this kingdom will perish because of a very fierce struggle between relatives about the succession to the throne.

"At this time seafarers [i.e. the Dutch East India Company] will come to Java to trade. They will interfere in the war. And they will close off the country from all sides and they will finally gain victory, after which they will divide the kingdom. One part will be returned to Padjang and will be called Njakra Wati Surja. This era will be called Sangkara because these times will be violent. Tax will be paid in [local] money and reals, because on Mount Padjan I was given *melati* flowers.

"After four kings have reigned for a period of sixty years over this kingdom a time of confusion will come about. The wrath of God will come over Java, the prosperity of the country will disappear, and great disasters will follow one after the other. God's wrath will increase from year to year. The upper classes will be cursed and the people will be needy. The people will not be able to live peacefully in their houses, and they will be living at the side of the roads and they will wander aimlessly in the market-place. The upper classes will be cruel to the common people, who will also become immoral. Truth will disappear and lies only will be spoken. Honest men will no longer be found, and many will be poor. Women also will have lost all their shame. The justice of the King will be uncertain, labile, and not severe enough. The type of tax he will demand will change but the amount will increase all the time. Masses of ... buffaloes, cows, horses, calves, weapons, lances, and daggers, will be paid in tax. Money and the English coins will be exported from the country, and during wartime no food will be found because the harvest will fail and the country will be flooded. It is not certain where the King will reside. His commands will be disastrous for the people. In short, the government will be bad, and it will be as if the devils are ruling. Two seafarers of high rank, who are rich and courageous, will now become powerful in Java. After suppressing the people they will disappear again. Disasters will occur more frequently and will no longer be prevented. The people will move about aimlessly. They will move to the north and to the south and backwards again. They will finally die without having made the pilgrimage [to Mecca]. There will be many robberies committed by hardened highwaymen. But now also the end of this kingdom is near. There will be eclipses of the sun and the moon, and rain, wind, earthquakes, typhoons, and ash rains will come about. The seasons will be confused. And everywhere there will be war and rebellion. The enemies [i.e. the Dutch] will continuously change their tactics. They will become very powerful. Many of them will come to Java and they will act more and more daringly. All this will take place because on Mount Padjan the meal was served by Njai Endang, the nun.

"But then, oh my son Pagedongan, there will appear Si Tandjoeng Poetih [i.e. the *Ratu Adil*—the Saviour]. This prince will be pure of heart. He originates from Mecca and he is a descendant from one of the *walis* [i.e. the first missionaries who brough Islam to Java] of God. The name of the King will be Raden Amisan and his power will extend over the whole of the earth. Now there will be no more crime and all people will be like one family. This king will only desire to lead the people in calling out God's name, but not to command armies, because God alone will act as the great leader in battle. He will destroy the enemy and also everybody who rejects the appointment of this priest-king. Now justice will take its course. But also the king will forgive and give pardons. He will be fair and just. He will refuse to accept the goods of the people, because he is not interested in gathering treasures, but he will attempt to further the interests of his subjects. He will only charge one dinar on four *bouws* of land. This will happen because on Mount Pandan I was offered *seroeni* flowers. There will be prosperity in the whole of the land and the people will be contented. The people will have no difficulty in feeding and clothing themselves, because clothing and gold will be cheap. Also much gold will be brought to Java from overseas. There will no longer be dishonesty, and although there will be no police patrols, theft will disappear. Thieves will not disappear because of magic, but because they will be punished by this priest-king. He will command respect and everybody will fear him. Nobody will have anything to do with criminals and therefore the highway robbers will disappear. The gamblers will run into bad luck, and the criminals will flee into the forests. Cursed by the Almighty they will come to the mosque where, fearing the revenge of God, they will be converted.

"He [the King] will be like *gula djawa* [a type of brown sugar] and he will look like the *kenanga* [scented flower]. There will be no treasures in his palace because he is very gentle and generous to his people, yes, to all the people on earth. No longer will there be beggars. He will have them all brought together and he will give them food and clothing, and houses. He will continue to be generous to them and with the help of God they will all soon be prosperous and happy. They will all like to obey his commands and they will all love him. His commands are like gleaming precious stones ... [The kingdom of Tandjung Putih will disappear again. A period of unrest and lawlessness will exist until the coming of another Messiah called Eru Tjakra. After one century another period of confusion and internecine warfare will occur.] This confused state of affairs will come to the notice of the King of Pringgi [Holland], who will attack with an army that is immensely large. The noise made by these soldiers is like the sound of the sea when the high tide comes in. He will meet all the *boepatihs* [royal governors] in battle and will defeat them all, one after the other ... The whole of Java will finally be conquered. People from other countries who come to trade in Java will be pillaged. The King will rule with great severity over the Javanese and will let them feel his superiority. Once a year he will return to Pringgi, taking as tribute a number of families with him, while he will send a number of his own people to Java.

"Finally the great King, the *boepatih* of Ngroem, hears about this usurpation and supression. He is very angry and immediately calls for his *patih* [rank immediately below Regent]. He says: '*patih*, I hear that the island of Java has been conquered by people from the island of Pringgi and that one of them has put himself up as king. But he has not yet recognized me as his overlord, nor has he personally come to submit himself. Moreover he causes great confusion there, pillaging the merchants and transporting people as prisoners, about a thousand men each year. But the island of Java belongs to me. My forefathers did found a colony there ... We must therefore prepare for war and you, *patih*, must immediately depart for Java, taking a large number of men with you, and drive out the people from Pringgi. If they resist, destroy them to the last man and don't return until you have driven all of them out.' The *patih* immediately equips a force of four hundred thousand men which embarks in two thousand ships. With this force he goes to Java ... After the whole army has landed the war of annihilation will begin. All the people from Pringgi will perish and their bodies will be thrown in the rivers, which will be completely filled ... "

[During the twentieth century, the last part of Jojobojo's prophesies changed and the King of Ngrum became the Japanese, who would drive out the Dutch. The Japanese would stay in Java for the duration of the life cycle of the *mais* plant. After that Java would be free again.]

J.A.E. Wiselius, *Djaja Baja zijn leven en profetieen*. (Koninklijk Instituut voor de Taal-Land-en Volkenkunde van Nederlands Indie. Bijdragen) Derde Reeks. Zevende Deel. 1872, pp. 172-207.

37 T. Roorda: The beginning of the Rebellion of Dipanegara, according to a Javanese manuscript, 1860

[The story begins with the banishment by the English of Sultan Mangkubuwono II in 1812. He was succeeded by his son Mangkubuwono III, who was particularly fond of two of his sons, the eldest, called Dipanegara (or Diponegoro), and the youngest, Raden Mas Bagus Suradja. But when the Sultan offered Dipanegara the rank of crown prince he refused and asked that his younger brother Suradja be appointed instead. Dipanegara offered to act as guardian. This was agreed to by the Sultan and ratified by the Dutch colonial government, and when Mangkubuwouo III died in 1814 he was succeeded by his youngest son Suradja, who was then barely thirteen years old and took the name Sultan Bagus Djarot. Prince

Dipanegara and Prince Mangkubumi were appointed as his guardians.]

The King [Sultan Bagus Djarot] loved his elder brother Dipanegara very much and from time to time visited him in Selaradja. Dipanegara was equally fond of his younger brother and came to see him at least every three weeks. Prince Mangkoeboemi was a man of weak character and only acted as a guardian, but he was on good terms with Prince Dipanegara.

The King was barely thirteen years of age and his mother loved him so much that she gave in to all his whims. In order to develop him rapidly into an adult she gave him a number of pretty girls for company and he was trained and instructed in the lustful arts by his wet-nurse. This sinfulness did not cause any concern [at the court], but when Dipanegara heard about it, he wrote his mother the following letter: "Mother, I write you this letter because the way you are bringing up my younger brother, the King, leads him into sin. Do not let him go too far, but let him practise moderation. Do not let him commit sins. This will later go against him, because he who sins against God will experience the dire consequences". Although the mother replied that she would take heed, the young King continued to be brought up by her in lustfulness and luxury, and she gave in to everything he desired.

He married his cousin, a daughter of the former prime minister, Danoeredja, who had been murdered by the King in the palace because he was suspected of treason.

Somewhat later he ordered an extremely beautiful gold-plated carriage to be made; and when it was ready he ordered all his soldiers in the court to dress themselves in the European fashion and to accompany him on his pleasure tours. A hundred men had to ride in front and a hundred in the rear. He also ordered that they were to exercise within the walls of the palace and he wanted to drive everywhere within the palace precincts in every direction, with the result that the homes of the officials were demolished in order to make way for the new road. And to the east, west, north, and south, everything—whether it belonged to the upper classes or the common people—was damaged. The common people felt very unhappy. Many coconut trees were cut down to make way for the new road. Also outside the palace walls everything, including the Soeranatan [the meeting place of the Suranatas—a corps of armed priests] was destroyed. The people became disillusioned with the King. "What kind of a king is this? What strange ideas! And the great unhappiness he causes! He does not care about the unhappiness of the common people. The future looks grim."

In the mornings the King would go out riding in his gold-plated coach, dressed in sumptuous clothes, and with a detachment of cavalry in front and behind. The coach would go so fast that it would strike the riders in front; many fell from their horses and some even died. When told about this he did not care. It happened almost every day. On his return to the palace he drank alcoholic beverages as if they were water. He was not interested in acting virtuously, but completely surrendered himself to his pleasures and vanity. He forgot his Maker, the Creator of heaven and earth, but he always showed respect for his elder brother, Prince Dipanegara.

Dipanegara was a very pious person, who spent day and night praying in his chapel. Only on Thursday evenings did he go to his living quarters, but in the morning he would return to his chapel to pray and read the Qu'ran. This chapel was at Selaradja, where there was a beautiful park with a large flat black rock in the midst of all sorts of beautiful flowers and a pond with goldfish. The Prince recited the Qu'ran with a lovely and melodious voice, and when weary from the reciting would read the histories of the conquests of the old kings.

He reflected on the behaviour of his younger brother, who had been elevated to the throne and who now had become a fearless sinner, letting his passions run riot, ignoring the precepts of religion, and not caring to retain the grace of God. "My brother", he said, "does not care for the grace of God; I fear that he will lose it. I read here in these books about kings who have lived in luxury but whose lives were only of a short duration." ...

He invited his younger brother to visit him in Selaradja. When the young Sultan read the letter, he felt in his heart, "My brother Dipanegara is displeased with me. I have brought this upon myself."

The King went quickly to Selaradja and, not wishing to be accompanied by a large number of retainers, he only took forty men with him, and instead of his robes of state he wore old clothes. On his arrival in Selaradja his older brother came to meet him at the outer gate. They shook hands and, holding hands, they went inside and sat down on the big black rock in the shadow of a *komuning* tree [a large, shady tree].

Dipanegara said: "The reason, my royal brother, why I invited you here is that yesterday I read in the book *Nasihat-al-moeloek* the story of ancient kings of Arabia and other Western countries who were happy and unhappy ... " [Dipanegara then told his brother about various kings in the past who had been struck down by God because of their iniquitous lives.] Dipanegara, speaking in a friendly tone, said: "My royal brother, think about these stories which I have read to you from the books."

The young King thanked him and, realizing that his brother was reprimanding him, made all sorts of good promises, but they were feigned. He quickly took his leave and returned to his court, where the next morning he again went out in his coach to have fun.

In Selaradja the Prince ordered that all his subjects should say their prayers. "Whoever does not pray, I will drive away, and I will have their houses destroyed, be they old or young."

Prince Dipanegara continued to live the life of a holy recluse in a cave in the Silarong mountains, which he had equipped and prepared for the purpose. He often stayed there in quiet seclusion. He also liked to go on pilgrimages to holy places. And from time to time he went into the loneliness of Pamantjingan, Paranwedang, Parangkoesoema, the Potiman cave, and the Kamal cavern. Only taking two boys with him, he went along the seashore to the southern mountains to seclude himself in the Soeralamang and Saroengga caves. He did not want to wear beautiful clothes and wore a black coat and black trousers. He tried to attain the dignity of a *wali*, God willing. He did not want to lead a life of luxury and pleasure, arguing, "How long does one's life on earth last? At the highest only a hundred years, but the life in the other world is without end." And it was on that that he held his hopes, thinking, "If I come to die burdened with sin, then I will be damned. Yes, who will save me, when I am in hell having to suffer eternal punishment? The Qu'ran is the guide for a happy life and a holy death."

The Prince called his subjects together and let them read the Qu'ran, after which he treated them to a meal. He was very sympathetic to the fakirs [mendicant ascetics] and the poor; and he supported the needy and orphans. When persons came to him to ask permission to go on the pilgrimage to Mecca, he would provide them with their travel needs. He acted in this way in accordance with the precepts of the God-given Qu'ran ...

[Dipanegara went to visit a poisonous cave where he was subjected to various trials, which he believed were a sign that God had forgiven him for his previous sins. Some time after the return of Dipanegara to Selaradja (December 1822), the Sultan's life came to a sudden end.] The King went to his harem where he sat down among his wives. His mother sat very close to him. He ordered the *gamelan* [Javanese orchestra] to be played and its enchanting sounds could be heard. Songs were performed with lovely voices and the King enjoyed himself very much.

The King ordered the serving of the food, which had come from the outside from his uncle, Prince Mangkoeboemi. But the King could not enjoy the meal because he was shivering all over. While he put his hand out for a piece of meat, he said to his mother: "Why is it that I am so tired and listless?" When the meat was still on his tongue, he fell forwards with his face on his plate. He became unconscious and then died. He was lying there motionless, like a chicken that had been attacked by a kite. The mother jumped up in terror and grasped her son, but he was no longer breathing. There were loud lamentations in the palace and immediately messengers were sent to the [Dutch] fort and Selaradja, and soon all the princes and *boepatihs* had heard the news.

The Resident arrived soon afterwards and wanted an autopsy. Prince Dipanegara was deeply moved, and with tears in his eyes he said: "What did you expect, my brother? You did not listen to my warnings. It was ordained by the Almighty that your life would be short. The Doctrine says clearly that a Muslim prince who is unjust will have a short life."

The Resident said: "It would be better if the autopsy took place soon. If he really has been poisoned, we will do our best to ensure that the poison will come out by means of medicines. If the poison comes out he will soon recover and live."

The Prince was opposed to this. "No," he said, "this must not happen because after all it is the will of the Creator. My brother the King is surely dead and why should his body be mutilated? Certainly, if he would come to life again we would rejoice, but if he remains dead then he will have a scarred body. We should console ourselves and acquiesce in the will of God."

The mother, however, insisted that the proposal of the Dutchman should be followed up, and the others agreed with her. Quickly the body was opened up in the lumbar region. But no blood flowed and all were sorry. The mother cried uncontrollably, sorry that she had agreed. But after some time she consoled herself with the thought that it had been the will of God. The body was then cleaned and after the performance of the normal observances was interred at Djimatan.

Prince Dipanegara remained three days and three nights in the palace and then returned to Selaradja.

After the Governor-General in Batavia had been notified of the sudden death of the Sultan, it was decided there that the son of the deceased King should succeed to the throne under the guardianship of Prince Dipanegara. After this decision had been received by the Resident a meeting was held, in the Residency house, of the princes and the Prime Minister and his *boepatihs*. Prince Dipanegara and Prince Mangkoeboemi were the last to arrive. All the important Dutchmen were sitting on chairs in a long row, but none of the Javanese. Almost immediately the Resident jumped from his chair and, suddenly confronting Prince Dipanegara with the order received from Batavia, he said: "Prince Dipanegara, this is a decision which has been received from Batavia. Take it, and please read its contents."

The Prince took it and, thinking about it, acclaimed the decision.

He was opposed to only one point; and after a moment of reflection he told the delegates from Batavia and the Resident: "Resident, I have a request, and I hope that nobody will oppose it. All I wish is that the Government should allow me to live as a *pandita* and *santri* [mystic and pious Muslim]. I am pleased at the elevation of my nephew to the throne, but I am not interested in becoming a guardian. I cannot do it. Let my uncle Mangkoeboemi become guardian of my nephew."

But the Resident did not agree with the proposal. Out of fear of the Governor-General he did not dare to change anything in the decision and he kept protesting to the Prince, but in vain. The Resident Bongos [literally "black spot on the face", a nickname for Resident de Salis] became incensed.

The Prince then said: "Send somebody to Batavia and let the elevation of my nephew be postponed for a while. There is no haste; let us wait for the reply from Batavia so that I may be relieved of my burden." The Resident agreed and the coronation of the King was postponed until word had been received from Batavia.

The Queen Mother was very disquieted that the elevation of her grandson did not take place because Prince Dipanegara was obstructing it, and the other princes agreed. Would he himself want to become king? The princess was very worried that nothing would come of the coronation of her grandson. "What will happen to me, when Prince Dipanegara takes over the government? After all he is the son of a concubine." The Queen Mother did not understand things correctly; her fears were untimely and she misinterpreted the situation ... [The Queen Mother established close contact with the Dutch Resident de Salis and, trying to convince him that Dipanegara was a troublemaker, who himself was after the throne, she urged that her grandson should be crowned forthwith without waiting for the reply from Batavia. Other important courtiers such as Danureja and Wiranegara supported the Queen Mother's allegations.]

Finally the letter from Batavia arrived and a meeting was held in the Residency house of all the princes and notables. The request of Prince Dipanegara had been granted by the government; and he was very pleased. The elevation of the new Sultan, however, was postponed for a few days ...

[Prince Dipanegara returned home and went to his cave at Silarong to pray and meditate.] When he had been at Silarong for three days he heard the sound of successive cannon shots such as was the custom in honour of the arrival of a letter.

"Let us go home quickly," he said to his squires, and sped to Selaradja. When he arrived he said: "Did you hear the shooting? I wonder what it would be about."

Kertjaja said: "Lord, I have been to Sindoedjaja where I heard that Your Lordship's young nephew is being confirmed and installed as sultan."

For a while the Prince remained speechless; he became glowing red, his lips were trembling, and he said to himself: "What could be the reason for not inviting me to the coronation of my nephew? It must be another mean trick by this dirty Danoeredja, and Wiranegara and Mother." He remained silent and locked himself in his bedroom in Selaradja where he remained for three days and three nights. He felt deeply wronged, and said to himself: "It is as if I am no longer myself! I feel no longer human! Danoeredja, Wiranegara, and Mother treat me wrongly. I have no plans to take over the realm by force, but nevertheless they are suspicious of me and they secretly try to trick me." ...

[Dipanegara, after having consulted a religious teacher, finally calmed down and forgot about the affair. Not long afterwards the Resident de Salis was replaced by Resident Smissaert, who was able to establish good relations with all the princes, including Dipanegara. It had been especially impressed upon Smissaert by the colonial government not to upset Prince Dipanegara, who was left free to carry out his religious calling. He did not call at the court very often, although he was very fond of the young King, who was then four years old, and whom he sometimes took with him for the day to Selaradja.]

Some time later Wiranegara and the Prime Minister, Danoeredja, with the intention of playing a harmful trick on both princes (Dipanegara and Mangkoeboemi), made the Resident the following proposal: "If you are agreeable," they said, "it would be a good idea to extend southwards the road that runs to the west of the capital, from the market-place at Koetjen right through to Padakkan Mountain, and from there to Pandawa, Silarong, Pidjenan, and Mangir to the Praga River where it will connect with the road to Senepi; and to the north of the market-place of Pakoentjen it should run straight through the village of Tompean, where there is a garden with all sorts of fine fruit trees; and then it should go further northwards straight through the village of Ngloewes to the village of Terini, where it will connect with the highway. We believe that this will help future development because then the people who live to the south of the capital can travel northwards more easily."

The Resident replied: "The greatest objection I can think of is Selaredja. Think about it again carefully, which does not mean that I have already given my approval. Do not take this matter lightly, and if the Prince does not agree you should not persist. Do not force him, if he is unwilling, because it could have dire consequences and could become a cause of disturbance. I have made an agreement with Dipanegara that 'Whoever starts trouble will have to bear the consequences.'" The Resident further said: "Of all the princes of Mataram, nobody should be so bold as to offend this one, or the realm will undoubtedly be disturbed ... Think carefully about what I am saying, Danoeredja."

After Prime Minister Danoeredja and Waranegara had left the Resident's house and returned home they immediately discussed the matter and decided to have a road running from north to south pegged out. The Prime Minister, intent on causing trouble, wanted the road to run directly past the garden of Prince Dipanegara. He wanted to incense the Prince, who was already a little annoyed.

Dipanegara had laid out a garden in the village of Katompean, with all sorts of fine fruit trees, which were already in full bloom. People were sent from the market-place of Pakoentjen by the Prime Minister and led by Raden Brangta koesoema to trace the road northwards, and without any warning they put pegs straight through the garden. The gardener, who went to tell the Prince immediately, was asked by him who was in charge of the people who had put the pegs in. And when he replied that it was Brangtakoesoema, the Prince said: "Brangtakoesoema is certainly disrespectful in not having said a word to me about it. He is cheeky to me, because he has been sent by Danoeredja. He should have come and asked me. Go and pull all these pegs out and if Brangtakoesoema objects, hit him hard around the ears."

His servants rushed out immediately and pulled the pegs out of the ground, and when Brangtakoesoema objected he got a box on the ear from Dermadjaja. He ran away as fast as he could, leaving his horse behind. And when he reached the Prime Minister he told what had happened.

The Prime Minister, who was sorry and upset that Raden Brangtakoesoema had been boxed in the ear, went to the Resident and told him what had happened.

The Resident said: "Earlier I told you to treat the Prince with respect and to consult him in all matters. And now this fellow Brangtakoesoema starts to put pegs in without having first asked permission. Naturally Prince Dipanegara felt hurt and rightly the fellow got boxed in the ear." Danoeredja wanted revenge against Dipanegara.

Some time afterwards the court went to pay visits to the western part of the palace—the harem—where the Queen Mother was lying very ill. Prince Dipanegara also went and, sitting on a chair in the square in front of the mosque he asked the Prime Minister to appear before him and ... made clear his displeasure that he had agreed to the request of the Dutch for the rice fields of the village of Redjawinangoen. "Even if you wanted to agree, you should have consulted with me. Listen, Danoeredja, in order to get their favours, you render services to the Dutch and you make them presents of things which do not belong to you. You are doing well out of it. You have nothing to lose and can only gain." The reason why the Prince showed his displeasure so sharply was that he had made the man prime minister in the first place, with the agreement of the Dutch. However, in the heat of the moment Danoeredja forgot about his early beginnings, and he replied to the Prince somewhat sharply. And the Prince hit him with his slipper on the cheek. Danoeredja felt very offended, because many people were present. But he thought to himself: "Who can dismiss me from my post? If I stick with the Dutch, who would dare to do anything against me?"

[Danureja became a strong supporter of the Dutch, while Dipanegara, although not breaking his relations, stayed somewhat aloof from the colonial government. Another incident that incensed Prince Dipanegara was the appointment by the Queen Mother of a new *penghulu* (religious official). Dipanegara objected that such an appointment could only be made by the King or his legal guardian. After some rather nasty altercations, the Queen Mother finally gave in, and sent the new *penghulu* to Selaradja, where Dipanegara confirmed him in his position.]

Prince Dipanegara was very much offended because his mother handled all affairs with the Prime Minister, and with Wiranegara and the Dutchman, without consulting the Prince. Moreover, the Queen Mother was on very intimate terms with the Dutchman, from whom she had no secrets. Also in the evenings the Resident went often to the palace, but what he wanted with the Queen Mother nobody knew! "The court has lost its prestige," Dipanegara said to himself, "the kingdom is in decline." The Prince was very worried. He heard that the Queen Mother and Danoeredja were using indecent language. He said: "They are doing everything possible to discredit me with the Dutchman and they accuse me of trying my hardest to take over the throne. What shall I do to alienate her from the Dutchman?"

The Prince was very downhearted. From time to time he made pilgrimages to holy places. He was seldom home, staying mostly at Silarong. His behaviour caused the Dutchman and the Prime Minister to comment. The Queen Mother also felt suspicious and consulted the Prime Minister. "Listen, Danoeredja," she said, "what are the people saying about Dipanegara's plans? He is seldom home, and he always sits there in Silarong praying. I fear that he has something mischievous in mind, and wants to raise the flag of rebellion; and if this happens it will be difficult to put down. His behaviour is suspicious." The Prime Minister was out for revenge against Dipanegara because he was still smarting under the shame of having been hit publicly with a slipper on his cheek, and also because Dipanegara had been degrading him by telling everybody that he had become prime minister through his help.

So the Prime Minister wanted to confirm the Queen Mother in her suspicions and replied: "Your Highness could well be right. I have overheard people saying that the Prince wants to travel because, according to one of his servants, he has said he does not want to be ruled by the Dutch. He has said: 'The situation in this country is such that even for someone to become king the Company has to agree.' He cannot bear to be under somebody else. He is too proud. And he has said: 'The Europeans are continuously asking for rice lands, which in the end will mean that everything here will be in the hands of foreigners.'" The Prime Minister further said: "I have even heard about the plans of the Prince from one of my guards at the outer gate, whose father is a servant at Selaradja. This man has told me that Prince Dipanegara is planning to leave his main house and is going to live at Silarong."

The Queen Mother commented: "If that is the case, then he is planning something big, and wants to put himself up as king and rule the whole of Java. And even if he cannot succeed, we will have troubles. Well, Danoeredja, go and tell this immediately to the Dutchman. We have to take care that the Prince does not get away from us. If he escapes from his home there will undoubtedly be a rebellion in Mataram which will be very difficult for us to suppress, because the people in the villages support Dipanegara and he certainly will quickly get a large following. The common people will accept his authority." The Queen Mother was suddenly quiet, worried that perhaps she might be mistaken. She said to Danoeredja: "Go and discuss the matter carefully with the Dutchman and don't let there be any misunderstandings."

Danoeredja went immediately to the Resident, with whom he had a long talk. The Resident only nodded and did not speak, although he was pleased.

Prince Dipanegara felt very despondent. Many warned him that the Company was after him and that the Dutch were under the impression that he was planning to rebel. He was restless and could not eat during the day nor sleep at night. He told Djajamoestapa to seclude himself in the loneliness of Djimatan at the base of the grave of Sultan Agoeng. Djajamoestapa departed immediately together with one other man. He arrived there on Thursday evening and was led by the keeper called Kjai Balad to the foot of the grave outside the Tjoenkoeb [a structure over the grave around which curtains are hung], where he spent the whole of the night. Although suffering from the great cold he prayed all night long, hoping to receive a revelation—good or bad—for the Prince.

Kjai Balad came at dawn after he had performed his morning prayers and opened the door of the grave. The envoy entered and sat down at the base. After having cleaned the grave on all sides he sat down again and prayed, thereby showing that he was an envoy. When he had finished praying, he saw in the middle of the curtain a bloodstain, a round red space as large as a dinner plate. He looked at it intently and then went outside, where he asked the keeper Kjai Balad: "Kjai, what kind of red bloodlike stain is that in the middle of the curtain? Has it been there long? Or is the curtain always so red in the middle?"

Kjai Balad replied: "I am also struck by it, I am really amazed, because that red stain was not there yesterday. It is the will of the Lord that much blood will be shed in Java. It is a sign that there will be war. The will of God is irrevocable, be it concerned with prosperity or destruction. Nobody can avert his decision ...

[Jajamustapa returned home and reported to Dipanegara, who again sent him to other holy places to obtain any further signs if possible. After a long and adventurous journey Jajamustapa returned with further stories about divine revelations.]

After Dipanegara had performed his midnight prayers, he clearly heard a voice. He was startled, and when dawn broke he had Djajamoestapa fetched and told him: "The reason why I had you called is that soon after the performance of the midnight prayer at Selaradja, I very clearly heard a voice which said: 'Listen, you are permitted by God to become King! Take care not to indulge in self-exaltation, because if you sin that way it will not come to pass.' Was this the devil or the voice of an angel?"

Djajamoestapa replied: "I submit to the judgement of Your Highness, but in all probability it was an angel, because Your Highness had just completed the midnight prayer. If it was the devil"—and then the Prince interrupted: "Would that be the will of God?" ...

[The Dutch Resident who for some time had been spying on the movements of Dipanegara finally also began to mistrust the Prince's intentions. And in order to capture him he issued various invitations to Dipanegara to come to Yogjakarta. The Prince refused for some time, but when he finally went he took a hundred of his best soldiers with him and declined to enter the house of the Resident, fearing a trap.]

After the Prince had returned to Selaradja, he was told that it was commonly believed that the Resident in conjunction with the Prime Minister and the Mangkoealam—the Prince's grandfather— planned to attack him at Selaradja. The Prince was incensed, although he did not show it openly. He ordered that all the inhabitants of Selaradja should leave their houses at night and keep guard, armed with their lances, at the stockade surrounding the village, together with other village heads who supported him.

After the stockade had been guarded for a few nights, more and more villages came to know about it and all who loved the Prince came to keep guard. Soon there were three hundred men who during the day went home again. This could not remain unknown in the capital, where the whole affair was exaggerated and it was said that the Prince was recruiting troops and had ordered all the villagers to be on their guard. Moreover the Prince had set himself up as a *kraman* [i.e. as a rebel against constituted authority] and would leave his home in the month Soera and proclaim himself King at Silarong.

The Prince became very sad: "It is commonly said that I want to flee from here and proclaim myself king. It is not my intention to plunge the realm into disaster." He asked the eldest of his subjects: "What do you advise me? Everybody suspects me of wanting to put myself up as *kraman*."

They replied: "We leave this to the judgement of Your Highness; but one thing is certain, Prince, the Dutch will move against Selaradja. We leave it to Your Highness whether we should move against them or should keep ourselves prepared. We have also heard that people at the court of Danoeredja say that Your Highness is accused by the Dutch of getting your troops ready at Selaradja and that there are vast numbers of people present during the night. And they exaggerate and say that there are thousands. The Dutch are sending out spies during the day as well as the night."

The Prince said: "If that is the case then I cannot get out of it any more. But the Company will not get its way yet. I am still in Java and for that reason they accuse me of causing difficulties. Well, prepare letters for the inhabitants of the villages saying 'Who of you love me?' And go to the villages to recruit soldiers. My eldest servants shall have the rank of *Toemenggoeng* and they must have a letter with my seal, saying: 'This is documentary proof that I want you to occupy village lands by force'." The Prince further said: "I should not take half-measures. If I submit myself, the Company will certainly arrest me and send me outside Java. So it is better to take bold measures. A human being can have some happiness, and it is not to be expected that I shall live long any more."

Soon after this call by the Prince, masses of soldiers arrived at night, not only from the villages, but also from the capital. Soldiers of the Katanggoengs, Njoetras, palace guards and Pinilihs (legions of the Sultan) came to offer the Prince their allegiance. They said: "If Your Highness is going to depart from your home, then we will sacrifice ourselves for Your Highness."

The Prince answered: "I accept this with gratitude. But be unobtrusive and be careful." Also many princes and other members of the royal house came to see him at night, as well as many Mandoengs, Wirabradjas, Soeranatas, Soerjagamas, and Daengs [smaller corps of soldiers of the Sultan]; and people who lived west of the Winanga River came to submit themselves to the Prince.

The Prince let it be announced that all should come together in the night of the seventh of the month *Soera*, and that the next morning they should surround the capital ...

[Resident Smissaert, trying to prevent the outbreak of a rebellion, made an attempt to capture Dipanegara by sending a courtier, Sindunegara, to Selaradja to invite the Prince to come to Yogjakarta, supposedly to discuss his grievances. But when Dipanegara refused, the Resident became greatly angered and sent the same emissary back with the same request.] Sindoenegara left immediately, and he said to the Prince, who was surrounded by all his servants: "Your humble servant has been sent by the Resident to request Your Highness to come to the house of the Resident or, if Your Highness desires, to the Palace, or the house of Prince Mangkoeboemi, to have a discussion with the Dutchman. If Your Highness does not wish to come to any of these three places, would Your Highness state what he desires and the Resident will fulfil his wishes. It is hoped that this affair will not have any further dire consequences and that Your Highness will have pity on the people."

The Prince answered in a loud voice: "All right, since the Resident promises to comply with my wishes, I want him to get rid of Danoeredja and Wiranegara because they are a plague in the realm. As long as those two stay the Kingdom of Mataram will not enjoy any prosperity. Go and tell this to the Resident." ... [Soon afterwards Prince Mangkubumi arrived, having been sent by the Resident to induce Dipanegara to come to Yogjakarta. Prince Mangkubumi was to remain behind as a hostage. However, Dipanegara talked Mangkubumi into joining forces with him.]

The next morning Sindoenegara was again sent to Selaradja to invite the Prince, but this time he was followed by a large number of Dutch soldiers, who were to carry out a heavy attack and take Dipanegara prisoner and, if he resisted, to kill him. It was thought that this would be fairly easy as there were not very many troops in Selaradja and moreover these Dutch soldiers looked very aweinspiring. The Prime Minister and Wirjanegara, the son of Kjai Wiragoena, were also there, riding at the front of their troops.

After Sindoenegara, who had been sent to talk the Prince around, had arrived in Selaradja, he said to the Prince: "Prince, Your Highness's servant has been sent by Your Highness's friend the Resident to tell you that he will comply with your desires, and invites Your Highness to be present at the arrest of the Prime Minister and of Wiranegara. Moreover, the Resident leaves to you the decision whether they should be crushed to death or just killed."

The Prince replied: "If the Resident is really serious in agreeing to my demands, then let us go. I want to talk with the Dutchman."

While they were sitting there talking quietly and pleasantly, repeated gunfire was heard. The Prince was startled and, making a threatening gesture with his finger at Sindoenegara, he said in great anger: "What kind of advice are you giving me, Sindoenegara?" In great haste Sindoenegara took his leave, promising that he would have the soldiers withdraw. He galloped away with great speed.

Rifle fire was exchanged across the river. Both sides shouted warcries and were equally courageous. The Prime Minister Danoeredja led the battle and struck the enemy east of Tompean, while Raden Wiranegara hid himself near the spring near the lodge at Boeloe and ambushed the enemy. The battle was hard, with both sides fighting equally well. The battlecries and the cracking of the rifles sounded like a thunderstorm in the mountains. But the troops from Selaradja were swamped by the enemy. They defended themselves as well as possible with rifle fire, but the courageous enemy kept coming on. The fighting was so heavy that one could not distinguish enemy from friend. Soldiers were thronging around each other and the artillery kept on thundering. The attack came from three sides, from the south and from Tompean and from Boeloe where the artillery was stationed. Djajadirja and the leader of the *pradjoerit-panjas*, named Anon-wijaja, made a fierce attack on the Dutch, and many fell. But the Dutch kept on coming courageously and the artillery kept thundering as if it wanted the mountains to collapse. The battle continued unabated. Selaradja was full of people. The son-in-law of Dipanegara, the son of a *rongga* [official], fought fiercely. Djajaprawira attacked the Dutch furiously and many fell, but they kept coming, firing in file. As he had no rifle, he became frightened and fled. Djajadirja, the commander of the Wirabratas, full of fighting spirit, stood firm with his men. But the troops of the Company kept pushing forward. The sky was darkened by rifle smoke. Djajadirja evacuated the field with his men, but his horse was obstreperous and would not run fast. One of the Company's men ran towards him and hit him with his sword and Jajadirja died. When the troops from Selaradja were shelled from the right, they quickly withdrew. The struggle became too heavy; many died or were wounded and they became frightened. Prince Dipanegara and Prince Mangkoeboemi, who were at the head of their troops, came under heavy artillery fire and the troops scattered. Those who withstood the artillery also soon became frightened, as they were unprotected.

Prince Mangkoeboemi became uneasy and said to his cousin: "Boy, let us retreat. Perhaps God will help us later." Then Prince

Dipanegara and Prince Mangkoeboemi retreated westwards, crossing the River Bajem ...

T. Roorda, *Verhaal van de Oorsprong en het Begin van de Opstand van Dipanegara, volgens eeen Javaans handschrift*. (Bijdragen tot de Taal-Land-En Volkenkunde van Nederlandsch Indie), Nieuwe Volgreeks, Derde Deel, 1860, pp. 137-227.

38   H.J.J.L. de Stuers: Memoirs of Tuanku Imam Bondjol, 1850

Once there was a man called Toeankoe Moeda, who was the son of a priest named Toeankoe Radja Noedin, who hailed from Alahanpandjang, where also his forefathers came from. When he was thirty-five years old he decided to move his household to a better area, because in the place where he lived food was hard to come by and even water had to be carried from afar. As a result of God's special goodness he reached, together with his wife, two brothers, and two sisters, a lonely place at the foot of Mount Serdjadi. There he built a house and cultivated the soil, planting rice, palm trees, and other fruit trees. He also established a herd of cows and horses ...

After Toeankoe Moeda had lived there for one and a half years he deliberated with the chiefs and people of Alahanpandjang about a fortification and a mosque. After the decision had been made, everybody took part in the work and a fort was erected ... within which six houses and a mosque were built. It was given the name of Bondjol, which means that this fort was erected to maintain the true principles of Islam and to oppose all immoral and forbidden acts, and to tell the people that they should live in accordance with the rules of reason, justice, and morality. It was further decided to appoint judges or administrators ... and Toeankoe Moeda, Toeankoe Itam, Toeankoe Gapoe, and Toeankoe Halamat were unanimously elected. After that Toeankoe Moeda came to be called Toeankoe Imam by the people. These four judges followed the holy teachings of Mohammad and all their decisions were known for their justice ...

[After the death of the other judges Tuanku Imam became the sole ruler of Bondjol, which continued to grow in prosperity, attracting many people from other areas. As a result the fort had to be considerably enlarged.] After the construction of the fort had been completed and the armament had been taken care of, the people concentrated their efforts on commerce. Under these conditions of peace and solidarity the village of Bondjol continued to increase in prosperity. Merchants from surrounding districts came to trade. For a period of twenty-five years the inhabitants enjoyed all the benefits of solidarity, peace, and prosperity. There was no crime and no injustice; and everybody tried to remain virtuous and just, and not to sow discord.

In the middle of all this happiness, contentment, and prosperity, there all of a sudden arrived a man from Soengipoa named Padabongso, with the news that the Dutch under the command of Colonel Raaff had occupied the village of Samawang ... [This occurred in 1822. Tuanku Imam then gives an outline of the struggle between 1822 and 1831 when the Dutch slowly and after great difficulties were able to subdue most of Minangkabau. In 1831 the Dutch were nearing Bondjol, which was situated in the northern border region and which so far had remained outside the battle area.]

Then the village of Lawan in the district of XII Kotas was occupied. After a one-day struggle the Dutch had been able to subdue the people there. Then a man from Soengipoa ... named Toeankoe Tinggi submitted himself to the Dutch Government. A general peace was concluded with the people of the XII Kotas and the troops arrived in Soengipoa, where they camped in the market-place. Three days later a letter was sent to the region of Koempoelan and Alahanpandjang. On hearing the news about the arrival of the Dutch in Soengipoa the people of Alahanpandjang became worried, because Soengipoa is only twelve hours walk away. Many were frightened, but many also remained courageous. Some wanted to flee, while others prepared themselves to resist. In this unstable situation there arrived an emissary from Colonel Elout called Pandita Sari, who had delivered the letter to the Penghoeloe Datoe Bandhara. After Pandita Sari had returned to his region of Passi-lawas, Datoe Bandhara called Penghoeloe Datoe Sati, Toeankoe Imam, and all the chiefs of the people of Alahanpandjang to the market-place. After they had gathered there, a certain Toeangku Lebeh opened the letter of Colonel Elout and read it aloud; its contents were as follows:

> This is a letter from the Colonel of the Dutch troops, Elout, to the Penghoeloes Datoe Bandhara and Datoe Sati and Toeankoe Imam in the land of Alahanpandjang. I, Colonel Elout, make it known to you that the Dutch Government requests your country; if you want to surrender the country in peace, let all the chiefs come to us in Soengipoa to conclude peace. But if you do not want to surrender your land, take care, because we will soon march against your country.

When Toeankoe Lebeh had finished reading and all had understood the contents of the letter, the chiefs were divided. Some wanted peace and others wanted to defend themselves. But the majority were for peace, including Datoe Bandhara. Only Datoe Sati was opposed. He argued: "I do not want to conclude peace, because our country is too small and too sparsely populated to perform seignorial services for the [Dutch] Government."

Then Toeankoe Imam said: "Don't let there be division among you, but be united and true to each other in order to avoid a disaster." This admonition of Toeankoe Imam was, however, not heeded, and discord spread more and more among the people. This made Toeankoe Imam think, and he said to himself: "What is the use of staying any longer in Alahanpandjang, because the Penghoeloes are not united, and without them I have no say. It would be better for me to leave here with my wife and children ... " [Tuanku Imam went to Lubu-sikaping, while the other leaders of Alahanpandjang concluded peace with Elout on the condition that the Dutch Government would respect the religion and customs of the people and would not occupy the fort at Bondjol.]

When all this was agreed upon by both parties, the Dutch troops entered ... Alahanpandjang. The people had already prepared *atap* [split bamboo] to build houses for the Dutch at a certain place called Medang-sebah. But the Dutch refused to live there and, after having kicked out the people, occupied the houss and mosque of Bondjol ... During their one and a half months stay the Dutch troops took by force and without any payment the fruits, cattle, and fish belonging to the people.

Three days after Toeankoe Imam had gone to Loeboe-sikaping, his brother, called Radja Manang, arrived to inform him that the Dutch had occupied the fort of Bondjol and had turned the mosque into a barracks ... he also had been ordered by Colonel Elout ... to request Toeankoe Imam to come and see him. "It is well," Toeankoe Imam replied, "I will go to Colonel Elout ... " Immediately after his arrival in Bondjol, Toeankoe Imam together with his son Joesoef went to see Colonel Elout. The following conversation took place:

"Where is Toeankoe Imam?" asked Colonel Elout.

"That is I," he replied.

"Enter, Toeankoe Imam," said the Colonel. And Toeankoe Imam with his son Joesoef entered the room and as requested went to sit down beside Colonel Elout ... "How are you, Toeanku Imam?."

"I am well, sir."

"Where do you live now, Toeankoe Imam?"

"I live nowadays in Loeboe-sikaping. I fear the Dutch troops ... "

"You must not fear, the [Dutch] Government will not cause you any harm." He further asked: "How old are you now, Toeankoe Imam?"

"I am sixty."

"And I am sixty-one," Colonel Elout replied.

"So we are of the same age ... "

"You are already old, Toeankoe Imam. You must no longer work. It is better to enjoy your old age and to leave the carrying of responsibilities to the younger ones."

"I agree," Toeankoe Imam replied. "I shall follow your wise counsel and judgement, Colonel, and I hold myself at your disposal ... " [Tuanku Imam was replaced by Tuanku Muda whom the Dutch appointed Regent over Alahanpandjang. Elout left the area with the main body of his troops, leaving a small detachment to guard Bondjol.]

The Dutch troops remained in the mosque and houses of Bondjol ... They brought dogs and other dirt inside and took the fruits and cattle of the people. Yes, they even demanded all sorts of work from the population and large deliveries of rice without any payment. They meted out punishment daily. Once some government stores were brought from Si-pisang to Bondjol to be transported to Loeboek-sikaping. Twenty men from Alahanpandjang had to move these goods escorted by a sergeant and twelve soldiers. When they had gone half the distance and had reached a place called Soengisalassa, they asked to rest for a while in order to eat and to say their daily prayers. This was not allowed. When, however, one of the twenty carriers, named Dara Salam, ignored the refusal, one of the soldiers immediately fired a shot that hit him in the breast and killed him. The others were driven forward with the leash. And they walked in great fear for a whole day. After these goods had been brought to Loeboek-sikaping and had been stored in the mosque there, they returned to Alahanpandjang. On their return the commander [of Bondjol] had left for Pisang, and although everybody went home, this affair did not remain unnoticed.

The severe and arbitrary actions of the troops caused general discontent in Alahanpandjang and brought the people to a general meeting at Tandike where a great many unreasonable and arbitrary matters were brought up, matters made worse because the people had come to terms with the government after mutual promises had been made. These agreements had not only been thrown to the wind, but, instead of the peaceful and quiet rule they had expected from the government, they had been suppressed and mistreated. As a result it was firmly decided by all to take up arms, and to die rather than tolerate this any longer. Immediately, letters were despatched to all regions and it was agreed that on the third of the month Radjab (January 1833), each in his own region would rise up and kill all the soldiers.

In the morning of the third of the month Radjab (it was a Friday), about twenty hoeloebalangs [military leaders], led by two chiefs named Toeankoe Nan Garang and Radja Lajang, unexpectedly entered Bondjol. When they reached the mosque they attacked fiercely, killing within half an hour all the European and Javanese soldiers ... [Bondjol was able to put up such a fierce and courageous resistance to various large attacks that it was not until 1837 that the Dutch were able to reimpose their rule.]

After that General Cochius came from Batavia [at the beginning of 1837], bringing a number of soldiers with him. Neither side gave way. The Dutch troops shot fire shells which burned down the mosque and the house of Toeankoe Imam. This increased the anger of the people even more and they began to return the fire ferociously.

One morning around 3 o'clock when the people of Bondjol, tired from the continuous fighting, were resting for a few moments, the Dutch troops under the protection of a continuous artillery barrage took the opportunity to penetrate into Bondjol through a breach in the wall. Some African and Buginese soldiers suddenly appeared in Toeankoe Imam's harem. They wanted to drag some of the women with them ... The women began to screech tremendously. Toeankoe Imam woke up, took his sword and, accompanied by his son, Oemar Ali, went to the women's quarters from where the screeching could be heard. Fronting the soldiers, he [Oemar Ali] received a bullet wound in his thigh, but he kept on fighting ferociously. Then he was shot in his side; the bullet stuck in the flesh and, unable to bear the severe pain, he went home bleeding severely. Toeankoe Imam, although now completely on his own, kept hitting around him with his sword until the soldiers finally withdrew from Bondjol. Toeankoe Imam pursued them with his sword outside Bondjol, where he received a bayonet wound ... which made him fall down. When he received a second thrust, he immediately stood up again, hitting with his sword right and left into the soldiers, who fled back to their camp. Exhausted, and covered with thirteen wounds which bled continuously, causing tremendous pain, Toeankoe Imam was carried home by the people of Bondjol.

The following day around 5 o'clock the Dutch troops came very near the breach in the wall of Bondjol and attacked. The people were waiting for them and defended themselves courageously. The women also took to arms, aiding their husbands. The battle was so fierce that neither army could recognize the other, while the noise made by both sides echoed into the air. The battle lasted until 12 noon when the Dutch fell back on their encampments. The number of dead and wounded on both sides was great ... [A few days later] the struggle continued with increasing ferocity. The noise of the shooting never stopped and everything was covered by thick smoke. The Dutch troops succeeded in shooting various breaches in the wall and they burned down the bamboo bushes around Bondjol with fire shells ... The number of people killed on both sides was shocking. In Bondjol there were only fifteen *hoeloebalangs* [officers] left, who kept resisting day and night for another two and a half months.

About this time three *hoeloebalangs* ... came at night to see Toeankoe Imam and suggested that he should leave the village and go with them to the village of Merapi in order to discuss what should be done in this precarious situation. Bondjol was badly damaged, the batteries had been destroyed, and all the houses and trees had been burned down and fallen to the ground. Toeankoe Imam agreed with this proposal ...

When the Dutch soldiers saw that the village of Bondjol was deserted they occupied it immediately and restored the batteries. Two days later the Dutch troops moved against the village of Merapi. The people met them in the field. But after only a one-hour battle the Dutch troops retired to Bondjol and the people of Merapi returned to their homes. This was the end of the war. Two days later peace was concluded at Bondjol between two emissaries of Toeankoe Imam and the government.

Later Toeankoe Imam was invited by letter from Padang to go to a fortification in the mountains to meet the Resident there. When Toenkoe Imam arrived at the mountain, however, the Resident was not to be found. Escorted by a captain, another officer, and twelve soldiers, he was brought to Padang with his son and three followers. From there he was transported to Batavia where he remained for four months in the house of the Commander of the Balinese. After that he was transferred to Tjiandoer and eleven months later he was sent back to Batavia from where he was brought by warship to Ambon.

H.J.J.L. de Stuers, *ridder, De vestiging en uitbreiding der Nederlanders ter Westkust van Sumatra. Tweede Deel (Amsterdam: Van Kampen, 1850), Bijlage B. Memorie van Toewankoe Imam aangaande de komst der Hollanders in Sumatra's binnenlanden en de aldaar door hen gevoerden oorlog*, pp. 219-40.

39   H.T. Damste: Hikajat Prang Sabi, 1928

In the name of Allah, the merciful and loving! God be praised, I laud the Lord and I beseech the Lord to bless the prophet, and after the prophet his family and friends. This is a *hikajat* [story] about the conduct of the holy war. It has been commanded to conduct war in the path of Allah; it is the order of God, the very pure. The word of the Lord in the Qu'ran is clear and explicit, oh my brothers: "God has bought the lives and property of the believers. And the price is paradise. They shall go into battle to kill their enemies who will fall under their blows; the promises which have been made to them in the Mosaic law, the Gospel, and the Qu'ran will be fulfilled. After all, who can be more faithful to his promise than God? Rejoice in your covenant, it is the seal of your happiness."

Take heed, oh believers, of the word of my Lord! God, the Lord of all the worlds, has made it such that he has bought the faithful to let them fight the unbelievers. He did not only buy them to carry out their religious duties and to make their living by gaining profit; no, he has bought the believers in full. Think about this, brothers, who are destined for salvation! Indeed, goods and souls were bought by him, which are to be surrendered for the holy war ... after this verse, in which He says that He is buying you, is it proper, brothers, to be diffident about carrying on the war against the unbelievers, to suspect this sale, and to want to behave freely and to act according to one's pleasures? You cannot commit a breach of contract ...

Be very devoted and do not worry! You will get God's help. "Paradise is in the shadow of the swords", this tradition is also very well known ... This is a road sign to the very beautiful Paradise, which is a haven of comforts. This is the order of things in the afterlife, which is different from things in this world. "The eternal life is to be found in the drinking of the cup of death." God gives eternal life after death, oh brothers. Listen again to the following verse which I will read to you about the blessings and pleasures which He will readily give you: "Oh, believers, shall I teach you the means to escape your deep suffering? Believe in God and in His prophet, fight under the banner of the faith, liberally sacrifice your life and goods; that is your road to happiness, if you want to know. God will forgive your sins. He will lead you into the gardens where streams are flowing. You will enter into the exquisite Garden of Eden where you will enjoy the greatest happiness."

The easiest way for the faithful is, according to the directions of God, the great Lord, to do battle in the path of Allah ... then all sins will be forgiven and wiped out, even if they are as numerous as the foam in the surf on the beach, and he will grant the Paradise of Eden, a region of feast and pleasures. There one will get everything that is desired immediately. The Lord gives special pleasures to those who served the cause of the holy war. He will give them heaven, paradise, which glows with an unforgettable light! There will be seventy heavenly nymphs and in addition to that, girl servants. God's reward being so great, is it proper to be slow in taking up battle against the unbelievers? Anybody with good eyes does not throw away gold to pick up iron! When listening to the wiles of the devil, one will mistake diamonds for iron. People have no interest in fighting the unbelievers. It is as if our superb religion is neglected and is no longer dear to us, and nobody any longer runs warm for it. It is as if we confess a false religion when doubts can arise about the need to wage war against the unbelievers ... "Obey Allah and his prophet." It is your duty to follow the commands and interdicts. Trust God and the prophet when the time comes that the soul and matter end; do not worry about the dissipation of your property, and of those in authority follow the congenial king! Do not take notice of the lures of the devil! Do not follow his sinful desires, because they withhold you from living in accordance with the commands of the Lord. They hold you back from your duties, so that you will not get into a war with the unbelievers.

Listen to me, *teungku abang* [brother religious teacher], so that you will be aware of the wiles of the devil, which are manifold ... Nobody can cope with the tricks of these unbelieving spirits. Even if the faith is destroyed, nobody cares. The devils, who command you to live under the Company [the Dutch], speak as follows: "Surrender yourselves to God! You cannot put up any resistance. How could you? Supposing you are going to fight, then your rice sheds, children, wives, and your many and beautiful possessions will stay behind! Let us stay here in the village and takes things as they are ordained by the Lord. Let us go later when the unbelievers have retreated some distance." Do not listen to these sophistries of the devil. But trust in God and the prophet! Immediately after the unbelievers occupy the country, rise up and do not acquiesce! Do not hesitate any longer, but go into battle and follow the prophet!

We may not keep quiet, living in this country, and enjoy ourselves. [Holy war] is the duty of every individual just as much as the *sembahjang* [daily prayers], which must be performed at all the set times if you belong to the [Islamic] community. But the *sembahjang* and the *poeasa* [fast] are alone not sufficient if one does not go to the holy war. The poor, old and young, small and big, *keutjhi* and *waki* [various types of leader], even slaves, are bound to go to war ... Also listen to the word of God that commands you to take money with you for the holy war: "Use your goods to support the faith. Do not cause your downfall by your own hand. Do good. The Lord loves those who are charitable". Be serious about paying for the holy war. It is also your duty to surrender your goods and remember "that you cannot fulfil your duty without giving something". If you do not give anything of value and you do not yourself go, then wait until you are pushed into purgatory. Listen so that I can explain to you what God says in the Qu'ran: "Tell those who are piling up gold in their coffers and refuse to use it for the support of the faith that they will suffer painful tortures. When the time comes, that gold glowing from hell fire will be laid on their foreheads, their sides, and loins, and they will be told: look at it, here are the treasures which you have accumulated; enjoy them" ...

Let us all be thankful that the pleasures which God gives us never abate. These divine pleasures continue to flow without interruption, but the greatest pleasure given by God's blessing is bestowed upon the pious poor who go to war. If nobody had made war against the Dutch they would have taxed every head; not one *sagi* [area] would have remained free, and they would have made demands on everybody. In the lands they have conquered, the following high taxes are levied: five dollars are to be paid for one *haih* of land; they ask one dollar per person when a child is born in the country and one dollar per person when somebody dies. One out of seven days has to be worked for them. This is the *adat* [custom] and the law of the unbelievers and this situation exists in the lands of the Malays and Singkil, and also in Palembang and the Padang region. And nobody stands up to them! People of good family obey the unbelievers and none of them go to war; all of them surrender themselves to the *kafirs* [unbelievers]! When they [the Dutch] levy taxation they give a *tahil* [1 tahil = 0.054 kilograms of precious metal] to a few of them [i.e. indigenous rulers and officials] and to keep their hold on the country they do not mind paying out *katis* [1 kati = 625 grams].

And that is the reason that nobody goes out to fight. Many can already be considered as having become unbelievers. Not one is strong in his faith, which is a sign that the world is coming to an end. The *teungkus* have been completely fooled by the spirits, and those who obtained a great deal of knowledge no longer make use of it. When the devil is at work a voice inside the *teungku* speaks as follows: "Oh, *teungku*, how could you go into battle? Who would take care of the people?" And he whispers to the *teungku*: "Who will take care of the castrated billy goat? ... Who will administer the *zakat* and *tehlil* [religious taxes]? Why should you nervously put yourself to haste? This war goes slowly and will still take a long time; why should you rush to the lowlands? It would be better if you go later when the problems in the country have faded!" These are the wiles he employs against the *keutjihs*, *teungkus*, and *wakis*, with the result that the people begin to think: "Our *teungku* has not gone down to the lowlands. Why then should we make great haste? What is so special about this war then? Perhaps this war is not necessary after all? Let us stay put for the time being! If there was an obligation to fight, the *teungku*, who is a religious teacher, would have followed it up because he is a learned man who is reading day and night, holding discourses from the *kitabs* [Islamic religious texts] and the Qu'ran, in which after all everything about the holy war is contained." This is how the people argue, even the *keutjhis* and *wakis*. The people as well as the *teungkus* have been fooled; the *keutjhis* solely concentrate on administration and the *teungkus* are busy with *kenduris* [religious feasts]. Everybody works at his job and nobody any longer thinks about the holy war. Everybody is completely taken up with making his living; some occupy themselves with gambling, but the command of the Lord is neglected. One follows his own inclinations and stays home ...

It is definitely your duty to fight the unbelievers, and you may not associate with them! Allah's command is to kill them, so do not go around with these unbelievers. Even just looking at them causes already a feeling of guilt. Where does there exist a pure and true relationship with God? There is no faith in their hearts any more, because they call the unbelievers *"tuan"* ["sir"]. Going to the unbelievers is the same as concluding a pact of friendship, and whoever shakes hands with an unbeliever has no longer any faith; he has already said *"tuan"*! He talks about all sorts of things to the *kafir*, he has himself become a *kafir*, and he will be called that in this world. Why do you continue to live with them? Why, gentlemen, don't you think? *Kafirs* are the enemies of God!

Let us have a look at the other side of the picture and the great troubles people have who live under the government of the *kafirs*. But still you do not follow the prophet! These unbelieving children of whores [the Dutch] are of a wicked disposition; some people they hang; they ruin our religion; moreover they sell everybody into slavery; they kill all the dignified *ulebalangs* [noblemen] in the regions! And the *campakas* have become defoliated and have withered away. When nobody fights against the Dutch the punishment later will be great. They kill all *peutuas* [elders] to the last man! A section of the people they transport to Batavia, others they take to Europe; the young ones are destined to become soldiers, while the aged have to become sailors. They make a great mess in the country, and they immediately appropriate everything they find; they take all property and divide it among the people who have come with them in the same way as they give pay to the soldiers ... They confiscate everything that belongs to people who are not living within the [Dutch-controlled areas], but the people who have subjected themselves are presented with a different bill: the damned *kafirs* have laid down that they will take half of the property of the total population to pay for their expenditure. They say that they have suffered heavy losses which are impossible to calculate! "You must cede half of your property; the other half you may have yourself. This is the custom of the Company, and if you do not comply, then you can go away." They leave you one half and that with a great deal of fanfare, and if it is brought before the court, they will take the lot. The wretched unbelievers are changing the laws until nothing is left of them. Moreover they force you to do guard duties. All weapons they confiscate, and they hit you when you object. Even if you have hidden the weapons they will find them.

In order to get hold of these weapons they have devised the following scheme: they introduce gambling and opium-smoking, and some set themselves up as toll-collectors as in Java. With great devotion they encourage the people to gamble. And three to four hundred men may come to gamble in the hope of gaining a fortune. The losers will only retain their bodies; everything else they have brought with them will be taken and stored away. The unholy *kafirs* execute the other part of their plan: They let their friends take goods in pawn, only accepting pikes, rifles, lances, and sabres, and they supply as many dollars as desired ... After they have taken all weapons, they spy around and take in money; everything they scrape together—they press and look everywhere. And when there are no more weapons in the country, the time has come for them to change the laws. Where are you all, great and small, old and young? They make the law, the damned *kafirs*, and they rule with new methods. "You all have to participate in the business of the Company! Do not disobey the *tuan beusa* [Dutch official]. Whoever, will disobey will have his head split in two and his body pierced." This is what the *kafir* dogs say to the crowds in the presence of the people of the west coast [i.e. the Minangkabaus, who at that time were preponderant in the colonial police force in Atjeh] ...

After they have got what they wanted, they keep on taking whatever they desire. They call all the beautiful young girls to the fort, leaving not one of the adult virgins who look pretty, and choose their concubines from among them. They take whoever they take a fancy to. Good women become completely corrupted. The actions of the Dutch are criminal. The bridegroom sits home alone, because the *kafirs* have taken his wife. This is what half the Dutch do. Others go about it in a different way: as soon as the man has gone out, they come up to the house, open the door and go and look for the bride. They go behind the *klambu* [mosquito net] and sleep with the woman. They have hung up their hat on the stairs as a sign [this refers to traditional Achinese beliefs about the way the Dutch were supposed to act in Java]. If you go upstairs they will kick you and throw you out in no uncertain manner. If the husband becomes angry, they bind his arms and legs crosswise with sharp irons. You may go and report the behaviour of the soldiers to the Company: "What is this, *tuan*, the soldiers just satisfy their lusts and fornicate! They take all the young virgins as well as all the married women, they overpower the whole of the people. What about your good intentions now?" Then the *kafir* will answer glibly, arguing: "Oh *peutuas*, listen, the laws of the Company are as follows. In all the countries we have obtained we have introduced a system of equal sharing: all the crops in the fields and the property in the villages is to be shared equally with the owner. So far as the women are concerned, they are partly shared by the husband and partly by the soldiers. You people should not be jealous, because this is how things are done under the Company. You *teungkus* should not complain about this: you spent the night with them but during the day, gentlemen, they are for the soldiers."

The *kafir* dog, of the rank of controleur [lower-ranking Dutch official], calls up all the women of rank, the wives of the *ulebalangs*, who are still wearing *subangs* [earrings] in their ears because they are young. He tells the husband: "I have been here for some considerable time now, and I want to conclude a pact of friendship with you. We live here in your land together and we should discuss what work there is to be done. Your wife has never been here to see me yet. Why don't you send her for a day? I would like to see her very much!" The *ulebalang* thinks: "He tells me to bring my wife, I believe that it would be unwise not to comply. The Company wants to see her." The *ulebalang* then goes home and orders a number of dishes to be made ready, telling his wife: "You have to go to the *Belanda* [Dutchman]. Go to the fort tomorrow or the day after tomorrow so that he will get to know you." The wife is then very pleased. If you say to a woman that she can go out, she needs no further encouragement. She picks up the dishes and is soon on her way to the fort. On her arrival the *"tuan"* receives her properly. He presents her with *sirih* [betel nut], food, and all sorts of sweets and tasty dishes, such as those sugared things. When the reception is finished and the food has been cleared away, he presents flowers. After that he sends everybody home. He gives clothes of pleated gold and expensive flower arrangements. After he has offered these gifts he says to the woman: "Let there be much love between us, little sister; come and look us up again tomorrow or the day after tomorrow." The woman then goes home in a sprightly mood, after he has accompanied her to the gate of the fort.

About a week later he takes the matter up again and asks her to come. The woman goes again to the controleur in the *kota* [town]. Again he gives her presents, and tells her to come the day after tomorrow. And the day after tomorrow she returns again, saying nothing about it any more to the *ulebalang*. She can no longer be held back or forbidden, and the woman is driven impetuously by feelings of love. The *kafir* then says to the woman immediately after she arrives: "How long do I live here already in this land and in your village, but nobody loves me; it is as if I am being disparaged wherever I go. If you love me, then do what I ask: go inside the *klambu* and lie down. That is what I would really like, because I am so desirous of you." Hardly has the woman heard this than she goes inside, giving rein to her lusts without asking any questions. This is how women act when somebody is seducing them. The *kafir* also slips quickly inside and so they are both together behind the *klambu*. They lie down and pursue their lusts. After he has got what he wanted, he sends her back home. But the next morning he tells her to come again. The woman is happy and does come again; and so it goes on, with the woman running in and out of the *kota*. And when her jusband forbids her, he has done wrong according to the ideas of the Dutchman, who says: "The husband has no right to judge! You have no right to forbid her!"

Here is another example of the burdensome legislation of the Dutch *kafirs*. One out of seven days must be worked for the prince, day and night. That is the kind of law they introduce: women and men, small and big, old and young, they force to comply; they make *ulebalangs* work, even the *potjut* [high-ranking nobleman] from the big house! They treat everybody the same: one cannot distinguish any more who is *potjut*, who is Si Laba, who is a slave, and who is a lord. The *kafir* levels everything down. *Keutjhi* and *imeum* [ranks] do not count any longer, and they mix up *wazis* and *mantris* [officials]. The opium-smoker becomes frantic, he becomes sick because they do not allow the supply of opium; he has not got enough to smoke and becomes very restless.

People who want to travel are also very much encumbered. If they have no passport, even when they are only planning a short trip, they are arrested and their goods are taken. Even if one only goes to somewhere close for a short time, a quarter of an hour for example, or even if one is in haste because of difficulties with work—however important it may be, if you have no passport you are not allowed to go; they absolutely refuse and you are not allowed to travel. You cannot get done what you want, and even if you want to make footsteps as tiny as those of a louse, you will be halted. The divine law disappears, the *adat* deteriorates, and nothing remains of religion. However, what has increased very much since the Dutch *kafirs* have come is gross stupidity. This is how the government is of those who are damned by Allah; oh blessed ones, I am not exaggerating, it is exactly as I am saying; I am not boasting and I do not get any profit out of it.

If you do not believe it, then go and see for yourself; depart today for Java. In Padang and in Deli as well as in Batavia in Java the divine law is not honoured. In every country where the Dutch remain, the women live as prostitutes and those who are married commit adultery, and even if the men know that they are adulterous they are not able to forbid this wretched business ...

H.T. Damste, *Hikajat Prang Sabi* (*Bijdragen tot de Taal-Land-en Volkenkunde van Nederlandsch-Indie.*) Deel 84, 1928, pp. 549-63.

The genesis of the modern Indonesian nationalist movement

By the beginning of the twentieth century Liberal colonial education policy had created the nucleus of a new indigenous elite, consisting mainly of Dutch-trained Indonesian doctors, teachers, and government administrators and clerks. The higher nobility for some considerable time considered these new positions in the colonial service to be far below their social status, and most of the sons of the higher *priyayi* (indigenous administrators usually of noble origin) continued to seek appointment in the far more prestigious—in Javanese eyes—*Inlands Bestuur* (Native Regional Government Service). The majority then of this new elite originated from the lower *priyayi* and even commoners (*see* document 40).

The appearance of this new elite caused friction in both indigenous society and colonial society as a whole, because neither the majority of Europeans nor the higher indigenous nobility were prepared to grant indigenous doctors and teachers the socio-economic recognition due to their educational qualifications, which were often far higher than those of European and native officials.

Many of the European "old-timers" in the colonial service as well as most of the Javanese regents considered the new indigenous intelligentsia as a threat to their authority and their privileged position, and as a whole paid only lip-service to the ideals of the Ethical Policy, which advocated that Western-educated Indonesians should be "associated" as much as possible with Europeans, not only in cultural terms but also in a social and economic sense (*see* document 25). Indigenous doctors and teachers received salaries which were far below those of most *priyayi* administrators; they were snubbed socially; and whenever Indonesians managed to acquire the educational qualifications required for higher positions in the civil service they were put on a side-track and prevented from taking up a leading function.

The frustrations suffered by the new elite are illustrated in documents 41-42. Kartini was the daughter of the Regent of Japara, a progressive Javanese nobleman who was one of the few higher *priyayi* with a Dutch education. She stressed the need for a modernization of indigenous society, although opposing a wholesale imitation of European civilization. Kartini emphasized the need to improve the lot of Indonesian women and is highly revered in modern Indonesia as the great pioneer in their emancipation.

Ahmad Djajadiningrat came from a progressive noble family in Banten (West Java) and was one of the first Indonesians to enter and complete the Dutch High School (*H.B.S.*). He became one of the showpieces of the Ethical Policy and as a moderate nationalist advocating evolution rather than revolution he occupied important posts in the colonial civil service, was a Member of the *Volksraad*, and a member of various important government commissions.

Curbed in their ambitions and influenced by Western ideas of social justice as well as by developments in India, China, and Japan, some of the Western-educated Indonesian intellectuals turned to nationalism and the eventual destruction of the colonial system as a solution to their problems and the sufferings of the people. In 1906 Dr Mas Wahidin Soediro Hoesoedo, a retired *dokter-djawa* (native doctor), travelled widely throughout Java to raise money for a study fund for needy Javanese students. He strongly believed that the Javanese could advance themselves only by means of Western education and by invigorating their own culture. Dr Wahidin's efforts met with little response from most of the *priyayi*, but he was enthusiastically received by the students of the medical school (*S.T.O.V.I.A.*) in Batavia (Jakarta), who were highly critical of racial discrimination in the colony and the preferential treatment given by the colonial government to the indigenous nobility. Spurred on by the example of the Chinese and the Eurasians, who were organizing themselves to further their own group interests, some of these students came to the conclusion that it was high time to establish a modern organization for the advancement of the people of Java. As a result the first modern Javanese organization, called *Budi Utomo*—High Endeavour—was born on 20 May 1908 on the premises of the *S.T.O.V.I.A.*

In criticizing the *priyayi* for failing to look after the interests of the people and in bypassing this traditional indigenous leadership class as well as their elders, the student founders of *Budi Utomo* committed a revolutionary act considering the still strongly hierarchical socio-political framework in the Java of 1908 (*see* document 43). However, the new organization was soon swamped by *priyayi* who impressed their conservative stamp on it and *Budi Utomo* remained initially non-political and concentrated on educational and cultural issues. It was not until 1917 that *Budi Utomo* adopted a political platform demanding a parliamentary government, universal suffrage, a uniform legal system, religious neutrality, and the creation of equal opportunities for Indonesians in the social and economic field. The following year it joined a group of radical European and Indonesian Members in the *Volksraad* that demanded the immediate introduction of self-government. *Budi Utomo*, however, remained politically moderate and its importance in the nationalist movement seriously declined during the 1920s until it finally in 1935 amalgamated itself with another moderate political party, the *Persatuan Bangsa Indonesia*—the Indonesian People's Union—to form a new party: the *Partai Indonesia Raya*—*Parindra*—which believed in political evolution rather than revolution and concentrated on the educational and economic development of the Indonesian people.

Many of the more radically inclined members soon left *Budi Utomo* and later joined the *Indische Partij*—the Indies Party—a radical organization which demanded full independence for the Indies. While *Budi Utomo* was Java-centric, the *Indische Partij* was Indonesia-wide in its approach and attempted to combine all races in the colony in its fight against colonialism (*see* document 44). The *Indische Partij* was founded in 1912 by the Eurasian E. F. E. Douwes Dekker, a distant relative of the famous Eduard Douwes Dekker ("Multatuli"), the author of *Max Havelaar* (*see* document 6). In March 1913 the party claimed a membership of seven thousand, the vast majority of whom were lower-class Eurasians.

The better-situated Eurasians, who on the whole were employed in the middle and some of the top ranks of the colonial civil service, stayed aloof, and in 1919 founded the *Indo-Europees Verbond*—Indo-European Union—which threw in its lot with the Dutch empire, hoping in this way to perpetuate their privileged position in the colony. The majority of Indonesians did not join because they resented the superior attitude with which most Eurasians treated the indigenous people, while the Chinese as usual carefully avoided becoming embroiled in politics and concentrated on tending their business interests.

The ideal of Douwes Dekker to create a vast national, multiracial, anti-colonial block proved impossible to realize. Moreover in 1913 his party ceased to exist when the colonial government refused to accord it legal recognition and exiled the three main leaders, Douwes Dekker, Dr Tjipto Mangunkusumo, and Suwardi Suryaningrat, to the Netherlands on the grounds that they had endangered peace and order by writing subversive propaganda (*see* document 45).

Most of the Eurasian followers of the *Indische Partij* joined the strictly Eurasian organization *Insulinde*, which because of continuous in-fighting remained politically ineffective. Only in 1919 when Douwes Dekker was allowed to return to the Indies was *Insulinde* given a new lease of life. The organization changed its name to *Nationale Indische Partij*—National Indies Party—and became increasingly radical in its actions, with the result that its leaders were in and out of jail. In 1923 the colonial government after four years of "consideration" refused to approve the statutes of the *Nationale Indische Partij*, which now ceased to exist.

40 The social origin of S.T.O.V.I.A. students and graduates, 1875—1904

	students	graduates
	Sons of higher native officials	
Radja	1	—
Pangeran	3	1
Regent	10	6
Patih	14	3
Head-*jaksa*	7	3
Under-collector	17	3
Wedono	61	11
Head-*penghulu*	17	7
Native army officer	16	7
Total	146	41
	Sons of middle-ranking native officials	
Jaksa	12	4
Assistant-*wedono*	41	12
Dokter-djawa	37	5
Teacher	93	22
Mantri	83	19
Vaccinator	11	2
Native veterinary surgeon	1	—
Total	278	64
	Sons of lower native officials and private persons	
Clerk	25	8
Prison warder	3	—
Telegraph operator	5	1
Typograph	2	—
Draughtsman	1	—
Supervisor	3	1
Soldier	7	1
Village head	30	11
Trader	7	—
Farmer	16	3

Tradesman	12	1
Pilot	1	—
Watchman	3	1
Tram conductor	2	—
Cart driver	2	—
Village police	1	—
Labourer	10	2
House servants	10	2
Officials on half-pay	2	—
Private without profession	67	13
Profession unknown	110	11
Total	319	55
General Total	743	160

Jaarlijks Verslag School Tot Opleiding van Inlandse Artsen, 1904-1905 (Batavia: 1906). Biljlage no. 10.

41 R. A. Kartini: Letters of a Javanese Princess

Father sent a note to the government on the subject of education. You must know that many of the native rulers rejoice at the actions of the government. The Javanese nobles are in the favour of the government here and in the motherland, and everything possible is done to help them, and to make them blossom to perfection.

The aristocracy sees with sad eyes how sons of the people are educated, and often even elevated to their ranks by the government because of knowledge, ability, and industry. Sons of the people go to European schools and compare favourably in every respect with the high and honourable sons of the noble. The nobles wish to have rights for themselves alone; they alone wish to have authority and to make western civilization and enlightenment their own. And the government helps and supports them in this, for it is to its own advantage to do so.

As early as 1895 there was a decree that without the special permission of His Excellency the Governor-General no native child (from six to seven years old) who could not speak Dutch would be admitted to the free grammar school for Europeans. How can a native child of six or seven years learn Dutch? He would have had to have a Dutch governess, and before he is able to learn the Netherlands language, the child must first know his own language, and necessarily know how to read and write. It is only regents who do not have to ask permission for their families to go to the European schools; most of the native officials are afraid of receiving a "No" in answer to their request and therefore do nothing ... I remember well from my own school days that many European children went to school who knew as little Dutch as I, and I hardly knew any.

Father says in his note that the government cannot set the rice upon the table for every Javanese, and see that he partakes of it. But it can give him the means by which he can reach the place where he can find food. That means is education. When the Government provides a means of education for the people, it is as though it placed torches in their hands which enabled them to find the good road that leads to the place where the rice is served ...

Father is very proud of his ancient noble race, but right is right and justice is justice. We wish to equal the Europeans in education and enlightment, and the rights we demand for ourselves, we must also give to others. This putting of stumbling-blocks in the way of the education of the people may well be compared to the acts of the Tsar, who while he is preaching peace to the world, tramples underfoot the good right of his own subjects. Measure with two measures, no! The Europeans are troubled by many traits in the Javanese, by their indifference and lack of initiative. Very well, Netherlander, if you are troubled so much by these things why do you not do something to remedy the cause? Why is it that you do not stretch forth a single finger to help your brown brother? Draw back the thick veil from his understanding, open his eyes; you will see that there is in him something else besides an inclination for mischief, which springs principally from stupidity and ignorance ... Here before you lie the innermost thoughts of one who belongs to that despised brown race. They are not able to judge us, and the things we do and leave undone.

Do they know us? No, even as little as we know them ...

The Hollanders laugh and make fun of our stupidity, but if we strive for enlightenment, then they assume a defiant attitude towards us. What have I not suffered as a child at school through the ill will of the teachers and of many of my fellow pupils? Not all of the teachers and pupils hated us. Many loved us quite as much as the other children. But it was hard for the teachers to give a native the highest mark, never mind how well it may have been deserved.

I shall relate to you the history of a gifted and educated Javanese. The boy had passed his examination, and was number one in one of the three principal high schools of Java. Both at Semarang, where he went to school, and at Batavia, where he took his examinations, the doors of the best houses were open to the amiable schoolboy, with his agreeable and cultivated manners and great modesty.

Everyone spoke Dutch to him, and he could express himself in that language with distinction. Fresh from this environment, he went back to the house of his parents. He thought it would be proper to pay his respects to the authorities of the place and he found himself in the presence of the Resident, who had heard of him, and here it was that my friend make a mistake. He dared to address the great man in Dutch.

The following morning notice of an appointment as clerk to a controleur in the mountains was sent to him. There the young man must remain to think over his "misdeeds" and forget all that he learned at the schools. After some years a new controleur or possibly assistant controleur came; then the measure of his misfortunes was made to overflow. The new chief was a former schoolfellow, one who had never shone through his abilities. The young man, who had led his classes in everything, must now creep upon the ground before the one-time dunce, and speak always high Javanese to him, while he himself was answered in bad Malay. Can you understand the misery of a proud and independent spirit so humbled? And how much strength of character it must have taken to endure that petty and annoying oppression?

But at last he could not stand it any longer; he betook himself to Batavia and asked His Excellency the Governor-General for an audience; it was granted to him. The result was that he was sent to Preanger, with a commission to make a study of the rice cultivation there. He made himself of service through the translation of a pamphlet on the cultivation of irrigated crops from Dutch to Javanese and Sundanese. The government presented him in acknowledgement with several hundred guilders. In the controleur's school at Batavia, a teacher's place was vacant—a teacher of the Javanese language be it understood—and his friends (among the Javanese) did all in their power to secure this position for him, but without result. It was an absurd idea for a native to have European pupils who later might become ruling government officials, perish the thought! I should like to ask who could teach Javanese better than a born Javanese?

The young man went back to his dwelling-place; in the meantime another Resident had come, and the talented son of the brown race might at last become an assistant *wedono*. Not for nothing had he been banished for years to that distant place. He had learned wisdom there; namely, that one cannot serve a European official better than by creeping in the dust before him, and by never speaking a single word of Dutch in his presence. Others have now come into power, and lately when the position of translator of the Javanese language became vacant it was offered to our friend (truly opportunely), now that he does not stand in anyone's way! ...

I know an assistant resident who speaks Malay with a regent although he knows that the latter speaks good Dutch. Everyone else converses confidentially with this native ruler but the Assistant Resident—never.

My brothers speak in high Javanese to their superiors, who answer them in Dutch or in Malay. Those who speak Dutch to them are our personal friends; several have asked my brothers to speak to them in the Dutch language, but they prefer not to do it, and Father also never does. The boys and Father know all too well why they must hold to the general usage.

There is too much talk about the word "prestige", through the imaginary dignity of the under-officials. I do not bother about prestige. I am only amused at the manner in which they preserve their prestige over us Javanese.

Sometimes I cannot suppress a smile. It is distinctly diverting to see the great men try to inspire us with awe. I had to bite my lips to keep from laughing outright when I was on a journey not long ago and saw an assistant resident go from his office to his house under the shade of a gold umbrella, which a servant held spread above his noble head. It was such a ridiculous spectacle! Heavens! if he only knew how the humble crowds who respectufllly retreated to one side before the glittering sunshade, immediately his back was turned, burst out laughing.

There are many, yes, very many Government officials who allow the native rulers to kiss their feet, and their knees. Kissing the foot is the highest token of respect that we Javanese can show to our parents, our elderly blood relatives, and to our own rulers. We do not find it pleasant to do this for strangers; no, the European makes himself ridiculous in our eyes whenever he demands from us those tokens of respect to which our own rulers alone have the right.

It is a matter of indifference when residents and assistant residents allow themselves to be called *Kandjeng*, but when overseers, railroad engineers (and perhaps tomorrow, station-masters too) allow themselves to be thus addressed by their servants, it is absurdly funny. Do these people really know what *Kandjeng* means?

It is a title that the natives give to their hereditary rulers. I used to think that it was only natural for the stupid Javanese to love all this flim-flam, but now I see that the civilized, enlightened Westerner is not averse to it, that he is daft about it.

I never allow women older than I to show all the prescribed ceremonies to me, even though I know they would gladly, for though I am so young, I am a scion of what they consider an ancient, noble, and honoured house, for which in the past they have poured out both blood and gold in large measure. It is strange how attached inferiors are to those above them. But to me, it goes against the grain when people older than I creep in the dust before me.

With heavy hearts many Europeans here see how the Javanese, whom they regard as their inferiors, are slowly awakening, and at every turn a brown man comes up who shows that he has just as good brains in his head, and just as good heart in his body, as the white man.

But we are going forward, and they cannot hold back the current of time. I love the Hollanders very, very much, and I am grateful for everything that we have gained through them. Many of them are among our best friends, but there are also others who dislike us, for no other reason that [that] we are bold enough to emulate them in education and culture.

In many subtle ways they make us feel their dislike. "I am a European, you are a Javanese", they seem to say, or "I am the master, you the governed". Not once, but many times, they speak to us in broken Malay, although they know very well that we understand the Dutch language. It would be a matter of indifference to me in what language they addressed us, if the tone were only polite. Not long ago, a *Raden Aju* was talking to a gentlemen, and impulsively said, "Sir, excuse me, but may I make a friendly request: please, speak to me in your own language. I understand and speak Malay very well, but alas, only high Malay. I don't understand this *pasar* [market] Malay." How our gentleman hung his head!

Why do many Hollanders find it unpleasant to converse with us in their own language? Oh yes, now I understand; Dutch is too beautiful to be spoken by a brown mouth ...

Raden Adjeng Kartini, *Letters of a Javanese Princess*, tr. A. L. Symmers (N.Y.: Norton, 1964), pp. 56-61.

42 Ahmad Djajadiningrat: Memoirs, 1936

The position of the government's *dokter-djawa* was at that time [at the beginning of the twentieth century] considered about equal to that of *mantri* [overseer], such as *mantri* for the water supply and police *mantri*. It is understandable that the *dokters-djawa* who accomplished such a long and difficult study were not content with this situation. The higher European and also the native B.B. [*Binnenlands Bestuur*—Local and Regional Government Service] officials were not concerned in the least to treat these doctors with a little more consideration. It was therefore not surprising that on occasions they became rebellious, in particular to countrymen who stood far below them in intellectual development. When I was still a young regent I once attended a party in a club in a remote part of the country, where the guests were consuming too much hard liquor. Among them was the local Regent and a *dokter-djawa*. The Regent now and then treated the *dokter-djawa* somewhat haughtily. After he had drunk a great deal, the latter said to the Regent: "You have become regent by the grace of God. I on the other hand have become a *dokter-djawa* through my own will-power ... "

In the year 1902 it was not yet the custom for a native to dress partly or completely in European style. Even the regents still wore the national dress, that is, a *kain* [long piece of cloth which is draped around the body], a Javanese-style coat, and a headdress. They did not wear shoes, but slippers. I was dressed in that way when as Regent I made a tour of Java for the first time. In Soerabaja I stayed at the Hotel Simpang, at that time one of the top hotels ... One evening after having visited one of my acquaintances I came back to the hotel fairly late and the dining room was already full ... When I entered I heard somebody say ... in Dutch: "What kind of a monkey is that?" I calmly took my place at the big table and had hardly started to eat—with fork and spoon of course, because I was not in a *pesantren*—when I heard from the same table the remark: "Look, look, he eats with fork and spoon ... " There was cholera in Soerabaja at the time. I did not dare to drink water and so I ordered half a bottle of wine. Again there came a remark from the same corner: "Blimey, he drinks wine!" Across from me there sat a fairly elderly gentleman who seemed to find these coarse remarks very impolite. Annoyed, he suddenly stood up and walked around the table towards me. When he stood behind me he said aloud: "Sir, may I introduce myself? I am Garstens, former Resident of Pasoeroean. I can see on your face that you can understand Dutch. The remarks of these young people behind you greatly annoy me." Again there came a remark from the same table, although now more in a whisper: "What do you know, he also understands Dutch!" I was only slightly angered at this boorish behaviour ...

[The People's Credit Service] was an institution which was particularly well suited for leadership by indigenous intellectuals, because they could have acted as an educational lever for the indigenous population. This was unfortunately not realized, because this service was used as a transit office for indigenous academics. A native who had managed to pass the Higher Civil Service Entrance Examination was usually placed temporarily in the People's Credit Service in a low-ranking position. If he was found satisfactory, he would be promoted through the ranks. If he reached the stage where the next move upwards meant a position of leadership, he would— even if he had the capabilities for such a post—be transferred to another branch of the civil service where, although not losing financially, he would not be entrusted with a position of leadership.

Therefore no educated Indonesian was able to give his utmost and the best years of his life to this service, which was of such great value to the indigenous population.

I have never been able to understand the attitude of the government with respect to Western-educated indigenes who wanted to work in the civil service. Over and over again it was argued by European officials that Article 67 of the Colonial Constitutional Regulations [which opened all government positions to all races, providing the necessary educational qualifications had been obtained] could not be applied because from a Western point of view the native officials were still not up to standard. But when there were indigenes who in all respects had the same qualifications as the European officials, who supposedly were so keen to work together with native officials of the same educational and cultural level, there were no openings for them in the native civil service. When the first Javanese who had passed the Higher Civil Service Entrance Examination in the Netherlands applied here for a position in the civil service he was put on a side-track. The resolute and determined Governor-General van Heutz wanted to see this young Javanese, who held the same qualifications as European officials, placed in the European civil service corps. But already the question where he should be stationed as a European official was not easy to solve ... Finally this young man, of course, ended up in the transit office for Indonesian academics ...

Ahmad Djajadiningrat, *Herinneringen van Pangeran Aria Achmad Djajadingrat*, (Batavia Kolff, 1936), pp. 236-37; 241-42; 261-62.

43 Soewarno: Letter of Secretary of Founding Committee of Budi Utomo to the press, 23 July 1908

For a long time now we (the students of the *S.T.O.V.I.A.*) ... have thought about the possibility of improving the situation of our people, in particular the lower classes. We were and are still fully aware of the difficulty of our task, but this is not the reason why we remained quiet. We did not expect actual opposition from our countrymen, but rather we feared that they would completely stay aloof if we came forward with our ideas. How many well-educated men with initiative and energy have not already tried to create an association to improve the intellectual development of the Javanese? A case in point is Soedirokoesoedho, who travelled throughout most of Java presenting the holy cause to almost every *prijaji*. But alas, all these people were bitterly disappointed in their expectations. It should therefore not be surprising that we were rather hesitant to follow the example of these courageous men and take our case to the native officials.

One of the prescribed duties of the *prijaji* is supposed to be to help the common man, to raise him from the darkness of ignorance so that he will be better equipped in the struggle for life and will be able to compete more successfully with foreigners. But it is well known that the lower *prijaji* in particular are unable to free themselves from the pressing yoke of servitude. They always succumb to pressure from above because they feel that opposition would be an act of irreverence and that it would damage the prestige of their superiors. So when the higher *prijaji* cannot be won over to our side, our cause is surely to be rejected by at least half of the lower officials.

We had to take careful note of this evil, which is apparent almost everywhere and extremely obstructive to a successful outcome. We felt that the best way to tackle the problem would have been to practise casual therapy, i.e. to take away the causes; and the most effective way would in our opinion have been to convince the people deeply and to make them realize the urgent need for an association which unites us, which acts vigorously and presents itself to the outside world as something that is here to stay and of which serious notice will have to be taken.

But this we could not force on people. And therefore we considered it wise for the time being not to propagate our ideas among the older generation. Instead we decided to approach the young people who live under the same pressures as we do. The obvious thing to do was to appeal to the feeling of love for our people of those who thought like us, that is our comrades in the Native Agricultural and Veterinary Science School at Buitenzorg [Bogor], in the Training Schools for Native Officials at Bandoeng, Magelang, and Probolinggo, in the Native Teachers' Training Colleges ... whom we could expect to understand us better, so that our voice would not be calling out alone and in vain in the wilderness. We could also expect that they, as the future advisers of the lower classes, would be willing to do their utmost in the service of the prosperity of their people and country. And we were not mistaken in this. Our ideas were generally accepted and supported by them, because already for a considerable time young Javanese students have been keen to do something for our great people of Java, of which they are only a very small part. After all the happiness of our people is our happiness; its development is also our development; its downfall is also our downfall.

Furthermore, the fact that a number of native officials and private persons have joined us spontaneously is sufficient proof that there are many who are sympathetic to our ideas and that they believe our association is feasible ... we are not planning as our first and immediate task to clear the Augean stable. Probably also the abolition of the *hormat* regulations [prescribing the particular type of homage to be shown to native and Dutch officials] will be incorporated in the programme. But education must be the first point on the platform.

How we are to reach our objectives will have to be decided in more detail in the coming *Poeasa* [Fast] month at Jogjakarta where a central committee will be elected. We invite every organization that has the same objectives to send representatives to this general meeting. Also the statutes will still have to be decided. It goes almost without saying that the young people who while still at school were forced by circumstances to do the thinking will not lead the association. Older, equally genuine, and experienced men, whom we can trust, will have to lead us. Only then can we act, and show our countrymen that there is also character and will-power hidden in the Javanese people.

In the last few days some newspapers have featured interesting articles on the activities of the three *Raden Adjengs* of Japara [Kartini and her sisters] and the Regents of Japara, Temanggoeng, Karanganjar, and Koetoardjo, etc. Their [progressiveness] is fortunately well received by the press. We were happy to read about this, because now the great difficulty of "not being understood" by the appointed leaders of the people is no longer there, and we can abandon our doubts. The leaders now appear to have the same ideas as we. They want to go in the same direction, and what is simpler and more efficient than to go the same way together? This will in the first place avoid the cutting-up of our forces, which is an important prerequisite for the success of our attempts. Combination and full co-operation have so far been lacking. But now, when voices are raised from all sides, and many feel the need to combine, one must really try to make this association as strongly and widely based as possible.

We have immediately informed the three *Raden Adjengs* of Japara about our association and its objectives and we have requested them to establish a local branch, while at the same time we made it known that we also supported their own efforts. We are also taking measures to inform and keep in close contact with the various leaders of our people [regents]. We hope that this co-operation will result in a strong organization.

It is true that this initiative should not have been taken by us, who are younger in years, and we do not accuse anybody of having forsaken his duties. The time for action was apparently not yet there. But now perhaps the dawn of a new life for the Javanese has come. In any case, the time for sleeping has now undoubtedly passed. And if the leaders also now remain aloof, inactive, and do not want or dare to put themselves at the head of this movement, then we ourselves will be forced against our will to get down to business without them. However, we believe that this will not be necessary.

S. L. van der Wal, *De opkomst van de Nationalistische beweging in Nederlandsch-Indie, een bronnen-publikatie* (Groningen: Wolters, 1967), pp. 39-41.

44 E. F. E. Douwes Dekker: The Indies Party, its nature and objectives, 1913

What is the objective of the *Indische Partij*? ... The answer is found in Article 2 of the Constitution, which reads as follows: "the purpose of the *Indische Partij* is to awaken the patriotism of all the people of the Indies for the country which feeds them; and to induce them to co-operate on the basis of political equality in order to bring this Indies fatherland to prosperity and to prepare its people for independence ... " Let us begin [by explaining] the last words, which have caused so much fear: "to prepare the people for independence". I doubt whether there is much to fear from these words. In fact we are doing nothing else than subscribing to the government programme. Is it not true that the government in semi-official and perhaps also official statements [has indicated that it] actually desires to gradually develop the colonies to the same level as the mother country? What else can this mean politically than that the colonies will be prepared for statehood? What type of state? Is only self-government envisaged, which in a colonial situation means something very different from independence? Or is perhaps the new state to remain under the sovereignty of the mother country, whatever mother country this may be? Of course [the latter] cannot be true. Unless the colonial political programme, the colonial political task that the mother country has taken upon itself, is a fraud; unless we are given a stack of marked cards; and unless there are dishonest intentions, a mother country that advertises its colonial rule in such a way cannot mean anything else than that the final objective of its policy will be to grant independence. The government should therefore have no objection to our programme. But if she did object, we would have shown up her [real] intentions. And if we were forced to change this aspect of our programme, there would still be sufficient time to do so. Furthermore, we would know then that we were fooled in believing that the government was honest. We would have forced the government of the Indies to take a public stand ... And we would then no longer have to doubt that ... we would be refused our civil rights always ...

I have been asked whether the *Indische Partij* is evolutionary or revolutionary ... The penetration of every new idea brings with it reforms. As we plan to put an end once and for all to the colonial situation, the *Indische Partij* is definitely revolutionary ... Revolutionary action enables people to achieve their objectives quickly. Surely this is not immoral ... The *Indische Partij* can safely be called revolutionary. Such a word does not frighten us ...

[The next point raised by Douwes Dekker was the creation of an Indies nationalism based on the national unity of all races in the colony. Pointing to Austria-Hungary, Russia, Switzerland, and the United States, Douwes Dekker argued that a national multi-racial society could also be achieved in the Indies.] Truly, it should not be so very difficult to imagine such a unity, at least not for those Indiers who are of mixed blood. I admit that it would be more difficult for Europeans, but also among them some can be found who can be put up as examples to the majority. There is a difference in the way in which Indiers of mixed blood and Europeans look at the pure Indiers, the natives. The Europeans, that is the best and noblest among them, consider natives persons intelligent people, who after higher intellectual training are perfectly capable of becoming a great credit to humanity. The Indiers of mixed blood, however, should see a little more in them. They should consider the natives as their half-brothers. They will find in the character of the natives so many traits that are similar to their own. After all they are themselves partly native, and an Asiatic, Eastern people. There is no doubt that if the natives are educated both morally and intellectually and are granted equal political rights and equality before the law, a general intellectual association will come about that will make the idea of a united people possible ...

[Douwes Dekker also stresses the need for a more Indonesia-centric education.] It is a fact that we do not know our fatherland ... It is true that we do not need to know our own cultural history to determine the price of Java coffee or sugar on the Amsterdam market. On the contrary it might even obstruct the drainage [of profits] from the Indies ... We know to the last detail about such interesting facts as the Remonstrants and Counter-Remonstrants [two political-religious factions in seventeenth century Holland] and that Jacoba of Bavaria fled dressed in men's clothes—but about our own fatherland we know nothing or very little ... What do we know about Modjopahit [fourteenth century Javanese empire], which at its zenith had colonies in Ternate, Pasei, and had its ships sail to Cambodia and even China to trade, causing the land of Java to prosper? We know nothing about such things ... What do we know about the grandiose ideas that must have fired the imagination of the thousands of artists who built the Boroboedoer [vast Buddhist shrine in Central Java], the Prambanan [Hindu temple complex in Central Java], and the many other temples? ... What do we know about the beauty of the ornamentalism, the mysticism of line and form that encompasses a world of aesthetic thought in the golden era of our architecture? ...

[Turning again to the problem of the pluralistic colonial society Douwes Dekker argues that national unity is possible.] How can the fraternization of the Indies races and subgroups occur? This is only possible through intellectual development. Economic differences, varying interests, yes, even class differences will to a certain extent remain, but racial differentiation will and must disappear. An intellectually developed person does not ask for the place where one was born. Only the ruling classes with their stupid prejudices do this because in accentuating racial divisions they see a means to maintain their privileged position ... Reason reaches across all racial barriers. People with the same education are attracted to each other. A people is divided into several strata because of different levels of intellectual development. The evidence for this is to be found in our own society. We have friends among the natives, who we feel are in no respect below us intellectually. Do we in our dealings with them notice their race perhaps? ...

There is nothing we need so much as self-assurance and self-confidence. We must get rid of our timidity. It is a hindrance to us, it damages us. On the contrary, we must feel in us a strong sense of our own worth, a realization that we are not inferior to anybody. Then there will develop in us a strong moral pride in being ourselves, which will disdainfully suppress in us every desire to put ourselves forwards as different from what we really are ... This will prevent us from becoming renegades. Renegades are small, miserly people who only deserve our contempt. Every Indier should be staunch and proud of being an Indier. He should be proud that he can and may be himself ... When a mother country during long centuries of colonial rule has had no other objective than to exploit and squeeze its colony dry for its own benefit, and when in all these long centuries ... it has not succeeded in accomplishing its task of creating a nation, then its colonial policy and its colonial morality are rotten. And it would be in the cause of morality to push down what is on the point of collapsing from internal decay. This is of course what the *Indische Partij* aims at in its struggle against racial superiority and racial discrimination ... It will give the final push to make the tree of racial discrimination crash to earth ... *But when Indiers of mixed blood complain about this racial superiority they must take care not to become guilty themselves of the same sin with respect to the natives*. They must realize that artificially inculcated ideas of belonging to the ruling classes do by no means give them the right to look down on a class of Indiers with whom they are bound together with unbreakable chains ...

The *Indische Partij* does not support any particular religion. The *Indische Partij* is of the opinion that religion should remain outside the scope of our and any other political organization ... The *Indische Partij* will struggle against all expressions of religious sectarianism and all attempts to create religious hate. Instead it must preach the religion of brotherhood ...

[Douwes Dekker stressed the need for Indiers to take a greater interest in technical education and to strengthen such qualities as self-control and intellectual courage. Equality of all races before the law was an important platform in the programme of the *Indische Partij*.] The abolition of legal inequality will cause very great problems. But no problem can be too big to keep us from acting justly ... Taxation legislation will have to be completely revised because the natives, that is the Indiers with least capital at their disposal, pay a great deal more than the prosperous whites. Under the existing system the emphasis is on taxing poverty and only as an afterthought does one think about the satchels filled to the brim with gold ... The abolition of legal inequality will also result in a change in the judicial system. Some experts warn against such a reorganization. One does not know what to do with the *adat* [customary Indonesian] law. But there are also experts of equally high standing who advocate the introduction of a uniform legal system ...

Legal inequality also exists with respect to land ownership. There was once a big loudmouth who declared that it was a feather in the cap of the Dutch nation that it had left the natives undisturbed in the possession of their land and had protected this land against alienation ... In reality it is the big capitalists who have enjoyed the loving care of all successive governments ... The natives if they have to suffer from hunger can now at least do so in their own dilapidated huts. By God Almighty, it must be a great feeling to starve in your own house ... Why then are the people not prosperous if the possession of land is hailed as such a source of riches ... ? Why ... do the natives earn in proportion no more from their land than a tradesman? ... If the natives desire to obtain the same rights enjoyed by the other more privileged groups of the population, then they must from their side also be prepared to share exclusive rights to land with everybody who complies with the conditions laid down by law. I cannot see why an Indier of mixed blood may not be the owner of land in the same way as a native ...

[The *Indische Partij* demands the right for Indiers to defend their own country.] What is our purpose in training the Indiers to defend themselves? It is nothing less than a patriotic duty which they should fulfil and which they should be granted. At present we are not capable of defending our own country. Why not? Only because the Netherlands nation is apparently so convinced of its shortcomings in the fulfilment of its colonial task that it does not *dare* to put its trust in the gratitude of the people. *The government is afraid of us and will take great care to prevent us from getting arms in our hands* ...

[The *Indische Partij* also condemned the pluralistic nature of the colonial education system.] At present we have separate schools for Europeans, for Chinese, for natives, and within a short time we will also have schools perhaps for half-whites, three-quarter whites, full noblemen, half-noblemen, and God knows for whatever other aristocratic gradations there may be. The *Indische Partij* wants a uniform education system, one type of education for everybody ... The white children can learn a great deal in all fields from the darker-coloured children. The native children are much keener to learn; they are much quieter than the white children ...

E. F. E. Douwes Dekker, *De Indische Partij, haar wezen en doel* (Bandung: Fortuna, 1913), pp. 2-50.

45   The Indische Partij in Action

1. R. M. Soewardi Soerjaningrat: If only I were a Netherlander, 1913

At present there exists an abundance of newspaper articles which propagate the idea of staging a big feast here in the Indies to celebrate the centenary of the Independence of the Netherlands ... I can easily understand the feelings of Netherlands patriots of today who want to celebrate such an important date. After all, I am also a patriot, and in the same way as the genuine Netherlands nationalists love their fatherland, so do I love my own fatherland more than I can express in words. What a joy, what a pleasure it would be to be able to commemorate such a very great day. I wish that for a moment I could be a Netherlander, not a naturalized Netherlander, but a real pure son of the Greater Netherlands, completely free from foreign stains. How would I rejoice when later in November the long-awaited day would arrive, the day of the Independence celebrations. How I would rejoice when I would see the Netherlands flag together with the Orange banner flutter in the wind. I would join in the singing until I was hoarse from the *"Wilhelmus"* [the Dutch national anthem] and the *"Wien Nederlands Bloed"* [another national song popular at the time] ... All these manifestations would make me feel proud. I would thank God in the Christian church for his goodness. I would send to heaven a wish, a petition for the maintenance of Netherlands power also in the colonies ... I do not know what else I would do; but I would feel capable of anything. I would indeed wish to organize the coming celebrations on as wide a basis as possible, but I would not want the natives of this country to participate in this commemoration. I would forbid them to join in the cheering during these festivities. I would even close off the area where the festivities took place so that no native could see our elation at the commemoration of our day of Independence.

It would seem to me somewhat impolite, coarse, and improper, if we—I am still imagining that I am a Netherlander—let the natives join ... First of all we would hurt their finely attuned feeling of honour, because we would be commemorating our independence here in their country which we keep in subjection ... Wouldn't we think that these poor slaves would hunger for the moment when, like us, they would be able to celebrate such an occasion? Or are we perhaps of the opinion that because of a long-practised spirit-killing policy of suppression we have killed all human and spiritual feelings in the natives? We would certainly fool ourselves, because even the most primitive peoples curse all forms of imperialism. If I were a Netherlander I would not celebrate the commemoration of independence in a country where we refuse to give the people their freedom ... Especially in these times when the people of the Indies are engaged in finding their feet, although they are still only half awakened, it would be a tactical mistake to show this people how it should eventually celebrate its independence. In this way one would stimulate the passions and unconsciously develop the desire for freedom, the hope for independence in the future ... If I were a Netherlander now at this moment I would protest against the idea of this commemoration. I would write in all the newspapers that it was wrong. I would warn the other colonists that it would be dangerous to hold Independence celebrations in these times. I would dissuade all Netherlanders from offending the people of the Netherlands Indies who are awakening and are becoming bolder. It might cause [the people] to become impudent. Truly, I would protest with all the power that is in me. But ... I am not a Netherlander. I am only a brown-coloured son of this tropical land, a native of this Netherlands colony and I would therefore not protest ...

Putting all irony aside ... the centenary celebrations of the Independence of the Netherlands say something for the everywhere so highly regarded fidelity to the fatherland, in this case of the Netherlanders. I wish them the greatest enjoyment in their national commomoration. But what I and many of my countrymen object to is mainly the fact that here we have another case where the natives must pay for something that does not concern them in the least. What benefit will the celebrations, which we are all helping to stage, bring us? Absolutely none. At the highest we will be reminded that we are not a free people ... I feel therefore far more for the idea mooted in the native daily *Kaoem Moeda* and in *De Express* of forming a committee of educated natives in Bandoeng, where the idea for a commemoration was born ... which on the day of the celebrations will send a congratulatory telegram to the Queen in which at the same time it will urge the abolition of Article 111RR [this article in the Colonial Constitutional Regulations controlled the right of political association] and the speedy establishment of an Indies parliament ...

R. M. Soewardi Soerjaningrat, *"Als ik eens Nederlander was"* (Onze Verbanning, Schiedam: 1913), pp. 68-72.

2. Tjipto Mangoenkoesoemo: Power or fear, 1913

Yesterday we were very fortunate: the assistant public prosecutor came to our office and took possession of the writings of R. M. Soewardi Soerjaningrat, our secretary. Without wanting to challenge the Justice Department or the police, I must say that we felt proud.

Was this seizure meant as a demonstration of power? Does the poor deluded government really think that we will be discouraged because we are confronted by superior might? On the contrary, it will stimulate us to provoke that superior power, to force it to do its utmost to get us down. The stronger its action, the stronger our power will grow.

Was it fear that already at this stage forced the government to stop our power? If so, it is a compliment for our secretary, because it would follow that the "libellous article of the muddle-headed R. M. Soewardi Soerjaningrat", to quote the *Bataviaasch Handelsblad* [conservative Dutch newspaper], was not insignificant after all. So, after all, one of these "intellectual pariahs" has stood up whose "confused writings" are considered to be able to bring the "dull, indolent masses of natives" into motion. This would not be very pleasant for the Netherlanders.

There is still a third possibility. We do not believe that the product of an "intellectual pariah" can draw the attention of the higher European authorities unless these authorities had been hit in the soft underbelly. We suspect that the "libellous article" contained something that was offensive to our white masters. We cannot remember that a European newspaper was ever prosecuted because it offended us. But then, of course, the "amoral" native people are after all only a nation of slaves who therefore would not be easily offended. But it is still possible that the prosecution of a [European] newspaper for sowing racial hatred might eventuate. If this prosecution does not occur, it is clear that there is *no* justice here. Happily, *we* cannot be blamed.

The time has come to take a stand. We call on our brothers, the Young Javanese, to take careful note of the reactions of the European press. From what we have already seen, it appears that they want to challenge us. We have already been told: "We are the strongest, and so you must keep your mouth shut; we are the possessors of your land". This is simply misusing power to stop us from speaking, because they do not want to hear anything unpleasant. But by Allah, this won't be so easy. Our Committee firmly intends to continue the struggle to the end by intellectual means—we are, of course, not allowed to arm ourselves! Brothers, support that Committee! ... While later everybody who calls himself a Netherlander will be in a festive mood listening to toasts and speeches ... about the sweetness of freedom, the same sweet freedom will be taken away from our own brother Soewardi.

Tjipto Mangoenkoesoemo, *'Kracht of Vrees'*, (Onze Verbanning Schiedam: 1913), pp. 73-75.

The Islamic Movement

Islam, which gradually began to penetrate the Indonesian islands in the fourteenth century, was never able to replace traditional Indonesian civilization in its entirety. This was particularly so in Java. Admittedly Islam brought change to Java, but its impact was often not very deep and many elements of traditional Javanese culture can still be seen fully alive today.

Islam came to the Indies after it had first filtered through the civilizations of Persia and India and was therefore presented to the Indonesians in a familiar mystical garb. And in most parts of the Archipelago the conversion to Islam was initially little more than a formality. The royal courts and the nobility still adhered firmly to the traditional culture into which some select Islamic concepts were gradually absorbed. The islamic law never succeeded in completely supplanting the *adat*, nor was the Islamic concept of theocracy ever accepted by the traditional ruling classes; and whenever *ulama* (Muslim teachers) attempted to interfere too drastically with the traditional social and political status quo they were ruthlessly suppressed. Later during the colonial period the Dutch consistently supported the nobility and the *adat* chiefs against any encroachements on their authority by "fanatical" Muslims.

At the village level many of the old traditions were gradually covered with an Islamic veneer. Animist and Hindu/Buddhist beliefs and practices continued alongside and often were closely intertwined with the performance of Islamic religious duties. In many ways, then, Java was not Islamized, but Islam was Javanized (*see* document 46).

Still, more orthodox Islamic pockets have existed since the fourteenth century in the coastal areas of Java, from where they have gradually spread their influence into the interior, mainly through the establishment of *pesantren*, centres of orthodox religious learning. Document 47 contains a survey of the number of *pesantren* in various parts of Java in 1831 as well as a description of the teaching methods and types of books used in these institutions. This proselytizing process intensified during the second half of the nineteenth century when as a result of improved communications more Indonesians made the pilgrimage to Mecca, where they were imbued with the more authentic spirit of Islam. Many of these *haji* (pilgrims) on their return to Java set up *pesantren* to spread the true faith.

Yet the number of *santri*—pious, more orthodox Muslims—remained relatively small compared with that of the *abangan* (the more syncretic nominal Muslims). It was the Dutch missionary Poensen who was among the first to point out this important distinction between *santri* and *abangan* (*see* document 46). This primordial cleavage within Javanese society was popularized in the 1950s by the American anthropologist Glifford Geertz in his book *The Religion of Java*.

During the nineteenth century when the West was beginning to penetrate more deeply into indigenous life, the orthodox Muslims began to react more strongly against colonial rule. Muslim teachers preached hate against the *kafir* (unbeliever) colonial government and its European and native servants; and it condemned Western concepts, methods, science, and education as *haram* (heretical). An interesting example of this strong anti-colonial feeling in the *pesantren* is provided by Ahmad Djajadininvrat, who as a young man spent some time in one of these teaching institutions in Banten (*see* document 48).

From the beginning of the twentieth century, however, a number of *ulama* took up the challenge of the West in a far more positive manner. Influenced by modernist Islamic ideas from the Middle East, these Indonesian Muslims set about with great energy and zeal to stave off the threat posed by both Western secularism and Christianity.

Islamic reformism or modernism was an attempt to revitalize Islam in its struggle for survival against the ever-increasing impact of Western political and intellectual superiority. This Islamic renewal had been gaining strength during the second half of the nineteenth century in the Middle East, particularly in Egypt, where such prominent Islamic scholars as Djamal-al-Din-al-Afghani and his pupil Mohammad Abduh through their writings and activities had exerted a far-reaching influence throughout the whole of the Islamic world.

According to these reformers the decline of Islam as a political power and as a civilization was due to the fact that it had not been able to keep up with intellectual and social developments in the rest of the world. During the ages the orginally simple and rational core of the Islamic faith—the Qu'ran and the Hadits—had been overgrown by such a burden of irrational beliefs and superstition that any intellectual progress had become impossible. Muslims had succumbed to heresy, which was the major reason why Islam no longer was able to fulfil its divinely ordained purpose of being the most powerful community on earth. To enable Islam to rise again, al-Afghani argued that as a first step religion should be cleansed from impurities and heresy. He also dreamt about the re-establishment of a powerful empire uniting all the Muslim peoples of the world under the one great caliph (pan-Islamism) and advocated direct political action. Mohammad Abduh was less sanguine in his approach and emphasized religious and educational reform.

Most of the efforts of the Indonesian Muslim reformers went initially into the remodelling and reconstruction of the existing Muslim education system, because the colonial education system was considered to be one of the greatest dangers to Islam. As Snouck-Hurgronje (*see* document 25) had foreseen, the lack of religious instruction in government schools and the closer contact of students with Western thinking and ideologies tended to "emancipate" them from Islam. In particular students from a *prijaji* or *adat*-conscious background, where orthodox Islam had never been able to penetrate fully, succumbed more easily to the lure of Western rationalism and secularism. But also among students with a more orthodox Islamic background a weakening or even a complete abandonment of the faith was not uncommon. The other danger to Islam was the proselytizing efforts of the Christian missions, which since the relaxation from the middle of the nineteenth century of the old-established rule forbidding missionary activity in predominantly Muslim areas, had penetrated into many parts of Java and Sumatra, establishing schools and hospitals.

Between 1909, when the first modern Islamic school was established in Padang (Minangkabau), and 1942, Indonesian Muslims created a vast network of modern educational institutions ranging from elementary schools to university. In 1934 there were in Minangkabau alone 452 modernist Muslim schools with 25,292 pupils.

It was also under the aegis of Islam that the first modern organized Indonesian mass movement—the *Sarikat Islam*—was established. The *Sarikat Islam* was founded in 1912 and under the energetic leadership of Tjokroaminoto, a fiery and charismatic speaker, it rapidly grew out into a vast movement with branches all over Indonesia, claiming 2.5 million members in 1919. Most of the rank and file were *Abangan* and not particularly inherested in furthering the cause of Islam, which was one of the major platforms. But rather they saw the *Sarikat Islam* as a sounding-board for their social and economic troubles, viewing the charismatic Tjokroaminoto as the long-promised *Ratu Adil*, who was on the verge of inaugurating an era of prosperity and happiness.

While the national leadership consisted on the whole of modernist Muslims, who considered Islam as the only proper vehicle to further the national and economic interests of the people, the local leadership was rather motley in its composition, consisting of religious teachers of the old and new orthodox variety, disgruntled school teachers, union leaders, native officials, and unemployed school-leavers, who all had their own personal axes to grind.

This uneven commitment to the Islamic cause on the part of many of the local leaders and the rank and file caused serious problems of discipline and eventually resulted in the disintegration of the movement.

The initial programme of the *Sarikat Islam* was politically very moderate and stressed that the main purpose of the organization was to further the interests of Islam in Indonesia and to work for the social and economic advancement of the people in co-operation with the government's Ethical welfare programme (*see* document 49).

A deterioration in economic conditions during and immediately after World War I and, even more important, the infiltration of Communists into the movement drove the *Sarikat Islam* into a far more radical direction. This caused a serious split in the party between the more conservative Muslim elements led by the modernist leader Hadji Agus Salim and the radicals led by the Communists. Attempts by Tjokroaminoto to find a *modus vivendi* between the two groups, by claiming that in terms of social and economic objectives there was very little difference between the precepts of the Qu'ran and Marx, failed to heal the breach. And finally in 1923 the Communists were ousted from the organization, taking with them the vast majority of the rank and file, who apparently were more interested in finding an immediate solution to their social and economic problems than in religion.

In 1923 the organization constituted itself into an official political party—the *Partai Sarikat Islam*. While the *Sarikat Islam* under the leadership of Tjokroaminoto had attempted to accommodate the whole spectrum of Indonesian nationalist aspirations within its organizational structure, the *P.S.I.* became more specifically Islamic in its objectives. Like other Islamic organizations it strongly objected to the secular nationalism of leaders such as Sukarno, Hatta, and Sjahrir and strove for a free Indonesia with a constitution based on the precepts of the Islamic law (*see* document 50).

The *P.S.I.*, however, only played a comparatively minor role in the Indonesian nationalist movement during the late 1920s and 1930s. In 1939 the party joined the nationalist agitation for the establishment of a full parliament in the Indies. But the *P.S.I.* was further weakened when Kartosuwirjo and his followers, who accused the party of compromising too much with the secular nationalists, separated themselves (*see* document 51). (In 1948 Kartosuwirjo founded the *Darul Islam* [Islamic state], which fought both the Dutch and the Indonesian Republic.

After the rapid decline of the *Sarikat Islam* in the early 1920s the leadership of the Islamic revival movement passed to the *Muhammadyah*, an organization founded in 1912, which concentrated its efforts in the social and educational field and refused to become directly involved in politics. The objectives of *Muhammadyah*, as laid down in its constitution, were to spread the true Islam among the Indonesian people and to improve the religious life of its members by means of holding public meetings to discuss religious subjects; the founding and maintaining of modern Islamic schools; the founding and maintaining of mosques for public religious services; and the publishing of religious books, newspapers, and tracts.

Taking a leaf out of the book of the Christian missions the *Muhammadyah*, in addition to founding schools, also established hospitals, orphanages, and organizations for poor relief. Its efforts met with a great deal of success and in 1925 there were already twenty-nine branches with four thousand members; eight Dutch-Native Schools; a teachers' training college; thirty-two vernacular primary schools; and fourteen *madrasah* (religious schools)—altogether including one hundred and nineteen teachers and four thousand pupils. Two clinics had also been established, one at Yogjakarta and one at Surabaja, and an orphanage and house for the poor at Yogjakarta.

By 1929 membership had grown to sixteen thousand and the *Taman Pustaka* (publishing section) had during its fifteen years of existence published and distributed seven hundred thousand books and pamphlets. Also the *Aisjijah*, the women's branch of the *Muhammadyah*, had made considerable progress and by 1929 counted forty-seven branches and fifty groups with five thousand members, supporting thirty-two schools for girls with seventy-five teachers.

In 1938 *Muhammadyah* had 852 branches with 250,000 members; it maintained 834 mosques and *langgar* (prayer houses), 31 public libraries, and 1774 schools, some of which received subsidy from the colonial government. At that time the organization had also 5516 male and 2114 female *muballigh* (missionaries) in the field. Document 52 contains excerpts from one of the national congresses of *Muhammadyah*.

Another important modernist Islamic organization was the *Jong Islamieten Bond* (the Young Muslims Union), which had been founded by Hadji Agus Salim to protect Islamic students in Dutch high schools and institutes of tertiary learning from the evil of secularism. The *Jong Islamieten Bond* became more directly involved in politics, opposed the secular Indonesian nationalist youth organizations, and refused to join the *Indonesia Muda* (Young Indonesia) organization, which had amalgamated within itself most of the earlier regional youth groups such as *Jong Java*, and *Jong Ambon*, etc. (*see* document 53).

The progress made by Islamic reformism caused conservative religious scholars to organize themselves also along Western lines. In 1926 a number of prominent *ulama* in East Java founded the *Nahadatul Ulama* (Association of Scholars) in Surabaja (*see* document 54) for the purpose of furthering the cause of traditionalist orthodox Islam and to encourage believers to adhere strictly to one of the four *madzhab* (i.e. the traditionally recognized legal interpretations of the Qu'ran) as opposed to the stress placed by the modernists on individual interpretation. The organization planned to work towards achieving unity among the *ulama* who adhered to any of the four *madzhab* and would scrutinize *kitab* (religious books) for their orthodoxy. Moreover the *Nahdatul Ulama* was to spread the faith by every means allowable within the law; to further Islamic education; to take care of the running of mosques, prayer houses, and *pesantren*; to engage in pious works such as giving support to widows and the needy; and to further agricultural, trading, and industrial enterprises in so far as this was not in conflict with the law. The organization spread rapidly throughout Java and also established breaches in Borneo. By 1942 the number of branches had grown to 120.

Similar to the *Muhammadyah*, the *Nahdatul Ulama* was ostensibly non-political, although in the schools and boy scouts sections the nationalist spirit was very much cultivated. Both organizations, however, became somewhat more politically orientated towards the end of the Dutch colonial period. And it was largely on the initiative of K. H. Mansur, the *Muhammadyah* leader, that in 1937 the *Madjlisoel Islamil A'laa Indonesia* (Council of Indonesian Islamic organizations) or *M.I.A.I.* was founded. The *M.I.A.I.* was a federation of Islamic organizations, and although it was primarily religious, the membership of such parties as the *Partai Sarikat Islam* naturally brought the organization into closer contact with politics.

46 C. Poensen: Letters about Islam from the country areas of Java, 1886

There was a time when hardly anything was known about the religious thinking and activities of the native world. The natives were blandly dismissed as "superstitious Mohammedans"; and the Dutch

East India Company and the later Netherlands Government agreed with this conclusion and made it the basis or main principle of their policy ... This situation has changed completely in the last few years ... and now one hears not only that Islam exists in Java ... but also that there is a so-called Javanism—a term that, although perhaps not entirely correct, has been coined to describe the mixture of the old Javanese animism, Hinduism, Mohammedanism etc ...

The Javanese are all (with an unimportant exception) *Mohammedans*. This is what the government says and what the natives themselves say, as well as what reality teaches us ... and the *pesantren* and the pilgrimage are continuously spreading a better understanding of the true spirit and essence of the Islam ... How true this is could be seen recently when Raden Ario Tjondra Negara made a point about the *salat* in connection with the performance of religious duties on Friday. A man such as Dr Juynboll [Dutch Islamic expert] rejected this explanation, but later was found to be wrong ... So we should now ... begin to get some inkling of the meaning Islam has in present-day Java and of what is happening in the world of the *pesantren* scholars and the *hadjis*, and the influence they exert on the masses. These large masses are completely manipulated by them. And although they [the masses] continue to live in stupidity, heresy, and poverty, they in fact know, especially in the eastern and southern parts of the island, little more about Islam than the circumcision of the children, fasting, not to eat pork ... that there are ... a number of feast days ... that all *prijaji* are naturally Mohammedans and that all Christians are *kapir londa* [unbelievers] ... But all this ignorance and foolishness will gradually diminish, and this is already to be noticed in some classes. The result will be that the masses will become stronger in their Islamic beliefs and its teachings will be better known. In short the people will become better Mohammedans.

But to have a proper understanding of the situation it is necessary to make a distinction between the *formal* and *inner* life of the people. And the *inner* life of the masses, the *prijaji* of course excepted, can at present hardly be called Mohammedan. What do we mean by this? For example, the Netherlands people we can call both formally and inwardly a Christian nation ... The whole of life and thinking—the public spirit—of the people is permeated by Christianity, although many do not think and act in a Christian manner. In this sense the Javanese people cannot be called a Mohammedan nation. It is true that *formally* the religion of the masses is, however defective it may be, undoubtedly Mohammedanism ... but *inwardly* there are other and older forces still at work. This has become clear especially during the last few years. And it is not possible to understand fully the inward life of the people if one concentrates solely on the outward forms and ceremonies of Islam ... The only way to understand this is to observe carefully the more intimate religious customs, manners, and actions in the daily and homely sphere, to talk with the people, etc. It will become clear then that *outwardly* the people certainly must be called *Mohammedan*, but that *the inner soul* is motivated by a religious feeling that expresses itself in all sorts of non-Mohammedan ideas and practices, and that the people do not yet live and think in a Mohammedan way. [It will become clear] that we are dealing with a Mohammedan people, which is and wants to be called Mohammedan, not because it prefers Islam and is permeated by its spirit, but because it has to be Mohammedan and finds it difficult to be anything else, because all the ruling powers desire it that way, and this is difficult for the lower classes and the better situated as well to oppose.

In the daily life prayers can be heard in which the names of all sorts of spirits are called, while the name of *Allah* is either lacking or is treated equally with those of the many other [spirits]. People can be seen to bring offerings to the spirit of the village, and to other spirits in rocks, trees, graves, caves, rivers, etc., while in their own mosque they never bring a single offering to *Allah*. One also will learn that the people divide themselves into two classes: the *bangsa poetihan* and the *bangsa abangan* [whites and reds]. The first group consists of a fairly small number of people who could be called "pious", orthodox Mohammedans, although their orthodoxy too could be questioned sometimes. The other group consists of the vast majority of the people, who are not Mohammedan in their religious thinking and actions, but who live in accordance with the precepts of their forefathers. They can do well without Allah, the only exception being when a wedding is to be performed before the *penghoeloe* [Muslim religious official] ... and when one is forced to recite the Mohammedan creed. And then after all Allah is only a new Lord, who has been added later, and with whom one is not as familiar yet. On these occasions one calls out loudly that Allah is the only one, while at home in a far happier frame of mind offerings are prepared for the village spirit ...

If more evidence is wanted, one should observe the villager when he is sick, when somebody dies, when his wife is pregnant or in childbed, if he wants to undertake something special, for example to transport a buffalo or cow to another village, or to build a house or something of this kind. One should even spy upon thieves, when they decide to go and steal somewhere, and how they then need the protection of special spirits in order to carry out their plans unnoticed, to become invisible and go without interference. But Allah ... Yes, the villager uses formulas, called *rapals*, in which Allah's name is mentioned, but he has to share this honour with many others! ...

In my previous letter I spoke about the more intimate religious actions in the daily life of the natives. As in this month a number of religious actions must be performed, this is a good occasion to look at them more closely. The month Sja'ban (Saban in Javanese) is especially dedicated to the memory and veneration of the dead and it is therefore also called the "*Roewah* month", the month of the spirits ... Most of the Europeans would not know about this ... And yet there is hardly a religious duty that is so generally performed by the natives as this *roewahan*, or the veneration of the dead with a sacrificial meal ... Certainly, the festivities at the end of the fast [lebaran] are much better known by Europeans, because they cause a greater stir and movement among the natives than their spirits or All Souls day.

But all this movement and stir still do not provide us with a proper gauge to estimate what is important in the inner life of the natives. The Javanese *roewahan* is a real Javanese religious feast with an Arabic name, but Javanese or Polynesian in origin. Already before the coming of Islam were the dead venerated here ... How do the natives celebrate the commemoration and veneration of the dead? ... [The celebration] consists of a meal, although some of the better situated give first another meal—*kendoeren*—near the *poenden*, a sacred grave, of the village. The closest neighbours and people who are encountered more or less accidentally are invited to the meal ... A special preparation of rice—called *sega poenel*—seems to be generally considered necessary for such a meal. The rice is served in eight *ambeng*—certain quantities of rice on special plates—to the guests who sit on mats around a ninth *ambeng* in the middle of which a small banana tree has been planted. Poorer people will have to be content with two or four *ambeng*. Each *ambeng* is dedicated to a particular spirit such as that of Adam, Eve, Mohammad, Fatimah, and imaginary personalities such as heaven and earth, etc., because the food must be considered as an offering ... Once everybody is sitting happily around this food the meal cannot start until after the oldest person present, or preferably the modin [religious official who calls people for prayers], has uttered the so-called *oedjoeb*, i.e. a declaration that all the friends present ... old and young ... are witness that the host has prepared this meal in eight *ambeng* dedicated to Adam, Eve, etc. in order to obtain their blessing—called *sawab pandonga*, for house and family ... And when this speech has ended he ... will ask the guests to start eating ... The offering made in this way is considered to be partly in honour of the dead and partly for the benefit of the living. The idea behind this is that the dead are close to the living and can either protect them or—in the case of neglect or disregard—can harm them.

There are also people who bring offerings on the 30th of the month Roewah, that is the day before the beginning of the fast, for the specific purpose of honouring the dead. This is called *ngintoen donga* and *megengan*. The first term means that "prayers are sent" for the benefit of the deceased. This also occurs after the fast on the 1st of the month Sawal early in the morning. The second word derives from *megeng*, i.e. to prepare onself for the fast, and it actually means "the performance of the ceremonies for the preparation of the fast" ... Sometimes the housewife will at the same time prepare a few *sega apem*—i.e. small pancakes made of rice flour, yeast, and sugar—and the first one that comes out of the pan will be considered sacred and may not be eaten by anybody. A coin is put in the middle and a second pancake is put on top ... This double pancake is put away and is destined for the deceased; it is called *kedoekoeng-ing lelampah* or ... a travelling hat. It serves to protect the deceased while travelling to the regions of eternity, because he is surrounded by dangers and bad spirits sometimes will surprise the traveller and cause him to lose the right way ...

You have of course already noticed yourself that the natives also in the fulfilment of their duties during the month Roewah have not renounched their peculiar syncretism, and it should be clear how far they are orthodox followers of the Arabian faith. We have already pointed out that the veneration of the spirits is a remnant of the pre-Islamic era, of the era when the name of Allah was as yet totally unknown to the natives, and when numerous offerings, as is still happening today, were made to the spirits of nature, the spirits of the deceased and—because of the influence of the Hindus—to the gods of the Hindu pantheon. All this has not yet been forgotten, and one has simply added Allah of the Islam and his prophets and saints and a religion has been formed, consisting of the original Polynesian, Indian, and Arabic ideas ...

Polygamy and the harem are the cancer of family life; and also in Java we learn every day that this is true ... The "small man" usually has only one wife, although there are some who have two. In the higher classes the largest number is four in accordance with the Islamic law. But there are also some who have only one wife, while they sometimes have a number of concubines. It is well known how easy it is for the "common man" to change wives. And there are many men who after having been divorced have lived together with many wives—we know of a case of twenty and another of thirteen different wives ...

The nature and character of the people still exert an influence on many occasions in family life. The woman is here not a "slave", as may be the case elsewhere [in the Muslim world], and shows herself everywhere without a veil. In line with local customs the woman has often still a great deal of power in the house. And although the man

may be the head of the household, the woman is the neck on which the head turns in the direction she desires ...
Most European inhabitants only know that the fast has begun when their servants ask to borrow some money, or pre-payment of their wages, or for permission to give a meal—*djagongan*—in the evening, or to buy clothes ... Those who, however, are a little more familiar with the life of the natives are reminded [of the fast] every night for the thirty days of this month by the shouting of the *santris* [*pesantren* students] ... What is this shouting about? It is praying and glorifying God with Arabic chanting. After the *waktoe-Isja* [evening prayer], it is the praying period of Ngisa, which begins when the twilight is disappearing, the *bedoeg* [drum] is struck with a special beat for this occasion. This is called *tidoer* [sleep] and it serves to call the people together for the *tarawih* prayer ... i.e. a prayer which ... is interspersed with *rekas*, with bowing. One can hear this at about seven o'clock in the evening during the whole of the month. One of the elders leads the prayer, which is loudly ... repeated through all those present. After the *tarawih* prayer has finished, readings are held from the Qu'ran, called *daraessan*. This *daraessan* can last until midnight, after which each *santri* in turn treats his colleagues to coffee and cakes ...
The fasting month commences as soon as the new moon is visible. One is obliged to fast from the beginning of the day, i.e. from the moment a white thread can be distinguished from a black one ... until sundown. With the exception of children below the age of seven, the sick, travellers, and soldiers at war, one is obliged to abstain completely from eating and drinking, bathing, in short all sensual pleasures, for example also smoking, *sirith*-chewing, kissing, and even the brushing of teeth, etc. But nobody, so the Prophet is supposed to have said, is allowed to harm his health ...
And so one keeps Allah to his word that he wants to make things easy for the people ... and by excessive eating and drinking some of our natives compensate themselves at night for the deprivations of the day. Mostly our natives eat after sundown—this is called *boeka*—and just before the morning—which is called *sahoer*. And they sometimes eat more and more dainty food than usual. I have also met now and then pious persons who only ate once and very simply at about one o'clock in the morning. There are officials who only fast on the first and last day of this month ...
Especially the 21st, 23rd, 25th, and 29th of this month are important days in Java. The night of the 27th is called the night of fate—*lailat'oel quadri*. According to the legal scholars, numerous miracles occur during this night. It is best to pray during this night rather than any other night ... After sundown on these five days the so-called *Malemmans* take place. In the principalities it is customary

that food is distributed to the people on the 21st by the Sultan, on the 23rd by the Crown Prince, on the 25th by the princes at the court, on the 27th by the Vizier, and on the 29th by the *toemenggoengs* [officers]. It is said that this is done to commemorate Mohammad who, after having secluded himself in a cave, did not want to eat the food that had been prepared for him, but gave it to his followers.

The villages celebrate these *Malemmans* in their own way. The offerings are said to be especially dedicated to the prophet Adam on the 21st, the prophet Noah on the 23rd, the prophet Abraham on the 25th, the prophet Moses on the 27th, and the prophet Mohammad on the 29th. At sundown one sees everywhere men and boys running towards the house of the village chief, and it is not long before one hears many voices call out loudly *"inggih"* ["yes"], repeatedly, agreeing with the explanation of the *modin* ... as to the meaning of this offering, to whom it is dedicated, and to what purpose.

The offering also consists of a meal in which all male inhabitants of the village participate ... who each in turn take care of the food (i.e. a fifth of the participants have to take care of the food for one of the five nights), which has to be brought to the house of the village chief, who usually himself gives his share on the fifth night ...

On the 29th and 30th those whose parents are deceased—or as others say: everybody who has to take care of a grave—are busy with the preparation and baking of *sega apem* or rice flour cookies ... which are made in large quantities because they are already eaten from four or five o'clock on the afternoon of the 30th of Ramadan, thus actually before the fast is finished. But this is the custom in the village. Mutual visits are made during which these rice cookies are presented to the visitors, who eat as many as they like and take the rest home with them. But as this happens to each in turn nobody actually gains a great deal. Only *kijaji* or *santri* just take without returning anything and it sometimes happens that these people have vast quantities of these cookies at home, which they dry and keep, and later eat or sell ... But more still has to be done. On the last two days of the month the men go and clean the graves ...

Very early on the morning of the 1st of the month Sawal a bath is taken, the cattle are washed, nice clothes are put on ... and the graves are visited and an offering of flowers is made. These flowers are scattered on the graves, prayers are said, sometimes fireworks are lit, after which one goes home to eat ... After that the necessary visits are made to the village chief, the *goeroe*, the *modin*, and every other old or worthy person ... And this is the end of the fast for the vast majority of people ...

C. Poensen, *Brieven over den Islam uit de binnenlanden van Java* (Leiden: Brill, 1886), pp. 2-8, 13-17, 28-29, 32-36.

47 J. A. van der Chijs: Report of 1831 on indigenous education

The Resident of Batavia reports that in his region there existed a large number of so-called native schools which, however, did not teach anything else than the parrot-fashion reading or rather intoning of the Qu'ran, while some pupils were also taught to write with Arabic characters. This education was given by priests [*sic*] who, although they were not supervised, all followed the same methods. For their trouble they enjoyed a salary the size of which depended on the wealth of the parents of the children. Some children, particularly orphans, were educated free of charge.

Buitenzorg [the present Bogor]. There were no permanent schools, but in some places the children of natives were instructed either by priests or other natives mainly in the reading and writing of Arabic characters. This education, however, was very defective.

In Cheribon there were 190 *pesantren* with 2763 pupils who, however, learned nothing else than to read the Qu'ran and some other Islamic books. In some *pesantren* instruction was also given in writing with Arabic characters. The pupils were duty-bound to work part of the day for the *goeroe*, who was recompensed for his troubles by the fruits of their labour. Those natives who desired to learn to read and write Malay and Sundanese asked for help from one of their relatives or friends. Most natives of standing would send their children to a *pesantren* for some years. Every *pesantren* had from one to a hundred or more pupils, depending on how highly the *goeroe* was regarded by the population, either on the grounds of his piety or because of his knowledge. The *goeroes* were mainly religious ministers.

Tegal. About a thousand children were instructed in the reading of the Qu'ran and the reciting of prayers. Only few priests were familiar with the Javanese script. The Regent of Tegal reported that it was always very difficult to provide his children with a different type of education and the available teachers were very deficient. Since the English interregnum, some good results had been obtained even by those sub-standard means. Before that time there were even children of regents who could neither write nor read.

Pekalongan. There were nine *pesantren* in which the children of chiefs and of a few Javanese of lower status received some religious instruction. The teachers (priests) were happy with what they were given voluntarily by the parents and with the *sedekahs* [religious meals] to which they were sometimes invited.

Semarang. There were only *pesantren* here too. They were divided as follows:

> Regency of Semarang 95 *pesantren* with 1140 pupils
> Regency of Kendal 60 *pesantren* with 928 pupils
> Regency of Demak 7 *pesantren* with 519 pupils
> Regency of Grobongan 18 *pesantren* with 365 pupils

The *pesantren* were not only visited by children but also by adults of both sexes. Few reached the stage where they understood what they learned to read. Some *goeroes* also gave instruction in the reading of the Qu'ran in the Javanese language.

Kedoe. There were five schools which gave some instruction mainly in religious subjects. Children of chiefs, who stayed longer at school than the children of commoners, also received instruction in the reading and writing of Arabic and Javanese characters. Many children of chiefs, however, learned this by their own volition outside school with the help of relatives or other capable people.

Bagelen. In various villages there were priests, who gave very deficient instruction in religion. The most important of them was *kiai goeroe* Koetoebo at Alang Alang Ombo, who had been given a fairly large piece of land by the court of Jogjakarta for his troubles.

Banjoemas. There were only religious schools and very few at that. The teachers were even less capable than on the north coast. A few sons of regents received instruction in the reading and writing of Roman characters at the Residency office.

Rembang. There were various *pesantren.* The priests who acted as teachers did not get any salary, but lived from gifts which during feast days were given to them by their pupils or the parents.

Soerabaja. The following statistics were presented. In the Regency of Soerabaja and Japan there were 410 *langgars* [small prayer houses used also for religious instruction], with 4397 pupils, of which 355 were girls. In the district of Grissee there were 238 *langgars* with 2603 pupils; and in the district of Bawean there were 109 *langgars.* Whoever had some wealth and could read Arabic usually set up a *langgar* beside his house, in which he himself became the teacher, first for his own children and those of relatives and later also for other children. People with some wealth but who could not read Arabic employed a priest from the outside. A decline in wealth or loss of interest, etc., often caused such schools to disappear again.

The Regent and other important chiefs, if they wanted their children to learn reading, writing, and arithmetic, used private teachers. The instruction in the *langgars* lasted usually from three to four years.

From Bawean many children taking sums of thirty to forty reals with them went to Pasoeroean to further their education. They would usually return after two to three years.

Madoera. There were thirty-four *langgars* in Soemenep, ninety-seven in Pamekasan, and ten in the district of Madoera. The Sultan of Madoera considered these institutions as sufficient, because the Madurese were still in the lowest stage of civilization and the *langgars* were the appropriate institutions to develop their intellectual powers.

Besoeki. There were between five hundred and six hundred religious schools. Some young men in the retinue of the regents were taught to read, but some chiefs could not write at all.

Japara. There were ninety *pesantren* with 3150 boys and 326 girls.

The reason why there is little emphasis on the teaching of Javanese is that, according to the Qu'ran, human beings are incapable of understanding any other subjects before they have completely familiarized themselves with the teachings of religion. Also anybody who had completed his studies in Mohammedan doctrine and then had gone on the pilgrimage to Mecca was considered a scholar for whom all other knowledge was unnecessary.

Important is the description of the teaching methods in a *pesantren* by a native commission at the time, consisting of the Regent of Pati, the head-*djaksa* [legal official] and the head-penghoeloe [religious official] of Japara. I quote as follows:

> The first instruction in the *pesantren* or *pengadjian* is in the *alip-alipan* or the Arabic alphabet. Then a book called *toeroetan* is used, which explains the various characters used to form the words contained in the Qu'ran. The next step is the reading of the Qu'ran and then in succession the book *semoro-kandi*, which explains the doctrine, and the book *kitab sitin*, which teaches the accepted way of prayer.
>
> Instruction in these *pesantren* is more concerned with the reading than the writing of Arabic. There are many who can read it well. The main purpose is the reading of the Qu'ran, and therefore writing is considered unnecessary.
>
> The persons who teach in these *pesantren* are usually the best-trained persons in religion in the villages and *kampoengs* [urban native quarters]. The parents send their children to be educated by these persons who, on the basis of doctrine, are obliged to teach the children without requesting any payment. However, they are recompensed by voluntary gifts.

Most of the children who visit the *pesantren* are of lower-class origin. However, there are also some children of chiefs who receive their education there, but they sit separately. Girls go to the *pesantren*, but less than boys. The girls are usually taught by the wives of the teachers, or also sometimes at home by their parents.

Very seldom are the children of regents educated in the *pesantren*. Usually they are educated by priests belonging to the Regency, who carry the same Suronoto.

The number of youngsters who visit these *pesantren* reaches in the case of the larger *pesantren* to about one hundred and fifty, while in the smaller ones the minimum is ten. In this Residency, however, there are no large *pesantren*.

The *pesantren* teachers, when there are a large number of students, are assisted by the most advanced youngsters. Generally they use their own children for this purpose.

Very seldom is it found that the pupils, yes, even the most advanced ones, understand what they read, because it is in Arabic. However, the Qu'ran is understood by means of the *kitab tapsir*, which is a translation into Javanese of the Qu'ran.

The *goeroes* or teachers usually receive the following gifts. Every Thursday evening the *santri* [pupils] who are taught in the *pesantren* go out to visit the people and after chanting prayers are given alms, ranging from ten to thirty *duiten* [brass coins], which they bring to their goeroes, who usually buy oil with it to burn in the *pesantren*.

When a young man or a candidate for the priesthood has advanced to the stage where he has read through the whole of the Qu'ran, he is obliged to offer his teacher a meal to celebrate the occasion, consisting of rice and other native dishes, as well as a quantity of money ranging from ten to thirty *duiten*. This money is known as *oeang selamat*.

Each year after the *poeasa* [fast] has ended, every pupil presents his teacher with five *katis* of rice. This gift is called *pitra*.

Every year after the rice harvest the parents give part of the rice—usually from two to eight bunches—to the teacher. This gift is known as *djakat*.

When a boy gets behind with his studies, then from time to time he must give some oil for burning. This gift refers to the fact that his intellectual capacities are in need of enlightenment.

When the school building needs some repairs, the pupils have to contribute from one to thirty *duiten* towards the cost.

The students are also obliged to give a helping hand without being paid when the house of the teacher or the schoolroom, the so-called *langgar*, needs repairs. At all times they also have to be ready to carry out other work for their teachers.

J. A. van der Chijs, *Bijdragen tot the Geschiedenis van het Inlandsch Onderwijs in Nederlandsch-Indie* (Bataviaasch Genootschap. Indisch Tijdschrift van de Taal-Land-en Volkenkunde. 1864-1866), pp. 228-41.

48 Ahmad Djajadiningrat: Reminiscences about life in a *pesantren*

As I seemed to have an aptitude for the study of religion, many people advised my father to let me continue my studies. My father apparently liked the idea, because shortly afterwards he decided to send me after the coming *lebaran* to the village of Karoendang, where one of my cousins ... was running a *pesantren* ... The day came near when I would leave home again, this time to be introduced into the deeper secrets of Islam.

Until then I had always been dressed in short trousers, a jacket, and a small cap. But when it was decided that I would become a *santri*, I had to look very different. My head was completely shorn. This was done by my mother personally while the so-called *Abda'oe*, i.e. the little book containing a list of the names of the prophets and a part-genealogy of the last prophet, was recited. My clothing was changed for a coarsely woven sarong, a white *kabaja* without buttons (*badjoe sangsang*), so that my breast would always be visible, and a cheap headdress. Like other *santris* I was given ... some clothes, a small bag of rice, dried meat (*dengdeng*), and an earthenware pot to cook rice. Soap and towls were not included. So, fully equipped as a *boedjak* or *botjoh pondok* (*pesantren* student), I left my closest relatives full of courage and with the intention of not returning before I could be called *Alim* (learned in religious matters). Walking—as a *santri* should—I left Kramawatoe carrying my clothes, kitchen utensils, on a stick over my shoulders.

Close to the outskirts of Karoendang there stood at the side of a small stream a little brick mosque, which then had an *atap* [split bamboo] roof, but which is now tiled. Beside this small mosque there were a few small bamboo houses, which now have been replaced by small brick buildings. The one situated closest to the stream served me, my two cousins, and another ten boys or so as sleeping and cooking quarters and as study room. Almost the whole of the space was taken up by a large *bale-bale* [low bed] of bamboo covered with pandan mats on which lay some cushions. Near each cushion there was a small bamboo case (*kepek*), a few *kitabs* (religious books) and writing utensils. On the *bale-bale* we slept and wrote, laying on our stomachs. (Only older *santris* with parents a little better situated could afford the pleasure of having an empty kerosene tin as a writing desk.) Under our *bale-bale* all sorts of things were stored, such as food, kitchen utensils, firewood, etc. The only part of the building left free was for cooking.

I could easily have been given better housing, but my father insisted that I should lead the same life as the other *santris*. There were about forty pupils in my *pesantren*, and they came from various districts of Banten. The pupils were divided into two groups: one of older and more advanced students, and a younger group of beginners to which I belonged. The older ones were taught personally by the *goeroe*. The younger ones were instructed and supervised by older *santris* (the so-called *loerah pondok*) who were selected by the *goeroe*. Every *loerah* had his own area in the *pesantren* and his own students. One of my cousins ... was also a *loerah*. I would have liked to be under him; but our *goeroe* decided otherwise. He probably did have his reasons for this. I was given another *santri* as my *loerah*, who was a clever and very pious man, but whom I found a very unpleasant person. He was extremely anti-government and hated everybody who was connected with the government. Instruction was mainly given in two ways. The younger ones among us sat around the teacher, who recited and explained the text like a professor giving a lecture. Later everybody was given the opportunity to ask questions (this method of teaching is called *sorangan*). The older *santris* on the other hand came one by one with a particular text to the *goeroe*, who then would recite it, giving the necessary explanations. After that the student would have to read the text himself and repeat the explanations (*bandoengan*).

As the son of a [government] official I had to suffer a great deal from my *loerah*, who had little liking for the government. If for example I pronounced an Arabic word incorrectly he would immediately spit at me in a hateful way: "You will never learn it, because you have filled your stomach too much with rice which was bought with unclean money." (A government salary was in his opinion *haram*, i.e. unclean.) ...

Life in a *pesantren* is very different from that in a normal native household. Unconditional obedience to the teacher, a regular life, equality and fraternity among the students, are laws which are strictly maintained by the *goeroes*. Our daily activities were regulated as follows. We had to be in the mosque from five to six in the morning to take part in the morning religious service (*salat soeboeh*). Before the actual religious service commenced, we, the *santris*, had to sing aloud all sorts of pious songs (*sasalawatan*), which remind Muslims of their religious duties. [These songs] contained many hateful references to people of other religions. Sometimes also the Sultans of Banten were glorified in these songs. We were free from six to seven o'clock. Only some pupils whose turn it was had to clean the *mosque* and the *pondoks* [living quarters]. From seven to nine the older *santris* followed instructions from our *goeroe* and the younger ones from the *loerahs*. (Our *goeroe* in addition to instructing *santris* had other functions. He was a member of the council of *oelamas* [*priesterraad*] at Serang and he did not teach regularly every day but only a few days a week). After that we prepared and ate our meal, which lasted until about 11 o'clock. The *santris* had no plates, etc.

Instead we used a piece of the leathery bark of the *pinang* tree (*oepih*). Water was contained in earthenware *gendis* (jars) and we used empty coconut shells as cups. Of course we ate with our fingers.

On *pasar* [market] days we were allowed to go to Serang to ... beg for salt, *lombok* [red peppers], and other cheap food. The *santris* had to do this because there was never any money. If they wanted to eat something special, they were dependent on the generosity of other people. As I have already remarked, equality and fraternity were practised literally in the *pesantren*, so that my cousins and I, sons of native officials, were spoken to without any reference to our status by children of simple farmers. I considered myself then as their equal and I joined them in everything, even begging, in which I was always more successful than my co-pupils, perhaps because I was still small and looked different from the average *santri*. I did not only beg in the market-place but also sometimes in the villages. If, for example, I did not feel very much like cooking my own meal, then I went with a begging bowl (an empty coconut shell) along the houses, and often I did not only get some rice but also something tasty such as meat or fish, which was also enjoyed by my cousins, who always ate together with me. This begging sometimes led to naughty tricks unbefitting to a *santri*.

The first little book I was given to study was the Sittin (a small book written in Arabic with a Javanese translation printed between the lines), which dealt with the five pillars of Islam and other matters of importance to the Mohammedan. The lessons were given in the mosque.

In the evenings before going to bed the *santris* talked a great deal, discussing the events of the day and also telling jokes. Usually it was the native officials from high to low who were made the butt of the fun.

One evening I heard a *santri* assert: "I attended a *wajang* [puppet or shadow play] performance today."

Whereupon somebody else retorted: "But surely you cannot give a *wajang* performance during the day?"

"And yet", the first speaker said, "I saw Petroek and Nalagareng [clownish figures from the *wajang*] in a beautiful carriage." Apparently he had seen the Regent and the controleur. The Regent was in fact short and fat and the controleur was long and thin.

"And I", somebody else said, "have attended a *topeng* [masked dance] performance. I only saw Pentoel [clownish figure] but with an incompleted mask before his face. This Pentoel, with his conceited face, told the people that they—including the women and children—must have themselves inoculated against smallpox, because then they would never get it. He just acts as if he is a *setan koeris* (a bad spirit causing smallpox)."

"He may not be a *setan*", somebody else said, "but he certainly has met with such a *setan*." By Pentoel was meant the assistant *wedono* of the sub-district in which our *pesantren* was situated. He had a pock-marked face and a large nose ... This little story caused one of the younger *santris* to ask one of the *loerahs* whether inoculation was against the religious law.

"Of course," was the reply, "it is after all pus that you get into your body, and according to our religion pus is impure."

I made good progress with my studies so that after only a few months I was given a second booklet called Tafsiran (elements of Arabic grammar). This little book was not as easy as the first one ... It is said sometimes that the study of the *nahoe* (Arabic grammar) can send people out of their minds. It is at present one of the greatest obstacles to Javanese *santris*. The person who has mastered this [grammar] may call himself *"kijaji"*. My eldest cousin had succeeded in this and he was therefore allowed to teach Arabic. He was not older than eighteen, and of all the *santris* studying in our *pesantren* he was the only one who continued his studies in Mecca. And on his return he was recognized as a great theologian ...

In the moonlight on the grass in front of our *pondok* we learnt "oedjoengan" and *"mentjak"* (the first is fencing with a short wooden staff, and the second is a type of jiujitsu).

As the *santris* had to wash themselves ritually (*woedhoe*) at least five times a day for the *salat*, one would have expected that they and the *pesantren* would have been exceptionally clean. This is actually not the case at all. One could not find any more unhygienic people than the *santri* and more unhygienic conditions than in a *pondok-pesantren*. This should not be surprising if it is realized that the ritual washing, according to the letter of the law, is restricted to certain parts of the body. Moreover the way of life of the *santris* and the circumstances they live in are not conducive to the continuous practice of hygiene. The *santris* seldom wash their clothes and avoid soap when they do. Instead the cheap *lerek* fruits are used (these are round brown fruits which when put in water produce a little soap-like foam).

Ahmad Djajadiningrat, *Herinneringen* (Batavia: Kolff, 1936), pp. 35-38.

49 Tjokroaminoto: Speech at the Sarikat Islam Congress, 1916

We have done a great deal in furthering the interests of the native population ... I wish to point out at this congress that our association has among other things always co-operated with the government and has pointed out to it various matters that the people object to, various regulations that we consider are bad for the native population. And we must co-operate as much as possible in showing how the lot of the natives can be improved—how to increase the prosperity of our race, of our country of birth, the Netherlands Indies. We love our *bangsa* (people), and aided by the strength of the teachings of our religion we are doing our best to unite the whole or the greater part of them; we love the land that gave us birth; and we love the government that protects us. Therefore we have shed our timidity and we draw attention to everything we think is right: we ask for what we think will improve our people, our country, and our government.

In order to reach our objectives, to facilitate our work, and to realize our great plan, it is necessary to create legislation giving us natives *the right* to co-operate in the construction of all these regulations of which we are thinking at present. We sincerely hope for such legislation. It should no longer be allowed that laws and regulations are made for us, that one governs *without us*, without any participation from our side. Although we strongly desire and hope for change, we have never dreamt about the coming of a *Ratu Adil* or other absurd and impossible things. But we will continue to hope honestly and openly for the realization of self-government in the Netherlands Indies, or at least the birth of a colonial council, so that we can participate in discussions about government matters. Gentlemen, do not be frightened because we dare to use the word "self-government" at this meeting. We may use this word without fear, of course, because there exists a law—which should be read by every citizen—that also uses the word "self-government" (the Decentralization Law of 1903) ...

It is felt more and more in the Netherlands as well as in the Indies that self-government is necessary. It is felt more and more that it is not right for Holland to rule the Indies like a squire administering his lands. It is not right to consider the Indies as a cow, which is fed only because of its milk. It is not right to consider this land primarily as a place where people go for the sole purpose of profit. And now it is no longer right that the inhabitants, who are mainly natives, do not have the right of a say in a government that regulates their lives ...

We realize and completely understand that to institute self-government will involve great difficulties. This cannot be achieved immediately and at present it is still like a dream to us. In fact, however, it is no dream, but a continuous feeling of hope that can be fulfilled only if we apply ourselves to the utmost and use all possible means within the bounds of civility and honesty. In this way it is certain that self-government for the Indies will eventuate within ten years ...

Who would ever have dreamed that our "Central *S.I.*" would come about, which on this day has the power to collect here the representatives of dozens of local *S.I.* associations, that is, representatives of hundreds of thousands of natives from all parts of the Indies? Who would have dreamed that all these representatives genuinely desired to co-operate in furthering the interests of all castes, races, and needs of the fatherland? This is the fruit of these three years. How much more then shall we achieve if we really work with all that is in us and unabatedly during the next ten to twenty years? For us natives it is even easier to concentrate on the objective of self-government because the majority of our people have *one religion, the same belief, a genuine belief, the same view of life, the same faith, and the same needs and interests* ...

[Referring to the growing pressure of the Communists on the *S.I.*, Tjokroaminoto continues:] Among our people there are a few who are so obsessed with the idea of political action that they begin to think about impossible things and foolish schemes. These are signs of the times that we must note carefully and struggle against if necessary. On the other hand we must be pleased that these aberrations are coming into the open and that they do not remain hidden as a disease that might spoil a good cause ... All this does not mean that our expectations and desires are opposed to the interests of a greater Netherlands. Our objective is the unification of the Indies and the Netherlands, to become citizens of the self-governing "State of the Indies". We do not want to cry out: "Down with the government!" On the contrary, our motto is: "Together with the government and in support of the government to go in the right direction ...

Koloniaal Archief, *Sarekat-Islam Congres (le Nationaal Congres) 17-24 Juni 1916 te Bandoeng, Behoort bij de geheime Missive van den wd. Adviseur voor Inlandsche Zaken dd. 29 September 1916, No. 226* (Batavia: Landsdrukkerij, 1916), pp. 2-10.

50 Report of the meeting of the Partij Sarikat Islam held on 26 January 1928 at Yogjakarta, to commemorate its fifteen years of existence

In spite of the extensive propaganda of the last few months and perhaps partly because of the late starting-hour ... this meeting was only attended by about a hundred persons, among whom were representatives from only eighteen of the forty *P.S.I.* branches in Java. *Moehammadijah* was surprisingly not represented at this meeting, while at another meeting where the Qu'ran translation of Tjokroaminoto was scrutinized, the members of this association were present in large numbers. On the other hand *B.O.* [*Boedi Oetomo*], *P.N.I.*, *P.P.P.K.I.*, *Wal Fadjri*, and a few other unimportant associations were represented at this meeting. The *P.N.I.* and *P.P.P.K.I.* delegate was Dr Samsi from Bandoeng.

After the customary reading from the Qu'ran, on this occasion by H. Abdoellah Siradj, Panghoeloe Pakoealam, the Chairman, H.O.S. Tjokroaminoto, opened the meeting. He welcomed everybody sincerely, but in particular the delegates from the nationalist and Islamic associations, because their presence was of great importance in view of the discussions about the founding of a national bank and a *madjelis oelama* (council of religious scholars). The speaker then pointed out why 26 January should be considered the foundation date of the *S.I.* It was because on that date in 1913 the large *S.I.* meeting in the City Gardens in Soerabaja took place, after which the *S.I.* became widely known. Despite many difficulties, according to the speaker, the *P.S.I.* has until now managed to stay alive, and it never was dead, not for one moment. He was thankful to Allah for this, the Almighty. As only few members of the *P.S.I.* were present, he requested all other Muslims to participate in the "*sembahjang hadjat*" (a religious service for a special purpose) after the closing of the meeting in the Pakoealam mosque.

The speaker then invited H. A. Salim to give an outline of the history of the *S.I.* H. A. Salim began his talk with the remark that the Chairman had already pointed out that the *S.I.* had to struggle with many difficulties in its life. He was happy about this because all progress in life is the result of contrast and opposition. The fact that the *S.I.* experienced difficulties was actual proof that it was alive.

Before the *S.I.* was founded, the Javanese, according to H. Salim, were called the most docile people on earth. When the *S.I.* was founded many facets of suppression had already been defeated. After all the fact itself that the *S.I.* could be established was proof that the characteristic of "being the most docile people on earth" was already fading.

The founding of the movement in 1912 was not because suppression had reached its zenith just at that time. He explained that the [association] was founded on the example of what had happened in China. China had learned to acquiesce in the superior power of the Europeans, the fearful "foreign devils". But when the Japanese, a similar type of people, were able to make their importance felt, the Chinese found the courage to resist. Furthermore, there was the victory of Japan over Russia, which shocked the magical prestige of the West. All this led to the revolution of 1911, in which the old ruling dynasty was dethroned and the old humiliating institutions were demolished.

After that the Chinese felt a free people, equal to the Japanese and the Westerners. In this country they no longer wanted to be treated on an equal footing with the natives and they became rather arrogant to them. And the indigenous inhabitants who had come to accept three centuries of Netherlands rule as a matter of course were awakened when the Chinese, hitherto their equals, joined [the Dutch suppressors]. According to Mr Salim, this then was the reason for the awakening of the native people.

He admitted that *Boedi Oetomo* and the *N.I.P.* were older, but they could not be considered representative of the people as a whole because they recruited their members from certain classes.

It has sometimes been said that *S.I.* has continuously changed direction. This may be true, according to Mr Salim, but one thing runs like a red line throughout the whole life of *S.I.*, and that is the wish to see national demands satisfied. Mr Salim illustrated this point with the following simile: a baby that has just been born *cries*; a somewhat older child *asks* for food when he is hungry; an adult *looks* for it himself. The one cries, the other asks, the third one is trying to find, but in the final analysis all three of them are motivated by the feeling of hunger.

Then H. Salim outlined how at first *S.I.* was a type of complaints bureau, because at that time it was difficult for the common people to have justice done. This was partly because of the attitude of the higher authorities, who were not used to listening to complaints from the common people, and partly because no witnesses could be found who dared to tell the truth. In this respect *S.I.* had brought change.

This change in mentality was not only advantageous for the people themselves, but also for the government and the administration, because now one could get to the truth of the situation.

Also this awakening of the people had its advantages for the *prija-ji* class. Previously natives and Europeans with equal capacities and qualifications were paid on different scales. The speaker illustrated this point with examples from his own experience. Although he possessed the final diploma of the *H.B.S.* [Dutch High School], he was not able to get a position as clerk. But later when he had returned from Djeddah [where he had an important position at the Dutch consulate], he was offered a position of *commies* [medium-echelon position] with the *S.S.* [State Railways] at 150 guilders per month. When he mentioned that he was *gelijkgesteld* [literally, equalized: Indonesians with certain educational qualifications could opt to become Europeans before the law] with Europeans, it appeared that the salary would be 225 guilders per month. He politely refused the offer, because it offended his self-respect, and it was this fact which, according to the speaker, determined the future course of his life. But now this discrimination had stopped. And was this not of great importance to the intellectuals, Mr Salim asked.

Then the speaker touched on the difficulties the *S.I.* had experienced during its existence, such as the difficult years 1919-26, when the *S.I.* was attacked on both sides. The Communists tried to gain influence in the party with the result that the weaker brothers separated themselves. But the heaviest blow was the Section B affair [supposed attempt at open rebellion by a West Java branch of the *S.I.*], which killed the *S.I.* outside Java and caused many in Java to turn their backs on the association.

When the first *Al Islam Congress* was held in 1922 at Cheribon, one thought, according to Mr Salim, that the *S.I.* had already expired, because the influence of Tjokroaminoto, so it was said, had been broken.

The speaker, however, is convinced that the life of the *S.I.* is not dependent on the influence of Tjokroaminoto or anybody else, but on the will of the people. In any case the *S.I.* is today still fully alive. Admittedly the membership has declined since 1918 from about two million to at the most twelve thousand people, but on the other hand there is the advantage that now the *P.S.I.* has only convinced members. Our present motto is: *"Innamaloe'minoena ichwah"*, i.e. all Muslims are brothers, with the result that when we make a summons this does not solely concern the twelve members of the *P.S.I.* at Batavia or the twenty members in Bandoeng, but it concerns the whole of the Islamic people in this country. The commemoration of the *S.I.* is thus the commemoration of the new will of the people. In the beginning the motto of the S.I. was: *"Kerso, koewoso, mardiko"* ("will, power, freedom"), i.e. one must begin with the development of the will, because the will creates power and when that power is there, freedom will come by itself. This motto, according to Mr Salim, still needs to be adhered to strongly today. (Applause.)

Then Hadji Salim tried to explain that it was impossible for a people's movement to stay out of politics. One could hardly move without coming into contact with politics. Moreover it was not possible to properly execute the orders laid down by Islam without wishing to become involved in politics. Everywhere in this country one hit against that single thing called colonial policy. At first the *S.I.* was also not political, but it soon realized that it was necessary to become familiar with the world of politics.

Looking at it superficially, it is remarkable, according to H. Salim, that the ban on political parties in this country was lifted just after the S.I. became involved in politics. However, in reality, this is how things usually happen. History teaches that no government has ever granted new rights to its people voluntarily. The people always had to show clearly first that they strongly demanded such rights. The speaker pointed to the Magna Carta, which the King granted to the English people when it stood ready to act sword in hand.

The Prophet also, so H. Salim continued, was only able to make Islam great after he entered the political sphere. And the speaker pointed to the political treaties concluded by the Prophet in the interest of Islam with the people of Mecca and other tribes.

Islam is the legal basis for the whole of society including political life. And when the members of *Sarikat Islam* take Islam as the foundation of their actions, then this is not to use this religion as a type of mask (*topeng*), but indeed from the conviction that there is no better basis than Islam ...

Koloniaal Archief. *Uitvoerig Verslag van het Islamcongres te Djokjakarta 26-29 Januari, 1928. Geheim Mailrapport 332x/28.*

51 P.S.I.I. Congress held at Palembang, January 1940

This twenty-fifth Congress of the *P.S.I.I.* is of particular importance because it was influenced by the *Kongres Ra'jat Indonesia* [Indonesian People's Congress: see document 70] held the previous month in Batavia. In particular the action for an Indonesian parliament was strongly emphasized ... and the congress hall was decked out with red and white flags and a large banner inscribed with the words: "*Parlement Indonesia*". A large crowd was in attendance, while the women were accommodated separately in an adjoining school building ... where they could listen to the various speeches through loudspeakers. The scouts of the *Sarikat Islam* branch *Pandoe (Siap)* acted in their customary roles of guard of honour and stewards at the congress ... The Chairman of the congress was Mr W. Wondoamiseno ... who in accordance with the nature of the various functions sometimes delegated his function to Mr Abikoesno Tjokrosoejoso ...

After the singing of the "*Indonesia-Raja*" Mr Wondoamiseno opened the congress with an address in which he immediately outlined the major points to be treated by the congress: to direct ciriticism at existing conditions, which could only be overcome if Indonesians had their own parliament, and the need to strengthen the ties between the various population groups, preferably on the basis of Islam. Mr Wondoamiseno recalled that the problem of a fully fledged parliamentary system had been brought up as early as 1918 by the late Tjokroaminoto and that from the beginning the *P.S.I.I.* had agitated for such a parliament. He also pointed to the decision of the *Kongres Ra'jat Indonesia* in selecting the red-white flag and "*Indonesia-Raja*" as the flag and anthem of the unitary Indonesian movement.

Mr Abikoesno Tjokrosoejoso on the basis of a quotation from the book *Aufsteig und Niedergang der Nationen* [The Rise and Fall of Nations] by Hugo Marcus argued that the rise or fall of a nation depends on whether a nation is capable of acting at the right moment. When the right psychological moment is allowed to pass then the chance to rise to power is lost. The speaker used the Prophet Mohammad as an example of a person who was able to use the right psychological moment to bring unity to a divided country.

As a result of a letter received by *G.A.P.I.* and the *Kongres Ra'jat Indonesia* from the Colonial Commission of the *S.D.A.P.* and the *N.V.V.* [Dutch Socialist Party and Organization of Socialist Labour Unions] in the Netherlands, supporting the action for a parliament, Mr Abikoesno stated that it had been decided to shorten the duration of the congress in order to enable the *P.S.I.I.* delegates to return home as quickly as possible to make arrangments for further local action on the question of a parliament. He finished his propaganda speech by saying that he considered the present point in time to be important because the question whether the nation would rise to power or would completely decline was at stake.

It was announced during the first public session that in order to obtain a parliament more speedily, a spiritual mobilization by means of a fast was to be organized on Sunday, 18 February 1940. After the fast there would be held at midnight a *"salat at-tatawwoe"* (a recommended but not compulsory devotion) and a *"do'a qoenoet"* [prayer] would be read, while all *P.S.I.I.* branches would be instructed to continue the action for a parliament by means of public meetings and instruction courses. The text for the prayer would be chosen from the *"soerah Al-'Imran"*, a chapter of the Qu'ran which deals with a controversy with the Christians and the battle of Oehoed and which explains that the Muslims are invincible, although it may happen that they are humiliated for a certain period.

More explicitly Mr Abikoesno declared that this decision was the first step taken by the *P.S.I.I.* in the action for an Indonesian parliament. "Economic awareness and spiritual mobilization are the key to progress; and an Indonesian parliament is the way to achieve this. If this objective has been achieved, the drainage of capital from the country will stop, illiteracy will disappear, the true representatives of the people will deliberate about the country's affairs". Mr Abikoesno added: "Our action is not only just, but is also made compulsory by Islam."

The other speeches were largely based on the same theme: the establishment of a parliament was necessary to bring about improvements in economic and religious matters, because nothing in this respect could be expected from a colonial government.

It was also important to note the analysis made by Wondoamiseno about Islam as a religion which in contrast to Communism recognizes the right to individual private property, although with certain limitations.

It was announced during the last public session that the expulsion of Mr Kartosoewirjo from the party was endorsed by the Congress ... this means the definite separation of the group of *P.S.I.I.* members who under the leadership of Kartosoewirjo had set up the *Komite Pertahanan Kebenaran P.S.I.I.* [Committee for the Maintenance of Truth of the *P.S.I.I.*]. Kartosoewirjo was the Vice-president of the *P.S.I.I.* Council and was in charge of a party cadre training course which was to be established at Garoët. The separation of the Kartosoewirjo group had weakened the *P.S.I.I.* quite considerably in many parts of Java.

Although the party leadership stated that the *P.S.I.I.* had at present about twenty-five thousand members and that during 1939 more than five thousand new members joined, this organization is in a rather dormant state in many parts of the Netherlands Indies. Only a few branches such as in Palembang, the west coast of Sumatra, and Bolaang Mogonday in North Celebes, appear to be active.

If then in terms of size the *P.S.I.I.* is no longer what it once was in the past, its *spirit* still appears the same: it is discontented and critical about existing conditions and seeks refuge in the far future, in which Islam will not only be the basis of all religious activity but also of the system of government itself ...

Text of the special prayer for the spiritual mobilization

Oh, God! Owner of the Kingdom! You grant the Kingdom to whom You please and take away from whom You please, and You raise to prominence whom You will and humiliate whom You will; what is good rests in Your hand; truly You are almighty. You let the night penetrate the day and the day penetrate the night and You create life out of death and death out of life, and You provide in abundance whom You will.

Oh, God! Truly, we beseech Your help and Your guidance and we beseech You for forgiveness; we make an act of contrition to You and we believe in You; we surrender ourselves to You and we give You the highest praise; we thank You and we do not disavow our faith in You; we stay away from those who rebel against You and leave them.

Oh, God! In case this matter [i.e. a parliament] is good for me in a religious sense, and for my life and future, let it then be predestined for me and let me be predestined for it. And if it is bad for me in a religious sense and for my life and future, then keep it far away from me, and me from it. Let what is good be predestined for me wherever I may be. God, may You bless our lord Mohammad, our illiterate prophet, his descendants and companions, and give them peace ...

Koloniaal Archief. *Adviseur voor Inlandse Zaken aan den Gouverneur Generaal, 16 Februari, 1940, No 227/K-5. Geheim. Afschrift Vb. 30 Dec. 1940 Lt. X31.*

52   Report of the 23rd Congress of Muhammadyah held at Yogjakarta, July 1934

The twenty-third yearly Congress of *Moehammadijah* at Jogjakarta from 19 to 25 July 1934 was clearly affected by the adverse times [i.e. the economic depression]. Previous *Moehammadijah* congresses were great events, particularly when they were held in the founding city of the organization: Jogjakarta. Representatives, men as well as women, thronged together from the whole of the Netherlands Indies, and I was never more deeply impressed about how *Moehammadijah* with its numerous branches spans the whole of the Archipelago than when at the 1931 Congress I was present at the reception of all the representatives, from the remotest corners of Sumatra, Borneo, Celebes, and Java, who each in their own national dress and in their own language spoke their blessings over the Congress, ending with the Islamic prayer: "Blessed be you, and Allah's forgiveness and His gifts."

Although this twenty-third congress was announced as a *"Congres Akbar"*, i.e. a major congress, its organization was kept on a moderate scale and the attendance remained below expectations. Preparations had been made to accommodate six hundred male representatives, but only three hundred and three turned up. Naturally thousands of interested people from Jogja itself and surrounding places attended the public meetings and the enormous temporary congress building erected on the northern *aloon-aloon* [city square] was on those occasions almost totally filled by a crowd estimated at between seven and ten thousand people. The women, associated in the *Aisjijah* organization, met separately. The strict separation of the sexes advocated by *Moehammadijah* prevented the men, with the exception of the police, of course, from attending the women's meetings ... There was one public meeting attended by both men and women, but the latter were hidden behind screens of white cloth ...

After some considerable struggle Hadji Hisjam has been elected President of the head office. This may be considered as a fortunate choice because Hadji Hisjam is one of the peaceful figures in the national leadership of *Moehammadijah*. Moreover the decisions taken at the congress at Semarang in 1933 were confirmed—an important development, because it means that the struggle of *Moehammadijah* against all sorts of religious *adats* in the Outer Possessions ... has been approved and will be continued ... The congress has discussed the problem—current in many other national organizations—of sending young people overseas to study. A commission has been appointed to study this problem. There seem to be two trains of thought in *Moehammadijah* on this point: one group, considering the restrictions imposed by the government on educational expansion, wants *Moehammadijah* itself to get into education on a larger scale; the other seeks the solution in sending young people to Cairo, Mecca, Japan, and if necessary even to British India. But the mention of British India conjures up in the minds of many the unhappy experience of sending young *Moehammadijah* members to Lahore, the centre of the *Ahmadijah* movement [modern Islamic sect], with which initially friendly relations existed but which later became deeply hated ...

During the two public meetings in the evening, as has always been customary with *Moehammadijah*, no deliberations or debates were held, but the programme consisted solely of religious lectures. And considering the final objective of *Moehammadijah*, which is to make Islam victorious in all aspects of life, naturally political ideals sometimes came to the fore ...

The Chairman, H. Soedjak, presented a talk on the topic, "The Netherlands Indies is a Muslim country". This country has been Muslim since Raden Patah founded the realm of Demak and since the Nine Saints of Java carried out their missionary task. Until today the princes of Java have been Muslim rulers. The mosques and smaller prayer houses in all the towns and villages are proof that this is a Muslim country; even in the *Kratons* [palace complexes] of the princes of Solo and Jogja one finds mosques. The Muslim character of this country is also obvious from the dispensing of law. No judgements by the *Landraad* [regional courts] are pronounced unless first the Penghoeloe—the Muslim legal adviser—has been consulted. So why is an organization such as *Moehammadijah* still necessary? Because Islam has not yet penetrated this country completely. Islam must be brought to all inhabitants of the Netherlands Indies. Islamic doctrine should not only be heard at meetings and *tabligh*-meetings, but it should penetrate into the houses, yes, into the sleeping quarters. Only then will the objective of *Moehammadijah* have been achieved.

A speaker from Makassar talks about the subject of Islamic education. He argues that the progress of a people depends largely on its education. The people of this country are duty-bound to take their education in their own hands. The present deeply humiliating state of Islam is due to the fact that the Muslims are not true enough Muslims. It is the task of the educators to solve this problem. The hearts of the children, which are very receptive must be filled with Muslim ideals. Muslims should be deeply convinced of the idea that only their own initiative can bring improvements in the situation of Muslim nations. This is in accordance with the word of the Qu'ran (chapter 13, verse 12): "Allah does not change the situation of a people, until it changes its condition itself."

Mohammad Masboellah from Madoera spoke about world peace. Nations and rulers sometimes think that they control the world, but in reality only Allah rules. In his time Alexander the Great wanted to bring the whole of the world under his control, and at the present time the League of Nations is trying to bring the nations together, but dynamite and other means of destruction are more powerful than the League of Nations. More than thirteen centuries ago Muslims received the revelation in the Qu'ran as to how world peace can be achieved. One only has to remain true to the great truths embodied in the Muslim Creed (*Sjahadah*). The pilgrimage to Mecca and its complete equality of all races, nations, and classes make up the symbol of political and social unity which can flow from the unity of one creed. The Qu'ran says: "The faithful are brothers" (chapter 49, verse 10). If the true meaning of the pilgrimage has been understood, there is no need for a Peace Palace [Court of International Justice in the Hague], because then one recognizes that on the basis of Islam the whole of humanity can feel as one united whole and differences of race and nation will disappear. Also from the daily prayers prescribed by Islam, in particular from the Friday service, it appears over and over again that Islam stands for the equality of and peace among all people ...

"Young Muslims and Science" was the title of a lecture presented by Moehammad Earid Ma'roef, a young teacher at the Teachers' College of *Moehammadijah* in Jogjakarta, which as is well known produces religious leaders for the whole of the Indies. This Moehammad Farid Ma'roef has studied in Cairo for a number of years, which perhaps partly explains his attitude towards Western education. Furthermore, one should keep in mind that the *Moehammadijah* has always been wary of both the secular as well as the Christian character of Western civilization.

Mr Farid Ma'roef argued that it is necessary for the development of a nation to obtain knowledge in the widest sense of the word. Knowledge has brought the nations of America, Europe, and Japan to their position of power in the world, and lack of knowledge has caused the peoples of the East to fall behind. The Muslim peoples must make it their objective to lift themselves from their state of decay by means of modern knowledge. The Qu'ran itself exhorts Muslims to seek knowledge. And scholars are treated with distinction in the Holy Book. There are also many sayings by the Prophet in which the faithful are exhorted to engage in the arts and sciences. There was a time when Muslims diligently adhered to these prescriptions: in the Middle Ages under the Caliphs of Baghdad and Spain the arts and sciences were flourishing, while Europe was still steeped in stupidity and barbarity. But, although it is the duty of Muslims to obtain knowledge, there are great dangers in following Western science blindly. Western style education estranges Muslims from their people and their religion. This danger posed by the West must be countered by strengthening Muslim education. We must not look towards Europe for guidance, but to the highly developed Muslim countries such as Egypt, Palestine, and Syria where, owing to a strong Muslim consciousness, primary schools, secondary schools, and even universities have been established based on Islam; and where all branches of science can be studied free from the Western danger ...

Koloniaal Archief. *Geheim Mailrapport 984x/34.*

53 Proceedings of the 3rd Congress of the Jong Islamieten Bond (Young Muslims League), held 23-27 December 1927

When the Chairman had just completed reading the notices, a group of about twenty women, mostly young, but also with some adult and even old ones among them, entered the hall. In contrast to procedure at the previous congresses, they sat down in specially reserved places, which were only separated from the men by a narrow corridor, about half a metre wide. If it is recalled that during the second congress in 1926 when the girls were still forced to hide themselves from the sinful looks of the men behind a specially erected white screen, and Hadji Salim tore down this screen, even the Chairman was rather shocked, we are witnessing here an important evolutionary—if not revolutionary development—in the thinking of the members of this Islamic youth organization.

As is customary, the meeting began with the reading of a verse from the Qu'ran, which was then translated into Dutch ...

Wiwoho [president of the League] first welcomed the representatives of the government, and the Sunan [Sultan of Yogjakarta], and then all the participants ... The speaker pointed to the rapid growth of the *Jong Islamieten Bond,* which at the first congress had seven branches; at the second there were already ten, and now at this third congress it was a pleasure to announce that the number of branches had increased to fifteen, of which two were outside Java: one at Fort de Kock [the present Bukittinggi], and the other at Medan, while the number of members had passed the seventeen hundred mark.

This, according to the speaker, showed clearly that the League was not only viable but also that it fulfilled a strongly felt need among the younger Indonesian intellectuals ...

Mr Wiwoho then touched on the idea of unity that lately had become more popular among the intellectuals. The fact, however, that so far attempts to federate the various regional youth organizations such as Young Java and the League of Young Sumatrans had failed miserably made the speaker conclude that the idea of unity could only be realized in the future through a fusion of the various ethnic groups in Indonesia. So far as the youth movement was concerned, this fusion could only be based on one of the following two principles: on Islam or Indonesian nationalism, which in the view of the speaker meant that in the future only the *Jong Islamieten Bond* and *Jong Indonesia* [*Indonesia Muda*] would be viable and able to develop strongly (applause) ...

[Speech by Miss Soepinah] before beginning her talk Miss Soepinah first thanked Mr Salim for the action taken during the previous congress, which now enabled the female members of the *J.I.B.* to participate in the discussions as they no longer were required to sit behind a screen ... In her speech she upheld the Islamic faith, arguing that the fact that hitherto Mohammedan women—read native women in general—held a low position in society was not due to Islam, but to a lack of education. And so during marriage negotiations the older relatives did not take any notice of the wishes and desires of the woman concerned. According to the speaker, Islam gives equal rights to men and women, but the men are to be responsible for their families. Even the divorce procedure was not attacked by Miss Soepinah. However, she found it difficult to acquiesce in polygamy . She pointed out that here in Java polygamy customarily means that there is only one first wife, while the others, although legally married, are considered and treated only as concubines, which is actually a disguised form of prostitution. According to Islam a man is only allowed to have more than one wife if he is able to treat his wives on an equal basis in all respects. However, the speaker would rather see that also in the Islamic world monogamy would become the rule.

This first lecture by a girl member, which indeed was well done, received enthusiastic applause ...

[Speech by Hadji Agus Salim] Before starting on the subject under discussion, Hadji Salim repeated the advice given to members of the *J.I.B.* at previous congresses, that the Qu'ran must be studied. It would be wrong to think that study should only be carried out by the so-called clergy. Also the Qu'ran should be translated into all languages, so that everybody would be able to study its contents.

Then after having criticized the reticence of women and having praised the courage of the three girls who had spoken before him, he finally came to the actual subject of his talk, which was the importance of the *hadj* [pilgrimage to Mecca] to Muslims. He spoke at length and in great detail, but did not put forward any new views. In summary he argued that the *hadj* had a stimulating effect on believers, because it increased their thriftiness. Moreover the pilgrimage to Mecca, for which so many difficulties had to be overcome, was a great experience and very educational for the pilgrims. And finally every Mohammedan was duty-bound to go on the *hadj* in accordance with the fifth pillar of Islam. But what about the argument that so many millions were drained from the country? According to Salim these millions would otherwise be spent in different—and perhaps sinful—ways. One only needed to remember the World War when also a great deal of money was made by Mohammedans in this country, but as there was no opportunity to go on the pilgrimage, they squandered their surplus money on cars, gambling, and women, etc., etc ...

[Speech by] Mr Sam, the founder of the League and Registrar of the County Court in Jogjakarta, who presented a lecture on Islam and nationalism. The speaker commenced with a survey as to how nationalism was born in Europe and how it brought various countries to great might, but how finally this same nationalism caused the great European war. That type of nationalism, according to Mr Sam, should not be adhered to by a Muslim. Nationalism to a Muslim means love for country and people, but also for Muslims in other countries, yes, for the whole of humanity. The Qu'ran says that humanity is divided into various tribes and nations in order that they should recognize and appreciate each other. That type of nationalism the speaker considered infinitely higher than what has been meant until now by nationalism in the West. Of course one's own fatherland must first be made independent, or at least one should strive towards that objective. In the most difficult task of achieving this objective the National Council should be assisted, according to the speaker, by a number of "*core*" *members*.

The attitude which members of the *J.I.B.* should take with respect to non-Muslims is expressed in the *Surah*: "*Qoel, ja, ajoehal kafiroena*", meaning that everybody should confess his own religion without any hindrance ...

[Another speech by] Hadji Salim, who now spoke about Islam and socialism. The speaker explained in great detail why and how socialism came about in Europe and how various countries were at present already governed by Socialist majority governments. It looks, according to the speaker, as if in the near future most countries will be governed under this system.

According to the speaker many of the Socialist principles can be found in Islam. The only differences are: Socialism, at least in theory, denies the existence of nationalism, while Islam does not, but instead tries to unite the various nations as much as possible. Islam forbids the acceptance of interest, Socialism does not. Islam recognizes the right to private property, but makes the *zakat* [religious tax] obligatory and strongly recommends the giving of alsm. Socialism wants to nationalize as much as possible. Islam is actively defensive, while Socialism is offensive in nature (great applause) ...

Koloniaal Archief. *Het 3e Congres van de Jong Islamieten Bond gehouden op 23 t/m. 27 December 1927 te Jogjakarta.* Geheim Mailrapport 162/28.

54 Government report on Nahadatul Ulama, 1928

The above-mentioned association consisting of orthodox Mohammedan scholars has evolved from a committee which was set up in February 1926 in Soerabaja in order to send a delegation to Ibn Sa'oed to confer about the interests of pilgrims from the Netherlands Indies and about the demolition of the holy graves by the Wahhabites.

This committee at the time despatched a telegram to the King of the Hidjaaz, the Sultan of Nedjd, asking him whether he would be willing to receive this mission, and when the Islamic World Congress (*Moe'tamar al Alam al Islami*), which had been announced by His Majesty, would take place.

The setting-up of this committee, of which people such as Kjahi Hasjim from Djombang and H. Abdoel Wahhab from Soerabaja, who are strictly orthodox, are members, must be seen as a reaction to the mission of Tjokroaminoto, H. Mansoer, and H. Soedjak to Mecca and against the kind of reform advocated by the association *Moehammadijah* and the objectives of the modernists in general. This committee has by now gradually evolved into an association called the "*Perkoempoelan Nahadatoe'l Oelama*" "the evolutionary urge of religious scholars", which held its first congress during the Islamic Congress in Mecca (*Moe'tamar*). This first congress was characterized by the strong opposition against the Wahhabites and there was violent agitation against the pilgrimage as long as the Wahhabites were in control of the holy cities. At this congress, which liked to be considered as the highest organ of the Javanese Muslim world, a few resolutions were passed concerning religious and Mohammedan legal questions such as the decision that a believer must adhere to one of the four schools (*madhabs*), that is of asj-Sjafi'i, Ahmad ibn Hanbal, Malik ibn Anas, or Aboe Hanifah, while also the sequence was indicated in which the works of Sjafi'ite scholars should be consulted in case of disputes.

This resolution was solely a reaction to the modernists who do not feel bound to any particular school or the works of any particular scholar, but who on the contrary declare themselves to be capable of deducting religious precepts from the Qu'ran and tradition which, as is well known, is not allowable from an orthodox point of view ...

From a report about the last day of the Congress of the Nahadatoel Oelama at Soerabja on 13 October 1927

I estimate that about two hundred people were present, all of them religious scholars. The chairman was Kjai Hasjim ... The most remarkable thing about this meeting was that while the scholars attacked each other vehemently about matters that to outsiders appeared futile, they all agreed about really important things. Moreover it looked as if the *oelama* wanted to come into the good books of the government, because almost without exception they bestowed excessive praise on the government's religious policies, adding every time that without the protection of the government Islam would be under great pressure; and they requested the government to continue this policy, i.e. to guarantee the freedom of true Islam without interfering in the actual religious aspects.

During the public meeting held in the evening in the mosque at Ampel, which was attended by an estimated fifteen thousand people, the government policy was highly praised as the only correct, just, and suitable one for Islam. And the behaviour of those people who wanted to misuse religion for political purposes (this referred, for example, to the *P.S.I.*) was criticized.

Although the speakers were too guarded to mention any names, the praises sung of people who adhered to the four orthodox and safe *madhab*, in contrast to those who do not do so "or belong to one of the numerous other *madhab*" ... makes the position obvious. Like the *P.S.I.* (one of the speakers said: "the misuse of religion for political purposes leads to Digul [concentration camp in West-Irian]"), the *Moehammadijah* is considered an ememy against which one would like to deploy the government as an ally ...

The orthodox *oelama*, when questions of religious finesse are not involved, are realists and practical conservatives who have a really classical ability to portray the existing situation as legal. They still have the support of the masses. And there is a sharp contrast between the handful of people who listened to [Hadji Agus] Salim's nationalistic speeches at Pekalongan (which they did not understand) and the enormous masses of people gathered in and around the mosque at Ampel, milling around to hear a non-Muslim government being praised! It must be admitted that curiosity must also have been a factor.

At the closed meeting only Javanese scholars were present, with the exception of the Director of the Egyptian school (*Madrasah Assasijah*) in Soerabaja, Ahmad Ghanain al Amiri (who in his speech underlined the loyal and political character of the association), and Moehammad Abdul Aleem Siddiqui Quadiri from British India (who in beautiful Arabic exhorted people to stay true to orthodoxy and warned against the modernist know-alls, in particular the *Ahmadijah*) ...

The most important were the discussions about marriage regulations, divorce, child marriages, and the mosque trust funds ... The practice of divorcing a woman soon after marriage or when she is getting older is strongly condemned as being opposed to the spirit of Islam ... The *penghoeloe* of Tangerang takes the strongest possible stand against child marriages, emphasizing the moral and social evils of this institution ... The *N.O.* requests the government to introduce at least one and a half hours of religious instruction into its schools according to the Sjafi'ite interpretation ... It was pointed out that the government was not unaware of the fact that the number of pupils in the village schools was declining because of the lack of religious instruction ...

Koloniaal Archief. *Geheim Mailrapport 261x/28.*

Communism

Communism was brought to the Indies by Dutchmen who in 1914 founded the *Indische Sociaal Democratische Vereeniging* or *I.S.D.V.* (the Social Democratic Association of the Indies). Among its founders were such international Communist stalwarts as Sneevliet, who later under the pseudonym Maring played an important role in the founding of the Chinese Communist Party.

In order to spread the Marxist ideals more widely among the indigenous masses the organization proceeded to infiltrate with some considerable success into existing indigenous nationalist organizations such as the *Sarikat Islam* and the *Indische Partij*. And it was able to attract to its ranks a number of able young Indonesian leaders such as Semaun, Alimin, and Musso. Another influential Indonesian Communist leader at this time was Tan Malaka, who had come into contact with Marxism in the Netherlands where he was studying at the Teachers' College in Haarlem. On his return to the Indies he played an important organizational role in the movement. He was banned by the colonial government in 1922 and became a Comintern agent in Asia. Tan Malaka returned to Indonesia towards the end of 1944 and became a prominent revolutionary leader. By this time he had broken with the Comintern, but his attempts to establish a National-Communist government in the Indonesian republic failed. He was murdered in 1948, probably by anti-Communist republican guerillas. Document 55 contains excerpts from a number of private letters by Tan Malaka to van Wijngaarden, a Dutch friend from the Teachers' College, in which he exposes his views on colonialism, capitalism, and Communism.

By the end of 1916 whole branches of the *Sarikat Islam* had come under Communist control. The most prominent of these was the Semarang branch led by Semaun, which rivalled in importance the head office of the *Sarikat Islam* in Surabaja, led by Tjokroaminoto.

The continuous pressure of leftist leaders to drive the *Sarikat Islam* into a more radical direction caused strong opposition from the more conservative and more directly Islamic-orientated leaders, causing a serious split in the movement. This caused the Communists eventually to dissociate themselves from the *Sarikat Islam* and to set up their own mass movement. In 1920 the *I.S.D.V.* changed its name to *Partai Kommunis Indonesia—P.K.I.*, or the Indonesian Communist Party—and in 1921 decided to regroup all leftist *Sarikat Islam* branches into "Red" branches. Finally at the *Sarikat Islam* Congress in 1923 the *P.K.I.* was ousted from the central organization of the movement and set up its own *Sarikat Rakjat* (People's Association) branches in direct competition with the *Sarikat Islam*. This *P.K.I.* decision contravened the directions of the Comintern, which in 1922 had re-emphasized the importance for Asian Communist parties of using the "block within" tactic, i.e. working within existing nationalist mass organizations.

Soon the messianic expectations of the masses were transferred from the *Sarikat Islam* to the *P.K.I.*, because the majority of Indonesians were not interested in specifically Islamic questions or Pan-Islamism. The people used the *P.K.I.*, as initially had been the case with the *Sarikat Islam*, as a vehicle for their protests about deteriorating economic and social conditions; and the *Sarikat Rakjat* branches were generally far more highly valued as local complaint bureaux than as dissemination centres of Marxist doctrine.

But also the *P.K.I.* leadership was often less than doctrinaire. Sophisticated leaders such as Tan Malaka, with a sound grounding in Marxist theory, were few; and most of these had been exiled by the colonial government by 1923. In particular most of the medium echelon and lower level leadership had joined the party rather for pragmatic reasons and was drawn from widely different social and educational milieux. Some were urban intellectuals and semi-intellectuals who were disgruntled with their socio-economic status; others were traders or farmers hit by the post-war depression, or well-to-do villagers, often orthodox Muslims, who complained about the burdensome taxes; others again were *ulama* (Islamic teachers), who opposed *kafir* rule; or government officials who had been treated unjustly by the colonial authorities. This rather uneven commitment by the party leadership to the Marxist cause worried the national party leaders a great deal, as it caused serious problems of discipline. It was on Tan Malaka's suggestion that indoctrination courses were set up to overcome this problem—the so-called *Sarikat Rakjat* schools, of which there were thirty-eight in Java with 2100 pupils in 1924-25.

However, these attempts at indoctrination were unable to stem the often undisciplined and unco-ordinated activities of party members, which culminated in the abortive and ill-conceived insurrections in Banten (West Java) and Minangkabau (Sumatra) in 1926-27, insurrections easily suppressed by the colonial authorities.

An official investigation (*see* document 56) into the causes of these uprisings shows how diverse the objectives and expectations of the participants were and that in many respects these rebellions were very similar to their counterparts in the nineteenth century. Uprisings had also been planned in other parts of Indonesia but did not get off the ground, usually because they had been prematurely discovered by the colonial intelligence service. As the report of the Resident of Blitar (East Java) shows (*see* document 57), the motives underlying the planned action appear to have been far more pragmatic or nationalist than Marxist. An investigation held in 1927 as to the social and educational background of a sample of captured Communist leaders indicates that the *P.K.I.* leadership on the whole originated from the lower classes and had little education behind it (*see* document 58).

These Communist-inspired rebellions caused a wave of harsh suppressive measures by the colonial government. Of the 18,000 persons initially arrested, a few were sentenced to death and executed while 4500 were sent to prison. The colonial government, which hitherto had been fairly lenient in the treatment of radical nationalist offenders and had allowed a number of them to go into exile in Holland or other countries, now took a much harsher line, and 1308 Communists were sent to the infamous Tanah Merah prison camp at the Upper Digul River in West Irian. This suppressive policy and the greatly increased vigilance of the *Politieke Inlichtingen Dienst* (Political Intelligence Service) effectively prevented the *P.K.I.* from rising again during the remainder of Dutch rule.

55   Tan Malaka: Letters to D. J. L. van Wijngaarden, 1920-1921

Tellorawa, 16 Febr. 1920.
Dear Dick,
   I got a shock when I received your letter. I am jubilant that the old cynical, humorous Dick all of a sudden shows himself as one of the fiercest opponents of all ideologies and parties. Never just parrot the opinions of others. This does not mean that I fully agree with you. Also I am still seeking, or rather I am investigating. I have already chosen my main direction in social and religious life, if I may describe the latter in this way. At present I am occupied with the question: "Is the supernatural possible?" I am at present living among a mystically inclined people, and one of these days I will strike a real mystic. There are charlatans, but there are also some who are convinced. And the latter you have to look for, because they do not show themselves off in public.
   I also feel that I have found how to look at society. We live at a

time when the various philosophies of life are clashing. The idea that this will produce chaos is unconditionally destined to be supported for a shorter or longer period. Good and bad after all are relative concepts. What is usually called good is what complies with the demands of the times. And that is Communism, to which we, Dick, because we are still open-minded, must direct ourselves. It is useless to argue that it will not succeed or that it is chimerical. Also we cannot consider the criminals who can be found among the Communists as professing true Communism, because the fact that there are also honest ones is proved by the arming of the whole of the world against this damnable system. For the time being the political reality is that it will be victorious in the whole of the world or that it will remain one of the strongest organizations, which will be built up even further. Until ... yes, until perhaps, as is the fate of everything or every idea in this world, it will after having reached its zenith begin to decline and finally disappear from the world.

As you see, I am only an onlooker—I am waiting. And I will leave my remarks at that for the time being and will refrain from trying to refute your arguments. Surely you can read about Marxist doctrine yourself. And if you had done that, then you could never have said that the Communists are destructive and the members of the S.D.A.P. [Dutch Socialist Party] are workers. I say again I do not have to refute your ideas because this has already been done so often. I also know that not long before my departure [from the Netherlands] many young people as well as others began to think very differently about this.

Also here the Europeans never take the trouble to fully understand the people. It has always been like this [in the Indies] and it is still like it. That is what is generally felt. If there is some ferment among the people then it is considered the work of agitators and false leaders. And the thousands of Europeans will remain blind to the true nature of the movement and the real needs of the people. [According to the Europeans] they [the people] live *senang* [happy] lives and have no wants. They are stupid. You cannot do anything about it. And whatever argument is put up, the inevitable reaction is: they are not yet ripe, etc., etc. ... In other words, what you are saying is not true. So I no longer talk about this to Europeans. It would be useless. And then in addition there is the feeling of racial superiority. It is impossible for them [Europeans] to give up their old position and power. One becomes lazy in movement and thinking and if I stay too long among the Europeans here I will become completely stupid. In Holland one tried now and then to talk about various things, but here the only topics of conversation are salaries, profit bonus, and leave. Nothing else. I am not exaggerating, Dick, and I am not trying to belittle your compatriots. If you were here

you would also become like that. In my opinion you people do not belong here. I do not want to be nasty, Dick. The climate, the people, and civilization here are different, if I may say so, and nobody of course thinks about adaptation to the majority. Instead one does nothing; one lets everything be done by others, one acts the great lord, one roars, yes, kicks, which is considered the best way to keep up prestige. East is East, etc. ... but that is not entirely true. It is not impossible for Nordic man to understand the man from the East and vice versa. Believe me. Well, Dick, if you write to me, I will of course always reply. I am always pleased to receive a letter from you.
As ever,
Yours, Ipie

Telorawa, 19 May 1920
Dear Friend,
I was very pleased to receive your letter. You must forgive me that I am somewhat late in replying. I really cannot help it. At present I have to work very hard. I am almost all day on the job and I regularly get up at half past four to study. Furthermore, recently I have written three articles for the *Bolsjewist* paper in the Indies (*Het Vrije Woord*—so a Dutch paper). So, do I hate every Dutchman or white man? Believe me, I will always have respect for people who are concerned about the lot of my people. Dick, I understand very well what the difference is between national struggle and class struggle ...

Dick, you should not expect any panacea from the system of proportional representation which has been introduced in Holland [in 1919]. Do you really think that there will be even the slightest change so long as the means of the production process remains the same, and private property remains intact, so that a small proportion of the people lives at the cost of the masses, so long as education, the police, and the army are class institutions? Do you really think that a hundred Troelstras [Troelstra was a Dutch Socialist who led his party to the verge of revolution in November 1918], with similar loud mouths, a hundred times magnified but without a revolutionary and purposeful mass of people behind them, would ever be able to drive out the capitalists from their privileged positions? As long as the production process and private property are not changed, the existing social contrasts will remain, although personalities may perhaps be changed or moved.

Are you really so frightened, Dick, of these destroyers? Marx says (I cite from memory): "The organs of state of the bourgeoisie must not be simply taken over, they must be demolished". Surely one cannot get a *Titanic* by repairing the rotten ship *De Wilis* of the Rotterdam Lloyd? However, gentlemen such as Schaper, Vliegen and Ebert, and Scheidemann [Socialists] believe this; and because of their horse-trading with the rightists they have become so dependent on the military that it is impossible to speak any longer about reforms. So much for parliamentary government! Look also at Lloyd George-Northcliffe. It is all one kettle of fish!

Admittedly, these destroyers are not ideal Communists, Dick. But they create the conditions for Communism, in the same way as the dictatorship of the proletariat. What is happening now in Russia is only the beginning of a transition period and in the meantime a great deal is already being done to provide education for all children. Yes, even the hours that illiterates spend in school are counted as working hours and paid for by the State! Men such as Loenakarsky and Maxim Gorki are the guarantee for the future education of the people. You know that Gorki at first was opposed to *Bosjewism*, even very strongly. Only later did he come to support *Bolsjewism*, just as Krussin and Nogin, who now conduct trade for Soviet Russia with the representatives of the Western countries, were formerly capitalists. However, to go back to Gorki, you should realize that your friend Shaw before the war had exactly the same ideology as Gorki, Anatole France, Romain Roland, and many others. But who is now more useful to society? Is it the reflective Shaw, who because of the war began to glorify the nationalist-imperialist idea, or is it Gorki, who together with Loenakarsky has translated into Russian more than five thousand books of all kinds?

The monotony you fear so much under a Socialist system will not, I think, be so bad, providing that all aptitudes and gifts are allowed to develop without the obstructions that exist now. For that, however, peace and quiet are needed and Russians are not allowed this by capitalist Western Europe: all sorts of armies are directed against them. I would not be surprised if one of these days *Bolsjewism* will be suppressed. But that would not be its own fault. Its spirit will live one and, purified by struggle, it will appear again so that power will come into the hands of labour, so that people will no longer be ruled by depressions, speculations, and other niceties of that kind; in short, so that humanity will apply the natural resources for the benefit of the whole.

Well, I had better stop for the time being. Otherwise you may think perhaps that I have already been in Russia or a Socialist heaven ... Dick, expecting to hear from you soon.
As ever,
Yours, Ibrahim.
In all probability I will get 420 guilders per month soon. It fairly makes my mouth water. Would'nt that cause me to be quieter and stop shouting in *Het Vrije Woord*! Don't laugh. Others would be snapping it up.
Yours, Ipie

Telorawa, 4 Aug. 1920
Dear Dick,
I received your letter last night ... We certainly hold very different opinions, Dick. But that does not mean of course that we should have to become estranged from each other. On the contrary, it is just because of that that we can either help each other on the right track or strengthen each other in our opinions ...

Let me take you up point by point.

[Your argument] that the class struggle can easily degenerate into national struggle is of course true. But in fact I did not argue that the whole of the Indies nation has already reached the point of a class struggle. The Indies is only just beginning to struggle, and it is as yet not completely clear how and in what direction it wants to go. But when it realizes that the whole of the capitalistic world is united against the colonized and the proletariat then it will automatically extend its arms towards the rest of the world proletariat.

Dick, I do not want to become personal. Moreover I know my friend Dick only too well. But when you say that you do not seek your salvation in the treasures of the world, such as proportional representation, but rather in God and your soul, then I must counter this by saying that millions and millions of people cannot do this because they are slaving from morning to night for a few capitalists. They are not sure whether they will have the barest necessities of life, while there is abundance in the world. They are devoid of any sort of higher education and civilization, etc., etc., etc.

You cannot actually take Holland as a normal example, because it is supported mainly by trading and colonial capital, which is less oppressive than industrial capital. Moreover Holland gains a great deal from its colonial possessions. You should look at the Ruhr, Saxony, and the extensive mining districts in England; and you should look around in Java, British India, and Egypt, where millions are sacrificed at the cost of the soul, yes the lives of millions. And this is putting it mildly. I am not even mentioning child labour, the labour of women, the destruction of family life, war, imperialism. And all this for the sake of surplus value, i.e. the blood of the workmen.

The question of being a "minority" is not important, although it is the hobbyhorse of the bourgeoisie and its servants in the West. According to you the Communists are in the minority; and you are right, because nine-tenths of humanity are capitalists or their sympatnizers or servants. They do not realize this, and even if they do, they are too weak or too disinterested to rise up, or they let themselves be taken in by the inexhaustible store of capitalist bribes.

You say you do not like to rule, nor do you yourself want to be lorded over. Correct. But if the latter is your objective, what would you do if you were not as lucky and capable as you are now? Would you then have to be the eternal victim of somebody with money? You consider all governments, restrictions, and organizations as evil and "an insult to the royalty of our free soul". The *Bolsjewists* think exactly the same and they only differ from you in this, that this royalty of the free soul cannot come into being as long as there are haves and have-nots, as long as nine-tenths of humanity must slave for the sake of a number of idlers.

The *Sanembah Mij* [a Dutch plantation concern] now earns according to a rough estimate 5 million guilders on an investment of 1½ million guilders. Of these 5 million guilders 65 per cent goes to the shareholders in Holland, while the coolies who work all day long earn 46 cents per day. Morality, refinement? Oh, my dear soul. Gambling, adultery, all the vices of man are encouraged [among the workers] ... as long as they work. This is the purest form of capitalism.

The Bolshevists want first to create the conditions for the soul to be free and royal.

Also the "improvement of the human race" [which Wijngaarden mentions] is contained in the programme of the Communists, and not only on paper—something will actually be done. Read about the attempts of Maxim Gorki and Loenakarsky. Read about the direction that modern education is taking, that is, education is to be for everybody, and to fit in with practical life, so that not only conceited gentlemen clerks and ink coolies are being produced. Selection, specialization, and individualization will be applied. I tell you again, read about it, and then you will realize that the "reforms" you want so much will of necessity be implemented, together with the basis of freedom. It will take at least another generation before this "rebirth" will come about, but nothing will result from talking alone. We have to do something about it. We must demolish what we are opposed to; attempts to patch things up won't work. In fact Shaw's ideas are not that far removed from those of the *Bolshewists*, and like all the Russian intellectuals of all ranks who first considered the *Bolshewists* as a lower form of human, as adventurers and bandits, Shaw and other notabilities in England have come closer to them. Read the proclamation of these Russian intellectuals (professors, engineers, writers of note) to the Western intellectuals, to which Shaw has declared his solidarity.

It is always true that when things begin to go well the waverers rush to join the tail end of the movement.

Also [the Communists] have taken adequate measures in the legal field in order to increase the sense of justice. There are no longer class courts, where the simple but honest minds get lost, because the experts of the bourgeoisie have the monopoly of legal knowledge and subtleties ...

Time is needed for the renaissance, because first the State must disappear (Lenin says, die) and also the dictatorship, because the State and also the dictatorship of the proletariat are according to Marx a recognition and a result of the fact that the antagonism between classes is unbridgeable. In other words every State has something superimposed on it. In our system this means the rule of the workers, the majority, over a minority of capitalists; and finally the State must die off.

Before everything else time is needed, but that is what the Bolsheviks are not allowed by the capitalists of the world, who do not say "let us be constructive", but rather "let us fight", and send their slaves against them. They also say that these *Bolsjewiks* cannot do anything else than destroy, but they forget to mention that these despicable bandits when they came to power despite hunger, economic upheaval, and mass famine, have still been able to defeat the last capitalist armies, such as in Poland. And the common citizens of course do not give it any further thought.

I won't elaborate on this, Dick. All I want to say is that because of this fighting, the ideals can be destroyed, yes, that the task must be interrupted for the time being and be left for completion by other generations of Communists.

You despise dictators, you say (also including of course Lenin, Bucharin, Krassin, and many others, whom I certainly do not esteem less than Shaw). Although I agree with you, I must point out to you that dictatorship does not only mean to rule. This is only necessary for the present, because otherwise the ex-capitalists would certainly try to obtain military aid from inside and outside the country. The present dictorship of the proletariat, however, also contains the germ of Socialism, which will have to be protected for a long time before it can be completely purified from all vestiges of capitalism. You can also despise that, of course.

So, Dick, the Communists continue to argue that what is happening in Russia today is only the beginning of a transition period.

You sighed in your letter that it is such a horrible beginning. But let me tell you that this is nothing compared with the murder of millions in the last great capitalist war ... which was sustained by greediness, a greediness that will never be satisfied, a greediness that expressed itself and still does today in competition, speculation, and imperialism at the cost of the masses. That is the nature of capitalism; it cannot do otherwise.

Wait a little while and the *danse macabre* will certainly begin again. Only listen to the sabre-rattling in Asia and America. Wherever capitalism settles it cannot belie its nature.

You will perhaps say to me again: I agree with you. But that is

why we should have an inner rebirth. I would also say that, if I did not consider it to be Utopian ...
As ever Yours,
Ipie

Tj. Morawa, 5 Jan. 1921
Dear Dick,
... These are great times in which we are living. I count myself lucky to be alive at this time and I will try to be worthy of its spirit ...

6 Jan. 1921
With respect to your hate of the Catholic Church, I must tell you immediately that it is also part of my programme of action to destroy her. Only I do not go to the *S.D.A.P.* [Dutch Socialist Party] for help. Friend, that organization is not in the habit of destroying anything. The *S.D.A.P.* roars, but when it comes to deeds, it retires frightened of the consequences. It tries to mend things; it does not destroy, and therefore cannot build things, because in order to construct something solidly one must first flatten everything. Look at the Ebert party in Germany. What are they doing? Or rather what can they do, what can they achieve only by talking? Give it a little time and the Ludendorffs will come to the fore again with the ... Crown Prince. And give it a little more time and then also the *S.D.A.P.* will belong to the past like Liberalism. And even now it begins to look very much like it. They only chatter and temporize all the time!

About the Catholic Church we do not have to waste many words. It is simply an economic institution, Dick. This started as early as the pronouncement of the principle, "Render unto Caesar ... " Already then the pure glow of fire was being extinguished. A spirit of compromise is a spirit of regression, exactly like *S.D.A.P.*ism and Kautskyism. What do you expect if both ideals and riches are in the hands of the great lords? The Catholic Church is in my opinion also the meanest form of capitalist exploitation, because it drags in God. But that sort of Judasism you can find in every religion. I can save you the trouble of having a look at Islam or Buddhism and so on. I saw in Colombo—and it is supposed to be even better in the much-renowned Further India where it is maintained in a purer state—I saw in Colombo then a few priests who were beautifully adorned, although in yellow as a sign of supposed poverty. With their eyes downcast they held a sort of little bell, with which they called on the people to give alms. The Buddhist priests are not allowed to own property. But this disdain for filthy lucre goes apparently so far that in that Further India where Buddhism has remained in its purest form they use a gold bell instead of a copper one, just for good measure.

We may as well remain quiet about Islam, which also does not practise what it preaches. So far all practice seems to be mostly directed at filthy lucre, an excellent job, or riches. There is only to be peace for those who own the greatest amount of capital or the largest palace. There may be no change or disturbance of the relationship between the capitalist lord and the workers, between the ministers of state—or rather capitalist slaves and the masses. Peace among the brethren on this earth. That is the recipe in Christian Europe, Buddhist Further India and Brahmanist or Muslim India. Peace, as long as you slave your guts out for a handful of rulers or capitalists and their equivalents.

Once I even let myself be initiated, very secretly, because I was ashamed that I was so curious and wanted to see with my own eyes what Islamic mysticism was about. For days I submitted myself to a teacher. My conclusion was: that all this mysticism was in all probability nothing else than hocus-pocus or trickery or both. Bah, I am disgusted with all this trickery that is found wherever religion creeps in.

Not that I am opposed to virtue, which was also the objective of, for example, Islam. Yes, I say was, because virtue was the only objective when Mohammad himself still lived very soberly. But when his followers came out of the desolate desert and entered fertile lands and prosperous cities, then the well-known recipe came into vogue again: peace between the owners of property and the powerful and the exploited. Nature became stronger again than dogma. Then virtue became restricted and had to be restricted to the very few, who supposedly could not influence the whole.

I am all for virtue. But first we must prepare the soil in which virtue can grow and ripen. Virtue and peace are in my opinion only possible by way of revolution. And in fact the materialist Marx has really an idealistic background. But in the first place whatever obstructs virtue and peace must be destroyed. By now we should all have come to know what is good and what is bad, if not in a philosophical sense then at least intuitively. Everybody, it does not matter how stupid he is, knows immediately if something is just, isn't that so? He also would know what hunger is, and a child from the Jordaan [poor quarter of Amsterdam] would like to have a pair of nice skates just as much as a child from *het Spiegel* [more prosperous area]. Again Dick, until next month!
I will write to you soon.
As ever, Yours,
Ibrahim

H. A. Poeze, "*Tan Malaka. Een Indonesisch Revolutionair. Levensloop 1896-1922*" (Ph.D. thesis, *Faculteit der Sociale Wetenschappen, Universiteit van Amsterdam*, 1972), pp. 50-59.

56 H. J. Benda and R. T. McVey: Communist uprisings, 1926-27

The police have now stated that there was a total of approximately four thousand party members; this figure is far smaller than the number of people who bought membership cards at one time or another. This difference is easily explained, for a number of those who bought cards did not at the time know anything about a definite rebellion ...

The persons who were ready for action came from all sections of the population; there was in proportion an equal number of those possessing no land, common *desa* (village) people, *desa* heads, the more well-to-do, and religious leaders. There was a proportionally large number of *hadjis* and *djawaras* [religious people]. Only a very small number of officials or former officials joined in and there was not one administrative official or real intellectual among the active rebels. There were, it is true, two members of the regency council of Pandeglang among them and some *desa* heads. There were various members among the Chinese, but otherwise the latter kept cleverly in the background ... apparently the Communists are to be found particularly among the youth; they were sought there intentionally: "there were cards for sale for the young people", one of the participants in Menes has said.

Nevertheless there were very many middle-aged and old people among them. Women remained entirely in the background in this religious country. Despite this fact there were some who had bought cards and there was one female promoter.

Relations between the participants concur with the social structure of the society ... This is also proved by the fact that the number of members was increased by persons with a certain influence going over to the movement and bringing with them virtually all those who came under their influence. Nevertheless a group of this sort did not join all at once. The most prominent went over first, often members of one family which little by little joined in its entirety; only after this had happened did the hangers-on follow suit quickly or gradually. Soon after some influential person had been won a large increase in membership would become apparent.

The Causes of Rebelliousness

In analysing the causes of the rebellion three motives may be distinguished from each other: (a) grievances against the existing order; (b) expectations for the future; (c) the possibility of revolution.

The aggregate impression of the inquiry has been that the main causes of the rebellion were those under (b) and (c). It is certain that neither the economic situation nor the existing religious sentiments alone could have given rise to any serious reasons for unrest. The feelings which were intentionally motivated by a third party, and which otherwise also made the grievances weigh more heavily, are what tipped the balance.

Grievances

Nevertheless it would be incorrect and incomplete if we were not to mention everything which was capable in some way or other of moving things in the direction of discontent. In Bantam (West Java) too there are repercussions of the international events which bring disturbances in their wake everywhere.

Here too as elsewhere many experience the feeling of dissatisfaction and an undefined discontent which usually accompany what we call "awakening" or "becoming conscious". But this is neither more intense nor more important than the same feelings elsewhere ...

The rebellion broke out in what were economically the most prosperous areas (i.e. in West Java and in Minangkabau [West Sumatra] and many of the rebels could by no means be called poor. Special investigations have been made to discover whether indebtedness could have perhaps been the cause of refractoriness or despair but in this respect also it has appeared that the rebels were not as a rule among the most oppressed; there are fewer credit abuses in Bantam than elsewhere in Java ...

The list (of specific grievances) is not impressive ... it is quite obvious that they alone cannot have been the cause of the rebellion.

There is not a district in Java and probably not a country in the world where it would not be possible to compile exactly the same sort of lists. There has probably not been one period in Bantam's history when lists of this kind could not have been made, but this fact did not cause an uprising then.

Finally there have also been some personal questions at stake in the disturbances. The man who played an important part behind the scenes at Menes, the dishonourably discharged *desa* head Entol Enoh, bore a personal grudge against the *wedana* (district head) because, while he had been made to collect the back taxes of his *desa*, which he partly paid from his own pocket, and had then been discharged after all ... Personal motives of this kind are of course of little importance for the question as a whole.

The Promised Utopia

The Communists showed great skill and keen insight in the way in which they spread expectations of the success of the rebellion and promises of a Utopia. For every group they had ready a separate ideal suited to the group's conditions. This ideal was always called *Kemerdekaan* (freedom), but each group has its own ideas of what that meant.

The more well-to-do were promised a Utopia where they could keep everything they possessed, would not have to pay any taxes, and would even get positions with the new government.

The descendants of the sultan and the other title-bearers were promised the establishment of a new sultanate and "their own sultan"; this state was represented as an Islamic state to the religious orthodox.

The followers of the religious leaders who were preparing for the rebellion were enticed with the prospects of the glories of paradise, the reward which would await them as warriors victorious in Allah's name, or as martyrs who have died for his cause.

Where it was of service the common man was given visions of *sama rasa sama rata* (equality for all), but this did not often occur, as it proved sufficient to win the support of eminent citizens. However, everyone was led to expect the blessings of cheap rice or free rice and free transport in cars and trains, etc. But nothing much was said about distribution of property belonging to the wealthy because an attempt was made to get the wealthy to join also.

Side by side with the illusions of fortune for those who would rebel were of course the threats of those who would not. They would not partake in the advantages of Utopia; on the contrary they would be oppressed; their property would be confiscated for the founders of the new community.

The Possibility of Success

Even more important than the notions formed about a Utopia were those concerning the possibility of success of the rebellion.

The crux of the whole problem is that the Bantamese do not like rule, whether it be Dutch or other. And thus the main feature of the Communist action apparently consisted of impressing upon the minds of the population the possibility of rebellion succeeding. To put it even more forcibly, the Communists convinced the people that a rebellion would arise and that the *pergerakan* [movement] was strong and powerful, irresistible and inevitable.

Thousands of members were prepared, part of the police was on the side of the Communists, together with the majority of "the soldiers of Tjimahi" and "Batavia", likewise various prominent *gurus* (mystical teachers), among them the *kiai* of Tjaringin. This even made an impression on members of the constabulary. What will you be able to do with sixty men if we turn up with two hundred thousand? The rebels in Menes and Labuan were instructed that after the first rebellious actions "the soldiers of Tjimahi" would arrive and decide what was to be done with the officials who had not yet been murdered.

By intentionally suggesting that the rebellion must succeed the Communists were cleverly taking into account the milieu in which they were working. While the aid of Russia and China was promised elsewhere in Java, here it was the irresistible Mustafa Kemal who would bring real aid in airplanes. The reason why suggestions of the certainty of success are so dubious is that one of the conditions under which the holy war may or even must be started is that there must be a chance of success. Threats were often employed in this unusually vague description of what was going to happen.

Religion

Religion is, generally speaking, of such paramount importance in Bantam that a separate study of its influence on the movement cannot be considered out of place here. The opinion expressed by many, even prior to the uprising, that a mass rebellion—for this is what it became in the Labuan area—would not be possible in Bantam without the religious sentiments of the population becoming involved, has proved to be correct.

Whereas other areas endeavoured to liberate themselves of the foreign tyrant in order to attain the promised Utopia, many of the Bantamese wished to free themselves of the infidel tyrant in order to pay greater honour to Islam. *Perang sabil* (Holy War) was the means to this end.

The advantages expected in this world were the same in both cases and the propaganda was also mainly aimed at the realization of these advantages.

In troubled times the *dukuns* (faith healers), the possessors of *ngelmu* (magical knowledge), prove to play a not insignificant part. When there is a movement on foot or when there is unrest among the people, they know that they can convince the common man that he can become invulnerable by means of their half-religious, half-magical practices.

*H. J. Benda and R. T. McVey, eds *The Communist Uprisings of 1926-1927 in Indonesia: Key Documents* (Ithaca: Cornell, 1960), pp. 40-47.

57 The Resident of Kediri: Communist disturbances in Blitar, 1927

The native officials who once every twenty-five days presided at the village meetings had not noticed anything alarming, and neither had the staff of the many plantations experienced any labour troubles.

It was fear that stopped most people from informing the administration. The interrogation of people who joined the conspiracy, consciously or unconsciously or out of fear, has, however, thrown some light on the motives that made so many people join.

Neither the top leaders nor the masses have any idea about the particular direction colonial policy has taken in the last few years. Naturally there were complaints about the pressure of taxation, but when this question was pursued it appeared that it was mainly local taxes that were felt to be too heavy ...

Relatively, Blitar is a prosperous district with ample opportunities for employment, although coolie wages on the plantations are as low as thirty-five cents per person.

In my opinion a distinction should be made between the motives of the leaders and the followers, which are similar only to the extent that both groups consider that the time has come when, according to the old prophesies, Dutch power shall be thrown off.

The current view that the purpose of the *Sarikat Islam* soon after its foundation must have been to gradually undermine the government's authority is also applicable in this district.

The leaders, originally of the *Sarikat Islam* and later of the *Sarikat Rakjat*, always emphasized in the closed meetings that the traditional forms of etiquette towards government servants should no longer be adhered to. And these officials could not do anything about this as long as the criminal code was not contravened.

At the public meetings during 1925 the people were regularly told that the *"kemenangan S. R. soedah akan datang"* ["the *Sarikat Rakjat* will be victorious"] because of the suppression by the capitalists. The leaders have unfortunately succeeded in completely destroying the people's trust in and respect for the *Binnenlands Bestuur* [Dutch and Indonesian regional administrators] and they themselves now enjoy the trust and confidence of the people.

Both I myself and the Regent agree that among the top leaders there is not one who has not pushed himself forward in this way other than for purely selfish reasons. However, among the second-echelon leaders many have acted from the deep conviction that they were doing their duty with respect to their people and country by expelling the cruel government. This is the impression I gained from their naive replies and their deep disappointment about the turn of events. They have been misled and some have become insane, while one took drugs and another one committed suicide by hanging himself.

I can see only a gradual difference between the actions of the *Sarikat Islam* and those of the *Sarikat Rakjat*, although so far as the leaders are concerned it stands out that the leaders of the *Sarikat Rakjat* openly confess that they no longer believe in the authority of the Qu'ran.

Santri have thrown their Qu'rans in the *slokans* [ditches] and in general the masses are not very strongly attached to the doctrine of the Prophet.

While the proud people of Mataram mostly kept away from the *Sarikat Islam*, they have all joined the *Sarikat Rakjat*. According to the Regent the reason for this is that the *Sarikat Islam* originally began in Solo, while the ideology of the *Sarikat Rakjat* reminds them more of Dipanegara, who originated from Mataram [*see* document 37].

But there are also material ties with Jogja, because they receive their goods on time payment from the merchants in Kota Gede, who have nearly all joined the *Sarikat Rakjat* and have given financial support to the movement in Blitar. Earlier they also financed the foundation of the bicycle corps of the boy scouts.

Many rich land-owners joined in order to ensure that during the period of great instability which they foresaw would result from the possible success of the movement, they would get off lightly. A number of them approve unconditionally the mass arrests and the forceful measures of the administration.

Among those arrested are a number of well-to-do people, who gradually became convinced members of the *Sarikat Rakjat*. Initially they were told at the meetings that the *Sarikat Rakjat* wished to help them in these difficult times and they were promised a happy life ... if they joined. Next they were deluded into believing that they could no longer expect anything from the Netherlands Government, and finally they were persuaded or forced to join the plot.

The masses joined because the false hope of *sama rata sama rasa* [equality for all] was repeatedly held out to them, which after all according to the old prophesies is supposed to be the basis on which the Kingdom of the *Ratu Adil* is founded.

The so-called little man, who is only concerned with providing himself with the necessities of life, complains about the restriction on his freedom caused by regulations and the many kinds of taxation.

A number of regulations, in particular those stemming from the Regional Council, are considered to be obstructive and tormenting and the concomitant financial obligations make the people poor. The village chiefs mention in particular the market taxes, the transport dues, house improvement tax, and stamp duties and legal costs to be paid for building construction, marriages, and divorces.

Annoying regulations are, for example, the forest regulations, which try to compensate for a shortage of forest inspectors by restrictive rules. Then there is the regulation about the cutting-down of fruit trees, which is no longer appropriate, and the tax on fireworks, which practically stops the enjoyment of a harmless popular pleasure. But what hurts the sense of justice of the whole of the native population in all its gradations most is the house improvement tax, which is considered an interference of the government into something close to their hearts: the design and construction of their homes. Many improvements such as beautiful market halls, paid for by high taxes, and asphalted roads, paid for by road taxes, are called *"pengisep"* [literally, "sucking" (extortionate)], while the native officials are called *penindes* [oppressors].

People have taken a great dislike to the exaggerated interference by the government. The native Inspector of Public Works here met a well-to-do native at the house of an acquaintance in Kesamben, who after he had heard what position the visitor held, told him: "Then you are the enemy of the Javanese people." This was apparently a reference to the implementation of the housing improvement regulations.

I have by no means yet exhausted all the possible reasons for the resistance movement; I have only tried to give an explanation for the complete loss of trust of the native population in their chiefs, who in the first place are the executors of national and local regulations.

When this type of mentality is prevalent, village conferences in which the meaning of new regulations is explained are of no use.

An important role in the organization of the plot was also played by young people who had completed school and, lacking professional qualifications, rummaged around, sponging on the general population by writing letters of request or complaint.

A few village heads were of the opinion that the restless agitation of recent times must be ascribed to the undermining activities of *"Tyang inkang saged saged, namoeng boton wonten pandamelanipoen"* ["those people who are knowledgeable (educated), but unemployed"]. The fact is that many of the leaders of the top and second echelon are younger people who have failed in their previous professions or never had one since they left school. The fact that various teachers sympathize with this movement has been brought to light during the last few years also in Blitar. It would deserve serious consideration not only to strengthen the inspection of the Native Primary Education system, but also to change the curriculum in such a way that it was no longer solely designed to impart academic knowledge. The present education system does not satisfy the population's desire for practical knowledge, but instead it tends to uproot the pupils from their spiritual surroundings without giving them the capacity to move themselves up to a more advanced stage of living ...

The deeper causes of the unrest are, as is known, contained in the rapidly changing economic conditions as well as in the complete change in the spiritual attitude of the people ...

An undefinable spiritual power, which also has moved other peoples, is at present converting all feelings into deeds, caused by obvious defects in the social structure and by needs which are difficult to fulfil.

Plots such as have been brought to light in Blitar will be found in other area of Java, and I am definitely convinced that it would be foolish to believe that the masses stand completely aside from this movement ...

Koloniaal Archief. *Resident van Kediri aan den Gouverneur Generaal, 3 Maart 1 1927, no. 26, Zeer Geheim, Mailrapport 421 x/27.*

58 The Assistant Director of Education and Religion: The educational background of arrested Communist leaders, 1927

On the order of the Director of Education and Religion an investigation has been held into the background, age, education, and profession of Communist leaders who are to be detained. The purpose was to find out from what kind of social milieu these people originated, and whether there would be a correlation between the provision of education to the indigenous population and the appearance of political extremism. It was also investigated whether the native movement is essentially a reflection of an economic process, i.e. the birth of a native middle class.

The data were obtained from the official hearings and are based mostly on what the accused themselves were willing to release about their past. In addition, the degree of response differed a great deal, although all of them were probably concerned to present their curricula vitae in the most favourable possible light. The results therefore may not only perhaps be somewhat untrustworthy but also are a little vague, as the information obtained was often inexact and insufficient. Moreover the conclusions are based on a sample of only 331 persons. So, in summary, the conclusions do not have full evidentiary proof, although on the other hand they contain indications that are certainly useful to know.

The geographical origin of the 331 Communist leaders investigated was as follows: Java—294, or 88.8 per cent; other regions—37, or 11.2 per cent ...

According to race the 331 persons were divided as follows: Europeans—0; Chinese—6; natives—325 (among whom there was one female) ...

Age	Number
15-20	5
20-25	77
25-30	97
30-35	80
35-40	42
40-45	17
45-50	6
50 years and above	7
Total	331

As the average age is 29.7 years, it follows that the general impression that most of the Communist followers are young people is incorrect.

During the interrogations questions were also asked about the education that had been received. Based on the replies that were given, the following picture about education emerges:

	Received schooling	Not received schooling
15-20	5	0
20-25	73	4
25-30	89	8
30-35	60	20
35-40	31	11
40-45	14	3
45-50	2	4
50 years and above	3	4
Total	277	Total 54

Some of the fifty-four persons without schooling—who account for 16.3 per cent of the total sample—indicated that they had received some education at home. However, there is no evidence that this education was sufficient to enable them to read and write. If we include these few people among the illiterates, then 83.7 per cent of the Communists were found to be literate. According to the Central Bureau of Statistics no more than 5.91 per cent of the male native population in the whole of the Netherlands Indies is literate, while in the case of Java and Madoera this percentage stands at 5.07. Furthermore, the percentage of boys of school age who actually attended school in 1925 stood at 15.2 for the whole of the Netherlands Indies, and at 14.2 for Java and Madoera. It is clear from these statistics that the Communist leaders belong to the comparatively thin top layer who know the art of reading and writing, and that proportionally there were more illiterates among the older leaders than the younger ones, which of course was to be expected.

The 277 persons who had received some education attended a

total of 389 schools or special courses. As will be explained later, this was only partly due to people continuing their studies at more advanced schools. The fact that such a large number of schools was attended was caused for the greater part by the frequent changing of schools.

If the number of schools attended is divided according to type, the following picture emerges:

	number	%
Tertiary education	—	0
Secondary education	15	3.9
Vocational education	51	13.1
Primary education	323	83.0

Since the figures for persons having attended secondary and vocational schools are actual, the number of persons that only attended primary schools is 277 − 66 = 211.

Proportionally speaking, the Communist leaders had received the following types of education:

	%
Tertiary education	0
Secondary education	4.5
Vocational education	15.5
Primary education	63.7
Illiterates	16.3

There is some uncertainty as to the effectiveness of this schooling, because often the data do not show whether a school was attended for a limited period or for the normal duration of the course.

In so far as this was expressly mentioned or could be gained from the other data, in not more than 118 or 30.3 per cent of the 389 schools were the particular courses successfully completed. As this figure refers to 277 persons, it appears that at the highest, 42.6 per cent could have been in possession of a diploma, although in fact this figure is lower because a number of the more accomplished ones attended, for example, a vernacular primary school, a Dutch-Native School, and a vocational school in succession. Not one of the persons who attended secondary school was able to obtain the final diploma. Of the 51 persons who attended a vocational school only 15 or 29.4 per cent obtained the final diploma. In only 103 cases or 31.9 per cent of the 323 primary schools that were attended was the whole of the course completed.

However, it is well known that a high wastage rate in schools is a general phenomenon. In the highest class (grade seven) of the Dutch-Native Schools only between 43 and 50 per cent of the total number of pupils remain of those who seven years previously entered these schools. In the Second Class Primary Schools (vernacular) one finds in the third grade still 90 per cent of the pupils who entered these schools for the first time, while in top grade (form 5) only between 30 per cent and 45 per cent are left.

Although the educational achievements of the persons investigated so far as primary school is concerned were somewhat below average, they were not so bad as to be considered failures. On the other hand those who received more advanced education showed themselves up rather poorly; and furthermore their number is conspicuously small.

The vast majority then has only received primary education ... Of the 323 primary schools ... there were 99 where the language of instruction was Dutch—or proportionally speaking, in 30.6 per cent of the primary schools and 25.4 per cent of the total number of schools that were attended. Among these [99 schools] there were 73 Dutch-Native Schools or 22.6 per cent of the primary schools and 18.7 per cent of the total number of schools attended. The percentage of Communists who attended Dutch-Native Schools was 22; of these only 27 persons gained the final diploma, or 37 per cent of all persons who attended the Dutch-Native Schools, and only 8 per cent of the total sample of Communists investigated. These socially exclusive schools seemed to have been attended with less success when compared with the normal figure of wastage in the Dutch-language primary schools. If we add to this the rather poor performance in the schools of more advanced education, then the impression is that the intellectual capacity of the persons concerned is not particularly high.

The majority then of Communist leaders have been to schools where the vernacular was the medium of instruction ... However, the question as to how many have been in Dutch-language and how many in vernacular schools cannot be answered exactly ... At the highest 35 per cent and perhpas closer to 30 per cent of the total number of Communists [in the sample] have been in Dutch-language schools, of whom twenty-seven students have successfully got through Dutch-Native Schools and four have got through European primary schools, that is together thirty-one persons or 9.3 per cent of the total sample.

If it is taken into account that we are dealing here with so-called leaders and not followers, then the number of persons educated in Dutch-language schools is not particularly large. In any case it is too insignificant to establish a certain correlation between the incidence of Communism and the provision of Dutch-language school facilities to the indigenous population ...

So far as employment is concerned, 12 people indicated that they were never employed and 123 only had *one* profession. Of the remainder:

    117 held successively 2 different jobs
     47   3
     27   4
      4   5
      1   6

This is a total of 632 different jobs for 319 persons, or almost two jobs per person (Not included were changes in employers within the same profession or promotion within the same service. The holding of office in a trade union or sections of the *P.K.I.* or *Sarikat Rakjat* was also not included.)

These jobs can be categorized as follows:

	Number	%
1. Government Service	216	34.2
2. Western sector of the economy	138	22.0
3. Indigenous sector of the economy	215	34.0
4. Journalists	25	3.9
5. Teachers in private schools	38	5.9
Total	632	

Category 1 can be divided again as follows:

	jobs
(a) Central, local, or village government	41
(b) Public corporations or utilities	146
(c) Public schools	29
Total	216

Category 2, the Western sector of the economy:

	jobs
(a) Plantations	20
(b) Industry	20
(c) Commerce and transport	76
(d) Shipping	6
(e) Various professions	16
Total	138

Category 3, the indigenous economic sector:

	jobs
(a) Agriculture	47

(b) Industry 31
(c) Commerce 74
(d) Various professions 63
Total 215

Under category 3(b), of the thirty-one jobs, eleven were connected with the batik industry.

The majority do not indicate how long they worked in a particular job, and with respect to those who often changed jobs it is difficult to say what their actual profession was. It seems that they changed jobs with the same ease with which they changed schools. Thus the 215 jobs in the indigenous sector of the economy do not mean that 215 persons or 64.9 per cent of the Communists found their major means of existence in this sector. On the contrary most of them fell back on the indigenous sector for want of better jobs.

For this reason the category of persons who only had *one* type of employment deserves more attention. They were in the service of the following:

	persons
The government	20
Western enterprises	24
Indigenous enterprises	66
Various professions	13
Total	123

Only the group that was permanently employed in the indigenous sector can be considered with some certainty to have found the major means of existence there; they carried out the following types of work:

	persons
Agriculture	13
Industry	26
Commerce	16
Various professions	11
Total	66

It would be incorrect to consider all these sixty-six persons as belonging to the native middle class. In the first place five Chinese who were in business and secondly, twenty-six persons who worked as coolies in native enterprises have to be subtracted. Thus there were only thirty-five persons left, or 11 per cent of the total number of Communists in the sample, who were exclusively employed or carried on business on their own account in the native sector. The majority of them were farmers and traders. It is not possible to determine how large their various enterprises were.

If one wants to include in the definition of middle class everybody who at one stage, irrespective of how long, has worked on his own account, then also a number of people who fell back temporarily on the native sector must be counted. Of the 215 jobs under category 3 there are 113 cases where persons either worked for some time on their own little piece of land, worked on their father's farm, traded in agricultural produce, or had a *warong* [small shop]. If these 113 cases of self-employment are considered to be within the native middle class, then even the most insignificant types of business such as the sale of *sate* [skewered roasted meat] must be included, and no account is taken as to how permanently these people were self-employed in the native sector. If this unsatisfactory gauge is used, 17.9 per cent of the total number of jobs held must be considered to be native middle class occupations. It would be possible to determine how many persons were involved, but it would hardly serve any purpose because again they would have to be divided into persons who have remained in the native sector (and it is not possible to determine whether this category wants to get back to better-paid employment as soon as possible), and those who in the meantime have returned to the public service or Western private enterprise.

In any case it can be concluded that of the 632 jobs, 519 or 82 per cent refer to wage employment and only 40 or 12 per cent to self-employment ...

It is possible to determine from the data in which particular departments of the public service the majority of the Communists were employed. The 146 persons mentioned under category 1(b) were employed as follows:

	Number	% of total sample
Head offices of Central Government Departments	7	2.1
State Railways	29	8.8
Harbour Service	8	2.4
Postmaster-General	16	4.9
Health Service	13	3.9
Defence	5	1.5
Police	13	3.9
Topographical Service	4	1.2
Forestry	11	3.3
Pawn Shop Service	17	5.1
Opium Monopoly	1	0.3
Customs	4	1.2
Total	146	44.1

Another 29 persons or 8.8 per cent were employed in public and village education.

Thus the State Railways and Education were the major departments. If the total number of persons employed in the transport sector is added, the following picture emerges:

State Railways	29
Private railways and tramways	21
Native Transport	10
	Total 60

Or, proportionally speaking, 18 per cent of the total number of Communists or 9.4 per cent of the total number of jobs held were connected with transport.

Only in a few cases was it possible to collect data about the social origin of the accused, that is in cases where the persons concerned were forced by circumstances to fall back on their relatives, who are usually farmers. The general impression is that the Communist leaders originate from neither the higher classes nor from the middle classes, but rather from the poorer sections. The type of school most frequented also points to this. However, there is in addition a fairly large number of people of better background who have had bad luck or whose career has been ruined by their own fault. For example, there were four persons belonging to the higher nobility with the title Raden Mas and fifteen of the lower nobility with the title Mas or Raden; moreover there were seven *hadjis* [i.e. persons who had made the pilgrimage to Mecca]. Generally these people held lower-ranking positions in society.

Of the persons who were in wage employment only 58 held positions such as *toekang* [tradesman], *mandoer* or *mantri* [foremen], against which there were 380 copying clerks, labourers, and coolies. Another 71 teachers and journalists have to be added to the more prestigious category.

We were able to obtain some information about the reasons for the changing of jobs. Of the 196 persons who had more than *one* type of employment, totalling 509 jobs, there were 59 persons who kept completely silent on this point, while the remaining 137 gave reasons for one change of jobs but kept silent on the others. The following reasons were given: 38 persons were dismissed honourably or on their own request; 6 because of sickness; 28 dishonourably; 40 because of Communism; and 25 because of striking.

Sixty-five or 19.6 per cent of the Communists were dismissed at least once because of their political convictions and 8.3 per cent because of dishonourable actions. By no means were all able to obtain a new position quickly and in thirty-eight cases there was unemployment for a considerable time. It is not surprising that many fell for the offer made by persons who stayed in the background to work as teachers in the *Sarikat Rakjat* schools or as propagandists. And the paid functions of the labour unions, and the *P.K.I.* and *Sarikat Rakjat* sections were a blessing for many.

However, in addition to those who were driven into politics by hunger, there were also quite a few persons who sacrificed their careers to their convictions.

Before the present arrest 29 persons had already had a brush with the law, although the number of criminals is very small. Of these 29 persons, 18 were convicted for breaking the laws controlling the press and public speaking; 4 were convicted for breaking the laws concerning public assembly; and 11 (or 3 per cent of the total number of Communists questioned) were convicted for other criminal activities.

It is not possible to gain an exact picture of the organization of the *P.K.I.* from the interrogations, because in general the prisoners were fairly reticent on this point.

According to their own declarations, which are obviously incomplete, there were among them: 57 members of the *P.K.I.*; 38 members of the *Sarikat Rakjat*; 13 members of various labour unions; 14 office-bearers of *P.K.I.* sections; 16 office-bearers of *Sarikat Rakjat* sections; 21 office-bearers of various labour unions; 1 member of the Central Committee of the *P.K.I.*; and 17 propagandists. Various persons were members or office-bearers of various organizations at the same time. The *P.K.I.* seems to have been fairly strict with respect to the moral behaviour of office-bearers. At least in two cases mention is made that office-bearers were dismissed because of immoral behaviour.

Summarizing the various impressions gained, it can be concluded that the sample of Communist leaders investigated did not in general belong to the agrarian section of the community, and that only few were self-employed permanently in native commerce or industry. So they do not constitute a middle class in the economic sense. The majority are in wage employment in the public service or Western private enterprise and usually in lower-ranking positions.

If the term middle class is defined in the sense of not belonging to the nobility or the clergy, then these people according to European norms can only for a very small part be classed as belonging to the third estate; the vast majority belong to the fourth estate. According to native and especially Javanese norms, which proportionally grade position higher than prosperity, the demarcation line between third and fourth estate must be drawn somewhat differently. And only the coolies and day labourers would be classed decidedly as fourth estate, while clerks and other lower-ranking officials, who in Europe are classified with the proletariat, still belong to the lower *prijaji* or the third estate.

The vast majority have only attended primary school in which the vernacular is the medium of instruction. The number of persons who successfully completed Dutch-language primary and more advanced schools is small.

To apply the term native intellectuals to this group would be to exaggerate; all that can be said is that most of them are literate, unlike the majority of the population, who can neither read nor write. And only in that sense is there a connection between Communism and education, although there is no correlation between Communism and particular types of schools.

Koloniaal Archief. *Onder-Directeur van Onderwijs en Eredienst aan den Gouverneur Generaal, 19 December, 1927, no. Ax 20/1/14.*

The Indonesia-centric nationalist movement, 1922-42

With the *P.K.I.* out of action after 1926-27 its leadership role in the nationalist movement was taken over by a group of second-generation nationalists, who rejected both Islam and international Communism as the basis of their policies and instead emphasized the need for an Indonesia-centric approach in the struggle to gain independence.

The initiative for this new departure in Indonesian politics was taken by Indonesian students in the Netherlands, who were members of the *Perhimpunan Indonesia* (the Indonesian Association), a political-activist society that had been formed in 1922. It is difficult to overstate the historical significance of the *Perhimpunan Indonesia* because many of its prominent members, such as Mohammad Hatta, Sutan Sjahrir, Sutomo, Subardjo and Ali Sastroamidjojo, exerted on their return home a profound influence on Indonesian politics both in the colonial period and during the free Indonesian republic. Inspired by Marxist anti-colonial ideas as well as the non-cooperative movement in India, the *Perhimpunan Indonesia* in its action programme issued in 1923 emphasized self-reliance and self-help as the only feasible way to obtain independence; and it exhorted every Indonesian to strive for a free and democratic government without relying on support from outsiders. The organization also strongly condemned the various regional organizations that had emerged in imitation of *Budi Utomo*, because they caused unnecessary political division, and urged that all efforts should be directed at establishing a national Indonesian unity. In 1925 another important platform was added, which emphatically stated that Indonesian freedom could only be obtained by conscious, self-assured, and self-reliant mass action.

The ideas of the *Perhimpunan Indonesia* were disseminated in the Indies through its journal *Indonesia Merdeka* (*Free Indonesia*) and by its members on their return. During 1924-25 a number of so-called Study Clubs were established for the discussion and implementation of the programme of action outlined by the *Perhimpunan Indonesia*. The most radical of these clubs had been founded in Bandung by Sukarno and Anwari, both recent graduates in civil engineering from the Technological University in that city. The Bandung group was unequivocally opposed to co-operation with the colonial government and when in 1926 the *Perhimpunan Indonesia* in Holland advocated the establishment of a national Indonesian people's party in order to disseminate its ideas among the masses, it was a number of radical revolutionaries from the Bandung Study Club who took the initiative and on 4 July 1927 founded the *Perserikatan Nasional Indonesia* (National Indonesian Union). The founding committee consisted of Sartono, Iskaq, Samsi Sastrawidagdo, Budiarto, and Sunario, all former members of the *Perhimpunan Indonesia*; Sukarno and Anwari; Sujadi, the official representative of the *Perhimpunan Indonesia* in the colony; and J. Tilaar, an employee of a Jakarta bank. At the first national congress in 1928 in Surabaja, the party's name was changed to *Partai Nasional Indonesia* (the Indonesian National Party)—*P.N.I.*—and Sukarno became its first chairman.

The *P.N.I.* stood for the complete independence of Indonesia and the party programme stressed that non-cooperation, national unity, and self-reliance were the only means by which this ideal could be realized (*see* document 59).

While it is clear that the *Perhimpunan Indonesia* played a very important role in getting the non-cooperative radical movement off the ground, it was Sukarno who was able to give this movement, in particular the *P.N.I.*, the imprint of his own ideas, which were not always in accordance with the views and philosophies of other prominent and more Western-orientated leaders such as Hatta and Sjahrir, who were convinced Social Democrats and envisaged a Western type of parliamentary democracy for Indonesia.

Sukarno, on the other hand, was more complex in his political ideas. Influenced by an amalgam of traditional Javanese and Marxist concepts, he strongly believed that the modernization of Indonesia did not necessarily have to occur at the cost of losing the national cultural identity. In a typically Javanese vein he suggested a syncretic solution to the problem of division within the Indonesian nationalist movement and in a number of articles in the journal *Indonesia Muda* in 1926 he argued that it was both possible and feasible to unite the three major streams of political thought in Indonesia—Islam, Marxism, and nationalism—into a harmonious whole, without having to suppress any of these ideologies as long as they did not disturb the general harmony (*see* document 60). However, unity in the nationalist movement could not, according to Sukarno, be achieved on the basis of a Western system of parliamentary democracy with its tyranny of the majority (fifty per cent plus one). A system of decision-making that was far more suitable to Indonesian conditions was, so Sukarno argued, a federation of all nationalist groupings, using the procedures of traditional Indonesian village government where unanimous decisions—*mufakat*—were reached after a full process of deliberation and compromise—*musjawarah* (*see* document 61). Endowed with a charismatic speaking talent and considerable political acumen, Sukarno was able at the end of 1927 to have the major parties and groupings—including the Muslims—agree to join such a federation of all anti-colonial forces in the country, which came to be called *Permufakatan Perhimpunan Politiek Kebangsaan Indonesia (P.P.P.K.I.)*, or the Unanimous Consensus of the Political Organizations of the Indonesian People.

The *P.P.P.K.I.*, however, was too restricted in its activities by the *mufakat* principle to perform the great national deeds Sukarno had hoped for. The ideological differences within the federation were too sharp and only a few general and rather lame declarations were made (*see* document 62).

When in 1929 Sukarno was imprisoned by the Dutch, the *P.N.I.* disbanded itself and the *P.P.P.K.I.* quickly disintegrated. The *P.N.I.* ideals were incorporated in a new party—the *Partai Indonesia (Partindo)*—which was set up in 1931 by Sartono (*see* document 63).

But an important minority of the old *P.N.I.*, which always had been rather dubious about the views and methods of Sukarno, now became openly critical of the new party's programme. And although the *Perhimpunan Indonesia* in Holland (*see* document 64) deplored the split in the left wing of the movement and remained officially neutral in the dispute, some of its prominent members, such as Hatta and Sjahrir, severely attacked Sukarno for his one-man rule of the party, which had brought the organization into complete disarray after his imprisonment, and they dismissed his ideas about unification as chimerical, insisting that a class struggle was inevitable (*see* document 65). In particular, Sjahrir objected strongly to the cultural nationalism of Sukarno and his followers and argued that there was little to be found in traditional Indonesian civilization that could be of value in the twentieth century (*see* document 66). Moreover, the sweeping-up of the masses in which Sukarno so excelled and delighted seemed to be of little practical value to the more rationally inclined Hatta-Sjahrir group, which insisted that the first priority should be to train a corps of well-educated cadres to diffuse the nationalist ideals among the people. And to this end a rival party, *Pendidikan Nasional Indonesia* (Indonesian National Education), was founded by Sjahrir in 1932.

Sukarno, after his release from prison in December 1931, attempted to heal the breach in the radical revolutionary movement, but he was unsuccessful. The differences were fundamental and continued to divide the radical nationalists until long after Indonesia gained its independence.

Increased harassment by the colonial authorities of both the *Partindo* and the *Pendidikan Nasional Indonesia*, and finally in 1933 the exiling of the top-echelon leaders such as Sukarno, Hatta, and Sjahrir almost totally lamed the radical wing of the nationalist movement; and the *P.P.P.K.I.* expired in 1935, with the *Partindo* and the *Pendidikan Nasional Indonesia* following suit in 1936.

The vacuum left by the radical nationalists was now partly filled by the more moderate nationalist groupings, which as "co-operators" were represented in the various government councils such as the *Volksraad*. The most important "co-operative" party was the *Partai Indonesia Raja—Parindra* (the Greater Indonesia Party—which had been founded in 1935 as a fusion of two older organizations, *Budi Utomo* and the *Persatuan Bangsa Indonesia—P.B.I.—*the latter having been set up in 1924 by Dr Sutomo, an important national figure who had been one of the founders of *Budi Utomo* in 1908 and also played an important role in the *Perhimpunan Indonesia* in Holland. Like its parent organizations, the *Parindra* stressed evolution rather than revolution and concentrated on the educational and economic development of the Indonesian people, setting up banks, farmers' cooperatives (*Rukun Tani*), and advisory services (*see* document 67).

The decline of the radical-revolutionary parties and the division within the nationalist movement as a whole were strongly criticized in 1936 by the *Perhimpunan Indonesia* (*see* document 68), which pointed out that in view of the growing threat of Fascist Japan, all nationalist parties should unite in a national front to face both the imperialism of the West and of Japan. Soon afterwards the *Perhimpunan Indonesia*, expecting a more reasonable treatment from a Social Democrat Holland than from Fascist Japan, exhorted Indonesians to co-operate with the Dutch Government in the struggle against Fascism in return for political concessions.

The action programme of the *Perhimpunan Indonesia* was taken up by the *Gerakan Rakjat Indonesia—Gerindo—*a radical nationalist party set up in 1937 to counteract the activities of the *Parindra*. The *Gerindo* was led by younger leftists such as Mohammad Yamin and Amir Sjarifuddin and was joined by many former *P.N.I.* and *Partindo* members. Its platform was very similar to that of the old *P.N.I.*, with the important exception that the principle of non-cooperation was dropped as unrealistic in view of the international situation.

However, the rejection in 1938 of the Sutardjo petition by the Dutch Government (*see* document 21) made it clear that much greater pressure was needed to extract political concessions from the

Dutch. This drove the various nationalist organizations together again and in 1939, on the initiative of the *Parindra*, the *Gabungan Politik Indonesia—G.A.P.I.* (Indonesian Political Union)—was founded, which reiterated the need for co-operation between the Netherlands and Indonesia in the fight against Fascism. This co-operation, however, could only be effective if Indonesians were given a greater stake in their own country and as a first step the *G.A.P.I.* demanded that Indonesia should be given a full parliament. "*Indonesia berparlemen*" ("Indonesia with a parliament") became the catchcry of the nationalists during 1939 and 1940 (*see* documents 69, 70, and 71), but the action was to no avail.

The stubborn refusal of the Dutch to give in to Indonesian political demands and the rebuttal of the Indonesian offer of help in the coming Pacific war caused many Indonesian leaders to turn their backs on the Dutch and to seek an accommodation with the Japanese about their political aspirations (*see* document 72). And during the fateful months of December 1941 to March 1942, when the colonial armed forces fought the Japanese invaders, the Indonesians as a whole kept aloof as disinterested bystanders.

59 Report of a meeting of the Partij Nasional Indonesia held at Bandung, 27 October 1929

At 8.30 a.m. the Chairman, Gatot Mangkoepradja (*P.N.I.*), opens the meeting, which is attended by about two thousand people, of whom about three hundred are women. He announces that because of the expected great interest by the public two public meetings will be held at which the same items on the agenda will be dealt with:
1. The right of assembly and association outside Java, by Mr Iskaq;
2. Illiteracy, by Mamadi;
3. Non-cooperation (self-help), by Gatot Mangkoepradja;
4. Religion, by Ir Soekarno.

After the customary expressions of welcome and gratitude, the Chairman requests the meeting to stand for a moment to sing "*Indonesia-Raja*", after which Mr Iskaq is asked to speak ... The public is somewhat bored by the way the speaker presents his talk; he is moreover three times interrupted by the police.

Mr Iskaq related that before 1919 the Indies people did not have the right of assembly and association; but when this was finally granted in 1919 regulations were instituted which in practice made it impossible to make full use of this right ...

The speaker mentioned the arrest by the police of Adang (member of the *P.N.I.*), but when he wanted to elaborate, the police requested the Chairman to tell the speaker not to continue with this subject.

Ostensibly with great calm, the speaker continued and spoke about the regulations forbidding the holding of meetings. He also wanted to criticize the attitude of the judges when dealing with cases of infringement of these regulations, but he was interrupted by the police.

He further talked about the powers of the heads of local government in the Outer Possessions, who were empowered to stop leaders of political parties from entering their region. And he mentioned the latest case in point, that of H.O.S. Tjokroaminoto, who first had been refused entry into the west coast of Sumatra, but later had been given permission on the condition that he would not hold any meetings ...

Accompanied by enthusiastic applause and shouts of: "*Bapak toeroen*", "*Hidoep Partij Nationaal Indonesia*" [literally, "Father (term used for older and important persons) is coming", "Long live the Indonesian Nationalist Party"], which lasted for a few minutes, Ir Soekarno appears on the platform. He first expresses his joy and gratitude for the enormous interest shown for this public meeting of the *P.N.I.*, which as on the many previous occasions is again an irrefutable proof that indeed everywhere in Indonesia the national spirit (*soemangat*) has spread, the national spirit which later will bring about the freedom of Indonesia (applause) ... He then presents a very clear explanation of the meaning of non-cooperation, which can be used either as a matter of principle or on an incidental basis. The *P.N.I.* adheres to non-cooperation as a matter of principle. In order to reinforce his arguments and also to keep the public spellbound, he often repeats emphatically the following words: "*Tidak maoe tjampoer dalam soeatoe apa djoega dengan Pemarentahan Blanda*" ["We must have nothing to do whatsoever with the Dutch Government"], which is of course every time answered with shouting and applause.

He then refers to the two places on the Council of the Indies to be filled by natives (*Inlanders*) (he says: "*Inlanderrrr*"—laughter), and hints at the mentality of Mr Koesoemojoedo [one of the appointees to the Council of the Indies]. He further says that he could not care less whether such heroes would be members of the Council of the Indies; even if there are a thousand Koesoemojoedos in the Council of the Indies, the *P.N.I.* does not want to have anything to do with government councils ... Why does the *P.N.I.* adhere to the principle of non-cooperation? Because the *P.N.I.* is convinced (*Insjaf dan berkejakinan*) that colonial rule is bad everywhere in the world and is the result of a clash of interests. Laughingly he tells the story that a friend offered him a seat in the *Volksraad*, saying that the daily allowance of 30 guilders was not to be despised. His answer was that even with a daily allowance of 100 guilders or more he would not want to become a member of the *Volksraad*. In short he is and will remain a non-cooperator.

The *P.N.I.* will not ask for anything, but will put its trust in its own power and adhere to the principle of "self-help". Whatever may happen in the world and however loud the thunder may rumble and however bright the lighting may flash, the *P.N.I.* will not retreat (applause).

The *P.N.I.* must live up to its symbols, red-white and the buffalo head, because red means courage (*Berani karena benar*), white means innocence (*Soetji*), and the buffalo head (*Kepala Banteng*) means self-reliance (*Mertjaja pada kakoeatan sendiri*) (applause).

Because of this and also the fierce activity of the *P.N.I.*, he is often accused of hating the Europeans (*Koelit-putih*); this he does not deserve because he does not hate the Europeans, but he hates colonial rule ...

Then he changes to the subject of religion. In particular religious associations have argued that the *P.N.I.* is opposed to religion (*bertentangan*). The speaker argues that these statements are not true and are nothing else than libellous accusations. The *P.N.I.* adheres to a position of neutrality with respect to religion. This is logical, because the *P.N.I.*, although keeping religion in high regard, has nationalism as its ideal. To the *P.N.I.* it does not matter what kind of religion a person adheres to, be it Christianity, Islam, or any other religion. As long as one is an Indonesian one can become a member. He asks the religious associations not to obstruct him unnecessarily in the future (*bikin sakit hati*), because he also leaves them alone. Moreover, to criticize and obstruct one another was useless, because it would not bring them one step closer to the ideal of *Indonesia Merdeka* (the Freedom of Indonesia). All religions surely would support the ideal of freedom. In order to illustrate his argument he quotes from an article in *Fadjar Asia* entitled "*Orang djaman sekarang gila*" ("Today's people are mad"), which describes the homage shown by members of the P.N.I. to the party flag as mad and non-religious. He explains that the flag is only a symbol, and that one does not pay homage to a piece of white-red cloth with a buffalo head on it but to the spirit (*soemangat*) of *Indonesia Merdeka*. He says: "Yes, I have so much respect for our national flag that when I am *bingoeng* [upset, confused] I give our flag a military salute." (Laughter and applause.)

Against the accusation in the newspaper mentioned that the *P.N.I.* is anti-Islam because it is opposed to polygamy, he argues that the *P.N.I.* does not intend to root out polygamy but rather wants to spread the idea of monogamy in order to improve the position of women.

At the end of his speech he said that he had received an anonymous letter (he called it *soerat kaleng*), which he read out aloud to the meeting. In short the writer of this letter asked Soekarno whether in view of the increased repressiveness of government measures he would continue to speak out so bravely, or would he, as the writer feared, become a case of *"Ati brandi, kaki lari"* [literally, "courage and run"].

When he read out this letter Soekarno became obviously incensed and shouted angrily: "What is this letter talking about? After all here is Soekarno standing in front of you all; and like Abi Tjandra Birawa [a figure from the *wayang*] he will not let himself be discouraged; *mati satoe, datang doea, mati doea, datang empat* (when one goes, two will come in his place, when two go, four will come in their place)." (A great deal of shouting and applause.) He further explained that this letter did not originate from a religious association but from one of his enemies. So he ended his speech and left the platform ...

Koloniaal Archief. *Afschrift Mailrapport, Geheim, 1080x/29.*

60 Sukarno: The quest for national unity, 1926.

The *Boedi Oetomo*, the "late" *Nationaal Indische Partij* which is still "alive", the *Sarikat Islam*, the Minahasan Federation, the Indonesian Communist Party, and many other parties—were either motivated by the spirit of nationalism, Islam, or Marxism.

Is it possible for these spirits to cooperate and form a common front against the colonial authorities and combine to form one great spirit, the spirit of unity which will bring us to greatness?

Is it possible in a colonial situation for a nationalist movement to join with an Islamic movement, which is part of an international struggle? Can Islam, a religion, cooperate in facing the colonial authorities with nationalism, which is primarily concerned with the nation, and with Marxism, which is based on the philosophy of materialism? ...

We say with firm conviction: "Yes, it can be done". Admittedly nationalism does not concern itself with factions which do not follow in "the desire to live as one" with the people. It is true that nationalism belittles all factions which do not feel as "one group, one nation" with the people. And it is true that nationalism fundamentally opposes all forms of action which do not originate from the "common experience of the people". But it should be kept in mind that the men who built the Islamic and Marxist movements in our country did have a "desire to live together as one" with the men who built the nationalist movement. They felt to be "one group and one nation" with the nationalists, that all groups in our movement: nationalists, Muslims, and Marxists alike, have a history of shared experience behind them, a common fate of being deprived of freedom for hundreds of years ...

The nationalists who are reluctant to seek contact with Marxists and work together with them show great ignorance of history and of the way the world's political system has evolved. They do not realise that the Marxist movement in Indonesia and Asia generally has the same origins as their own movement. They forget that the objectives of their own movement are often similar to those of the Marxist movement in their country. They forget that to oppose those of their countrymen who are Marxists is to reject comrades in the same struggle and to add to the number of their enemies. They forget or do not understand the significance of the policies of their fellow fighters in other Asian countries, such as the late Dr Sun Yat-Sen, that great nationalist leader who happily and wholeheartedly cooperated with the Marxists, even though he realised that a Marxist organization of society was still impracticable in China because the necessary conditions did not exist ...

We are convinced also that we can bring the Muslims and the Marxists together, although the differences of principle between these two are really very great. We are very sad when we recall the blackening of the Indonesian sky several years ago when there was a civil war-like clash, an outbreak of enmity between Marxists and Muslims, when we saw the forces of our movement divided into two factions warring with each other.

This split represents the blackest page in our history. While our movement should have been growing in force, this conflict resulted in the useless dissipation of our strength. It set our movement back by decades.

Alas! How strong our movement would now be if this conflict had not occurred. Our organization would certainly not be as inadequate as it is now; our movement would undoubtedly have advanced further than it has, no matter how great the obstacles in its path.

We are convinced that there are no important obstacles to Muslim-Marxist friendship. As we have explained, true Islam has some characteristics of Socialism. It is true that Socialism is not necessarily Marxism, and we know that this Islamic Socialism is different from Marxism—because Islamic Socialism is spiritual, while Marxist Socialism is based on materialism. But it is sufficient for our purposes to show that true Islam is Socialistic in character.

Muslims should not forget that Marxism's materialist interpretation of history can often serve them as a guide when they are faced with difficult problems of economics and world politics. Moreover, they should not forget that historical materialism as a method explains events that have taken place in the world, that it is a means of predicting future events, and that it can be extremely useful to them!

Muslims should not forget that capitalism, the enemy of Marxism, is also the enemy of Islam! This is so because what is called surplus value in Marxism is fundamentally the same as usury in the teachings of Islam. Surplus value is that portion of profit which rightly belongs to the workers who produced it. This theory of surplus was worked out by Karl Marx and Friedrich Engels to explain the origins of capitalism. It is this surplus value which is the basis of capitalism; in attacking surplus value, the Marxists are attacking capitalism at its very roots!

The true Muslim should immediately realise that it is wrong to regard Marxism which opposes surplus value as an enemy. He will realise that true Islam also struggles against such things; and that true Islam strongly forbids usury and the taking of interest ...

Marxism, which was previously so violently anti-nationalist and anti-religious, has now altered its tactics, especially in Asia, so that its previous bitter opposition has turned into comradeship and support. Today there is friendship between the Marxists and the nationalists in China, and between Marxists and Muslims in Afghanistan.

Marxist theory has also changed. In fact it had to; Marx and Engels were not prophets who could determine eternally valid laws. Their theories have to be changed with the times; they must be adapted to fit a changing world if they are not to become bankrupt. Marx and Engels themselves realised this and in their writings they often showed that they had changed their minds or changed their interpretation of certain events of their time ...

This ability to make tactical and theoretical changes explains why the "younger" Marxists, whether they are "patient" or "tough", especially the younger Marxists in Asia, are all supporters of genuine nationalist movements. They know that in Asia, where there is no proletariat in the European-American sense, their movement must change its character to fit in with prevailing conditions of life. They know that the Marxist movement in Asia must employ different means than in Europe, and that they must "work together with petty-bourgeois parties", because the prime target here is not to achieve power but to fight feudalism.

The workers in Asia can only organize a socialist movement, if these countries are free, and the workers have national autonomy. As Otto Bauer said, "National autonomy is a goal which must be pursued by the proletariat in its struggle, because it is very necessary for its policies". That is why national autonomy is something which must be put before all else by the workers' movement of Asia. That is why it is the duty of the working class in Asia to work with and support all movements aimed at achieving national autonomy, irrespective of the philosophies of these movements. That is why the Marxist movement in Indonesia must support our nationalist and Islamic movements which also have national autonomy as their goal ...

Sukarno, *Dibawah Bendera Revolusi* I, (Jakarta, 1963), pp. 6-7.

61 Sukarno: Towards the Brown Front, 1927

Some time ago Zentgraaff of the *Soerabaiasch Handelsblad* [conservative newspaper] propagated the idea of a white front to put up a stronger opposition against the "native" masses, which in their various organizations are beginning to gain steadily more power—at the cost of the prestige of the white man, which in the past was sufficient to protect the usurper against the "murderousness and bloodthirstiness" of the indigenous people.

His voice went on calling in the desert, and did not get a positive reaction from the white press in our country. The *sana* [other] party answered in the negative and dismissed the idea of a white front.

The attitude of this press can be explained in two ways: we could say that the white man in fact wants to strive towards fraternization and a mutual appreciation between the brown and the white man. Or we could explain it as follows: it is felt that just because of the formation of a white front, just because of this consolidation, one would weaken oneself; it is felt that the formation of a white front will irrevocably cause the birth of a "brown front", which could throw its numerical superiority into the balance, and would be impossible to neutralize by a tightly organized group of white men on its own.

Which of these explanations would be the more plausible one? One could argue against the first explanation by saying that in the past one never felt the need for fraternization. The white man carefully kept himself separate; he kept away from everything that was not "white", he dismissed all overtures from our side; he has constructed a society which has no points of contact with the Indonesian one. Why then suddenly these lovely smiles? And why these ideas about brotherhood?

We Indonesians find this suspicious!

The second hypothesis is supported by the fact that these profuse expressions of brotherly love occur just at the time when we Indonesians, through marshalling our power in various organizations, have managed to gain strength; at present we are no longer just a mass of illiterates but a mass of organized illiterates, who know that what we lack in scholarly knowledge, in organization talents and techniques, is amply compensated for by our numbers.

We Indonesians certainly realize that relations will continue to deteriorate, because we have become increasingly conscious of the power that rests in our numerical superiority, while the prestige of the ruling power has continued to decline. We realise that the drawing of a mathematically exact demarcation line between the brown men, who desire power, and the white men, who want to hold on to power, means that a climax is being reached in the deterioration of the relations between the brown men and the white men. But we also understand that the character of the struggle will depend on how accurately and quickly the antithesis is put; and that the better this antagonism is understood, the more exact the purpose of the struggle will be.

If we understand this, then the next step we Indonesians must take becomes clear.

Assuming that we are prepared to accept and make our own everything that is reasonable; and that we are even willing to learn from our opponents—although in an amended form and in accordance with our interests—then we should follow up the advice of Zentgraaff.

If a "white front" weakens the position of the Europeans in our country, then it follows naturally that *a "brown front" will reinforce our position*!

What is rejected by the opponent can only be good for us. We must create a powerful political force, which is possible only if we pursue realistic policies. Such a force can only be achieved through the formation of a brown front.

Let us hope then that this brown front will eventuate. Let us hope that all Indonesians realize that a lack of unity has been the cause of our defeats in the struggle against the West. They should learn from the history of our national degradation, from the court intrigues of the Mangkoerats, from the fighting during the times of Mangkoeboemi and Mas Said, from which not the Indonesians but only the Dutch ended up victorious.

The foreigners should not be confronted with thousands and thousands of "natives"; they should not have to struggle against millions of brown people; no, they should be confronted by the one indivisible Indonesian people—yes, by the one indivisible Indonesian nation!

But how can this be possible if in reality our people is divided over so many organizations, which all have their own ideologies and methods of struggle?

First of all: I must warn against any attempt to achieve a unification of all these parties. One should fully realize that it is impossible to shackle within the one single organization a people of fifty million souls living in a highly variegated social structure. And even if this were possible, there would be superimposed on Indonesia a kind of ideology and a spiritual poverty which would exclude a free and independent existence and would condemn our people to carry the yoke of slavery until Doomsday.

Therefore we must work towards a federation, which must leave intact the personality, the individuality, the character of the member parties. And the link that is necessary to bind the parties together must be a very loose one. It should not be oppressive, in order not to detract from its durability. It should be like the loose ties which bind the various parts of the British Empire together. Its strength should lie in its flexibility.

The agreement to be reached by the Indonesian parties can therefore not be one based on principles. Otherwise the members would have to submit themselves to a certain ideological discipline, which would mean a sacrifice to some extent of the independance and freedom of action on the part of the member parties.

Such a federation, which does not insist on ideological discipline nor force the member parties to sacrifice their freedom and independence for the sake of the federation—such a federation is possible. Yes, such a federation is possible when one is satisfied with *incidental* co-operation, that is, when it is unanimously felt by the members that such action would be urgent. Co-operation, for example, would be given in the case of the right to hold public meetings, about the penal sanctions, about the mass arrests resulting from [the use by the Governor-General of his] exorbitant powers; co-operation with respect to our student martyrs in Holland. We Indonesians, should be ashamed that over and over again our attacks on the penal sanctions and the capitalistic sugar industry are successfully parried. We should be ashamed that after hearing about student razzias or arrests none of us immediately packed our cases to find out at first hand further particulars; and that until now we have not been able to infuse some force into our movement!

Let us hope therefore that the *Permoefakatan Partij Politiek Indonesia* may be born soon. And that we, realizing the difficulty of our task, may find strength in each other in order to form an indivisible nation, to create a free and sovereign community of independent [organizations]. Let us forge the iron chain of the brown front! Let us be One!

Sukarno, *Dibawah Bendera Revolusi* (Djakarta: 1963), pp. 37-40.

62 Report of the 2nd P.P.P.K.I. Congress held at Solo on 25 December 1929

Seated behind the table on the platform were, among others: Dr Soetomo, President, Ir Anwari, Secretary, M. Soendjoto, Mr R. Ng. Soebroto, R. Roeslan Wongsokoesoemo, Soekaris, Abdullah, Dr Samsi, Mr Singgih, R.M.A.A. Koesoemo Oetoyo, Ir Soekarno, Dr Soekiman, Mr Ali Sastroamidjojo, Gatot Mangkoedipradja, M. H. Thamrin, R. Oto Soebrata, and Mr Hadi. Moreover all indigenous intellectuals of any political importance were present, originating from widely differing backgrounds ... Only the higher-ranking members of the self-governing princely houses were not present. *All* indigenous associations of any importance were represented, including the National Council of the *Perkoempoelan Politiek Katholiek Djawa* [Catholic Political Association of Java].

Mr *Handoko*, the Chairman of the Welcoming Committee, opens the meeting with a word of welcome. Then Ir *Anwari* reads out a number of telegrams including one from the Chairman of the S.D.A.P. [Dutch Socialist Party], "which for thirty years has struggled by legal means for the independence of Indonesia".

Dr *Soetomo* opens the meeting with a word of thanks to the hospitable city of Solo. He also expresses his gratitude to the European press because it always slanders the people's movement and to the Chinese press for its faithful support of the movement. He stresses that it is the duty of the indigenous press to first consult the *P.P.P.K.I.* before publishing anything about the movement.

Then he directs himself to Mr *Saronto*, who the previous evening had asked what *Boedi Oetomo* had in fact been able to achieve. Dr Soetomo puts him sharply in his place. Against the argum-nt of *Saronto* "that nothing had changed", the speaker gave a number of examples to illustrate how much things in fact had changed. He said that a number of regents often came to visit him not on official business but just to drink a cup of coffee. After the government had instructed the regents to wear the old feudal robes of state and carry the old feudal symbols of power, one regent had told him: "I went out with my yellow *songsong* [umbrella] in front of me, dressed in my robes of state. The people gathered around shouting, 'Look, the regent is getting married!' I put my *songsong* away, covered the car with cloths, and drove home rather embarrassed." Another regent told the speaker: "I was really thrilled to be able to get my *koeloek* [cone-shaped head-dress worn at the Javanese court] out of mothballs! But now my young son runs around the *kaboepaten* [dwelling of the regent] with it saying 'I am Dipanegara.'" (Laughter.) According to the speaker it is not true that nothing has changed. On the contrary, *things are moving so fast that the problem is no longer:*

how do we awaken the people but rather are we strong enough to tone down the powerful spirit of the people? Previously Indonesians were accused of only being interested in finding employment in the civil service, but now one has to appeal desperately to the younger generation to enter the civil service in order to co-operate with the foreigners in building up society.

Boedi Oetomo has made the nobility a part of the people's movement. It has been due to *Boedi Oetomo* that the "Indonesian" first estate, instead of being an obstruction which later would be demolished by the people, has become a valuable element in the people's movement ... [Dr Sutomo then continues his speech emphasizing the need for the establishment of a united and Indonesia-wide modern labour union movement, which should be led by intellectuals.]   Ir *Soekarno* has been pleased to accept the invitation of the Advisory Council to speak about the need to establish a farmers' union. In fact, he argues, such a speech should be held in the villages and not in the *kota* [city] where it would have the same effect as a *wajang* performance in a European club. He therefore asks the intellectuals who are present to disseminate his ideas in the villages ...

According to Professor van Gelderen [Dutch economist] the wage level in the cities is determined by the situation in the villages, because the largest portion of foreign capital has been invested in agriculture. If we want to combat the evil outgrowths of capitalism then we must take a stand against agrarian capitalism. The speaker then explains the various stages of imperialist capitalism and his story is taken almost word-for-word from the third editorial in *Het Volk* [Dutch Socialism newspaper] about the colonial programme of the *S.D.A.P.* ... the peasant has always been worst off. And the speaker outlines the burdens of indigenous feudalism.

After the coming of the white man and foreign capital another burden was added: forced deliveries of goods and forced labour, and later the Culture System and seignorial services. The third burden is an internal matter: the enormous population growth. With 270 people per square kilometre it is almost the most densely populated area in the world. It is not surprising therefore that according to the report of Dr Huender the Javanese are living below the breadline.

The misery of the people has led in the past to many uprisings such as the one by the *Padri* the one at Banjermassin, and by Dipanegara. However, today one has become wiser and follows a different way, i.e. through the modern labour union movement.

There are two diseases, one an external one and the other internal. The second one, overpopulation, can be remedied as follows:
1. By expanding the *sawahs* (e.g. by means of irrigation).
2. Improvement of agricultural production methods.
3. The creation of employment possibilities.

4. Emigration.

The only remedy against the first disease is to organize and set up labour and farmers' unions. The time has come to combine the people's power in the same way as Rama organized the monkeys [reference to the Ramayana epic].

The speaker mentions that modern capitalism furthers the idea of inheritable private property, because it disperses power. Many then look laughingly at R.M.A.A. Koesoemo Oetoyo [an important official in the People's Credit Service], the great fighter against communal land ownership. The speaker notices this and says: "I know very well that many think differently about this, but I, Soekarno, have my own theory about this and I maintain that I am right." He tries to illustrate his point with statistics about the number of villages with communal land ownership.

On the basis of the Meyer Ranneft-Huender Report [official investigation into the tax burden on the indigenous population, 1926], the speaker argues that the people of Java, who have a net income of 140 guilders per family per year, that is, eight cents per person per day, are the most heavily taxed people in the whole of Asia ...

The speaker also argues that the peasants suffer particularly because of the sugar industry that uses their land. These lands, which according to the Meyer Ranneft-Huender Report produce about 140 guilders per *bouw*, are rented for 70 guilders. In addition there is the fact—the speaker wants to be quite honest about this—that the Indonesian people have the great fault of not being able to handle money: the money received from rent is immediately consumed and the people go hungry. Sugar is a poison for us. It is the worst of all poisons, the worst of the worst, which we must combat first and with all our might. The speaker then elaborates on all the ruses and devices used by the sugar industry to get hold of land above the legal limit: "We must combat the sugar industry in its present form until it has disappeared."

Then there is the following debate: *Roro Wadining* demands strict answers to the following questions arising from the speech by Soekarno:

1. How does the *P.P.P.K.I.* plan to replace the indispensable capital of the foreign capitalists which it opposes?
2. Will the *P.P.P.K.I.* go into agriculture itself?
3. In what way does the *P.P.P.K.I.* envisage achieving a situation where commerce, which is now totally in the hands of foreigners, will be partly again in the hands of compatriots?
4. Is the *P.P.P.K.I.* planning to equip ships in order to take control of the transport of raw materials and agricultural produce from Indonesia and the import of industrial goods into Indonesia, which according to the speaker is such a highly profitable business?

Wignjo asks how Ir Soekarno plans to implement the inter-Indonesian emigration.

Safioeddin (from Djember, *P.S.I.*) supports Soekarno's call to make his speech known in the villages, but he is very sceptical whether this would be practicable because in the countryside even the smallest remark of this kind causes the people to call you a Communist and they practically avoid you. And although his village is not exactly small he has during the last three and a half years had many difficulties. Therefore the training of cadres on a large scale is necessary. If there are only one or two leaders in a village they are powerless ...

R. Pandji Soeroso (the *Volksraad* Member) feels that he should speak because his name has been mentioned.

He argues that a powerful organization is needed ... He gathers that both speakers have the following programme in mind: 1. Proletarians unite! 2. The nationalization of industry. 3. Struggle against capitalism. He concludes that the *P.P.P.K.I.* is Socialistic and asks whether this is true ...

Mr Thamrin announces that Ir Soekarno does not wish to speak.

And after Mr Soeroso, who points out that he has not received an answer to his question, is refused the right to speak, the Chairman closes the meeting ...

Koloniaal Archief. *Geheim Mailrapport 72x/1930.*

63 Report of the first public meeting of Partindo held at Batavia, 12 July 1931

The first public meeting of the *P.I.* has caused considerable interest. The large hall is completely filled to the extent that hundreds of people have to be refused entry. Among the approximately 1500 people in attendance there are approximately 150 ladies. Behind the dais on which the leadership is seated there is the red-white flag, which shows in the middle the abbreviation "*P.I.*" in large black letters ...

At 9 a.m. the President of the National Committee, *Mr Sartono*, opens the meeting. In his speech he expresses satisfaction at the large attendance and hopes that the *P.I.* will be sympathetically received by all layers of society.

The *P.N.I.* had been brought down by the authorities, which meant that the nationalist movement had lost its left wing. In these dark days a few nationalists, believing in the ideal of *Indonesia Merdeka* quietly founded the *P.I.*...

Work-programme

In line with its objectives, the *Partai Indonesia* shall:

I

1. Generate the awareness that a free Indonesia is the right of the Indonesian people, and that this will certainly be achieved if our people are properly organized in political groups which together will translate their power as an unfree nation into a national policy.
2. Strengthen the feeling of unitary nationalism.
3. Strengthen the feeling of Indonesian unity and pursue a policy based on a united fatherland, a united nation, and a united purpose.
4. Deepen the knowledge of national history in the widest sense of the word, and disseminate feelings designed to honour and respect Indonesian national heroes and leaders.
5. Improve the people's law (*adat* law) in the widest sense of the word and persuade the government to use legal principles which are based on the will of the Indonesian people.
6. Take away the present obstructions to personal freedom: freedom in one's own house and yard, freedom of self-expression by means of the printing press, freedom of religion, freedom of association and to hold public meetings, freedom from mail censorship.
7. Take united action to have removed from the Criminal Code the articles which threaten political and labour union leaders; co-operate with other parties to obtain proper judicial and prosecution procedures.
8. Make a study of and compose a draft constitution which reflects the will of the Indonesian people.
9. Strengthen the ties between Asiatic peoples and improve the political situation of colonial and semi-colonial peoples.

II

1. Further the advancement of society, which must be based on self-help and independence.
2. Improve the commerce of the Indonesian people.
3. Improve the industrial development of the Indonesian people.
4. Ensure that the farms of the Indonesian people will have the necessary capital available and ensure the establishment of national banks.
5. Promote as much as possible the use of articles manufactured by the Indonesian people themselves.
6. Establish co-operative societies.
7. Oppose usury and inculcate thriftiness and simplicity.

III

1. Combat illiteracy.
2. Establish independent national schools and courses.
3. Promote national independent education in such a way that a completely nationalist-orientated education system ranging from primary to tertiary level will be created.
4. Publish journals, books, and pamphlets for the benefit of the people.
5. Improve the position of women.
6. Promote Indonesian trans-migration.
7. Help to strengthen the land rights of the people or restore them, and have the right of free disposal fully recognized.
8. Further the establishment of farmers' organizations and labour unions.
9. Devote attention to public health.
10. Combat child marriages, the use of opium and alcohol, and prostitution ...

Mr Soedarmo Atmodjo presents a lengthy discussion about national education. He argues that in a colony there are always clashes of interest between the rulers and the subjected people. The government schools as well as the private schools subsidized by the government do not take account of the demands of a truly national education. The *P.I.* intends therefore to further the establishment of schools which take account of national interests.

Mr Winoto speaks about the economy and argues that in addition to political interests, the economic interests of the people must be promoted. So the *P.I.* is planning to establish an information office, to advise the people on commerce, agriculture, etc. He particularly points to the usefuliness of co-operatives. The speaker warns people about the dire results of certain popular customs such as holding too many *Slametaus* [parties], and the thoughtless borrowing of money from usurers, and advises the audience to live more soberly. In order to further national industry, local goods made by the people should be bought, and not imported goods ...

Mr Sartono comments on this point by saying that the party will continue to make propaganda for *"swadeshi"* [Hindu word for "indigenous". Gandhi led this movement urging Indians to consume nationally produced goods], and he urges the ladies to prefer homespun materials to imports from Paris.

Mr Soejoedi begs the meeting's pardon for wearing a Palm Beach suit. His subject is non-cooperation and he points to the success of this movement in Ireland and British India. The *P.I.* is non-cooperative in the sense that it does not want to participate in the various representative bodies, which can hardly be considered to represent the people. The *Volksraad* is only a pseudo-parliament based on a very imperfect system of elections. If the nationalist movement would gain a victory at the elections, this would be made useless by the government's right to appoint a number of members. Moreover the *Volksraad* is only an advisory body and its decisions can be ignored. In a subjected country even a fully-fledged parliament would be of little importance for the nationalist movement and the speaker mentions the Egyptian parliament as a case in point ...

Under loud applause *Mr Mohammad Yamin* approaches the dais ... Government officials whose salaries have been reduced by 5 per cent are protesting against this curtailment and are sure that they will be paid their full salary. Indonesia has lost 100 per cent of its freedom, but we are also sure that freedom must come. Freedom must be achieved by organizing a mass popular movement. And although it will be difficult to organize 60 million people, the speaker reminds the audience of the words of *Ir Soekarno* not to withdraw for the obstacles which have been put in the way of the popular movement. He makes a comparison between nationalism in a free country and in a colony. While in the first case nationalism grows like a beautiful flower, in the second instance it struggles upwards like a *djamboe kloetoek* [fruit tree] that is covered by parasitical vines. The speaker refers to the dictum of Professor Snouck Hurgronje: "There are too many ants licking at the honey jar". However, the remedy against the problem as suggested by this scholar is a mass exodus (applause).

The speaker argues that nationalism and democracy are the backbone of the freedom struggle and he rejects the nationalism of Notosoeroto [a well-known Indonesian supporter of the Dutch Commonwealth idea]. *Indonesia Merdeka* cannot be achieved through action in the *Volksraad*, but only by the action of the people themselves. Self-help is the only means to obtain the right of self-determination, particularly since the policy of trust [in Dutch promises] has failed and has been replaced by a policy of distrust, *politiek tjoeriga* ...

Koloniaal Archief. *Verslag van de openbare vergadering van de Partai Indonesia op 12 Juli 1931.* Geheim Mailrapport 794x/31.

64 Open letter from the Perhimpunan Indonesia, 8 November 1931

To the Indonesian People!

The greatest economic crisis that has ever been known in world history has also dislocated the colonial economy of the imperialists. In the repressed colonial and semi-colonial countries it is especially the enslaved masses of workers and peasants, who have no rights, that are hardest hit. The imperialist rulers of Indonesia have lately intensified their terrorizing campaign against the revolutionary resistance of the masses, which is the direct result of the deterioration in the economic condition of the Indonesian people. Mass retrenchments by the public service and private enterprise; salary reductions, which are especially severe for the lower officials; a decline in exports; a considerable fall in the price of indigenous produce, which has reduced the national indigenous income to the minimum; rigorous economizing in all branches of the government service in order to achieve a balanced budget, while at the same time taxes have been increased in all sorts of ways—all these are factors which have radicalized the Indonesian masses, and have thus created all the objective conditions for the development of a wave of revolutionary mass action against Dutch rule in Indonesia.

At this point in time when the Dutch imperialists are intensifying their policies of robbery and starvation, it is very sad to see that a split has occurred in the left wing of our national freedom movement, just at this time when A STRONG UNITED REVOLUTIONARY FRONT is more necessary then ever because the bourgeois-national groups are showing a dangerous tendency to consolidate their power in order to strengthen the ruling imperialists. The reformist policies and the highly dangerous opportunism of the bourgeois, liberal, narrow-minded nationalist groups are taking on dangerous proportions.

The *Partai Bangsa Indonesia*, the *Boedi Oetomo*, *Pasoendan*, and other *petit-bourgeois* parties of the same mentality, which are a refuge for half-hearted co-operators and non-cooperators, aspiring capitalists and industrialists, self-contented intellectuals and cultural nationalists, prosperous officials and private citizens, are in fact hostile to revolutionary action.

These organizations and groupings have always played an obstructive role in the mass national freedom movement, as is obvious from their attitude during the *P.K.I.* and the last *P.N.I.* affair, because they benefit directly or indirectly from the PRESERVATION OF COLONIAL RULE AND THE MAINTENANCE OF THE CAPITALIST "PEACE AND ORDER".

Therefore they pursue a misleading policy of reformism and opportunism that is ostensibly Socialist in principle, and they attempt, by means of misleading, radical phrases such as dominion status, the development of national banks and industry, and the consolidation of power in a bourgeois-controlled national united front, to involve the working masses, the peasants, and the labourers in their bourgeois action. They only want to parade the Indonesian masses as the star pupil in order to further their own historical, capitalist, and *petit-bourgeois* interests, and thereby at the same time to aid the imperialist rulers in the economic exploitation of the Indonesian masses!

At present there is again an urgent need for us to form A UNITED REVOLUTIONARY FRONT, in order to be better equipped in the coming exacerbated class struggle between the imperialist groups, which are supported by the Social Democrats, *petit-bourgeois* nationalists, *prijaji* and intellectuals on the one side, and the Indonesian peasants, workers, and proletarian intellectuals on the other.

Concomitant with the need for a realistic revolutionary united front, there is the urgent need to clearly establish the principles of our freedom struggle, on the basis of which the present split may be mended. It is at present necessary more than ever to give the PROPER GUIDELINES to the defenceless and leaderless masses. These guidelines have already been drawn up in the last edition of our journal *Indonesia Merdeka*, in which we wrote that national freedom must be seen as identical to the ABSOLUTE LIBERATION of the Indonesian masses, i.e. political, economic, and social liberation. In this journal we gave an advance warning not to fall for the possible illusion that after the foreign imperialist rulers have been chased away the coast will be free for another system of suppression of the masses by our own bourgeoisie, capitalists, *prijaji*, and dictatorial intellectuals!

We must therefore build up a revolutionary mass organization which is based on the principle: WITH THE MASSES AND FOR THE MASSES.

And the masses are not the small group of intellectuals, and the other privileged classes, but the large strata comprising the nation, the farmers, workers, the landless, and the proletarian intellectuals, who form 90 per cent of the Indonesian people.

Therefore the interests of these groups are the interests of the INDONESIAN NATION.

Thus the correct policy to achieve national independence must be based on the interests of the masses and the Indonesian Independence Struggle must therefore be inextricably tied to the struggle of the masses!

Viewed in this light, then, our action must make the Indonesian masses realize that only the unconditional national liberation of Indonesia will create the possibility of fully developing the potential power of the Indonesian people for the benefit of the masses. Our mass action must result in a massive combination of the lower strata of the Indonesian people in a struggle for a concrete objective. The masses must be made aware of their power and their task. They must be made more conscious of and familiar with the most effective methods to be used in the struggle.

Only an organization that has this major outline of revolutionary action before it can consciously accept the consequences of all its deeds and actions. Its mass propaganda must be directed at ALL INDONESIANS WITHOUT EXCEPTION, who, although they are not aware of it yet, have an interest in the achievement of the national liberation of Indonesia ...

In all these actions we must not lose sight of the concrete objectives of our freedom struggle, of which the most important one is: THE NATIONALIZATION OF THE LAND, OF ALL THE IMPERIALIST INDUSTRIES, PLANTATIONS, AND MINES, AND THE ABOLITION OF PRIVATE DOMAINS AND LANDLORDISM, for the benefit of the people, that is: the workers, farmers, the landless, the proletarian intellectuals. The control of the whole of the people's economy must be in the hands of the working masses as a result of the unconditional surrender of ALL POWER TO THE PEOPLE!

Decisive leadership in the nationalization of the land must be vested in workers' and peasants' councils, elected on the basis of popular suffrage; there must be the future perspective of peasants voluntarily combining in order to increase the productivity of the land taken over by them, although also the State will use its means to achieve this purpose. Moreover our freedom struggle must concentrate on the right of self-determination of the nation; on obtaining the right of free speech, the right of association, and the right to hold public meetings; the abolition of the government's right of arbitrary imprisonment; and the introduction of social service legislation (legal determination of minimum working hours; unemployment, old age, and sickness insurance; the assurance of hygienic labouring conditions). It must obtain equality before the law of men and women (politically, economically, and socially); and lighten the burdens of taxation on the workers and poor farmers, so that the latter can use most of their production for themselves, to further the establishment of unions and farmers' organizations, to further the establishment of people's agricultural, consumers', and production cooperatives ...

If in this way our political principles are exactly determined, then we can do nothing else but struggle relentlessly against the foreign Dutch imperialism and its social-democratic support, and the bourgeois-nationalist props on which Dutch imperialism is basing its power.

We must especially involve the students and the people's youth in our struggle, who must always be in the forefront of the mass revolution! The connection with the mass party and the close cooperation of the nation's youth—inherently radically inclined—is of great importance for the Indonesian freedom movement!

So our programme of action must contain within it all the elements that point to the final objective of our struggle.

Naturally, as we are in Europe away from the actual front line, we do not want to be so presumptuous as to suggest how such a programme should be implemented in detail. All that is necessary is that our co-fighters for the independence of Indonesia should leave their own narrow confines and put themselves into contact with the popular masses, listening carefully to what they suggest and in consultation with them construct a programme, which must be a PROGRAMME OF STRUGGLE FOR THEIR DAILY NEEDS, and against all forms of exploitation! For example:

STRUGGLE AGAINST WAGE CUTS AND MASS RETRENCHMENTS!
STRUGGLE AGAINST INCREASES IN DIRECT AND INDIRECT TAXATION!
STRUGGLE AGAINST THE USURIOUS INTEREST CHARGED BY GOVERNMENT INSTITUTIONS AND PRIVATE INDIVIDUALS!
STRUGGLE FOR UNEMPLOYMENT BENEFITS!
STRUGGLE TO OBTAIN LAND AND EMPLOYMENT FOR THE THOUSANDS OF UNEMPLOYED FARMERS AND WORKERS IN THE VILLAGES AND CITIES!
STRUGGLE FOR GOOD POPULAR EDUCATION!

Finally a few words about the co-operation with Dutch organizations such as the *N.V.V.* [Socialist Unions] and the *I.T.F.* [International Transport Federation] by some Indonesian labour unions. In our opinion, we can only co-operate with those organizations in the colonialist countries that have not only unconditionally recognized the right of our country for immediate independence but also actively and strongly support our struggle for an independent Indonesia. Nice words are of little benefit to our people! The organizations in question, such as the *N.V.V.*, and the *I.T.F.*, and the *S.D.A.P.* [Dutch Socialist Party], and its small branch the *I.S.D.P.* [Indies Socialist Party], do not fall into this category. The *S.D.A.P.* has never been willing to recognize unconditionally the right of our country for immediate independence, and its leaders, such as Muhlenfeld, Stokvis, and others, have an important place in the colonial suppression apparatus.

We only need to point to the Social Democratic Congress in Brussels, which put Indonesia within the last category of colonial countries, those least ripe for independence, not in the least, of course, because our country is rich in profitable resources.

The actual policies of the international social-democratic movement, such as the actions of the "Labour" government in England with respect to India, and the French Government in Indo-China, show us that this policy which the *S.D.A.P.* wants to follow in our country arouses the hostility of every Indonesian who is really concerned about freedom, and it also has had the immediate effect that labouring masses of the world are gradually turning away from social-democracy.

This unavoidable hostility of the revolutionary nationalists is even more accentuated by the undeniable fact that the *N.V.V.* and *I.T.F.* leadership even refuse to struggle for the principle of EQUAL PAY FOR EQUAL WORK for our compatriots who work on ships. These leaders actually want to maintain the subjection of Indonesia, because they will also benefit a little from the enormous profits made by Dutch imperialism in our country. It is therefore our duty to warn our compatriots in the various labour unions against such co-operation, which can only lead to a strengthening of foreign rule and a weakening of the INDEPENDENT LABOUR UNION MOVEMENT IN INDONESIA.

In this political crisis we must guard ourselves first of all against the penetration of social-democratic ideas into our ranks, ideas and dark subterranean powers that intend to tear down and weaken our revolutionary front for the benefit of the imperialists. It is in this context that the urgency is seen of the need for the solid unification of all parties that are truly battling for the interests of the whole of the Indonesian people and an independent Indonesia.

It is therefore not our intention to judge how much the present split in the leftist grouping is justified, a split that hitherto has only led to personal altercations, to fruitless disputes, theoretical wrangling among leaders, and academic polemics about "self-help" and "non-cooperation", which have never been objectives in themselves and should never be made to be. So far we have not been able to observe any difference of principle between the *Partai Indonesia* and the independent groups, on which we could base our justification for taking a particular stand against one of these parties.

Future political developments will show us which parties will follow the correct revolutionary path, as we have outlined above.

To us, who as a revolutionary nationalist organization are not actually in the front line, it is only important which organizations and parties in our country, under whatever name, will put our guidelines into practice! Those are the groups that certainly will be accorded our fullest sympathy and moral and active support.

We express the hope, then, that when our co-fighter Ir Soekarno has been released from prison, he will find that the revolutionary united front, which he has built up with such energy and self-sacrifice, has closed its ranks again on the basis of our political principles, which are the only correct principles with which to realize the LIBERATION OF OUR LAND AND PEOPLE.

Perhimpunan Indonesia.
The Hague. 8 November 1931

Koloniaal Archief. *Open Brief van de Perhimpoenan Indonesia, 8 November 1931, Geheim Mailrapport 20x/32.*

65 Mohammad Hatta: The crisis of the P.P.P.K.I., 1930

As leaders in the struggle for the idea of Indonesian unity we were delighted at the birth of the *P.P.P.K.I.* Not that we ever had any illusions about the possibility of fusing all political parties into one large organization, so that the differences of opinion between political parties would disappear! No, we have never seen the ideal of Indonesian unity in that light. It would be absurd to believe that because of the rise of the *P.P.P.K.I.* arguments in Indonesian politics would no longer exist. Anybody who believes that this would be possible is living in the realm of dreams and fantasies. Such a political unity does not exist anywhere in the world, not even in the politically most homogeneous nation. Indonesia would truly be a rare exception if it managed to create such a miracle, and in that case we would become rather dubious about the capacity of the Indonesian leaders and of our people to discern political differences, and we would have reason to despair about our national future.

No, the idea of Indonesian unity has nothing to do with uniformity of political thinking. It poses the idea of a united and indivisible Indonesia and of a united and indivisible Indonesian people. The propaganda for unity must be concerned with the education of the masses into Indonesian citizens; and the population groups of the various islands must be made to realize that they belong to one and the same nation, the *Indonesian* nation ...

Our delight about the establishment of the *P.P.P.K.I.* as a sort of political concentration was caused mainly by the fact that we hoped that this body would develop itself into a representative organ of the Indonesian people, into a true Indonesian national parliament, in which the voice of the people can be heard ...

Two years have now passed; and instead of a consolidation of national power, we can see that a greater confusion of political ideologies has occurred and that there are signs of a crisis. What then are the reasons for this?

A superficial observer of the Indonesian national movement, or one who dreams about a policy of [ideological] unification could perhaps ask us in amazement with what right we could speak about the crisis of the *P.P.P.K.I.* He could direct our attention to the undeniable fact that recently everywhere and at almost every meeting people are speaking about unity. He could remind us how the youth organizations, which until recently were proud of the island of their origin, have hastened to disband themselves and have thrown themselves into the mighty stream of the unitary movement ...

These facts will not be denied! But they cannot camouflage the signs of crisis in the *P.P.P.K.I.*, which are of a serious nature. Two facts are coming strongly to the fore: there is an ideological crisis and there is a manifestation of powerlessness ... ideological confusion has occurred since in wide circles of the *P.P.P.K.I.* one began to believe that the idea of unity must also be realized in politics. There is a strong tendency present to make the *P.P.P.K.I.* into a supreme [political] organization rather than let it develop into a national parliament ...

Mohammad Hatta, "*De Crisis der P.P.P.K.I.*", in *Verspreide Geschriften* (Jakarta: van der Peet, 1952), pp. 418-21.

66 Sutan Sjahrir: Out of Exile, 1949

For my relative unpopularity in nationalistic and intellectual circles in Indonesia, I can largely thank what they call my "Western inclinations" and sometimes even my "Hollandophile" sentiment. I have always known that such attitudes were inevitable in every nationalist movement that pits itself—as an independent movement—against a ruling nation. Masaryk was obviously anti-German, the Egyptians anti-English, and so one finds among us an always growing anti-Dutch—and even anti-Western—disposition or ideology.

This disposition is, in fact, strongest among some intellectuals and petty bourgeois, and hence precisely among those who are not yet active contributors to the political movement. In these circles one finds the most unreasonable attitude toward Westerners, and especially toward the Dutch. Most of them are civil servants or white-collar workers, and because they are afraid of losing their jobs, or because they pay too little attention to political affairs and too much attention to the subordinate but connected issues, they merely grumble bitterly to one another. Although I understand this, I have never been sympathetically inclined toward such an attitude, and I have never wished to make any concessions in this direction ...

For me, the West signifies forceful, dynamic, and active life. It is a sort of Faust that I admire, and I am convinced that only by a utilization of this dynamism of the West can the East be released from its slavery and subjugation.

The West is now teaching the East to regard life as a struggle and a striving, as an active movement to which the concept of tranquility must be subordinated. *Goethe teaches us to love striving for the sake of striving*, and in such a concept of life there is progress, betterment, and enlightenment. The concept of striving is not, however, necessarily connected with destruction and plunder as we now find it. On the contrary, even in *Faust*, striving and struggle have the implication of constructive work, of undertaking great projects for the benefit of humanity. In this sense, they signify a struggle against nature, and that is the essence of struggle: man's attempt to subdue nature and to rule it by his will. The forms that the struggle takes indicate the development and refinement of the individuals who are engaged in the effort.

What we need is not rest—or death—but a higher form of living and of striving. We must extend and intensify life, and raise and improve the goals toward which we strive. This is what the West has taught us, and this is what I admire in the West despite its brutality and its coarseness. I would even take this brutality and coarseness as accompanying features of the new concept of life that the West has taught us. I would even accept capitalism as an improvement upon the much-famed wisdom and religion that make us unable to understand the fact that we have sunk to the lowest depths to which man can descent: we have sunk to slavery and to enduring subjugation.

What we in the East admire most in the West is its indestructible vitality, its love for life and for the fulfilment of life. Every vital young man and young woman in the East ought to look toward the West, for he or she can learn only from the West to regard himself or herself as a centre of vitality capable of changing and bettering the world.

The East must become Western in the sense that it must acquire as great a vitality and dynamism as the West. Faust must reveal himself to the Eastern man and mind, and that is already going on at present.

It is, I suppose, not so unusual that I am sometimes called a "half-Westerner", and that I am often distrusted by those who are fanatically inclined towards Eastern civilization and culture, and who reject Western "materialism". It is true that I hate self-deception and submissiveness, and that instead I support the desire and courage to live the life that the West represents.

This does not, however, mean that I idealize the West as it now is. On the contrary, I am quite aware that there is deceit and decay in the West as well, but I nevertheless feel that it represents an improvement over what is generally and commonly implied by the term "Eastern". What I value most highly in the West is its resilience, its vitality, its rationality—and it is only rationality that can possibly control human life ...

Sutan Sjahrir, *Out of Exile* (New York: John Day, 1949), pp. 115, 144-46, 159-62.

67   Report of the 2nd Congress of Parindra, December 1938

The President of the National Committee, Mr R.M.H. Woerjaningrat, invites the public to rise in memory of the late Dr Soetomo, the founder of *Parindra* and pioneer of the Indonesian movement, and Mr Soepratman, the composer of "*Indonesia-Raja*". Then the speaker reviews the situation in the world, Indonesia, and finally of the *Parindra*.

It is difficult to obtain a proper picture of the international situation after the recent happenings in Europe. The powers are stepping up the armaments race and a new world war can break out at any time. This is not surprising because the policies of most countries are based on materialism, with the result that armed conflict cannot be avoided.

This situation is even more difficult for the colonies ... If the colonial power loses the war, the colonies are automatically surrendered. But what would happen if the colony itself was attacked and the colonizing country stayed out of the war? The colonies are still being considered as chattels, and the speaker refers to the Brussels conference where decisions were taken that contravened the principle of self-determination of nations.

The *Parindra* strives towards unity and does not like conflicts. The *Parindra* is looked on as an association of the upper classes. This is not correct. On the contrary, it acts on behalf of the common people (shouts of *hidoep* [hear, hear]). For example the party has established *Roekoen Tani* [farmers' associations] in the villages. Another thing: *Parindra* is not a Javanese association. All Indonesians are accepted as members and the official language is Indonesian (shouts of *hidoep*).

It has been the wish of Her Majesty the Queen that the colonial government should be just, and recently Her Majesty has advocated a "moral rearmament". If this is taken to heart by us, the conditions in the colonies will improve.

The *Parindra* programme should concentrate on:
1. Setting up *Roekoen Tani* branches everywhere so that the Indonesian economy will remain agrarian, which means that at the same time the capitalist system will be kept at bay.
2. Combating illiteracy.
3. Making Indonesian mothers aware of their motherhood in terms of the *Parindra* spirit.
4. Improving the administering of justice for Indonesians.
5. Striving for a change in the composition of the representative councils. The people must have more representatives in these councils and the fact that the membership of the regency councils is largely composed of government officials is undemocratic ...

The next speaker is Mr L.N. Palar, who on behalf of the *Sociaal Democratische Arbeiders Partij* [Dutch Socialist Party] and the *Nederlands Vakverbond* [Dutch Socialist Federation of Labour Unions] expresses the hope that the contacts between political associates in the Netherlands and the national movement in this country will remain strong. And the speaker points to the colonial platforms and colonial working programmes of both parties ...

After the intermission the *Volksraad* Member R.P. Soeroso speaks on the subject of "Unemployment and Indonesiation".

This problem, according to the speaker, is urgent and of great importance for Indonesia in connection with the large increase in population, particularly in Java (about half a million per year). Indonesia has become an essential link in international trade and has therefore also become part of the capitalist system, with the result that the country is now subject to variations in economic conditions and unemployment, which are felt more strongly in Indonesia because the country is agrarian-based and dependent on exports. The measures taken by the government with respect to emigration are not sufficient to cope with the population increase. Also the area under cultivation in Java does not increase in proportion with the increase in population and therefore secondary industry must be expanded. Employment must be diversified and the ability of the people to cope with the struggle for life must be improved. The open-door policy of the government certainly causes employment diversification, but at the same time it weakens the economic independence of the people.

Owing to the impact of the economic depression on the sugar industry and the plantations in the Outer Islands, many contract labourers have been sent home and the number of unemployed has increased because of the economizing policies of the government. And although the Department of Economic Affairs has taken numerous measures to improve the cottage industries, they are not effective enough in lowering the number of unemployed.

The speaker then talks about the problem of unemployment among the young people, which endangers the existing social system while the number of young unemployed increases every year ... The speaker then makes the following proposals:
1. Unemployment statistics should be gathered. If this is too difficult, statistics of "skilled labour" should first be compiled and then of "unskilled labour".
2. The economic position of the people should be strengthened by:
    (a) the construction of various public works, which will absorb a number of unskilled labourers. The money for this could undoubtedly be found. The speaker said that two or three years previously he would not have believed that at present the

government would be able to spend so much on defence.
(b) the furthering of secondary industries. The government should ensure that Indonesians themselves could become industrialists so that profits would remain in the country and investment capital be created ... For example the government could advance loans for the establishment of small enterprises such as fruit and fish canneries.
3. The Indonesiation must be intensified both in the civil service and in private enterprise.
4. Emigration of the people of Java to the thinly populated Outer Islands.
5. Lands granted under hereditary leases must return to the people after the leases have expired.
6. Unemployment insurance must be set up.
7. Maximum working hours must be established in the civil service as well as in private enterprise.
8. Minimum wages must be laid down.
9. Financial help should be given to the unemployed.

M.H. Thamrin is applauded when he begins his talk on "Defence and the division of defence costs" ... Every independent country is spending extra money on armaments in order to be able to defend its freedom. The situation in Indonesia is such that there is nothing for the Indonesian people to defend and the cost of defence should therefore be totally born by the rulers. If the Indonesian people is to be drawn in, then it must first be convinced that everything should be sacrificed for the greatness of the country and people. But then the people must first be given a stake in the country far larger than they have today. The people must also be trained to protect themselves against the horrible consequences of modern warfare, but such a training can only be successful if the people have become fully convinced of the necessity to defend their own rights ...

Are the rights of the Indonesians so important and precious that they will make people defend them to the death? The Indonesian people are not independent, and they have no right of self-determination. Their interest in the defence of the country is small and their rights are few ...

"In conclusion," the speaker argues, "as long as the situation in Indonesia and the position of its people do not improve considerably, and as long as the Indonesians do not have the right to improve the humble situation of their land and people, it will not be just and proper to let the Indonesians sacrifice their goods and lives in order to maintain present conditions."

Koloniaal Archief. *Geheim Mailrapport 196./39.*

68 Report of the Perhimpunan Indonesia closed meeting held at Leiden on 12 June 1936

In the small meeting hall, which was almost totally filled, there were about forty people in attendance, of whom three were women. Recognized were: Raden Mas Abdoel Madjid Djojoadhiningrat ... , Mas Soewarso ... , Mas Sidartawan ... , Mas Doelhak ... , Goesti Ketoet Djelantik ... , Raden Mas Soegeng Notohadinegoro ... , Raden Prijono ... , Gele al Rasjid Haroen ... , Mas Harjono Adi Tjondro ... , Raden Mas Ariono ... , Amir Hamzah ... , and Raden Soenito ...

The meeting was opened at about 9 o'clock by Mas Soedario Moelawadi (also named Moekim) ... The speaker ... announced that the *Perhimpoenan Indonesia* had felt the need to call this meeting in order to discuss various problems concerning Indonesia and to spread more propaganda among the younger Indonesian students. He first presented a short survey of the general political situation in the world. He then outlined the economic difficulties confronting the capitalist countries in Europe, which also affect the colonies. The Netherlands, according to the speaker, is in economic difficulties, which one is trying to solve by all sorts of means, such as economizing and pauperization—the policy of this government not only here but also in Indonesia. Roestam Effendi [Indonesian Communist Member of the Dutch Parliament] has highlighted in various speeches in parliament the policy of exploitation of this government. Because of the growing pressure of the danger of Fascism the colonial problem is becoming even more difficult. How should we defend ourselves against this? The only possibility is to set up a political national united front of all leftist and rightist national parties in Indonesia. The *Perhimpoenan Indonesia*, the party which has the motto, "The Indies free from Holland", must now take the leadership. More than any other organization we have fought and are still fighting against the colonial exploitation by our rulers; against the policy of keeping the Indonesian people stupid, of treating them as a third-rate nation. Various organizations and associations are trying to work for an independent Indonesia, but they are totally apolitical in this. We must realize that these organizations, however useful they may be, will not achieve anything in the final analysis. The *Perhimpoenan Indonesia* shows its true colours and is a purely leftist national movement, and she must take the lead in order to bring about a concentration of all forces that can work together to achieve a free Indonesia ...

In connection with the future conflict in the Pacific in which the Netherlands will undoubtedly become involved, we must determine our position now. Because of the attitude of imperialistic Japan, the point has been reached where our colonial rulers in Indonesia have no say any more in economic matters. Japan brings in as many goods as it likes. The trade conference between the Netherlands and Japan, which was announced with so much fanfare, has totally failed. However, we must not underestimate our colonial rulers, because they are backed by the British and the Americans, and the way the situation is now, also by the French fleet. A solidly united national Indonesian people will be able to withstand these powers. As at the moment the hate against the colonial rulers in Indonesia is general, the time can be considered to be ripe for our task of setting up a national front in which all national forces are united. There will have to be a common struggle against colonial rule, exploitation, hunger, misery, and educational deprivation. It will be a heavy struggle, but it is our great duty. With an exhortation to join the *Perhimpoenan Indonesia*, the only organization that struggles for a free Indonesia, the speaker ended his talk ...

Raden Mas Hadiono Koesoemo Oetoyo ... made a short, rather disconnected speech in which he emphasized that it would not be possible to combine all parties in Indonesia into one national front, and that in any case the tempo at which this would occur was too slow. He discussed the programmes of the various national organizations and youth groups and the encouragement given to them by the colonial rulers in order to keep the Indonesian masses divided. He urged that the *Perhimpoenan Indonesia* should speed up its actions.

Then Djojoadhiningrat spoke. He first hailed the beautiful speech of Moewaladi and dismissed the opinion of Oetoyo that it would be impossible to set up a national front. In the struggle for an independent Indonesia there are two streams, one of which is to the right and can get away with a few things with the colonial government, but the other is leftist and is a thorn in the side of our colonial rulers. The rightist stream submits requests, but the leftists demand. We must follow Western tactics. In the West also there is a great deal of division, but in the struggle against Fascism a united front has been created. Only look at France and Spain. This has happened because Fascism is considered as the common enemy, which can only be defeated by concentrating all opposing powers. In Indonesia we consider the colonial rulers as the common enemy, who can only be defeated by a combination of all national powers. Without this union the outcome of the final struggle can never be in our favour. We must struggle to achieve equality with our rulers. To request, as various right-wing organizations have done, that Indonesians will have the right to become army officers is senseless. We must demand the establishment of a people's militia, because such a people's militia can help us in the final struggle for an independent Indonesia with their arms and can even be of decisive importance. It will not be long now before the great struggle in the Pacific will break out and then the *Perhimpoenan Indonesia* must have a definite plan of action ...

The next speaker was Masdoelhak, who agreed completely with the previous speakers. He also advocated the establishment of a national front in order to wage the final struggle against the colonial rulers. If all parties were willing to compromise on some of their principles, agreement could well be achieved. In the final struggle the Western, in our case the Dutch, revolutionaries must co-operate and we must work towards that purpose. The speaker suggested to the Chairman that the discussions of this meeting should be published in a pamphlet and sent to our fighters in the Indies.

Then Djojoadhiningrat spoke again. He agreed with the ideas of Masdoelhak about the co-operation of the workers in the Netherlands. This point had the full attention of the *Perhimpoenan Indonesia* and Roestam Effendi would, when the time came, take care of this matter ...

Koloniaal Archief. *Geheim Mailrapport 619x/36.*

69 Manifesto of the Gaboengan Politiek Indonesia, 20 September 1939

The plenary session of the *G.A.P.I.*, held on Tuesday evening 19-20 September 1939 in Jakarta, and attended by the representatives of:
1. GERINDO, 2. PERSATOEAN MINAHASA, 3. PARTIJ ISLAM INDONESIA, 4. PERSATOEAN PARTIJ KATHOLIEK INDONESIA, 5. PARINDRA, 6. PASOENDAN, 7. P.S.I.I. being of the opinion that:
1. in view of international developments there is an ever-growing threat to the security of the government in the Netherlands Indies and Indonesian society;
2. and that it would be most appropriate to effect co-operation between the Indonesian people and the Netherlands people;
3. and that this co-operation should be effected by way of granting the Indonesian people more rights in conducting the government of the country;
Resolves:
1. that the members of *G.A.P.I.* shall not take action independently but shall be prepared to work together with other organizations under the aegis of *G.A.P.I.*;
2. that a government ought to be instituted with a parliament

elected by and from the people and that this government is to be responsible to parliament;
3. if what has been stated under 2 can be conceded within a previously determined period of time, the *G.A.P.I.* is prepared to urge the Indonesian people to give as much support as possible;
4. to notify all layers of the Indonesian people of this resolution, calling on all Indonesian movements and the press to support it.

Jakarta, 20 September 1939
The Secretariat of *G.A.P.I..*

S.L. van der Wal, *De Volksraad* ... , p. 403, note 3.

70 Indonesian People's Congress, 23-25 December 1939

Unlike at the *G.A.P.I.* meeting of 1 October 1939, this time the congress hall was decked out with nationalist flags and slogans that propagandized the demand for a parliamentary form of government. The whole organization this time was also very different from the rather matter-of-fact atmosphere of the first *G.A.P.I.* congress. The Congress Committee entered in solemn procession, flanked by uniformed members of youth organizations and preceded by the flags of the various bodies. Military-sounding orders were shouted when they entered and the public rose in deference, singing *"Indonesia-Raja".*

The large attendance consisted mainly of intellectuals and the people from the lower middle classes, among whom were many women. The indigenous organizations and the press were very well represented. Some members of the *Volksraad* as well as departmental officials were present. However, no interest was shown by the Europeans. The Congress Committee consisted of the representatives of the various organizations that have joined *G.A.P.I.*, while Raden Abikoesno Tjokrosoejoso, the general secretary of *G.A.P.I.* and chairman of the executive committee of the *P.S.I.I.*, acted as chairman of the congress ...

In his speech the Chairman, referring to a statement by Chamberlain, expressed his hope that after the conclusion of the present war changes would occur in the Netherlands Indies. "Whatever the outcome of the struggle may be, the world of tomorrow will not be the same any more as the world of today ... all nations will be granted their rights." Mr Abikoesno emphasized the need for the "Indonesian people" to unite and ended his speech by calling on the Netherlands to grant the wishes of the people ...

In this open session the following resolutions taken during the

closed sessions of the congress were made public:
1. As from 24 December 1939 the Indonesian People's Congress has become a permanent body. 2. Its purpose is to increase the happiness and prosperity of the Indonesian people. 3. The first step towards the achievement of this goal is the establishment of an Indonesian parliament. 4. *G.A.P.I.* is to be the executive body of the congress. 5. Membership is open to organizations and political parties. 6. Decisions will be arrived at democratically, i.e. by majority vote. 7. The drafting of the programme is to be delegated to a commission ... 8. A fund is to be opened and gifts are to be accepted to finance the activities of the congress. 9. The action for an Indonesian parliament will be continued under the direction of the *G.A.P.I.*, which will issue general instructions as to the action to be taken. It is to be solemnly announced that the red-white flag has been accepted as the symbol of unity, and that *"Indonesia-Raja"*, which was composed by the late Soepratman, is to be the national anthem. The Indonesian People's Congress legalizes the use of the Indonesian language in the various representative bodies, and it exhorts in particular the various organizations which are represented in these councils to continue to use the Indonesian language. The Congress urges support for the Indonesian press and the national press bureau ...

Rather striking was the presence at the congress of Achmad Jacobi gelar Datoek Simaradjo, who spoke on behalf of the *Madjlis Tinggi Kerapatan Adat Alam Minangkabau* ... the well-known association of Minangkabau *adat*-chiefs. And although the appearance of this Datoek will perhaps only be supported by a part of the Minangkabau *adat* chiefs, the fact that this organization has joined the congress demonstrates in a way the "Unity of Indonesia". The same can be said about the expression of adherence given by the representative of the *Geredja Merdeka Minahasa*, the independent Minahasan Church.

In the speech of the representative of the *M.I.A.I.*, the federation of Islamic organizations, the following paragraph is rather important: "that the objective we have in mind may be achieved speedily, because the many outstanding problems concerning Islam can only be solved satisfactorily when Indonesia has its own parliament" ...

Dr Ratu Langie draws attention again to the problem of "drainage". And because of the present growing interest in nationalist circles in this problem, it can be expected that new attempts will be made to obstruct the transfer of business profits overseas and to further the Indonesiation of the public service to prevent millions of guilders flowing from the Indies in the form of pensions ...

The chairman of the indigenous Roman Catholic organizations, Mr Kasimo Endrowahjono, concerned himself with the difficult social problem of the need for minimum wages. Although many indigenous leaders apparently believe in "Statism", i.e. the power of the State to considerably improve by means of legislation the lot of the citizens and especially to improve the standard of living of the masses, it cannot be denied that more could be done to combat without delay and more systematically any abuses in the wage structure ...

The lecture of Mr Aroedji Kartawinata about "The Burdens of the People" exemplifies how the *P.S.I.I.* poses as the advocate of the poor by bringing its grievances to the fore. The examples used by Mr Kartawinata, which nearly all refer to the Outer Possessions, could also be an indication that the *P.S.I.I.* has lost a great deal of ground in Java, and is only still important in a few parts of the Indies.

The most important speaker was Dr Soekiman, who presented a clear and sober explanation of the development of the parliamentary system in Western Europe. My impression was that he tried to impress upon his listeners the need to keep in mind the fact that the evolution of a country's governmental structure into a parliamentary structure can be a slow process, and that a rejection of their demands should not discourage them from going on trying. It is important to notice that Dr Soekiman also strongly emphasized that a powerful defence structure should be organized in the Indies to repel a foreign enemy. However, this could only be done in his view on an Indonesian national basis, for which the independence of the country was a necessary condition. The speaker concluded that if this condition were satisfied, "We would be mad not to co-operate with the Netherlands" ...

A number of other proposals submitted by members of the congress were dealt with in the closed sessions, of which one submitted by the *Perhimpoenan Peladjar Indonesia* (*P.P.P.I.*), the well-known students' organization, caused an incident. Section 4 of this proposal read as follows: "If the government rejects out of hand this demand for a parliament, then all members of the various councils [i.e. colonial representative councils] who have joined the Indonesian People's Congress should by way of protest withdraw themselves for a certain period from the elections." Also these students (apparently referring to the well-known slogan of the *P.N.I.* in 1929: "*Indonesia Merdeka Sekarang*"—"Indonesia Free Now") want to change the slogan "*Indonesia Berpalement*"—"Indonesia with its own parliament"—to "*Parlement Indonesia Sekarang*"—"An Indonesian Parliament Now". Although this proposal was received with a great deal of sympathy and applause, it was immediately rejected by the congress, and the students' delegation rather demonstratively left the meeting ...

This action for a parliament was criticized as a matter of principle by two prominent indigenous figures: Hadji Agus Salim, the leader of the *Pergerakan Penjedar*, and Dr S.G. Moelia, the *Volksraad* Member. The two large organizations of indigenous public servants, the *P.P.B.B.* and the *V.A.I.B.*, kept themselves completely aloof from this action ...

One of the most important resolutions of this first "Indonesian People's Congress" was that: "*the action for a fully fledged parliament shall be continued*". It is still too early to give a definite appreciation of this action and similarly it is not yet possible to indicate how it will develop. The enthusiastic beginning of this movement for a parliament must be followed by a period of reflection during which it will become apparent that the many parties united under the banner of the *G.A.P.I.* must have different views as to the final implementation of the parliamentary idea. Whatever the case may be, what I consider so far as the most important result of the *G.A.P.I.* action is the fact that it has succeeded in gaining the support of the most diverse parties for a common ideal. Never in the history of the indigenous political movement has unity been so strong as now ...

S.L. van der Wal, *De Volksraad* ... , pp. 496-502.

71 Petition of G.A.P.I. to the Governor-General, 9 August 1940

We the undersigned:
1. R. Abikoesno Tjokrosoejoso
2. R. Soekardjo Wirjopranoto
3. Drs Adnaan Kapau Gani

constituting the Secretariat of *G.A.P.I.* (*Gaboengan Politiek Indonesia*), Kwitang 12 Batavia-C, acting in this matter on behalf of the *G.A.P.I.*, have the honour to submit respectfully to Your Excellency the following resolution taken during the plenary session held at Batavia on 8 August 1940 ...

1. *Starting from the assumption*:
(a) that permanent peace and the progress and prosperity of humanity can only be achieved and maintained by the complete political, democratic, and social democratization of society;
(b) that in view of the present worldwide struggle between democracy and totalitarian Fascism it is necessary to defend and reinforce democratic principles and to introduce them where they do not yet exist;

2. *Considering*:
(a) the fact that the Netherlands and therefore also Indonesia participate in the war on the side of the democratic countries;

(b) and that this fact implies that both countries are fighting for the victory of the principles of democratic freedom over the suppressive methods of totalitarian Fascism;
(c) and that therefore the introduction of democratic principles, although for the time being only in relation to the Indonesian constitution, will put the relationship between the Netherlands and Indonesia in the proper context of and in harmony with the stated objectives of the war;
(d) that to join the side of the democracies is in agreement with the democratic principles advocated by the National Movement of Indonesia, the speedy realization of which is demanded in the manifesto mentioned above;
(e) that therefore the democratization of the constitutional organization of Indonesia will reinforce the moral as well as the total power of resistance against the arbitrary and repressive policies of totalitarian Fascism;
3. *Declaring itself prepared*:
to co-operate and consult with the government and political parties of all the population groups in this country in order to achieve the complete democratization of Indonesia;
4. *Urges the government*:
as a first step towards the general democratization of the country to democratize government by means of introducing within the near future, making use of its emergency powers, the following constitutional reforms:
(a) As an intermediate stage in the achievement of a full parliament, the *Volksraad* should be transformed into a parliament, the members of which are to be elected from and by the people using an electoral system which guarantees a fair representation of the various population groups;
(b) to transform the departmental heads into ministers to be responsible for their policies to the transformed *Volksraad*, i.e. the parliament.
5. *Calls*:
on other political, social, and cultural organizations to express their agreement with this resolution ...

S.L. van der Wal, *De Volksraad*, pp. 523-24.

72 Views of an indigenous lawyer on the Indonesian political situation in 1940

While it is already difficult in normal times for Europeans to gauge the inner life of the Indonesians, this is even more difficult in this time of worldwide confusion, because they [the Indonesians] rather pretend to be unmoved—while in fact they are very much moved—in order to stay out of all conflicts and difficulties. And indeed the Indonesians are very much on edge. Everything that happens around them, be they small or big things, they absorb carefully; they discuss these things with their friends in the greatest secrecy and they keep the impressions they have gained to themselves as a great treasure. They mistrust everybody who may ask about their views and they evade the question with such answers as: "After all it is wartime."

They have now grasped the meaning of Longfellow's words: "Think, others see as well as you", and they wisely keep their mouths shut. Europeans who especially now pretend to completely understand the psychological make-up of the Indonesians will one of these days only be disillusioned. At this time the "real face" of the Indonesians and what is hidden behind it is a mystery to the Europeans, and even more an Eastern mystery. The face will only express what the Europeans wish it to express. And this is even more so because the Dutch have always taught the Indonesians to appreciate *nolens volens* [whether they wanted to or not] all blessings which were brought down from above, and to acquiesce in everything in accordance with the recipe: *"chez vous, sans vous, sur vous"* ["with you, without you, above you"]. And at this particular time they just maintain their passive attitude partly because of force of habit, and partly because of necessity. It is therefore very doubtful whether the Indonesian expressions of adhesion to the Netherlands and the House of Orange are the result of a true understanding of Indonesian interests and an intense feeling of fellowship. Similarly, it is to be doubted whether the various collections for defence purposes were responded to spontaneously by the Indonesians or whether a certain amount of compulsion was used. It should also be taken into account that the voluntary collection for the needy in Mecca has had very little response from the people.

The disposition of the Indonesian people towards the Dutch and the Netherlands Government is dependent on a great many factors, such as differences in race, culture, religion, intellectual development, and differences in interests and purpose. These in themselves cause differences in the judgement of and the attitude to the Netherlands Government. This disposition is dependent on the extent to which the interests of individual or groups of Indonesians are served by the maintenance of Netherlands rule in these regions. The

Indonesians do understand very well that the Dutch need their expressions of adhesion and generosity for internal and external propaganda purposes. But why should they not participate? They have nothing to lose and can only gain ... After the outbreak of this war the government has indeed enlarged the number of privileged Indonesians. And this patronage was not only extended to those Indonesians who because of their unquestionable loyalty in the past and in the present towards the Netherlands Government indeed deserved to be rewarded, but also to those who earlier and even immediately before they obtained their certificate of loyalty had taken part directly or indirectly in disloyal actions against the government. The latter category will in spite of everything remain opportunists. In the hour of need one can count on them as little as or perhaps even less than on the other privileged class, which consists mainly of self-governing rulers, chiefs, and administrative officials of the rank of Assistant *Wedana* upwards, and which in general has the power over the people but no authority. This class will have to share the fate of the Dutch who have helped them into the saddle.

While the privileged class counts few intellectuals, the non-privileged class consists of many intellectuals and other Indonesians. The Indonesians in this last group can be distinguished into the politically conscious and those who are not politically conscious.

The politically conscious, in as far as they are organized, are to be found mainly in the *Gaboengan Politiek Indonesia (G.A.P.I.)* and the *Madjelis Islam Ala Indonesia (M.I.A.I.)* ... While the *Parindra* and the *Gerindo* set the tone in the *G.A.P.I.*, in the *M.I.A.I.* the main role is played by the *Moehammadiah* [sic] and the *P.S.I.I.*, while this last party is peculiarly enough also represented in the *G.A.P.I.*

The *Parindra*, which is pre-eminently an association of intellectuals, shows many inconsistencies in its policies. While it considers that the Indo-Arabs and the Indo-Chinese do have political interests in the Indies commonwealth, it tries at the same time to keep both groups completely out of the economic life of Indonesian society. It takes on a co-operative attitude towards the government, but in important matters it leaves the government in the lurch. It must also be pointed out that especially after the moral defeat suffered in the *Volksraad* because of Thamrin *cum suis*, it [the *Parindra*] now considers any compromise with the government as impossible, and this in spite of the fact that many of its members are higher and lower government officials and that the government is taking account as much as possible of its desires. [Motions by Wiwoho, Sutardjo, and Thamrin, dealing respectively with the democratization of government, the institution of an Indies citizenship, and the replacement in laws, ordinances, etc. of the words Netherlands Indies and Native by

Indonesia and Indonesian, were withdrawn by the proposers on 23 August 1940 on the grounds that owing to the government's recalcitrance there was no possibility of agreement on these matters.]

It [the *Parindra*] and all the other associations which are combined in the *G.A.P.I.* are of the opinion:
1. that even at this time the government in line with the policy followed by European capital wants to be friendly to the Chinese and the Arabs rather than to the Indonesians;
2. that the Commission Visman does nothing else than ridicule the political desires expressed in the *Volksraad* ... and even worse, it is trying to create confusion among the nationalist parties. [The Commission Visman or the Commission for the Study of Constitutional Reforms was set up on 23 August 1940 in order to study the political demands in Indonesia, to advise the government, and to consider the possibility and consequences of the introduction of an Indies citizenship and the replacement in legislation of the name Native by another term. The Commission's report was published in 1941 just before the Japanese invasion.]
3. that *"Indonesia berparlement"* ["Indonesia with a parliament"] ... cannot be achieved through negotiations. The interest gap between the people and the government, it is felt, cannot be bridged;
4. that the Dutch, who apparently without the help from the mother country can still manage their affairs in the Indies, can also do in all aspects without the help of the Indonesians, so that from its side it was logical to oppose the establishment of city guards and other defence measures.

The *Parindra* leaders are now following with more than usual interest what is happening in British India and South-east Asia.

The arrival of the Japanese delegation in this country was a welcome excuse to them to discuss with these foreigners all sorts of political and economic questions. [On 12 September 1940 a Japanese delegation arrived in Batavia led by the Minister of Trade and Industry, Kobayashi. The purpose of the delegation was to secure large supplies of vital war materials such as oil and rubber for Japan.] Messrs Douwes Dekker, P.F. Dahler, and Thamrin played an important role in these discussions. And there was some talk of exchanging blueprints on how the Netherlands Indies would be eventually governed within "the new order" aimed at by Japan. It hardly needs saying that these gentlemen used the political and constitutional set-up of the Philippines as a model. [Soon afterwards Douwes Dekker and Thamrin were arrested. Thamrin died on 11 January 1941 and Douwes Dekker was imprisoned and transported to Surinam (the Dutch West Indies).]

The members of the Japanese delegation have made good use of their stay in the Indies in more than one respect. The indigenous press receives financial help from the Japanese in the form of advertisements and other ways. It is generally known that the *Dagblad Radio* [newspaper] at Padang has been bought by Mr A. Madjid Oesman with Japanese capital and that Mr Mohammad Yamin is supposed to have applied for a licence on behalf of the said Madjid Oesman to establish a printing office ... which would be paid for by Mr Sakata, the representative in the Indies of the *Osaka Nichi Nichi* and the *Tokyo Mainichi*.

It must also be born in mind that Mr A. Madjid Oesman has been in Japan for four years to study political science, that he was a member of the Committee of the Pan-Asiatic Movement in Tokyo, and that during a demonstration in Tokyo he spoke as the representative of "*Indonesia Merdeka*" ... and unfurled the "red-white" flag as the flag of "Indonesia". He is married to a Japanese woman and professes to be a relative of Mr Sakata. In Padang he is treated with a certain amount of respect by the group of modernist Muslims and lately he has been assisted in word and deed by Mr Mohammad Yamin, the representative in the *Volksraad* for Minangkabau. Considering the inflammability of the Minangkabaus for new ideas, the government should be doubly vigilant.

How intense the Japanese propaganda is can be seen from the fact that pre-eminent leaders of the National Movement have been presented ... with the strongly pro-Japanese book *The Drama of the Pacific* by Major R.V.C. Bradley, while the Japanese Information Service in Tokyo takes the greatest trouble to make the prominent Muslims in Indonesia happy by sending them reading matter in Arabic. Indeed the Japanese Government spares no costs to familiarize the world with Japanese feelings and ideas. According to the semi-official newspaper *Nipon Dempo* 2,500,000 yen has been appropriated for the establishment of an "international cultural bureau"; 9,150,000 yen for a special diplomatic fund; 3,600,000 yen for maintaining relations with Japanese in foreign countries; 7,150,000 yen for the improvement of relations with the Manchukwo subjects. In addition to these official measures the Japanese Government has also created a so-called "Society for International Cultural Relations", which also receives strong financial support from the Mitsuis and the Misubushis, the real masters of Japan ...

The Indonesian nationalist leaders are convinced that the Japanese-Indies discussions will result in complete failure. Just to take one point of the discussions, it is not reasonable to expect that the Netherlands Indies Government would agree to admit at least 60,000 Japanese immigrants into the Indies. But Japan considers the fulfilment of this demand by the Indies as a *conditio sine qua non* for the continuation of the discussions.

The arrogant attitude of almost all Indonesian spokesmen during the deliberations in the *Volksraad* about the 1941 budget when the question of the status quo of the Netherlands Indies was brought up can be partly explained as a result of the general policy agreement which has been reached among the various nationalist parties, but also partly as an underestimation of the ability of the present authorities to control the [international] political situation. They are convinced that one of these days the status quo of the Netherlands Indies will be violated. And one cannot help being reminded of the words of Antoine Zischka, who wrote in his *Le Japon dans le monde* (page 63): "*Et si les indigenes, tout autour de Pacifique, n'aiment pas beaucoup le Japon, ils haissent les Blancs*" ["And although the indigenous people all around the Pacific might not love Japan a great deal, they hate the whites].

I am wondering whether the government has considered the possibility that as a result of an eventual Japanese-American war, an Indonesian Government abroad might be proclaimed, e.g. in Tokyo. After all in London there are also legal Polish, Czecho-Slovak, Belgian, Norwegian, and Netherlands governments. It may not be forgotten that there are leftist-oriented Indonesians abroad, especially in Tokyo, who are ready at the first sign to form a preliminary Indonesian government with the aid of a foreign power. The failure of the Indies-Japanese trade negotiations will be explained as an unsympathetic deed of the Dutch against the Indonesians ... who are opposed to export restrictions and licences ... because such measures are solely designed to "exploit" the people for the benefit of European and American capital. The arrival of the Japanese will be hailed as a happy event which will bring [the people] cheap goods. The rest will be done by the Djojobojo legend, which after all says that first Java will be ruled for a long time by the whites, then there will be a short period of rule by the yellow race, after which there will be independence. In executing its plans the *Parindra* is prepared to drop if necessary those members who work for the government. One should not lose sight of the fact that although Thamrin might not be so popular in his own circle, he is still the man who is recognized abroad as the leader of the nationalist movement ... and as such draws respect. He is a gifted politician who knows what he is doing. And like any other ambitious politician he believes in the doctrine that the purpose sanctifies the means. In an independent country he would go as far as to cause a bloody civil war and have many innocent victims killed in order to realize his ideals ...

While the *Parindra* draws its support mainly from the intellectuals, the members of the *Gerindo* belong mainly to the *petit-bourgeoisie*, while this party has also become a refuge for former members or sympathizers of the *Partai Kommunis Indonesia* (*P.K.I.*) and the *Sarikat Rakjat*. The ex-*P.N.I.* members have in line with the decision taken at the conference in Semarang in March 1940 spread themselves over the *Parindra*, *Gerindo*, *Parpindo*, *Moehammadiah* [sic] and *P.S.I.I.* in order to obtain the control over all these organizations in the long run.

They are all of the opinion that the government purposely gives preferential treatment to the Chinese and the Arabs and therefore that the intervention of Japan in the Netherlands Indies will not be unwelcome to them.

The Islam-oriented associations are complaining that the government has still not done anything to minimize the unequal treatment of Christians and Muslims. They are well aware of the fact that the British Indian Government has given its Mohammedan subjects all possible facilities to make the *Hadj* [pilgrimage to Mecca], such as the payment of passage money and shipping convoys in the dangerous zone. Compared with this the help granted by the government to needy Indonesians in Mecca appears to them as a drop of water in the desert. They have now come to the stage where they are indifferent to what the government elects to do for them. It is a fact that the National Board of the *Moehammadiah* [sic] and the *P.S.I.I.* in September last year held a closed conference with a few Japanese Muslims ...

Here follows a description of the political organizations and their membership ...

1. United in the *G.A.P.I.* (using a generous estimate)

	members
Parindra	10,000
Gerindo	5,000
P.S.I.I.	12,000
P.A.I.	3,000
Perdi	100
Pasoendan	10,000
Persatoean Katholiek Indonesia	5,000
Sarikat Ambon	1,000
Persatoean Minahasa	1,000
Persatoean Peladjar Peladjar Indonesia	300
Total	47,300

2. United in the *M.I.A.I.*

Moehammadiah [sic]	20,000
Persatoean Oelama Seloeroeh Atjeh	500
Nahdatoel Oelama	1.000
Pembela Islam [probably refers to Persis]	500
P.S.I.I.	(See under 1. above)
Total	22,000

3. Not associated with 1 and 2

Parpindo	200
Partij Penjedar	500
Persatoean Tarbijahtoel Islamiah	9,000
Persatoean Tionghoa Islam Indonesia	500
Persatoean Goeroe Goeroe Agama Islam	200
Persatoean Soepir Indonesia	1,000
Total	11,400
General Total	80,700

The number of politically or socially conscious Indonesians can be estimated at 200,000 or about 1 in every 300 inhabitants ...

It must be admitted that the government has done its best to induce the people of the Netherlands Indies to make common cause against the enemy. It has used new ideologies and slogans such as being bound by the same fate. The interests of the Chinese and the Arabs, who are people with a dual fatherland, are served by the maintenance of Netherlands rule over this country, because in case of victory of the totalitarian states and the eventual formation of an Indonesian Government they would lose many of their [present] rights. In any case they would have to be content with being foreigners in this "Indonesia". The indigenous people of this country have a very different frame of mind. Various answers will be given to the question whether the Indonesians are fully aware of being united in the same fate with the Netherlands people and whether ... they want this to continue and if not whether they will cordially accept it. The feeling of being united by the same fate and *"le desir d'etre ensemble"* exist and are indeed felt by the so-called privileged classes, or to use the words of Dr Meyer Ranneft, by the "the group of Netherlanders and indigenes who stand above the masses". But the existence of this [being united by the same fate] is denied and not desired by the vast majority of the 200,000 politically oriented Indonesians, while those not politically oriented could not care less whether there is a feeling of being united by the same fate with the Netherlands people or not. These people look at reality and are more than happy enough when they can lead a decent existence and are not overburdened with new taxes and new orders. They desire above all a just government.

Until now the government has only directed its attention to the expressed and unexpressed desires of the 200,000 politically conscious [Indonesians], and it has apparently been under the impression that if it gave in to their reasonable demands they would no longer make trouble. But nothing is further from the truth. Their desires can only be satisfied at the cost of the government. They will gratefully accept every concession made by the government but they will not stop until they are completely "boss in their own house". The well-intentioned measures of the government such as the appointment of some politicians to certain offices ... they take to be expressions of the weakness of the government, and they will draw the utmost profit from it. The present situation is too favourable to them to let it pass by unused ... The defence measures and the war materials ... are costing a great deal of money ... The masses, not knowing how to carry all the heavy financial burdens which are pressing on them, could eventually be placed in a position where they have to make a fateful choice. And this is the moment for which the political leaders are waiting. It will be welcomed as the moment when they will unasked for take matters in their own hands. It will be the beginning of the introduction of the new Japanese order in South-east Asia.

A chaotic situation may well occur if the government continues to bargain with the political leaders and their organizations. It is the duty of the government to push back the sphere of influence of the political leaders to its normal proportions. If the government does this, then it will notice that this sphere of influence is very small, because hero worship is still foreign to the Indonesians. The fate of the vast majority of the people, on which the government is actually dependent and which silently bears the heavy burdens put on them from above, deserves special attention. It [the people] wants a just government; and this justice cannot be given by either a Japanese or their own Indonesian government ... There is in my opinion still time for the government to neutralize the fatal influence of untrustworthy leaders on the masses by means of sound propaganda and heart-to-heart talks ...

S.L. van der Wal, *De Volksraad*, pp. 587-97.

Glossary

Abangan religiously syncretic and unorthodox Javanese Muslims.
Adat behavioural patterns, rules and customs left by the ancestors.
Anti-Revolutionaire Partij Dutch political party, neo-Calvinist, conservative.
Assistent Wedono Assistant District chief. See also *priyayi*, *Inlands Bestuur*.
Atap split bamboo.
Bahasa Indonesia Indonesian national language, largely based on Malay.
Bangsa people, nation.
Batavia seat of the Dutch colonial government, renamed Jakarta in 1945.
Batig slot budget surplus.
Belanda Dutch, European.
Binnenlands Bestuur Regional Government Service, consisting of a European and an Indigenous Branch. See also: *priyayi bupati*.
Boedi Oetomo (Budi Utomo) literally, Striving towards the sublime; a Java-centric, national organization of 1908.
Boven Digul concentration camp for Indonesian nationalists and Communists situated at the Upper-Digul river in West Irian (Irian Jaya).
Bouw 7096.5 square metres.
Budjang seasonal labour.
Bupati (or Bupatih) also termed Regent; originally viceroys of the Javanese court, later the highest rank in the Native branch of the *Binnenlands Bestuur*.
Company refers to the Dutch East-India Company or the Dutch colonial government.
Concordantie The policy of maintaining Dutch metropolitan standards and curricula in Dutch language schools in the Netherlands Indies.
Controleur lowest rank in the European branch of the Regional Government Service.

Darul Islam literally, the area of Islam; a fanatical Muslim movement (1948-63) attempting to establish an Islamic state in West Java.
Desa village.
Desa Lumbung village rice bank.
Digul see *Boven Digul.*
Doctorandus (Drs.) *Master of Arts.*
Doekoen (Dukun) soothsayer, medicine man, herbalist.
Dogcar horsedrawn carriage.
Dokter-Djawa School school for the training of indigenous vaccinators (1851); later a medical school.
Duit brass coin.
Gaboengan Politiek Indonesia (G.A.P.I.) Indonesian Political Union. A Federation of nationalist organizations (1939).
Gerakan Rakjat Indonesia (Gerindo) Indonesian People's Movement, a radical nationalist party (1937).
Goeroe (Guru) teacher.
Guilder approximately 3.30 $A in 1976.
Hadji (Haji) a person who has completed the pilgrimage to Mecca.
Hadji Mandoer money lender.
Haram contravening the Islamic law, unclean.
Hoofdenscholen special schools for the training of sons of the nobility planning to enter the colonial service (1870).
Hormat signs of respect and submission which commoners were required to show their superiors.
Ingenieur (Ir.) Master of Engineering.
Indier person living in the Netherlands Indies.
Indische Partij Party of the Indies; a radical multi-racial organization (1912).
Indische Sociaal Democratische Vereeniging (I.S.D.V.) the Social Democratic Association of the Indies; forerunner of the Indonesian Communist Party (1914).
Indo-Europees Verbond Indo-European Union; organization of Eurasians loyal to the Netherlands (1919).
Indonesia Muda Young Indonesia; radical-nationalist youth organization; also a journal of the same name.
Indonesia Raja (Raya) Greater Indonesia; Indonesian national anthem.
Inlands Bestuur indigenous branch of the Regional Government Service. See also: *priyayi, bupati.*
Insulinde from Latin, meaning Islands of the Indies; Eurasian political organization (1914-20).
Jong Islamieten Bond (J.I.B.) Union of Young Muslims; student organization set up to counteract the secularizing influence of Western education.

Jong Java Young Java; youth organization affiliated with *Budi Utomo*.
Kafir non-Muslim; unbeliever.
Kain long piece of cloth, to be draped around the body.
Kati 625 grams.
Kemerdekaan freedom.
Kitab religious book, manual.
Kiyayi Islamic scholar; see also *ulama*.
Kota town.
Kraton Javanese royal palace complex.
Langgar small mosque; a prayer house also used as a school.
Lebaran celebration after the ending of the fast.
Lumbung rice storage shed.
Madjisloel Islamil A'laa Indonesia (M.I.A.I.) Council of Indonesian Islamic Organizations (1937).
Mandoer (Mandur) foreman.
Mantri low rank in the Indigenous branch of the Regional Government Service.
Meester in de Rechten (Mr.) Master of Laws.
Merdeka free.
Muhammadyah reformist Muslim organization (1912).
Nahadatul Ulama Association of Scholars (1926); Muslim organization to counteract the Reformists.
Nationale Indische Partij (N.I.P.) successor to the *Indische Partij* (1912-23).
Nederlandse Handel Maatschappij Dutch Trading Company (1824).
Ngelmu magical knowledge.
Orang menumpang landless villager.
Padi dalem slowly maturing rice.
Padi gendjang quickly maturing rice.
Padri fanatical, puritanical Muslim reformers in Minangkabau (1800-1837).
Pandita mystic.
Partai Kommunis Indonesia (P.K.I.) Indonesian Communist Party (1920).
Partai Indonesia (Partindo) Indonesian Party (1931); radical nationalist.
Partai Indonesia Raja (Parindra) party of Greater Indonesia (1936); moderate nationalist.
Partai Nasional Indonesia (P.N.I.) Indonesian Nationalist Party (1927); radical-nationalist.
Partij Penjedar literally, party to increase consciousness; splinter group from Partai Sarikat Islam (1936).
Partai Persatoean Indonesia (Parpindo) Party of Indonesian Unity.
Partai Sarikat Islam Indonesia (P.S.I.I.) Party of the Islamic Association; evolved from the Sarikat Islam.

Pasar market.
Pasoendan Sundanese organization (West Java); mainly culturally orientated.
Pembela Islam journal published by Persatuan Islam.
Pendidikan Nasional Indonesia Indonesian National Education; radical-nationalist (1932).
Penghulu official in charge of Muslim religious affairs.
Pentjak Indonesian art of self-defence.
Perang Sabil holy war.
Perhimpunan Indonesia Indonesian Association; (1922); radical Indonesian students in the Netherlands.
Permufakatan Perhimpunan Politiek Kebangsaan Indonesia (P.P.P.K.I.) literally, Unanimous Consensus of the Political Organizations of the Indonesian People; (1927); nationalist federation.
Persatoean Goeroe Goeroe Agama Islam Islamic Teachers' Union.
Persatoean Katholiek Indonesia Indonesian Catholic Union.
Persatoean Minahasa Minahasan Union (North Sulawesi).
Persatoean Oelama Seloeroeh Atjeh Union of Islamic scholars of Acheh.
Persatoean or Persatuan Islam (Persis) Islamic Unity; reformist movement centred in Bandung.
Persatoean Soepir Indonesia Indonesian chauffeurs Union.
Persatoean Tionghoa Islam Indonesia Chinese-Islamic Union of Indonesia.
Persatuan Bangsa Indonesia (P.B.I.) Union of the Indonesian People; (1925); moderate nationalist.
Persatuan Tarbijahtoel Islamiah (Perti) Islamic Education Party.
Pesantren Islamic school; type of seminary.
Picul Measure of weight; varying according to produce; e.g. one picul of coffee is 255 lbs.
Poeasa (puasa) period of the Fast.
Politieke Inlichtingen Dienst (P.I.D.) Dutch Political Intelligence Service.
Pondok living quarters, Islamic school.
Priyayi class of aristocratic government administrators; sometimes also is used for Javanese upper-class.
Raad van Nederlands Indie Council of the Indies; supreme executive and legislative body headed by the governor-general.
Ratu Adil literally, a just King, who was popularly believed to inaugurate a millenium of justice and prosperity.
Regent see *bupati*.
Resident highest rank in the European branch of the Regional Government Service.
Roede (r) 3.767 metres.

Rukun Tani farmers' cooperatives; affiliated to the Parindra.
Santri pious, orthodox Muslims; also students in pesantren.
Sarekat Islam (Sarikat Islam) Islamic Association (1912).
Sarikat Rakjat People's Association; local branches of the Indonesian Communist Party.
Sate skewered roasted meat.
Sawah irrigated rice land.
School Tot Opleiding Van Inlandse Artsen (S.T.O.V.I.A.) school for the training of Native doctors; medical school in Jakarta. Evolved from the Dokter-Djawa school.
Sembahjang daily Muslim prayers.
Sirih betel nut.
Slametan festive meal on special occasions.
Sociaal Democratische Arbeiders Partij (S.D.A.P.) Social Democratic Labour Party; Dutch Socialist Party.
Swadeshi Hindi word for indigenous; Gandhi-led movement urging Indians to buy only locally produced goods.
Tegalan non-irrigated farm land.
Toean (Tuan) sir; lord; used only for non-Indonesians.
Oelama (Ulama) Muslim scholar, scribe.
Volksraad People's Council; proto parliament (1918).
Wajang Traditional Javanese puppet or shadow play.
Warong (Warung) small store.
Wilde Scholen literally, Wild Schools; schools run by Indonesians outside the official government system.
Zakat religious tax.

Index

Abangan, 236–37, 242–47. *See also* Javanese syncretism
Abduh, Mohammad, 237–38. *See also* Islamic modernism
Abdul Madjid Djojoadhiningrat, *raden mas*, 332–33
Abdul Wahab, *haji*, 270
Abikusno Tjokrosujoso, *raden*, 261–62, 335–36
Accountability law (1867), 76
Achinese nobility. *See* Ulebalang
Achmad Jacobi, *gelar datuk Simaradjo*, 336
Adat, 13, 86, 88, 93, 181, 210, 236, 238, 265, 336
Adat law, 11–12, 32, 318
Adatgemeenschappen, 125
Adnaan Kapan Gani, *Drs*., 338
Agricultural and Veterinary Science School (Bogor), 226
Agricultural extension services, 62–63, 68
Agricultural productivity, 94
Agus Salim, *haji*, 239–40, 258–59, 267–70, 272, 338
Ahmadyah, 265
Aisjyah, 240, 264. *See also* Muhammadyah
Algemene Middelbare School (A.M.S.), 152
Alimin, 273
Allah, 151, 161, 207, 214, 243, 245, 258
Ambon Association. *See* Sarikat Ambon
Ambtenaarstaten, 122. *See also* Graaff, S. de
Amir Hamzah, 332
Ancestral customs. *See* Adat
Animism, 242–47
Anti-Revolutionnaire Partij, 67, 77, 123, 139
Anwari, *Ir*., 302, 314

Appanage system, 180
Arab Union of Indonesia. *See* Persatuan Arab Indonesia
Arabic, 244–45, 248–51, 253, 255, 343
Arabs, 91, 95, 342, 345
Armed forces, oppressive behaviour, 204–6, 211-14; demand for indigenous army, 231, 331, 342. *See also* Defence
Arminius, 52, 53. *See also* Heyting, H. G.
Arudji Kartawinata, 337
Association, 135, 157–65, 215–16, 320; sabotage of, 220–25, 257. *See also* Ethical Policy; Snouck-Hurgronje, C.
Association of Scholars (Islamic). *See* Nahadatul Ulama
Atjeh War, 73, 76, 123, 181–82
Auto-Activity, 94, 230. *See also* Economic demand; Economic behaviour
Autonomous Ethnic Communities. *See* Adatgemeenschappen

Bagus Djarot, *sultan*, 188–92
Bahasa Indonesia, 329, 336
Bangsa Putihan. *See* Santri
Bataviaasch Handelsblad (newspaper), 234
Batig Slot, 7, 20, 35, 46, 61, 75–76
Batik industry, 91, 106
Baud, J. C., 8, 15, 18, 25, 35, 36
Bauer, O., 310
Benda, H. J., 284, 287
Berg, N. P. van den, 76
Binnenlands Bestuur (B.B.), 37, 41–42, 83, 86, 94, 121, 162, 192–200, 254, 288; maltreatment of indigenous population, 211–14;

superiority complex, 222–25; exclusion of Indonesians, 225
Boeke, J. H., 50, 56, 64, 97, 113
Bolsjewism, 277–78, 280
Borobudur, 229
Bosch, J. van den, *count*, 6–8, 10, 14–19, 22, 31, 34–36, 44–45
Boven-Digul, 173, 271, 275
Bradley, R. V. C., *major*, 343
British Empire, 313
British India, 46–47, 129–30, 181, 188, 265, 279, 282, 283, 319, 324, 342, 345
Brooshooft, P., 61, 65, 77
Bucharin, 281
Buddhism, 282–83
Budget Studies, 34, 50–56, 64, 97–113, 113–20
Budiarto, *Mr.*, 302
Budi Utomo, 127, 216–17, 225–27, 258–59, 301, 304, 308, 314–15, 321
Bupati, 3, 9, 23–24, 27, 32, 39, 41–42, 187, 192, 223–24, 227, 249, 251, 254, 288–89, 314. *See also* Inlands Bestuur; Priyayi; Javanese aristocracy; Indonesian elite

Caliph, 238, 267. *See also* Pan-Islamism
Capellen, G. A. R. van der, *baron*, 6, 180
Capital, indigenous, 84, 99, 104, 108, 109, 170, 331; foreign, 122, 130, 131, 170–71, 231, 316, 344; drainage of, 262, 280, 336
Capitalism, 70, 72–73, 279–83, 316, 328–30. *See also* Plantations
Carpentier-Alting, J. H., 128
Catholic church, 282, 336
Catholic Party. *See* Katholieke Volkspartij
Catholic Political Association of Java. *See* Perkumpulan Politiek Katholiek Djawa
Census. *See* Volkstelling
Centralism. *See* Unification
Chamberlain, N., 335
Chijs, J. A. van der, 248–51
Child marriages, 87, 272, 319
China, 287, 309–10; Revolution (1911), 258
Chinese, 14, 22, 28, 39, 63, 67, 85, 91, 95, 103, 155, 216, 217, 231, 258–59, 291, 342, 345. *See also* Usury
Christianity, 242, 307
Christian missions, 159, 238
Chronic diseases, 81–82
Civil defence, 331
Coffee, 15, 19, 22, 32, 34, 37, 46, 58, 67, 71
Cohen-Stuart, J. W. T., 165
Colijn, H., 123–25, 130, 135–40, 175–76
Colleges of advanced education, 152
Colonial Archives. *See* Koloniaal Archief
Comintern, 273–74
Commerce, indigenous, 50–51, 89, 91, 98–99, 109, 202, 318
Commissie tot Bestudering van Staatsrechtelijke Hervormingen (1940), 342
Commission for Constitutional Reforms. *See* Commissie tot Bestudering van Staatsrechtelijke Hervormingen (1940)
Committee for the Maintenance of Truth of the P.S.I.I. *See* Komite Pertahanan Kebenaran P.S.I.I.
Communism, 123, 153, 170, 172–74, 239, 257, 263; infiltration of Sarikat Islam, 257, 260, 273–300. *See also* Partai Kommunis Indonesia (P.K.I.)
Concordantie, 154, 176
Constitutional reforms (1922). *See* Grondwetherziening
Coolhaas, W. Ph., 22
Coolie Budget Investigation (1939–40), 65, 113–20. *See also* Budget studies
Co-operation, 304–5, 318, 321–25, 334, 337. *See also* Partai Indonesia Raya
Co-operatives, 319, 323
Corruption, 41–42
Council of Indonesian Islamic Organizations. *See* Madjlisoel Islamil A'laa Indonesia (M.I.A.I.)
Council of Religious Scholars. *See* Madjlis Oelama
Council of the Indies. *See* Raad van Nederlands-Indie

Court, J. F. H. A., de la, 154, 176
Cramer, Ch. G., 122
Credit needs, indigenous, 51, 62–63, 68, 70, 85–86, 93, 100, 102, 103, 105–6, 108, 112, 116–17. *See also* Usury; Desa Lumbung; Village banks; Pawn shops; Volkscredietwezen
Creutzberg, K. F., 123, 132, 133
Cultural nationalism, 302–3, 318. *See also* Sukarno
Cultural synthesis, 152
Culture System, 5, 7, 8, 16, 19, 30–36, 38–39, 43, 48, 71–73, 76, 91–92, 315; effect on Dutch secondary industry, 21, 44–45; effect on Dutch savings, 31; effect on Javanese working habits, 43–44; effect on rice production, 14, 18, 20, 26, 46; famines, 24, 29–30, 35–36, 39, 46; forced consignment system, 21; increase in communal land, 82; irrigation, 25; Liberal opposition, 15–17; maltreatment and excesses by civil service, 19, 22, 30, 37, 39, 44, 46, 66; modern education for indigenes, 13; need for indirect rule, 9–11, 14, 21; principles of system, 14–15; protection of Javanese against foreigners, 22

Daendels, H. W., *general*, 5–6, 10, 32
Dagblad Radio (newspaper), 343
Dahler, P. F., 342
Damste, H. T., 207, 214
Danureja, 189–202
Darsono, 122
Darul Islam, 240. *See also* Islamic state; Komite Pertahanan Kebenaran P.S.I.I.; Kartosuwirjo
Dencentralization Law (1903), 121, 256
De Express (journal), 233
Defence, 331
Deliberation. *See* Musjawarah
Demak, 185
Department of Colonies, 130, 133, 145
Desa Lumbung, 63
Desa Scholen, 151, 162, 167

Deventer, C. Th. van, 61–62, 76, 92, 122
Digul concentration camp. *See* Boven-Digul
Dipanegara, *prince*, 9, 18, 179–80, 188–202, 289, 314, 315. *See also* Java War
Djajadiningrat, Achmad, 223–25, 237, 252–55
Djamal-al-Din-al-Afghani, 237–38
Dokter-Djawa, 215, 223–24
Dokter-Djawa School, 33. *See also* School Tot Opleiding Van Inlandse Artsen (S.T.O.V.I.A.)
Dominion status, 144, 150
Douwes Dekker, Eduard, 31, 39, 217. *See also* Multatuli
Douwes Dekker, E. F. E., 217–18, 228–32, 342
Dualism, economic, 94–95. *See also* Plural society
Dukun, 80, 287
Dutch-Arab Schools. *See* Hollands-Arabische Scholen
Dutch-Chinese Schools. *See* Hollands-Chinese Scholen
Dutch East India Company, 3–5, 7, 9–10, 18, 179, 185, 240
Dutch Islamic Policy, 157–65
Dutch-language education system, 150–54; budget cuts, 154; entrance requirements, 152–53; indigenous demand, 152–54, 157–58, 160–61, 174–75, 219; incidence of communism, 294, 300. *See also* European primary schools; Hollands-Inlandse Scholen; Hollands-Chinese Scholen; Hollands-Arabische Scholen; Dutch-language secondary schools; Universities; Colleges of Advanced Education; Intellectual proletariat
Dutch-language secondary schools. *See* Meer Uitgebreid Lager Onderwijs (M.U.L.O.); Hogere Burger School (H.B.S.); Lyceum; Algemene Middelbare School (A.M.S.)
Dutch-native schools. *See* Hollands-Inlandse Scholen
Dutch-native Schools Commission (1927–30). *See* Hollands-Inlands Onderwijs Commissie

(H.I.O.C.)
Dutch parliament, 122, 124–25, 141, 148
Dutch queen, 125, 128, 141, 147, 149, 329
Dutch Reformed Church, 4
Dwidjosewojo, M. Wahidin, 128

Economic behaviour, indigenous, 93, 96, 110, 152, 156, 170. *See also* Economic development
Economic conditions, indigenous, 14–15, 18–20, 22, 24–25, 28–29, 30, 33, 35, 58, 60, 62, 64–65, 68–69, 70, 78, 90–96, 97–120. *See also* Culture System; Liberal colonial policy; Ethical Policy; Plantations; Wages; Gambling; Opium; Usury
Economic demand, indigenous, creation of, 93–94
Economic depression (1929–37), 64, 154, 264, 320–21, 330, 332; cuts in education, 175–76
Economic development, cultural obstacles to, 86, 110, 156, 170
Educational standards. *See* Concordantie
Education, 86, 96, 121; civic virtues, 156; dualism, 151, 154, 231–32; eradication of superstition, 155; expenditure, 170, 175–76; Indonesia-centric education, 229–30; industrialization, 166–67; minimum standards, 150; political and economic importance, 155–56, 170, 220, 226, 290; political radicalism, 153–54, 155, 170–74, 215–18, 290; subsidies, 151, 176; training of indigenous officials, 150. *See also* Vernacular schools; Dutch-language education system; Association; Indonesian elite
Education Council. *See* Onderwijsraad
Eerens, J. C. de, *general*, 19, 22
Egypt, 237, 279, 320
Engels, F., 310
Epidemics, 81

Eru Tjakra. *See* Ratu Adil
Ethical Policy, 61–65, 121, 123, 216, 256; state-owned enterprises, 72; financial aid to the colony, 76–78; effect on the economy, 93–94, 96; political and administrative reforms, 121–48, 228; education, 149–76, 215. *See also* Association; Indonesiazation; Industrialization; Irrigation; Transmigration; Indonesian elite
Eurasians, 152, 216–17, 229–32. *See also* Indo-Europees Verbond; Insulinde
European branch of regional government service. *See* Binnenlands Bestuur (B.B.)
European primary schools, 152
Evolution, political, 304
Expenditure, indigenous, 50–56, 97–113, 115–17
Exports, indigenous, 56

Fadjar Asia (journal), 307
Faith Healers. *See* Dukun
Farmers' co-operatives. *See* Rukun Tani
Fascism, 304–5, 332–34, 338–39
Fast. *See* Islam, puasa
Faust, 327
Federalism, 124, 138, 140
Federation of Indonesian Political Organizations. *See* Permufakatan Perhimpunan Politiek Kebangsaan Indonesia (P.P.P.K.I.)
Fock, D., 130, 150, 166
Food consumption, indigenous, 78–79, 91, 98–113, 117–20; calorific value, 118–19; albuminoids, 119; fats, 119–20; carbohydrates, 210; vitamins, 120. *See also* Malnutrition
Fransen van de Putte, I. D. 32
Froebel schools, 152

Gabungan Partai Politiek Indonesia (G.A.P.I.), 125, 147, 148, 262, 303, 334–39, 141–42, 345
Gambling, 88
Gandhi, 319
Gatot Mangkupradja, 305, 314

Geertz, C., 237
Gelderen, J. van, 315
Gelijkgestelden, 259
Gentle Persuasion. *See* Perentah Alus
Gerakan Rakjat Indonesia (Gerindo), 304, 334, 341, 344–45
Geredja Merdeka Minahasa, 336
Gerretson, F. C., 22
Goethe, J. W. von, 327
Gouvernementen, 121–22
Graaff, S. de, 121–22, 124–25
Graeff, A. C. D. de, 130–32, 139
Greater Atjeh Union of Islamic Scholars. *See* Persatuan Ulama Seluruh Atjeh
Greater Indonesia Party. *See* Partai Indonesia Raya (Parindra)
Grondwetherziening (1922), 124, 142
Grootambtenaarsexamen, 224–25
Gunning, J. H., 167
Guru, 252–57
Guru Ngelmu, 179, 183–84

Habbema, J., 149, 155–56
Hadi, *Mr.*, 314
Hadiono Kusume Utojo, *raden mas*, 333
Hadj, 84–85, 181, 191, 269, 345
Haji, 242, 284, 298
Hasjim, *kiyayi*, 270–71
Hasselman, C. J., 62, 78, 90, 95
Hatta, M. *Dr.*, 239, 301–4, 326–27
Helsdingen, C. C. van, 142, 147
Helsdingen, W. H. van, 141
Herendiensten, 28, 41, 48–50, 54, 68, 82, 83, 94, 180, 204, 210, 214
Heretical practices. *See* Islam, haram
Herzieningscommissie (1918), 124, 128
Het Vrije Woord (journal), 277–78
Heutz, J. B. van, 123, 150–51, 166, 182
Heyting, H. G., 34, 51, 92. *See also* Arminius
Higher Civil Service Entrance Examination. *See* Grootambtenaarsexamen
Hinduism, 245
Hisjam, *haji*, 264–65
Hoevell, W. R. van, *baron*, 31, 34, 39
Hogere Burger School (H.B.S.), 152, 216, 259
Hollands-Arabische Scholen, 152
Hollands-Chinese Scholen, 152, 175

Hollands-Inlands Onderwijs Commissie (H.I.O.C.), 153–54, 176
Hollands-Inlandse Scholen, 152; inefficiency, 154, 293–94; overproduction, 171, 173, 176
Holy War. *See* Islam, perang sabil
Homan van der Heide, J., 56, 60, 67
Hoofdenscholen, 33
Hormat system, 86, 226, 288
Hospitals, 81
House of Orange, 340
Housing, indigenous, 79–80, 97–115
Huender, W., 64, 91, 96, 315–16
Huizenga, L. H., 113, 120
Humanitarianism, 31, 65–66. *See also* Ethical Policy; "White man's burden"; Liberal colonial policy

Income, indigenous, 68–69, 89, 91–93, 95, 97–113, 115–16
Idenburg, A. W. F., 126, 128, 130–32
Imperial Council, 144
Imperial economy, 63
Imports, 58–59, 89–90, 94
Indebtness, rural, 85–86, 93, 97. *See also* Usury; Volkscredietwezen
Independence, 125, 129–30, 141, 228, 276, 286, 301, 306–7, 317–18, 320, 322–34, 337
Independent Church of the Minahasa. *See* Geredja Merdeka Minahasa
Indies' citizenship, 341
Indies' Party. *See* Indische Partij
Indies' Social Democratic Association. *See* Indische Sociaal-Democratische Vereniging (I.S.D.V.)
Indies' Social Democractic Party. *See* Indische Sociaal-Democratische Partij
Indigenous branch of the regional government service. *See* Inlands Bestuur
Indigenous law. *See* Adat law
Indigo, 15, 17, 18, 20, 23–24, 26–27, 32, 67, 95
Indirect rule, 165, 188–97. *See also* Inlands Bestuur; Binnenlands Bestuur
Indisch Genootschap, 43, 50
Indische Partij, 217, 228–35, 273,

308. *See also* Suwardi Suryaningrat; Tjipto Mangunkusumo; Douwes Dekker, E. F. E.
Indische Sociaal-Democratische Partij (I.S.D.P.), 324
Indische Sociaal-Democratische Vereniging (I.S.D.V.), 127, 273–74
Indo-China, 324
Indo-European Union. *See* Indo-Europees Verbond
Indo-Europees Verbond, 217
Indonesia Berparlemen, 147–49, 239, 261–63, 305, 334–39. *See also* Self-government
Indonesia-centric nationalism, 217–18. *See also* Non-co-operation; Self-help; National unity; Cultural nationalism; Partai Nasional Indonesia (P.N.I.); Partai Indonesia (Partindo); Pendidikan Indonesia (P.N.I.-Baru)
Indonesia Merdeka (journal), 301
Indonesia Muda (journal), 302
Indonesia Muda, 241, 268
Indonesian Association. *See* Perhimpunan Indonesia
Indonesian Chauffeurs' Union. *See* Persatuan Sopir Indonesia
Indonesian Communist Party. *See* Partai Kommunis Indonesia (P.K.I.)
Indonesian elite, traditional, 150, 152–53, 158, 215–18, 230; modern, 215–18, 225–27, 274, 335, social origin modern elite, 218–19. *See also* Priyayi; Bupati; Inlands Bestuur; Intellectual proletariat
Indonesian Islamic Association Party. *See* Partai Sarikat Islam Indonesia (P.S.I.I.)
Indonesian Islam Party. *See* Partai Islam Indonesia (P.I.I.)
Indonesian language. *See* Bahasa Indonesia
Indonesian mentality, 340–41. *See also* Javanese syncretism; Modernization; Economic behaviour
Indonesian national anthem. *See* Indonesia Raya
Indonesian national education. *See* Pendidikan Nasional Indonesia (P.N.I.-Baru)
Indonesian nationalism, genesis of, 162–65, 167, 171, 215–35
Indonesian Nationalist Party. *See* Partai Nasional Indonesia (P.N.I.)
Indonesian Parliament. *See* Indonesia Berparlemen
Indonesian People's Congress. *See* Kongres Rakjat Indonesia
Indonesian People's Movement. *See* Gerakan Rakjat Indonesia (Gerindo)
Indonesian People's Party. *See* Partai Bangsa Indonesia
Indonesian People's Union. *See* Persatuan Bangsa Indonesia (P.B.I.)
Indonesian private schools. *See* Wilde Scholen
Indonesian Republic, 273, 301
Indonesians in Japan, 343–44
Indonesian Students' Association. *See* Perhimpunan Peladjar Indonesia (P.P.P.I.)
Indonesian students in Japan, 265
Indonesian students in the Middle East, 265–66
Indonesian students in the Netherlands. *See* Perhimpunan Indonesia
Indonesians with European status. *See* Gelijkgestelden
Indonesian Union of Islamic Chinese. *See* Persatuan Tionghoa Islam Indonesia
Indonesian Unity Party. *See* Partai Persatuan Indonesia (Parpindo)
Indonesian Youth Organizations. *See* Jong Java; Jong Ambon; Jong Islamieten Bond; Indonesia Muda
Indonesia Party. *See* Partai Indonesia (Partindo)
Indonesia Raya (anthem), 261, 305, 329, 335–36
Indonesiazation, 162, 165, 215–16, 330–31, 336. *See also* Association
Industrialization, 63–65, 150, 330. *See also* Ethical Policy
Industry, indigenous, 50–51, 64, 90–91, 99, 103, 105, 106, 108, 318, 330. *See also* Batik industry
Inlands Bestuur, 5, 9, 10, 23–24,

27, 32, 37, 39, 67, 83, 122, 157, 215–16, 218–19, 338, 341; ranks, 218, 223; communism, 284, 288; loss of popular trust, 288–90
Insulinde, 217
Intellectual proletariat, 150, 153, 155, 170–74, 176, 239, 274, 290. *See also* Dutch-language schools; Hollands-Inlands Onderwijs Commissie; communism
International Transport Federation (I.T.F.), 324
Irrigation, 25, 58, 61–62, 67, 94, 315
Islam, 3, 4, 9, 179, 183, 301–3; anti-colonialism, 180, 207–14, 254–55, 308–11; doa quoenoet, 262; Hadits, 237; haram, 237–38; 253; impact of modern education, 157, 237–38, 266–67, 254–55; Japan, 345; kafir, 207–14, 237, 242, 274; kitabs, 210, 236, 241; madzhab, 241, 271; mysticism, 190–98, 236, 283; penghulu, 196; perang sabil, 182, 207–14, 287; pitrah, 106, puasa, 88, 103, 209, 227, 245–46, 251; reaction to Christian missions, 159, 237; right of private property, 263, 270; salat, 242; sembahjang, 209; Sjar'iah, 48, 181, 239; ummat, 260; walis, 185–86; zakat, 210, 270
Islamic Association. *See* Sarikat Islam
Islamic Boy Scouts. *See* Pandu (Siap)
Islamic Brotherhood. *See* Islam ummat
Islamic Education Party. *See* Persatuan Tarbyahtul Islamiah (Perti)
Islamic Fast. *See* Islam, puasa
Islamic Law. *See* Islam, madzhab, Sjar'iah. *See also* Islamic state
Islamic modernism, 157, 237–38, 264–70; education, 238, 240, 265–66; traditional opposition, 270–72. *See also* Muhammadyah; Jong Islamieten Bond

Islamic movement, 236–72. *See also* Islamic modernism; Sarikat Islam; Partai Sarikat Islam Indonesia (P.S.I.I.): Muhammadyah; Nahadatul Ulama; Jong Islamieten Bond
Islamic prayers. *See* Islam, do'a qoenut, rapal, salat, sembahjang
Islamic puritanism, 181, 202, 238. *See also* Padri War; Islamic modernism
Islamic religious texts. *See* Islam, kitabs
Islamic revelations. *See* Qu'ran; Islam, Hadits
Islamic schools. *See* Pesantren; Langgar; Madrasah; Islamic modernism
Islamic state, 202, 236, 240, 261, 263, 268. *See also* Darul Islam
Islamic teachers. *See* Kiyayi; Ulama; Guru
Islamic Union. *See* Persatuan Islam
Islamic World Congress. *See* Moe' tamar al Alam al Islami
Iskaq, *Mr.*, 305

Japan, 125, 182, 188, 266, 304–5, 332–33; propaganda in Indonesia, 342–45
Japanese-Russian War, 258
Java Bank, 133–34
Javanese artistocracy. *See* Priyayi; Indonesian elite; Inlands Bestuur
Javanese kings, incarnation of Wishnu, 183; court life, 189–99; despotism, 189–90; Islam, 236
Javanese social status system, 299–300
Javanese syncretism, 157, 183–88, 197–98, 236, 242–47, 302
Javanese view of history, 179, 183–88. *See also* Ratu Adil; Jojobojo; Messianic expectations
Java War, 9, 18, 179–80, 188–202; armaments, 199–202; tactics, 199–202. *See also* Dipanegara
Jojobojo, 179, 183–88, 344
Jong Ambon, 241

Jonge, B. C. de, *jonkheer*. 175–76
Jong Islamieten Bond, 240, 267–70
Jong Java, 241, 268
Junior High Schools. *See* Meer Uitgebreid Lager Onderwijs (M.U.L.O.)
Just King. *See* Ratu Adil

Kaoem Moeda (journal), 233
Kartini, *Raden Adjeng*, 215–16, 219–23, 227
Kartosuwirjo, 239–40, 263
Kasimo Endrowahjono, 336
Kat-Angelino, A. D. A., de, 143, 146 147
Katholieke Volkspartij, 61, 77
Kenduren, 244. *See also* Slametan
Ki Hadjar Dewantoro. *See* Suwardi Suryaningrat
Kiyayi, 247
Kobayashi, 342
Kol, H. van, 72, 95
Kolonial Archief, 172, 175, 257, 261, 264, 267, 272, 291, 300, 308, 317, 320, 325, 331, 334
Koloniale Raad, 122. *See also* Volksraad
Komite Pertahan Kebenaran P.S.I.I., 263
Kougres Rakjat Indonesia, 261, 355–38
Kusumo Judo, 306
Kusumo Utoyo, R.M.A.A., 314, 316
Kutoardjo, 50, 53, 54
Kuyper, A., 77

Labour legislation, 32, 67, 73–76 demand for inspection, 75
Labour unions, 239, 315, 319, 325
Land grants to nobility. *See* Appanage system
Land holdings, 68, 94, 97, 101, 106, 109, 112; communal land, 82–83, 103, 112; individual ownership, 82–83; rich land owners, 289. *See also* Share cropping
Land legislation, 32, 48, 67, 71, 231, 339
Landlords, 83–85, 95, 180
Land rent, 5, 10, 14–15, 50, 57, 68–69, 82–83, 96, 100–101, 103, 106, 108–9, 111–12
Landless peasants, 70, 78, 100, 101, 111
Landraad, 265
Langgar, 240, 250

Legal system, inequalities of, 231, 259, 323, 329
Lenin, 281
Liberal colonial policy (1850–1900), 5, 6, 7, 8, 9, 31, 61–62; economic stagnation, 60, 62; expenditure on infra-structure, 58; exploitation, 67–68, 70, 72–74; free labour versus compulsion, 43, 48, 67; future loss of the Indies, 47; modern indigenous education, 31, 32, 39, 215; private versus public enterprise, 31–34, 38, 46, 67, 71, 73; secure supply of land and labour, 47–50
Liberals, 122–30
Limburg-Stirum, J. P. van, *count*, 122–24, 126–35, 140–41
Literacy, 151, 169–70, 262, 305, 312, 319, 329
Livestock, 57, 68, 94–95, 100, 107–8, 112, 115
Loenakarsky, 278, 280
Lyceum, 152

Madjid, Usman, A., 343
Madjlis Oelama, 258
Madjlisoel Islamil A'laa Indonesia (M.I.A.I.), 241, 336, 341
Madjlis Tinggi Kerapatan Adat Alam Minangkabau, 336
Madrasah, 240. *See also* Islamic modernism, education
Magna Carta, 260
Mahdi, 179
Malnutrition, 65, 117–20
Mangkubumi, *prince*, 189–202
Mangkubuwono II (Sepuh), *sultan*, 9, 188
Mansur, K. H., 241, 270
Maring. *See* Sneevliet, H. J. F. M.
Marxist doctrine, 274–76, 301–3, 308–11. *See also* Partai Kommunis Indonesia (P.K.I.)
Marx, Karl, 239, 277, 283, 310
Mass education, 162, 166–67. *See also* Vernacular schools
Mataram, 200, 289
Matriarchy, 181
Maxim Gorki, 278, 280
McVey, R. T., 284, 287
Mecca, 181. *See also* Hadj
Medical care, 80–83
Medical training. *See* Dokter-Djawa School; School Tot Opleiding Van Inlandse Artsen (S.T.O.V.I.A.)

Meer Uitgebreid Lager Onderwijs (M.U.L.O.), 152; overproduction of students, 171
Messianic expectations, 179, 183–88, 274, 285–86, 288
Meyer Ranneft, J., Dr. 153, 172–74, 316, 346
Middle class, indigenous, 95–96
Midwives, 80–81
Minahasa Union. *See* Persatuan Minahasa
Minangkabau, 181, 202–7, 238, 274, 285
Mining, 63, 73
Ministerial responsibility, 125, 129, 130, 339
Modernization, 89–90; cultural obstacles, 79, 81, 84–85, 86, 93–94; on western lines, 327–28
Modjopahit, 185
Moe' tamar al Alam al Islami, 270
Mohammad, *prophet*, 202, 261–62, 264, 283
Moluccas, 3, 5
Money economy, 50–56, 69
Montessori schools, 152
Mufakat, 302
Muhammadyah, 240–41, 257, 264–67, 271, 341, 345
Mulia, S. G., *Dr.*, 338
Multatuli, 39, 42. *See also* Douwes Dekker, Eduard
Municipal Councils, 121, 125
Musjawarah, 303
Muslim. *See* Islam
Musso, 273
Mustafa Kemal, 287

Nahadatul Ulama, 241, 270–72, 345
Nationale Indische Partij (N.I.P.), 217–18, 259
Nationalism. *See* Proto-nationalist movements; Indonesian nationalism, genesis of; Islamic movement; communism; Indonesia-centric nationalism; Regional nationalism
National Indies Party. *See* Nationale Indische Partij (N.I.P.)
Nationalization, 317, 323
National unity, 302, 312–13, 318, 321, 326–27, 335, 338
Nederlandse Handels Maatschappij, 7, 17, 19, 21, 44, 133
Nederlands Vak Verbond (N.V.V.), 262, 324, 330
Neo-Calvinist Party. *See* Anti-Revolutionnaire Partij
Netherlands Association of Labour unions. *See* Nederlands Vak Verbond (N.V.V.)
Netherlands Trading Company. *See* Nederlandse Handelsmaatschappij
New imperialism (1870–1914), 181–82
Non-co-operation, 301–2, 304–6, 319, 325
Notosuroto, 320

Onderwijsraad, 168
Onze Verbanning, 234–35
Opium, 57, 69, 79, 88, 211, 214, 319
Opleiding School Voor Inlandse Ambtenaren (O.S.V.I,A.), 226. *See also* Hoofdenscholen
Osaka Nichi Nichi, 343
Outer-islands, 73, 306; expansion of Dutch control, 34, 73, 181–82

Padjajaran, 184–85
Padri War, 181, 202–7, 315
Pakualam, 258
Palar, L. N., 380
Pan-Asiatic Movement, 343
Pandu (Siap), 261
Pan-Islamism, 164, 238, 274
Partai Bangsa Indonesia, 321
Partai Indonesia (Partindo), 303–4, 317–20, 325
Partai Indonesia Raya (Parindra), 217, 304–5, 329–31, 334, 341–44
Partai Islam Indonesia (P.I.I.), 334
Partai Kommunis Indonesia (P.K.I.), 123, 274–300, 301, 308, 321, 345; uprisings (1926–27), 135, 173, 274–75; leadership, 274–75, 284–87, 288–300
Partai Nasional Indonesia (P.N.I.), 258, 302–8, 317, 321, 337–45; religious neutrality, 307–8
Partai Persatuan Indonesia (Parpindo), 345, 346
Partai Sarikat Islam Indonesia (P.S.I.I.), 239–41, 257–64, 271, 337, 341, 345
Pasundan, 321, 334, 345
Pawn shops, 57–58, 63, 103
Pembela Islam, 345
Pendidikan Nasional Indonesia (P.N.I.-Baru), 303–4
Pendopo, 168

People's Association. *See* Sarikat
  Rakjat
Perentah Alus, 12, 92
Pergerakan Penjedar, 338, 346
Perhimpunan Indonesia, 133, 301–
  4, 320–25, 322–34
Perhimpunan Peladjar Indonesia
  (P.P.P.I.), 337
Perkumpulan Politiek Katholiek
  Djawa, 314
Permufakatan Perhimpunan Politiek
  Kebangsaan Indonesia (P.P.P.I.),
  258, 303–4, 313–17, 326–27
Persatuan Arab Indonesia (P.A.I.),
  345
Persatuan Bangsa Indonesia (P.B.I.),
  217, 304
Persatuan Djurnalis Indonesia (Perdi),
  345
Persatuan Guru Agama Islam, 346
Persatuan Islam (Persis), 345
Persatuan Minahasa, 334, 345
Persatuan Partai Katholiek Indonesia,
  334, 345
Persatuan Peladjar Pelatjar Indonesia
  (P.P.P.I.),
Persatuan Sopir Indonesia, 346
Persatuan Tarbyahtul Islamiah
  (Perti), 346
Persatuan Tionghoa Islam Indonesia,
  346
Persatuan Ulama Seluruh Atjeh, 345
Pesantren, 160, 168, 224, 236–37,
  242, 246, 248–51, 252–55;
  teaching methods, 248–55;
  curriculum, 248–51, 254–
  55; life style, 250–55
Petition Sutardjo. *See* Sutardjo
  Kartohadikusumo
Philippines, 342
Pilgrimage (Mecca). *See* Hadj
Pilgrims (Mecca). *See* Haji
Plantations, 31–36, 38, 43, 46–
  48, 63–67, 71; conditions
  of coolies, 73–78, 95,
  113–28, 288, impact on
  indigenous economy, 70,
  84, 95; rent paid for
  village lands, 69
Plas, C. O. van der, 167
Pleyte, Th.B., 139–40
Plural Society, 229–32
Poensen, C., 237, 241–47
Poeze, H. A., 283
Political and administrative
  decentralization, 121, 150.
  See also Association;
  Unification; Volksraad;

Regional autonomy
Political Intelligence Service. *See*
  Politieke Inlichtingen Dienst
  (P.I.D.)
Political Suppression, 234–35, 275,
  305–7, 313, 318–19, 323
Politieke Inlichtingen Dienst
  (P.I.D.), 275
Polygamy, 86–87, 245, 268, 307
Population, growth, 33–35, 56–
  57, 62, 78, 94, 315, 330;
  movements, 78; birth rate, 78;
  density, 78; effect on
  literacy, 151. *See also*
  Transmigration
Portuguese, 3–4
Post, P., 168
Prambanan, 229
Press, European, 133–34, 232–34,
  314; Indonesian, 336, 342
Priangan, 3, 16–18, 24, 29
Priyayi, 9–10, 23–24, 27, 32, 39–
  40, 86, 90, 157, 180, 186,
  217–18, 225–26, 238, 242,
  259, 298, 322; religious
  tolerance, 161, 236; feudal
  suppression, 219, 223–26.
  See also Inlands Bestuur;
  Bupati; Hormat System
Priyono, *raden*, 332
Prostitution, 80, 214, 268, 319
Proto-nationalist movements, 179–
  214. *See also* Ratu Adil;
  Mahdi; Messianic expectations
Provincial councils, 121, 125, 129,
  131. *See also* Gouvernementen
Public health, 80–82, 96, 114, 121,
  319. *See also* Malnutrition;
  Medical care
Public works, 330

Qu'ran, 207–14, 237, 239, 248–51,
  257, 262, 266–67, 269, 289

Raad van Nederlands-Indie, 123, 130,
  132, 144, 146, 306
Racial integration, 228–32. *See also*
  Indische Partij
Racialism, 122, 134, 175, 215–18,
  220–21, 224–25, 229–32,
  258–59, 276, 311
Radicale Concentratie, 123, 128
Raffles, Sir Stamford, 5–6, 10, 32, 48
Ramayana, 316
Ratu Adil, 179, 181, 183–88, 238,
  256, 289
Ratu Langie, G.S.S.J., *Dr;*. 142, 336
Rebellions, 16, 18, 179

Regency councils, 122, 125, 129, 131, 329
Regent. *See* Bupati
Regional autonomy, 121–49. *See also* Adatgemeenschappen; Regency councils; Provincial councils
Regional councils, 121–22, 289
Regional courts. *See* Landraad
Regional Government Service, European branch. *See* Binnenlands Bestuur (B.B.); Indonesian branch. *See* Inlands Bestuur
Regional nationalism, 216–17, 241. *See also* Budi Utomo; Pasundan; Jong Java; Sarikat Ambon
Religious Neutrality, 159–60; in schools, 168, 272; in politics, 230
Religious Taxes. *See* Islam, pitrah, zakat
Renan, E., 164
Revolution, 71, 122, 131, 228, 321–25, 347; Netherlands, 126–27; Germany, 126
Rice production, 58, 92, 97, 99; effect of Culture System, 14, 18, 20, 26, 46; effect of Liberal System, 56, 68, 69; area under crops, 62; adat, 156
Ritsema van Eck, S., 140
Roorda, T., 188, 202
Royal Dutch Shell, 124
Rukun Tani, 304, 329. *See also* Partai Indonesia Raya (Parindra)
Russia, 278, 281, 287
Rustam Effendi, 332, 334

Salary scales, civil service, 259
Salt monopoly, 269
Samsi Sastrowidagdo, *Dr.*, 258, 302, 314
Santri, 236–38, 242–47, 253–55, 274, 289
Sarikat Ambon, 345
Sarikat Islam, 122, 238–39, 255–57, 273–74, 288–89, 308
Sarikat Rakjat, 274, 288–89, 295, 299; schools, 274, 345
Sartono, *Mr.*, 302–3, 317, 319
Sastroamidjojo, Ali, *Mr.*, 301, 314
Savings, indigenous, 84, 88, 102, 116–17, 156
Schmalhousen, H. E. B., 60

School fees, 152
School Tot Opleiding Van Inlandse Artsen (S.T.O.V.I.A.), 216, 218–19, 225
Scouting movement, 289
Second class vernacular schools. *See* Tweede Klasse Scholen
Seignorial services. *See* Herendiensten
Self-determination, 329, 331
Self-government, 121, 123, 129–32, 138, 141–49, 217, 239, 256, 261–63, 339. *See also* Indonesia Berparlemen
Self-help, 301, 318, 325. *See also* Perhimpunan Indonesia; Partài Nasional Indonesia (P.N.I.)
Semaun, 273
Senior high schools. *See* Hogere Burger School (H.B.S.); Lyceum; Algemene Middelbare School (A.M.S.)
Share cropping, 97, 108, 111, 115
Shaw, B., 278, 280–81
Shipping, 15, 95, 316
Singgih, *Mr.*, 314
Sjahrir, S., 239, 301, 302–4, 327–28
Sjarifuddin, A., 304
Slametan, 88, 97, 103, 105, 110, 156
Sneevliet, H. J. F. M., 126–27, 273
Snouck-Hurgronje, C., 150, 157–66, 182, 283, 320
Sociaal-Democratische Arbeiders Partij (S.D.A.P.), 61, 64, 65, 72, 122–23, 126, 134, 174, 270, 277, 322
Social-Democratic Labour Party. *See* Sociaal Democratische Arbeiders Partij
Social services, 323
Soerabaiaasch Handelsblad (newspaper), 311
Soviets, 323
Staats Spoorwegen, 259
Standard Scholen. *See* Tweede Klasse Scholen
Starkenborgh Stachouwer, A. W. L. T. van, *jonkheer*, 142
State railways. *See* Staats Spoorwegen
Statistics, reliability of, 62, 94
Stovkis, J. E., 174, 324
Study Clubs, 301–2
Stuers, H. J. J. L. de, 202, 207
Subardjo Djojoadisuryo, A., *Mr.*, 301
Sudarmo Atmodjo, 319
Suffrage, 124, 139, 323, 339
Sugar Industry, 14–15, 17–19, 26–

27, 32, 34, 37, 46, 58, 67, 95, 109; effect on indigenous economy, 57, 316; economic depression, 64; coolie wages, 70–71, 95, 111; indigenous production, 108
Sujadi, 302
Sujudi, 319
Sukardjo Wirijopranoto, *raden*, 338
Sukarno, *Ir.*, 239, 302–17, 325
Sukiman, *Dr.*, 314, 337
Sunario, *Mr.*, 302
Sun Yat Sen, 309
Supratman, 329, 336
Supreme Council of the Minangkabau Adat Association. *See* Madjlis Tinggi Kerapatan Adat Alam Minangkabau
Surinam, 342
Suroso, R. P., 174–75, 317, 330
Sutardjo Kartohadikusumo, 125, 141–47, 304, 341
Sutomo, *Dr.*, 301, 304, 314–15
Suwardi Suryaningrat, 217, 232–34
Suwarno, 225–27
Swadeshi, 319

Tanah Merah. *See* Boven-Digul
Tan Malaka, 273–83
Tariffs, 94
Taxation, 24, 27–29, 34, 50–51, 53, 57, 68, 72–76, 82–83, 92, 94–96, 98, 100–101, 103, 106, 108, 112, 151, 180, 185–86, 210–11, 288–90, 323. *See also* Land rent; Herendiensten; Toll-gates
Tea, 20, 32
Teachers' colleges, 33, 152, 154, 226
Teachers of mystical knowledge. *See* Guru Ngelmu
Technical schools, 150, 166
Technische Hoge School, Bandung, 302
Technological University, Bandung. *See* Technische Hoge School, Bandung
Tertiary education, 151, 152. *See also* Colleges of advanced education
Teungku. *See* Ulama
Textiles, imports, 57
Thamrin, M. H., 314, 317, 341, 342, 344
Tilaar, J., 302
Tjipto Mangunkusumo, *Dr.*, 128, 217, 234–35

Tjokroaminoto, R. O. S., 122, 128, 238–39, 255–57, 261, 270, 306
Tjondro Negoro, R. A., 242
Tobacco, 95
Tokyo Manichi, 343
Toll-gates, 180
Trade regulations, 64, 330
Training schools for native officials. *See* Opleiding School Voor Inlandse Ambtenaren (O.S.V.I.A.)
Transmigration, 61–63, 316, 330–31
Troelstra, P. J., 122, 126, 277
Tuanku Imam Bondjol, 181, 202–7. *See also* Padri War
Tweede Klasse Scholen, 151, 167; inefficiency, 294
Tyranny of the majority, 302. *See also* Sukarno

Ulama, 182, 209–14, 236–27, 239, 271–72, 274
Ulebalang, 182, 210, 213, 214
Unanimous Decision. *See* Mufakat
Unbelievers. *See* Islam, kafir
Unemployment, 65, 153, 330. *See also* Intellectual proletariat
Unification, 135, 139
Union of Indonesian Journalists. *See* Persatuan Djunarlis Indonesia (Perdi)
Union of Indonesian Students. *See* Persatuan Peladjar Peladjar Indonesia (P.P.P.I.)
Union of Islamic Teachers. *See* Persatuan Guru Guru Agama Islam
Union of Young Muslims. *See* Jong Islamieten Bond
Universities, 152, 173. *See also* Tertiary education
Usury, 28–29, 39, 63, 85–86, 93, 318. *See also* Chinese
Utopia, 285–87

Vernacular continuation schools. *See* Vervolgscholen
Vernacular schools, 99, 112, 150–52; absenteeism, 152, 167; financing, 150–51, 166–67; socio-economic obstacles, 152, 155–56, 167–68. *See also* Desa Scholen; Tweede Klasse Scholen; Vervolgscholen
Vervolgscholen, 151
Village banks, 63, 112

Village chiefs, 23, 24, 28–29, 49, 67, 69, 86, 284–85
Village community services, 50, 54, 97
Village councils, 129, 131
Village schools. *See* Desa Scholen
Vitalis, L., 8, 19, 22, 30
Volkscredietwezen, 121, 224–25, 316
Volksraad, 61, 122–30, 134, 137, 138–39, 141–45, 153–54, 174–75, 216–17, 256, 304, 306–7, 319–20, 330, 338–39, 341–43

Wages, indigenous, 27, 57, 60, 65, 67, 70–71, 91–92, 95, 96, 111, 115; minimum wages, 337
Wahabites, 270–71. *See also* Islamic puritanism; Padri War
Wahidin Sudiro Husodo, *Dr.*, 216, 225. *See also* Budi Utomo
Wal, Fadjri, 258
Wal, S. L. van der, 128–29, 132, 135, 139–42, 147–49, 166–67, 176, 227, 335, 338–39, 347
Wayang, 254, 315
Welter, C. J. I. M., 142, 147
Westendorp Boerma, J. J., 18
Western Dynamism, 327–28
White collar syndrome, 152–53, 176
"White man's burden", 61, 65–66
Wilde Scholen, 154, 319
Wijngaarden, D. J. L. van, 273, 275–83
Winoto, 319
Wiselius, J. A. B., 179, 183, 188
Wiwoho, 267–68, 341
Women, emancipation, 86, 240, 267–269, 307, 319, 335
Wondoamiseno, 261–63
World War I, 239
World War II, 305, 332, 338–47
Wurjaningrat, R. M. H., 329

Yamin, M., *Mr.*, 304, 320, 343
Young Indonesia. *See* Indonesia Muda
Young Java. *See* Jong Java

Zentgraaff, H., 311
Zischka, A., 344